The Economics and Politics of Accounting

The Economics and Politics of Accounting

International Perspectives on Research Trends, Policy, and Practice

CHRISTIAN LEUZ
DIETER PFAFF
ANTHONY HOPWOOD

OXFORD

UNIVERSITY PRESS

OXFORD
UNIVERSITY PRESS

Great Clarendon Street, Oxford OX2 6DP

Oxford University Press is a department of the University of Oxford.
It furthers the University's objective of excellence in research, scholarship,
and education by publishing worldwide in

Oxford New York

Auckland Bangkok Buenos Aires Cape Town Chennai
Dar es Salaam Delhi Hong Kong Istanbul Karachi Kolkata
Kuala Lumpur Madrid Melbourne Mexico City Mumbai Nairobi
São Paulo Shanghai Taipei Tokyo Toronto

Oxford is a registered trade mark of Oxford University Press
in the UK and in certain other countries

Published in the United States
by Oxford University Press Inc., New York

British Library Cataloguing in Publication Data
Data available

Library of Congress Cataloging in Publication Data
Data available

ISBN 0–19–926062–1

1 3 5 7 9 10 8 6 4 2

Typeset by Newgen Imaging Systems (P) Ltd., Chennai, India
Printed in Great Britain
on acid-free paper by
Biddles Ltd., King's Lynn, Norfolk

This book is dedicated to the memory of

Dieter Ordelheide

in recognition of his exceptional personality and
his outstanding contributions to accounting research, practice, and
the European academic community.

FOREWORD: IN APPRECIATION OF DIETER ORDELHEIDE

With the passing of Dieter Ordelheide, the academic accounting community has lost a champion, an innovator, a role model, and a very dear friend. In a short period of time Dieter became a key person in the network of institutions that now constitute the supranational space in which European-level academic accounting operates. Affiliated with the European Institute for Advanced Studies in Management, he played a vital role in designing the accounting research activities of the Institute. Deeply involved in the European Accounting Association, a body that had evolved out of the activities of the European Institute, Dieter had a vision of what that Association might achieve and he did his utmost to realize this. Foremost in his mind was the Association's involvement with the next generation of European scholars through the European Doctoral Colloquium in Accounting. He was determined that younger scholars should have more opportunities to be European than had been available to him. Through these and other related activities, Dieter Ordelheide became widely known and respected throughout the European academic community, and increasingly the international one. He was a voice that mattered—a voice of both wisdom and authority.

Born in 1939 in Bielefeld and educated at the Helmholtz-Gymnasium, Dieter Ordelheide began his research and teaching career in the early 1960s studying business administration and legal sciences at the University of Cologne, one of the leading institutions for these subjects in Germany. In 1966 he took up a research assistantship at the Ruhr University, Bochum, where he was taught and influenced by Professor Walther Busse von Colbe. He completed his Ph.D. on the modeling and simulation of maintenance systems, and in 1979 he successfully defended a habitation thesis concerning the efficiency of public agencies.

During the early 1970s he had been an affiliated student of the newly established European Institute for Advanced Studies in Management, Brussels.

In 1978 Dieter became a full professor at the Johann Wolfgang Goethe University, in Frankfurt am Main. Initially holding a chair in accounting and controlling, Dieter's interests focused increasingly on financial reporting. Indeed during the late 1980s and 1990s he increasingly specialized in the area of international accounting. So much so that in 1995 he assumed the newly created chair for international accounting at Frankfurt. With a widening circle of international academic contacts, Dieter Ordelheide established himself as one of the leading analysts and commentators on German accounting matters, both inside and outside the country. As Michael Power (2000: 342) has said: "He was both an ambassador for, and translator, of German accounting in the English speaking world ... as well as a national scholar preoccupied with the transformations required to implement the Fourth and Seventh European directives."

I still remember the time I spent trying to persuade Dieter to become more actively involved in the European academic accounting network. Hein Schreuder had stepped down from his professorial position at the European Institute for Advanced Studies in Management and we needed another person with vision, energy, and enthusiasm to continue the task of constructing a European academic space in the accounting area. Gerry van Dyck and myself thought that Dieter was precisely such a person. Associated with the Institute since his own days as a mature student, increasingly Dieter had become more involved with the institutions of that emergent academic space—the research workshops of the Institute, the meetings of the European Accounting Association, and so on. I remember outlining all of this to him and trying to persuade him to get more deeply involved. He listened, he questioned, and he thought. Clearly he was interested, so interested in fact that he wanted a little time to reflect on all the implications of such an involvement for his own career and personal interests. But that time was not too long. Dieter quickly called me to say that he positively wanted to get involved. So real was his interest that it was not long before he decided to change his chair at Frankfurt to reflect his new interest in International Accounting. Dieter had developed a conception of both his role in Europe and his role in Germany, with the latter being seen as one of trying to internationalize the national academic accounting culture. So enthusiastic was he with his new interests that Dieter had decided to reinvent himself.

Since that time his enthusiasm was evident to all. He played a key role in developing the respect with which the European Doctoral Colloquium in Accounting is now held—and he helped to provide a more secure funding base for it. He strove to create more challenging forums in which to discuss emerging research on understanding international and regional pressures for accounting change in Europe. Recognizing the need for more authoritative commentaries on international differences in financial reporting, he transferred the German tradition of scholarly commentaries on accounting matters to the international stage with the publication in 1995 of *Transnational accounting*, an enormous comparative project that he realized very quickly with the support of KPMG. A revised and extended edition was published in 2000. Not confining his interests to the academic world, Dieter took over my own position on the Accounting Advisory Forum of the European Commission and in this capacity played an influential role mediating between the national representatives, the Commission, and the increasingly significant international accounting agencies.

Dieter had a formidable intellect. He hated poorly conducted research, sloppy reasoning, and overly narrow analysis. But he also had an open and tolerant mind. Whilst many of his German academic colleagues were reluctant to embrace some of the newer intellectual developments in the international accounting research community, Dieter was questioning, at times cautious, but always appreciative of real intellectual insights that were grounded in serious analysis and sound research. In this way he became an avid reader of the research journal that I edit, *Accounting, Organizations and Society*, occasionally chastising me for publishing some of the more avant-garde papers but more usually enthusing about the way in which the political and sociological insights could help him to understand his own experience of both accounting and accounting regulation in action. In such ways Dieter Ordelheide had a very significant impact on the European academic accounting community, but equally, he was much influenced by it.

Over the years we worked very well together. Being aware of our differences, we were able to develop a deep trust in each other's views and judgments. Through working with Dieter I became aware of not only his formidable intellect but also his warm and extremely sensitive personality. Dieter cared for both people and ideas. He strove to help the young and the talented. He cared passionately for friendship. He was a very good person and is sorely missed.

The greatest tragedy is that Dieter had so much to live for. He was just about to embark on a new wave of projects and interests, as the academic representative on the German Accounting Standards Board, as President of the European Accounting Association and as the P. D. Leake Lecturer in Accounting at Oxford. But although all these activities were tragically cut short, he left us with a considerable legacy, one that will continue to shape agendas and influence our thoughts in the years ahead. His contribution was a very real and a very good one.

Central to Dieter Ordelheide's vision was a view of accounting research and knowledge as one of being engaged with the wider societies of which they were a part. While academic freedom and independence were of fundamental importance to Dieter, he never saw these as requiring an isolated academy. Precisely the reverse in fact. He was constantly impatient to demonstrate the potential that good knowledge could have for transforming and improving practice. Equally he was acutely aware of the need for a form of knowledge that could embrace, appreciate, and understand the nuances and complexities of practice. Dieter Ordelheide always had a notion of accounting knowledge that was sensitive to history, to institutional formations, and to wider cultural differences. To him such a form of knowledge was vital if we were both to appreciate and understand national differences in accounting practices and, over time, to move toward their transformation in the name of regional and international models.

Hardly surprisingly Dieter was therefore extremely interested in the melting pot of different national intellectual traditions that were slowly coming together to create a new European intellectual space. He was determined to play a role in this process in the accounting area, anxious to protect and preserve valuable attributes of certain national traditions whilst at the same time being open to the influence of more global intellectual pressures, whether these emanated from elsewhere in Europe or the United States.

On numerous occasions we discussed the common distinctive features of the different European intellectual traditions and the characteristics that were of value in any emergent European academic space. The following always tended to emerge as being important in these discussions:

1. There seems to be a widespread European tendency to contextualize phenomena. For instance, an organization is less-often conceived as a circumscribed entity, analyzed solely in terms of its internal dynamics than as an entity interacting with and in part a product of a wider socioeconomic context. European knowledges have been more inclined to see organizations and organizational practices as being embedded in wider configurations of institutional arrangements. Organizational knowledge in general and accounting knowledge in particular, therefore needs to be aware of and sensitive to these wider settings.

2. In Europe there has been a strong tendency for research to be open to a wider array of intellectual influences. With evidence of difference so manifest, there has been a willingness to tolerate more and different knowledges, thereby encouraging a greater openness in discussion and a greater appreciation of cultural diversities and specificities. Alongside concerns with economic analyses, Europe has added and encouraged interests in the contributions that can be made by legal science, sociology, literary criticism, philosophy, political science, and many other of the human and social sciences.

3. European bodies of knowledge tend to exhibit a greater sense of history. Even the knowledges themselves tend to be seen as being grounded in the contexts in which they develop rather than as isolated and abstract phenomena.

4. Possibly because of their greater historical sensitivity, European knowledges tend to have a greater sense of process, dynamics, change, and indeed the actions through which change and developments occur. Greater emphasis is placed on temporal understandings rather than only statics or at best, comparative statics.

Dieter Ordelheide's own research and publications exhibited many of these tendencies, not least his grounding of German notions of proper accounting in the Roman tradition of law (Ordelheide 1993), his discussion of the complexities of transforming national regimes of accounting in the name of European Directives (Ordelheide 1990) and the draft of his opening P. D. Leake Lecture in Accounting, which is published in this volume. All of these, like other of his writings, relate theory to institutional practice, draw on and actively utilize diverse intellectual traditions, revel in understanding historical and institutional context, and offer an appreciation of the ways in which accounting is an active product of a wider but understandable web of forces. Dieter Ordelheide offered deep, rich, and usable insights into the accounting condition.

Through his very active involvement in the creation and sustenance of European-level institutions in the academic accounting community, Dieter also played an important role in protecting, preserving, and facilitating the creation of such European knowledges in the accounting area. This is a contribution of lasting significance and one, I venture to suggest, of increasing importance at a time when there are ever-greater pressures for academics to concern themselves with more abstract, isolated knowledges.

Anthony G. Hopwood

References

Ordelheide, D. (1990). "Soft transformations of accounting rules of the 4th Directive in Germany," *Les Cahiers Internationaux de la Comptabilité*, 3: 1–15.
—— (1993). "True and fair view: A European and a German perspective," *The European Accounting Review*, 2(1): 81–90.
Power, M. (2000). "Obituary: Dieter Ordelheide (1939–2000)," *European Accounting Review*, 9(3): 341–3.

PREFACE

On Monday, May 29, 2000 Professor Dr. Dieter Ordelheide died at the age of 60. We lost an outstanding scholar and one of the most influential accounting professors in Europe. His impressive research contributed to accounting theory and practice in Germany and Europe. He shaped German group accounting and heavily influenced the opening of German accounting to recent international developments. In acknowledgement of these achievements, Dieter received an honorary doctorate from the Otto-Beisheim Graduate School of Management (WHU) at Koblenz/Germany in 1999. Over more than twenty years, Dieter Ordelheide has given much to the German and European accounting community, his colleagues, disciples, and students. He was professor out of vocation, with great passion and the extraordinary talent to fruitfully combine research and teaching. His remarkable insights, his way of thinking, and his outstanding personality will not be forgotten.

His numerous contributions to the accounting literature were in four areas delineating his main interests: (1) group accounting, (2) accounting theory, (3) international accounting, and (4) politics of accounting. We would like to briefly highlight his main contributions in each of the areas.

In the 1970s and 1980s, Dieter Ordelheide developed—jointly with Walther Busse von Colbe—a consistent conceptual framework for German group accounting. The basic idea was to redefine the boundary between the firm and the market explicitly recognizing groups, and to design group accounting rules that are conceptually equivalent to those applicable for legally and economically independent entities. The textbook, which he wrote together with Walther Busse von Colbe, became widely used and shaped German group accounting in practice and theory.

Dieter Ordelheide also proposed an innovative interpretation of the basic structure of accrual accounting. His "prospective accounting theory" is based on neo-institutional economics and in particular transaction cost economics. He argued that the transaction- and event-based representation of uncertainty in accrual accounting can only be understood in a world of information asymmetry and incentive problems. He viewed nonmonetary assets as (qualitative) risk indicators and their use in accrual accounting as a way to indicate changes in the underlying probability distribution of future cash flows. He argued that historical cost accounting, the realization principle, and the lower-of-cost-or-market rule can be reconciled with economic theory in a world of incomplete information and markets.

His third field of interest was international accounting. Dieter Ordelheide was one of the first to envision the implications of the globalization of capital markets for German accounting. Understanding that accounting is embedded in a country's legal and institutional framework, his position was to preserve those standards that fit the German system, but at the same time to be open for changes and international developments. He urged the German profession to be critical about the German status quo and to participate in the international standard-setting process. Demonstrating his international orientation, Dieter Ordelheide edited "Transnational accounting" (jointly with KPMG). It provides an in-depth description and commentary of the regulatory system and accounting standards of fourteen countries as well as the European Union and the IASC. In 1998, he broke ground with the second edition and it is very sad that he will not be able to see its forthcoming publication covering nineteen countries.

Inspired by his own involvement in standard-setting, Dieter Ordelheide's recent work focused on the standard-setting process and the politics of accounting. He viewed accounting as one of the core institutions of economic regimes and wanted to understand the social and political process that shaped this institution. In the last two years, he was working intensively on several research projects, which he planned to present at the 2000 P. D. Leake Lectures on the "Politics of Accounting." He was very proud to be the third speaker at this prestigious event at the University of Oxford and started from scratch "diving into" philosophy, sociology, and political science. The preparation for these lectures filled him with so much joy and fascination that they were one of the last commitments he gave up due to his grave illness.

This tribute would be incomplete if we did not mention his personality. Dieter Ordelheide had charm and wit and was full of joy of life.

To the assistants and research associates working at his chair, he was a wonderful teacher and mentor. He always supported them, but at the same time challenged their thinking in critical discussions without imposing his views. He encouraged them to attend international conferences and seminars. Most importantly, he helped them grow and develop "wings to fly on their own". His relationship with his assistants was very personal. The Christmas parties at his home, where all former and present assistants were invited, were clearly one of our annual highlights and an important social institution at the chair. The party usually lasted until late at night and typically "left a huge hole" in his wine cellar. In addition, he regularly invited them to spend the weekend at his house in Burgundy. These trips will remain unforgotten.

This volume celebrates and displays Dieter Ordelheide's interests in a wide range of approaches to accounting research. Its compilation is the result of the efforts and involvement of many people. The book was made possible by the generous contribution of KPMG Deutsche Treuhand-Gesellschaft AG and especially Professor Dr. Wienand Schruff and Dr. Hanne Böckem. The authors, all friends and colleagues of Dieter Ordelheide, gave generously of their time. Sandra Sizer Moore has done an outstanding job in editing the contribution of the non-native English speakers. Philipp Friedmann carefully translated Dieter Ordelheide's draft P. D. Leake Lecture from German into English. Dieter Pfaff's assistants, Silvia Allmendinger and Jochen Kühn, helped to get the manuscript into proper shape, contributing enormously to the administrative aspects of producing this volume. We also thank Oxford University Press and particularly David Musson, for their generous assistance and for publishing this book.

Christian Leuz, Dieter Pfaff, and Anthony Hopwood

CONTENTS

LIST OF FIGURES

LIST OF TABLES

LIST OF CONTRIBUTORS

Ray Ball, Sidney Davidson Professor, Graduate School of Business, University of Chicago

Wolfgang Ballwieser, Professor at the Institute for Accounting and Auditing, University of Munich

Michael Bromwich, Chartered Institute of Management Accountants, Professor of Accounting and Financial Management, London School of Economics and Political Science

Walther Busse von Colbe, Emeritus, University of Bochum

Ralf Ewert, Professor at the Faculty of Economics and Business Administration, Chair of Controlling and Auditing, Goethe University Frankfurt

Günther Gebhardt, Professor of Accounting and Auditing, Goethe University Frankfurt

Aaron Heilmann, Research Associate at the Chair of Accounting and Auditing, Goethe University Frankfurt

Anthony Hopwood, Professor, Peter Moores Dean, Saïd Business School, University of Oxford

Karel van Hulle, Head of Unit Accounting and Auditing, European Commission

Christian Leuz, Harold Stott Term Assistant Professor of Accounting, Wharton School of the University of Pennsylvania and Wharton Financial Institution Center

Stuart McLeay, Professor, University of Wales, Bangor

Doris Merkl, Research Fellow, School for Business and Regional Development, University of Wales, Bangor

Dieter Ordelheide (1939–2000), Professor, Chair of International Accounting, Goethe University of Frankfurt (1978–2000); Regular Visiting Professor at the University of Vienna and the Otto-Beisheim Graduate School of Management (WHU), Vallendar/Germany

Dieter Pfaff, Professor at the Institute for Accounting, University of Zurich

Michael Power, P. D. Leake Professor of Accounting and Director of ESRC Centre for Analysis of Risk and Regulation, London School of Economics and Political Science

Robert Verrecchia, Elizabeth F. Putzel Professor of Accounting, Wharton School of the University of Pennsylvania

Alfred Wagenhofer, Professor at the Institute of Management Accounting and Control, University of Graz

Stephen Young, Senior Lecturer, Lancaster University Management School

INTRODUCTION AND OVERVIEW

Accounting systems are embedded in a country's economic and legal framework, much of which is shaped by political processes. This web of interactions results in complex economic and political questions, which require accounting researchers to draw on numerous related fields, for example information economics, regulatory economics, sociology, and political science, to name just a few.

Although we have made considerable progress in the field of accounting, many fundamental questions about the economics and politics of accounting are still subject to debate. In this book, we reconsider several of these topics in the context of current debates and trends in accounting, giving special emphasis to international topics. It is our aim to introduce the reader to these current debates, but also to highlight important fundamental issues and to demonstrate what we can learn about them from recent advances in accounting. The book addresses six fundamental themes in accounting.

First, all organizations are sets of implicit or explicit contracts among individuals or groups of individuals, such as managers, investors, creditors, employees, auditors, and the government. These parties have different preferences as well as different endowments of capital, skills, and information, which give rise to conflicts of interest and thus to contracting and monitoring problems. Accounting information can address these problems and facilitate the design of contracts, such as corporate debt agreements and managerial labor contracts. The contracting and monitoring role of accounting has historically been very important for the development of accounting.

Second, accounting information can help the parties to make better decisions. For instance, it enables investors to forecast firms' future cash flows, which helps them to make investment decisions in capital markets.

The decision-facilitating role of accounting has received much attention in recent years. It is now perceived to be one of the key roles of financial accounting.

Third, recognizing the conflicts of interests, the parties want to know if they have received what they have contracted for. For example, outside investors want to know if they can trust the information they receive from firms and controlling insiders. This skepticism creates demand for auditing of the accounts and enforcement of accounting standards, which are explicitly or implicitly part of the contracts.

Fourth, the different parties often face similar information and contracting problems creating a demand for standardization. Standards ensure a minimum level of financial information, which can be used in decision-making or relied upon in contracting. Moreover, standards serve as coordination devices among individuals or groups of individuals and can overcome externalities in the provision of information. But there are also costs associated with the regulation and standardization of accounting. Regulators and standard-setters need to trade off these costs and benefits.

Fifth, in democracies, the obligation to prepare and disclose financial information requires the approval of the legislature or an authorized accounting standard-setting body, like the FASB or the IASB. Thus, standard-setting is a political process in which the different groups lobby for their interests.

Sixth, standard-setting is not only a national process but in times of global capital markets an international one. The international standardization of financial reporting across different legal and economic systems by supranational organizations is part of the movement toward a world economic system and raises special issues and problems.

Each of the subsequent chapters addresses one or several of these six issues. They provide the unifying backbone of the book and are further organized into three main parts.

Part I: On the economics and roles of accounting

The book commences with *Alfred Wagenhofer* providing an overview on the roles of financial accounting and posing the question what is it that we can learn from economic research in financial accounting (Chapter 1.1). In this line of research, accounting information is analyzed in settings that are characterized by information asymmetry and conflicts of interest. Wagenhofer discusses the major research findings and shows that analytical models are capable of addressing national as well as international reporting and disclosure issues. He also carefully weighs the benefits and limitations of analytical accounting models.

Chapters 1.2 and 1.3 focus on the role of financial accounting in providing information for investment decisions and security valuation. A key problem with regard to this role is the tradeoff between relevance and reliability of accounting information. As *Michael Bromwich* puts it, the trick is to incorporate expectations and information about future cash flows in accounting without leaving too much room for managerial manipulation. His chapter provides suggestions on how market values can be used to achieve this goal. He also reviews the current debate on fair-value and mark-to-market accounting in the context of this challenge. *Wolfgang Ballwieser* focuses on the decision-facilitating role of accounting as well, but points to the limitations of financial reporting. In his view, the capabilities of accounting in conveying useful information about firms' future cash flows is frequently overestimated. Although there is a long-standing debate on this issue, the contribution of Ballwieser is timely as he applies his arguments to current developments in accounting regulation.

In Chapters 2.1 and 2.2, we turn to the role of accounting in contracting and corporate governance. A fundamental question in this area is why contracts often use accrual-based numbers, such as earnings, rather than cash flows. Tackling this issue in Chapter 2.1, *Dieter Pfaff* discusses whether cash flow-based or accrual-based performance measures are better suited to provide incentives and control behavior in decentralized organizations. He reviews major research findings and highlights that performance measurement is a multiperiod problem. His chapter gives special emphasis to shareholder value-based measures, such as residual income or EVA, which have received much attention in corporate practice in recent years.

Ray Ball explores the link between corporate governance and accounting using the U.S. cross-listing of Daimler-Benz as an example (Chapter 2.2). He highlights the changes in Daimler's corporate governance around the cross-listing, essentially grafting elements of a shareholder value model onto its stakeholder structure, and discusses the resulting changes in its approach to financial reporting. More generally, his case study highlights the economic forces that shape accounting practice and drive accounting harmonization around the world.

Part II: On the regulation and enforcement of accounting

Are there theory-based recommendations for standard-setters and what are the cost and benefits of disclosure regulation? *Robert Verrecchia* (Chapter 3.1) tackles the first issue and reviews the disclosure literature to infer policy prescriptions that seem implicit in the results. He points out that the theory-based literature fails to distinguish adequately between analyses concerned primarily with narrow pathologies versus results that are sufficiently general that they extend naturally to broad policy issues. He attempts to make such distinction and discusses broad notions and ideas that originate from the theory-based literature in accounting that comport with casual empiricism.

Christian Leuz (Chapter 3.2) contributes to the second aspect of the question. He exploits special features of the German institutional environment to document empirically that competitive concerns govern firms' disclosure choices and that proprietary costs can be an important reason why firms withhold information, despite substantial capital-market benefits of disclosure. His chapter highlights that mandating disclosures can impose costs on firms and that these costs should be weighed against the social benefits of the desired disclosures.

Once accounting information is regulated, the standards have to be enforced. More generally, the conflicts of interests among the providers and users of accounting numbers generally imply that accounting information has to be verified, for example by an independent auditor. Auditing and enforcement pose many challenging questions. The book addresses two of them. First, standards may accord firms too much reporting discretion, which makes their enforcement difficult. Second, standards may have "no teeth" due to insufficient sanctions and penalties. The contribution of *Walther Busse von Colbe* (Chapter 4.1) addresses the first aspect. His chapter on accounting for purchased goodwill critically examines the new FASB standard (SFAS 142) and argues that it provides substantial room for manipulation, which raises doubts about its enforceability. Chapters 4.2 and 4.3 focus on the second aspect of standard enforcement, that is the role of penalties and auditors. First, *Günther Gebhardt* and *Aaron Heilmann* empirically examine the degree of compliance in Germany; an environment where standards are primarily enforced by auditors and shareholder litigation is rare. The study deliberately concentrates on a specific area, that is cash flow statements, to better identify noncompliance, but it exploits that in Germany, firms can choose between three different sets of standards, German GAAP, IAS, and U.S. GAAP. The results demonstrate significant noncompliance with the standards, despite unqualified audit opinions of all sample firms, and raise the question whether there is a need for an enforcement body or stronger sanctions as imposed, for instance, by shareholder litigation.

Second, *Ralf Ewert* (Chapter 4.3) reviews the analytical and empirical literature on the role of auditors in enforcing accounting standards. In particular, he analyzes the concern that combining nonaudit services and auditing for the same client may be largely responsible for recent accounting scandals and audit failures. He concludes that there is no evidence that a simultaneous offering of auditing and NAS to the same client unequivocally and systematically impairs auditor independence. In fact, there are instances where nonaudit services are likely to enhance the quality of the audit because they increase the auditors' capital that is at stake.

Part III: On the politics and standard-setting of accounting

The third part of the book starts with a chapter by *Dieter Ordelheide*. He goes back to first principles and explores the role of accounting in society. He analyzes the ontological basis of accounting and highlights their implications for research on the politics of accounting (Chapter 5.1).

The next two chapters deal with the fact that accounting regulation and standard-setting is a political process in which many groups have a vested interest. First, *Stuart McLeay, Dieter Ordelheide,* and *Stephen Young* (Chapter 5.2) examine the influence of three primary constituencies, preparers, auditors, and academic experts, on German financial accounting regulation during the implementation of the Fourth EU directive. The contribution provides evidence on the preferences of the three constituencies, the relative influence of their lobbying activities, and the interaction effects of agreement and disagreement among the lobbyists.

Second, *Stuart McLeay* and *Doris Merkl* (Chapter 5.3) examine the process through which accounting law was redrafted in Austria in preparation for EU membership. They identify changes in those aspects of accounting law to which the main parties could not at first agree, and hence to assess the *unconditional* influence of powerful groups that is exercised in circumstances where disagreement between the parties is already apparent.

In times of global capital and product markets, standard-setting is an international process that poses special challenges and questions. The last two chapters of the book recognize these developments and reflect upon the politics of European and international accounting policy processes.

First, *Karel van Hulle* (Chapter 6.1) provides an illuminating insider perspective on EU accounting regulation. He explains why the EU moved away from the idea of European harmonization through the Accounting Directives to the adoption of International Accounting Standards for all listed EU companies and provides important insights into the dynamics of EU standard setting-processes.

In Chapter 6.2, *Michael Power* focuses on a specific interest group, the academics. He provides an international comparison of the role of academics in the accounting policy-making process in Germany and England. He analyzes the nature of their involvement, the degree of institutionalization of their voice, as well as their influence on the process.

On the Economics and Roles of Accounting

Roles of Financial Accounting: Equity Valuation

1

1.1

Accounting and Economics: What We Learn from Analytical Models in Financial Accounting and Reporting

Alfred Wagenhofer

1. Introduction

Consider the following examples of financial accounting "insights": (*a*) investors always prefer more information to less; (*b*) more disclosure by firms is useful since it increases the amount of information in capital markets; (*c*) regulators must force firms to disclose information, otherwise they would conceal bad news; (*d*) if firms can "lie" in their disclosures without threat of being caught, they will do so, therefore markets must be protected from reacting to such information; (*e*) earnings management is a bad thing, and regulators should reduce accounting choices; (*f*) management evaluation should be based solely on controllable financial results; (*g*) effective auditing deters management from making erroneous financial reports.

The list can easily be extended. What these "insights" have in common is that they are wrong, at least in the general terms in which they are stated. It is mainly analytical accounting research that explains the reasons for this conclusion, and that suggests that more careful thinking on such issues is warranted. This chapter discusses the approaches taken by analytical research and the types of results that analytical models can achieve.

The objective is to reflect on the merits of analytical models in financial accounting research and to provide some arguments on why it may be useful to invest in doing, or at least appreciating, this type of research. Because most analytical models have their origins in economics, I refer to economics in the title of this chapter. However, the chapter is not concerned with the two-sided interrelationship between accounting and economics, as are for example Hopwood (1992) and Klamer and McCloskey (1992).

In discussing the advantages and disadvantages of analytical research in financial accounting, the chapter also addresses frequently mentioned prejudices. For example, models are highly stylized depictions of real accounting phenomena, focusing on a small part of the whole picture and ignoring many other aspects. The models also appear to rely on unrealistic assumptions on the underlying situation and on people's behavior. The results are seen to be driven by exactly those assumptions. Therefore, models are considered highly specific to the setting, not generalizable, and thus not useful in practice. In addition, many people find the mathematics unnecessarily complex and too difficult to understand anyway.

I wish to note two caveats at the outset: First, the chapter is not intended to give a full survey of the methodology and the results of analytical research in financial accounting.[1] I emphasize the applicability of the methodology, and select the papers discussed to illustrate arguments on the basis of subjective personal opinion. Although the focus lies on financial accounting and reporting, I include, where appropriate, analytical models that speak to both financial and managerial accounting, or can be interpreted in either way. Second, I consider analytical modeling in its own right. I make no attempt to evaluate analytical research against competing methodologies used in financial accounting research, such as empirical, experimental, historical, legal, sociological, and psychological research.

The remainder of the chapter is organized as follows: Section 2 surveys the main characteristics of financial accounting that provide essential ingredients of analytical models. Section 3 highlights some properties of analytical models used in financial accounting, including the types of results and their assumptions. Section 4 presents a few examples of models that are applied to specific financial accounting issues and provides the results of such models. Section 5 discusses the robustness of the results, empirical tests, and policy considerations. Section 6 concludes.

2. Characteristics of financial accounting information

Financial accounting and reporting is essentially a means to provide information. If information is to be useful, there must be uncertainty that can possibly be resolved by such information. To understand why accounting is useful at all, analyzing accounting information in the context of certainty would be clearly inappropriate. An information system provides signals that alter the likelihood of the occurrence of future events or states of the world that are part of a decision problem. A decision problem is characterized by states of the world, their probabilities, actions the decision-maker can choose, results of state-action combinations, and the utilities the decision-maker receives from such results. The usefulness of information can only be assessed in the context of a particular decision problem. Thus, the same information system may be useful in one context but not in another.

General-purpose financial accounting and reporting is designed primarily to provide information to people outside the firm, such as investors, creditors, and customers. These parties are presumably interested in that information and rely on it for their own decision-making. The firm prepares the accounting information, and hence is better informed than the users. Further, some potential users of information have conflicts of interest with the firm (or the managers representing it). The information asymmetry generates concerns because it is not necessarily in the firm's (or its managers') best interest to provide the information at all, or to provide it in an unbiased fashion. It is in such a context that disclosure and earnings management issues arise. Introducing an auditor as another player with asymmetric information and potential conflicting interests adds another layer of incentive issues to be considered.

These three basic characteristics—uncertainty, multiperson settings with conflicts of interest, and information asymmetry—are ubiquitous in analytical accounting models.[2] In fact, the early analytical accounting research was particularly concerned with understanding the implications of the different characteristics on the value of information systems.

However, there are several features of financial accounting systems that make them peculiar information systems. Accounting provides periodic information about the financial position of a firm. Accountants use accruals to provide information about transactions and events, not just cash flows. Accrual accounting allocates cash flows to particular periods under specific transformation rules. This information leads to the distinct accounting "language," such as stocks and flows, assets and liabilities, and income. The transformation rules include the realization principle, which defines when revenue is recognized; the matching principle, which states that expenses follow the respective revenues; and conservatism, which introduces a bias in the reported income.

Accounting generates summary measures of transactions and events that occurred during a period and of net assets at the balance sheet date. This process involves a great deal of aggregation, which is done via the recognition and measurement of assets and liabilities. Different valuation concepts are used. For example, some assets are measured at historical cost, others at fair value or market value, discounting is considered for measuring certain items and not for others.

Financial accounting and reporting is governed by standards or rules developed by standard-setters or legal bodies on a national or international level. The objective is to provide decision-useful information to the stakeholders of the firm, often by focusing on information that investors in capital markets demand, but also on stewardship. Financial reports are audited by independent public accountants. They are subject to scrutiny by the board of directors and supervisory boards, respectively, or by audit committees. In many countries there is some form of public oversight by private boards or by government institutions, and enforcement is carried out by such institutions or the courts. All these institutions are supposed to assure the quality of financial reports.

Accounting information competes with other information sources, which are provided either directly by the firm or generated by intermediaries. To be valuable, the information must have a comparative advantage over other sources, or at least a complementary value.[3] Indicators attesting that this is in fact the case are that investors and analysts usually generate earnings expectations and react to firms meeting or not meeting them, and that they also react to accounting scandals. Firms exert effort in managing earnings, which is costly and must be considered worthwhile. These features make accounting reports a special—and important—information system. Useful models in financial accounting attempt to capture some of these features.

3. Setting up the model

3.1. Typical model structures

Different economic model structures have been used to capture financial accounting and reporting issues. Most of them belong to the family of games with incomplete information.[4] These games are characterized by having at least two players with different information endowments and potentially conflicting interests. These characteristics fit well with the general setting in which accounting is embedded. The common solution concept for such games is the (Bayesian) Nash equilibrium. It requires that no player can gain by deviating from his or her equilibrium strategy, given his or her expectations about the other players and given the other players stick to their equilibrium strategies. In equilibrium the expectations are justified.

In the following discussion I distinguish between models that rely on precommitment of the parties and those that do not. The ability to precommit enriches the parties' action spaces and introduces a sequential rather than a simultaneous-move game. Models that emphasize precommitment include, most prominently, agency models that focus on contracts between a principal and agents. Usually, the principal is assigned the full bargaining power by assuming that she moves first and proposes a contract, but the agent can only decide whether to accept the contract. Contracts with creditors and the issuance of new capital are often modeled by assigning the bargaining power to the agent (firm and current owners, respectively). Formally, there are no qualitative different results.

Formally, the contract maximizes the principal's expected utility under the conditions that the agent accepts the contract and then reacts optimally given the contract provisions. The solution concept is constrained maximization, and is similar to the Stackelberg solution in economics.

Because of the focus on contracts, agency models are well suited to capture the relationship between the owners of a firm and its managers or between a firm and its capital providers. Management accounting is usually placed in the hierarchical organization of a firm. Thus, agency models play a major role in its consideration. In financial accounting, management performance and compensation issues are the most prominent application. Accounting information can serve as a performance measure in a compensation contract, giving the agent incentives to work in a desired way and providing (compensation) insurance to a risk-averse agent. If available before the action, accounting information may improve the agent's decisions to the benefit of the principal, but at the same time increase the incentive problem. A major insight generated by analytical models is that the value of information for each of these uses may differ. Therefore, designing a single accounting system requires a tradeoff between the effects on different uses.

In models that do not rely on precommitment, players maximize their welfare simultaneously rather then sequentially, relying on their information endowments and the expectation of others' reactions. The equilibrium solution is in reaction functions rather than in one player preempting others' decisions by precommitment. Models include general equilibrium models, signaling, disclosure, cheap talk, and bargaining games. Such models are useful for studying the effects of accounting information and financial reporting in capital markets or product markets without specific contractual settings. Moreover, in multiperiod settings, it becomes less palatable to assume that complete contracts reaching well into the future can be written or enforced. Thus, even if there are contracts, they capture only part of the relationships between players.[5]

Although both agency models and models that do not require precommitment have been used extensively to study accounting phenomena, the latter seem to have more potential to offer fresh insights. The results of simultaneous-move games are more likely to be surprising. Further, such games have the property that the outcomes can be discontinuous for continuous changes in underlying parameters. The solutions of agency models appear "smoother" because they are the result of the principal optimizing under constraints. Small perturbations of assumptions usually have only second-order effects on the result, and introducing another economic force into a model is likely to shift the original solution smoothly in one or the other direction. The modeling skills consist in finding combinations of countervailing forces at work that are of similar power so that they result in an interesting tension.

The early analytical accounting models analyzed predominantly managerial accounting issues.[6] However, recently, financial accounting has become the predominant realm for using economic models. This shift may seem surprising from a modeling point of view, since management accounting offers more degrees of freedom than financial accounting, which is much more constrained by institutional solutions and prevailing rules applied in actual practice. For example, depreciation schedules are usually considered in a financial accounting context. However, if a model results in a depreciation that is not observed in practice (such as the relative benefit depreciation schedule[7]), to over-come such criticism upfront, the setting can be framed in a managerial accounting context.

The increasing attention paid to financial accounting models may be due to the general increase in interest in financial accounting, to some extent driven by the internationalization of accounting standards and the empirical literature that requires theoretical hypotheses to test. Another reason may be that management accounting makes more use of agency theory settings due to the hierarchical organization within a firm. Financial accounting issues are much more frequently modeled in a simultaneous-game setting, which, as stated earlier, may be more promising for generating further insights.

3.2. Types of results

Analytical models provide a rigorous structure for analyzing accounting issues, they uncover forces that drive arguments and results, and they are explicit about the usage of accounting information in the modeled situation. A major strength is that such models aid in strategic reasoning, that is reasoning that occurs in situations in which parties act upon each other, inferring from observed results what information others may have, anticipating others' actions, and reacting optimally to those actions based on their available information set.

Models are particularly useful if they come up with interesting, at first sight counterintuitive results, results that we might not have thought of, or which look unexpected in the first place, but become obvious once the logic of the results is uncovered in the model. A typical example is that information can have negative value (even if the information system is costless). To avoid being exploited by the firm, the mere knowledge that the firm possesses superior information can induce another party to change its actions relative to a situation without superior information. This change of equilibrium actions can be costly to the firm, and the cost can be so severe *ex ante* that it outweighs a positive value of the information system for another use. The formal analysis of such situations makes it possible to pursue the direct and indirect effects that information may have on players' strategies, many of which would be much more difficult to consider without the entire rigor that the mathematical formulation requires. Of course, to be "interesting," such results should be not merely a narrow pathology of the model, but have broader implications.

Formally, there are two typical ways to derive prima facie counter-intuitive results: One is to show that an intuitively reasonable result does not hold either in general or under certain conditions. The other is to derive possibility results, that is an example of a constellation in which a counterintuitive result arises. Such results sharpen our understanding of phenomena and the conditions that are required to obtain them.

Structurally, agency models lend themselves to optimal solutions within the assumed set of constraints. If explicit solutions cannot be derived explicitly, which is often the case, then at least some properties or regularities of the solution can be stated. However, if this is difficult, another possibility for gaining some insights is by examples and numerical simulations.

More recently, comparing the performance of particular methods or solutions has gained acceptance.[8] This approach is more modest in its objective, because it tries to link an analytical model directly to observed practice rather than attempting to search for an optimal solution. Besides reducing complexity, this approach may present a way around the often highly specific optimal solutions of analytical models. For example, it may be useful to consider the effects of historical cost versus fair-value accounting in a specific situation, rather than optimizing over all perceivable valuation concepts. Or, going even one level lower, it may be interesting to consider effects of different fair-value concepts on parties' behavior.

These comparison models can sharpen our understanding of the effects and relative benefits of different concepts observed in practice. A major advantage is that such models are easier to bring into the classroom than are the models that seek to identify optimal solutions that are often far from those observed in practice.[9] However, the disadvantage is that it is not clear what the performance comparison of concepts, which can usually be shown not to be generally optimal, really implies. Trying to focus on such specific concepts may prevent one from seeing the larger picture. For example, it may well be that by directly comparing fair-value concepts, the conclusion emerges that one concept is better than another, but as it happens, the other concept is in fact part of the optimal solution of a larger problem that is not modeled explicitly. This potential shortcoming is reminiscent of the well-known *ex ante* versus *ex post* optimality of contractual agreements in agency models if *ex post* solutions are compared.

3.3. Acceptable assumptions

Assumptions are the key ingredient to a model. They define the space in which the model's results hold: Given the assumptions, the results follow logically. Usually, all relevant assumptions are explicitly stated, and they are the focus of critique. In this sense, they "drive" the results, and the results are sensitive to changing assumptions. However, there are usually implicit assumptions. Some are considered so common that readers are familiar with them, some relate to other points, such as how well functions behave. Still others are taken for granted, for example the natural contractual environment including the enforcement of contracts by the courts. These implicit assumptions should not have a major effect on the results, because otherwise the model would be incomplete.[10]

As with any model, assumptions are intended to capture the expected main (first-order) effects of model variables, leaving aside minor or second-order effects that would only add complexity without materially contributing to our understanding of what is going on. There is a tradeoff between realism or generality of assumptions and tractability of the model. Good modeling skills consist in finding a parsimonious model that captures major economic effects of the sort observed in reality, but a model that is still tractable. It makes a difference if actions and/or outcomes are assumed continuous or discrete variables. In particular, a binary support is much easier to handle mathematically, but it is not clear if two realizations are a good representation of three or more realizations. Several results may not occur simply because only two realizations are considered. It is also more likely that mixed strategies obtain in equilibrium in binary settings, which are harder to translate into practical terms.

An important modeling decision is which variables are assumed exogenously and which ones are endogenous to the model. Ideally, all first-order effects should be endogenous, because this enables one to analyze the interaction with other variables, or just to find that there is no interaction so that separation is possible. Obviously, at some point, exogenous variables must enter. It is often difficult to judge what constitutes a useful cutoff point between exogenous and endogenous.

In what they call the "exogenous issue trap," Christensen and Demski (2002: 439) emphasize that to analyze the information produced by accounting methods, the model should deliver an endogenous reason for why a firm engages in the underlying transaction in the first place. For example, to analyze inventory valuation methods, there should be an economic reason in the model that the firm wants to hold inventory. However, a potential downside of this claim is an increase in such a model's complexity.

Generally, agents' labor markets are rarely endogenized in agency models in financial accounting. The level of the agent's reservation utility (i.e. his alternative expected utility if he does not accept the contract) and his wealth are usually exogenous. The utility level might affect the agent's relative risk aversion, which many would consider an undesirable or second-order effect. To shield the agency problem from such effects, researchers often assume negative exponential utility functions. However, leaving the agents' labor market outside the model also ignores potential adjustments of the reservation utility in a multiperiod context, which could result from signals that, for example, allow other employers to infer agents' characteristics.

Few accounting models explicitly model negotiation. A reason is that bargaining models in economics have shown that the outcome is highly dependent on the assumed sequence of moves by the bargaining players, and that almost any outcome of a bargaining process can be supported by some set of assumptions. Therefore, bargaining power is exogenously assigned to the players.

Assuming a variable as exogenous does not necessarily imply that this variable does not have a great impact on firms and managerial decisions. Take as an example income taxes, which are exogenous in most decisions taken by managers on the firm level. Assuming the firm is not in a position to politically influence tax laws or their concrete interpretation by the fiscal authority, the tax authority basically acts as a principal by precommitting to a tax schedule. Then, there are few interaction effects. This implication makes the analysis of tax effects less "interesting" from a modeling perspective, and we in fact see few models that consider taxes explicitly.[11]

Costs that are determined from outside the model are another exogenous variable. Examples are costs of acquiring or disclosing information, or, more generally, transaction costs. Often, such models are considered unsatisfactory if the cost is essentially driving the results. The reason is that there is no strategic effect related to the cost, so that a major advantage of models, namely the study of strategic interaction, does not emerge.

In the early days of agency theory applications, many studies assumed certain shapes of functions, such as linear compensation functions, and analyzed the induced behavior of parties.[12] Later, researchers tended to search for general solutions. Restrictive assumptions made on utility, compensation, and probability functions were "unacceptable," except for some mild regularity constraints that were required for mathematical tractability.[13] Although this research provides many important insights into the usage and value of information systems in general, it is difficult to locate any accounting-specific content in it. For example, it is generally impossible to separate the optimal compensation into a performance measure (which I consider central of accounting) and a compensation function.[14] A monotone likelihood ratio property of the distribution function is required for optimal compensation to increase in output.

Over time, models grew in complexity so that they became difficult or impossible to handle mathematically. Therefore, in the early 1990s, previously "unacceptable" restrictive assumptions on the form of certain functions became acceptable. In particular, the LEN model has become a popular version of an agency model. It exogenously restricts the agent's utility function to negative exponential, it assumes linear production technology and a linear compensation scheme in the performance measures, and it assumes a normal distribution of the stochastic productive term. The main objection stems from the fact that, given a negative exponential utility and a normal distribution, the optimal compensation function is not linear. Thus, the assumptions are not fully compatible with each other. This observation raises the question of why one would want to study suboptimal settings in the first place.

Nevertheless, since many qualitative properties of a more general agency model carry over nicely to the LEN model, it is a useful model for generating new insights because of the dramatic increase in tractability. With the LEN assumptions in place, explicit solutions often become obtainable, direct comparisons of "optimal" solutions under one or another settings are possible, and interesting extensions, such as multi-action models, can be pursued in more depth. Of course, there are downsides, too. For example, assuming linear compensation functions prohibits analysis of other compensation schemes that occur in practice, such as management stock options or bonuses payable on reaching a target.

It remains to be seen what sets of assumptions may become "acceptable" in the future. A potentially promising avenue might be to include behavioral assumptions on the players' characteristics. Although preferences and taste formation are usually outside economic models, the usual rationality assumptions could be enriched by specific assumptions on the behavior and utility.[15] Considering the rise of behavioral economics and behavioral finance, such considerations may have a future in accounting. There have been a few papers that assume costs of reasoning, costs of allocating scarce time to several tasks, or empire-building preferences. More recently, Evans et al. (2001) show that honesty may have an effect on managerial reporting and could be incorporated by appropriate assumptions. Hirshleifer and Teoh (2002) analyze financial reporting to markets with not fully attentive investors. Other models rely on noise traders and similar constructs to arrive at useful results. What is important is that the patterns of behavior are described formally to be able to analyze its effects. The assumption of some kind of "bounded" rationality black box would not lend itself to economic analysis. However, assuming a certain kind of deviation from full rationality invites questioning why it is exactly this deviation rather than another. Appealing to psychological regularities may justify such assumptions. Such models would have merit if they can explain observable irregularities.

4. Some insights generated by analytical models

In this section I discuss a few examples of the insights generated by analytical models in financial accounting and reporting. These examples illustrate the flavor of these models and their arguments. The examples are drawn from more recent literature and are oriented toward capturing specific financial accounting properties.

4.1. The value of aggregated information

Aggregation is a major characteristic of accounting information. Virtually all financial performance indicators, including sales, profit, earnings per share, return on capital, and gearing, are based on highly aggregated information about transactions and events that occurred during a period. In the case of balance sheet items, the indicators use even earlier period information. Valuation is a means to transform transactions and events in a way to make aggregation possible.

Aggregation implies a loss of information content. The individual pieces of information carry more information about a state of nature or an act than does an aggregate, unless the aggregate is a sufficient statistic of the underlying information for a particular decision problem. However, it is rare that such a sufficient statistic exists, particularly if we consider the additional constraint that aggregation in financial accounting usually means to add or subtract values. Thus, one would expect that even after ignoring any information costs, aggregation is strictly disadvantageous.

This type of reasoning is inherent in the information content perspective of financial accounting.[16] This approach interprets accounting numbers as particular summary measures of underlying events. If an accounting procedure such as revenue recognition emerges as a sufficient statistic for the underlying information in a certain economic context, it is said to have some economic appeal (e.g. by saving potential unmodeled costs of information). Moreover, it becomes possible to compare different accounting rules with each other. However, this approach does not show the necessity of particular accounting procedures. It is difficult to think of aggregation as providing a strict advantage since the accounting procedure just rephrases and aggregates the original information. An underlying reason may be the fact that the sufficient statistic concept is perhaps too strong for deriving meaningful tradeoffs, but alternative concepts are not in sight. Thus, it is difficult to argue a strong advantage of aggregated accounting information.

How then might we explain the advantages of aggregation? One reason may be bounded rationality or limited information-processing capabilities, but then some users would have a comparative advantage in capabilities and could take advantage of disaggregated data, or they might apply a different aggregation than the one imposed by the accounting system. A more formal reason is that the value of information in an agency or game setting can be negative because the players anticipate the asymmetric information and adjust their reactions accordingly. This adjustment may result in a disadvantage of the informed player relative to remaining uninformed. The availability of only aggregated information, which is coarser contractible information, may reduce such a negative effect.

Consider a two-period agency setting in which the periodic performance measures are correlated (e.g. positively due to persistent noise or negatively due to tidiness of the accounting system). The agent's employment is governed by a two-period contract that can be renegotiated after the first period (i.e. the parties cannot commit that they would not renegotiate the contract at a later point if this is mutually beneficial). The correlation between the performance measures over time may, in fact, induce the parties to renegotiate the contract, but such a correlation can impair the incentives in the previous period because the parties anticipate renegotiation. Thus, a "ratchet effect" reduces the principal's utility. In such situations, the value of information can become negative under certain conditions, and using an aggregated performance measure in the contract may be beneficial (Indjejikian and Nanda 1999; Christensen et al. 2002). Aggregation essentially substitutes for the lack of commitment.

This reasoning applies more generally: Accounting information can help overcome contract imperfections such as a lack of precommitment or enforcement, availability of only short-term contracts, restrictions of the compensation function (as in the LEN model, in which nonlinear performance measures may be used to substitute for an inflexible—because assumed linear—compensation function), and the like. It is not surprising that fine-tuning accounting methods for this objective generates a close link between accounting and its usage in a certain organizational context.

4.2. Modeling conservatism

Assuming that some form of aggregation is required, the question arises how to aggregate information. This question leads to another accounting characteristic, conservatism or prudence. Conservatism biases accounting income toward lower income in earlier periods. It appears in different forms: Historical cost accounting does not recognize increases in value, but requires impairment in case the value declines. The lower of cost or market principle for inventory is similar. According to many accounting rules, certain intangible assets, such as research and development, are not recognized even if investment in these is economically similar to an investment in tangible assets. Expected losses are recognized if they become known, but expected gains are not recognized until they are realized (virtually certain). Another form of conservatism is to put more weight on lower estimates in case of doubt. This form is referred to in the IASB's Framework definition of prudence as "the inclusion of a degree of caution in the exercise of the judgments needed in making the estimates required under conditions of uncertainty, such that assets or income are not overstated and liabilities or expenses are not understated" (para. 37).

The usual arguments for conservatism in the standard-setting process include the following: Conservatism serves creditor protection if the distribution of dividends is limited to reported earnings (and retained earnings). It offers a tax advantage if taxable income is linked to financial statements. Conservatism reduces the expected litigation cost for the firm, its managers, and its auditors, provided that the costs are higher for an overstatement of earnings than for an understatement. What is often missing from these arguments is the tradeoff between the claimed benefits and potential costs due to conservatism including, for example, loss of unbiased information for forecasting or inefficient retention of money within the firm. More fundamentally, it is not obvious why the underlying rules that link economic consequences to accounting numbers exist in the first place. They are exogenously assumed.

Conservative accounting numbers are seldom applauded for measuring management performance. However, there are models that explain why conservatism may be a desirable feature for performance measures. One explanation is based on the limited liability of the agent. Kwon et al. (2001) show that the principal is better off designing an accounting system that reports a low accounting signal, given that the outcome is in fact low with a higher probability than a high signal given the outcome is high.[17] This effect is due to a subtle tradeoff between better information and compensation that must be paid to the agent. In a multiaction agency model, conservatism is an optimal property of an accounting system if the actions induce individual outcomes with different variances. Assuming outcomes are aggregated into a single performance measure, the optimal aggregation exhibits conservatism in that riskier outcomes are discounted relative to less risky outcomes (Wagenhofer 1996). In a similar model, Bushman and Indjejikian (1993) show that an accounting system is optimally biased if compensation is based on the accounting measure and the market price (as an unbiased measure). These findings are consistent with putting more weight on lower anticipated outcomes of highly uncertain events.

The arguments sketched here do not consider multiperiod effects that do exist because of the usual clean surplus condition of (much of) financial accounting. A different route for analyzing conservatism is to focus on the timing of recognition rather than on valuation in a certain period. Assuming that information is costly, it is worthwhile considering what events should occur so that it is acquired.

Given that the manager self-reports financial accounting information, he usually has an incentive to report favorable income because his compensation increases in the firm's income. Acquiring additional information after favorable information is reported, for example by an audit, is more useful in disciplining the manager's reporting incentives than acquiring information after an unfavorable report. This conditional recognition creates, on average, a kind of conservative bias (Christensen and Demski 2002: 349–56). A lower of cost or market rule can be optimal in a setting that provides incentives for an agent who puts effort into a production technology and controls the timing of sales in a firm. Combined with residual income as the performance measure and an appropriate interest rate, this rule achieves optimal incentives and no distortions of production and sales decisions taken by the agent (Dutta and Zhang 2002).

4.3. The value of earnings management

Earnings management comprises measures taken by informed managers to bias disclosed financial information. Managers are thus able to influence users of that information. Empirical studies and various accounting scandals are evidence of managers' incentives to manage earnings. Various people argue that earnings management should be prohibited or opportunities for it should be reduced. Doing so would protect users, particularly investors on capital markets.

However, assuming capital markets are sufficiently information-efficient, investors would be able to see through managed earnings. It is interesting to note that assuming this were the case, managers would not abstain from earnings management even if it were costly to them (Fischer and Verrecchia 2000). In game theory terms, there is no equilibrium without earnings management in such a game. This result is reminiscent of a prisoner's dilemma situation. The manager would be better off if he could convince the capital-market participants that he had not engaged in earnings management. However, since he cannot credibly do so, the market rationally expects a bias, and the manager has no better response than to bias his report until expectations about the bias are fulfilled on average. This result shows that it may be difficult to avoid earnings management. Moreover, in the same model, earnings management imposes a deadweight loss on the economy, and there may be good reasons to restrict it by setting stricter rules.

What about earnings management in an agency setting? Would a principal allow earnings management to take place in a situation governed by an optimal contract? Agency theory provides us with a powerful result, the revelation principle. It states that given some contract that induces earnings management, there exists another contract that achieves the same outcomes but induces truth-telling by the agent. Such a truth-inducing contract can be designed in such a way that the agent receives the same compensation for each signal he may have as he would get in the old contract. Formally, the revelation principle combines the agent's reporting function and the previous compensation function into a new compensation function. However, there is a cost associated with inducing truth-telling. Implicit in the compensation function is the principal's precommitment to use the reported information in a specific, (usually) *ex post* inefficient, way. The principal thus restricts herself to not making full use of the information, and sometimes to ignoring it all the way.

If the revelation principle holds, the principal cannot do better by giving the agent leeway for earnings management. However, the revelation principle requires several restrictive assumptions, including unlimited communication, unrestricted compensation functions, and unlimited precommitment.[18] Thus, to model earnings management in an agency setting, at least one of these assumptions must be abandoned. Finding that earnings management is part of the optimal solution suggests that it is beneficial. Giving incentives to the manager to avoid earnings management generally makes the principal worse off because, formally, it adds another constraint to the problem.

On the other hand, earnings management is usually disadvantageous to the principal relative to a situation in which earnings management can be restricted exogenously, because the manager uses it to his advantage. The principal has less control than she does without earnings management. However, there may be other reasons why earnings management still can have a positive effect on the principal's utility. One is that earnings management is available only under certain circumstances. Earnings management then implicitly provides information about these circumstances, and the principal can use this information to improve on the contract (Demski 1998).

4.4. Auditing and reporting

Another important characteristic of financial accounting and reporting is that financial statements are audited by an independent public auditor. Many models assume that there is an audit technology that can be acquired at a cost and which then delivers additional information in a prespecified way. Some of the more intriguing models assume the auditor is a rational, utility-maximizing person. Appealing to institutional audit arrangements, it is usually assumed that the auditor is paid a fixed fee, and the only sanction is if the auditor is caught not having fulfilled his task so that a penalty is imposed or a loss of reputation occurs. This setting, while supported by the institutional setting, is clearly a questionable exogenous restriction on feasible contracts with the auditor.

Consider the following model: The principal wants a manager to work hard, but is not able to observe the outcome until the time comes to pay the manager. Therefore, she depends on the manager's report on the outcome. She also hires an auditor to verify the report, but she cannot observe the auditor's effort or the outcome of the audit. Thus, she relies on the auditor's report as a basis to pay the manager. This quite natural setting has the (perhaps surprising) consequence that the principal can motivate neither the manager nor the auditor to work hard.[19] The reason for this result is as follows: Given the manager's report, the auditor chooses his report to maximize his fee—independent of the audit result. Therefore, the auditor has no incentive to incur audit costs. Anticipating the auditor's strategy, the manager chooses the report that maximizes his compensation independent of his effort. Of course, there are no incentives for him to choose a high effort. This result implies that there must be an additional institutional mechanism to control the auditor. If there is to be any incentive to provide sufficient assurance services, there must be a chance that the auditor could be caught issuing a clean opinion on a wrong report and would be penalized. Still, this threat cannot ensure that the manager always reports truthfully (Baiman et al. 1987). Suppose to the contrary that the manager always reports truthfully, then the auditor would not have any incentive to perform an audit, because he knows that the manager will tell the truth anyway. But, anticipating the auditor's strategy, the manager has an incentive to not report the truth. Therefore, equilibrium requires that the manager does not report truthfully in some instances.

Similar reasoning applies to the effects of increased auditor liability. Increasing the liability for audit failures provides greater incentives for the auditor to work hard, which in turn increases the quality of financial reporting. However, this result holds only if nothing else changes, which is seldom, if ever, the case. First, increasing the liability increases the auditor's expected cost and will usually increase required audit fees. The principal must trade off the increase in audit fees against the increase in quality. Second, an increase in audit quality may affect the behavior of other parties. For example, investors are less willing to spend resources to challenge the financial reports before the courts. Because this outcome is anticipated in equilibrium, it may in fact reduce the quality of financial reports and lead to a compensatory effect to the earlier increase in their quality.[20]

5. Using results

5.1. Robustness

A classical critique of analytical models is that varying the setting or specific assumptions slightly may have a substantial effect on the results. Complex interactions usually do not lend themselves to simple and robust solutions, so it is not surprising to find that the results are not necessarily robust.

Duopoly disclosure models provide a particularly neat illustration for nonrobustness. Suppose there are two firms competing in a product market and one of them has private information. Does this firm benefit from precommitting to disclose the information to its competitor truthfully? The answer is, it depends. Results turn on whether they are Cournot or Bertrand competition, and on whether common or individual information are assumed.[21] The information alters the production strategy of the competitor, which in turn affects the production strategy of the informed firm. The net effects obviously depend on the strategic interaction between the type of market competition and the type of information.

Therefore, to show that the results change for variations of the setting, and how they change, is an interesting result per se. As the discussion of virtues of games suggests, it is often the unpredictable behavior of solutions that generates new insights.

Nevertheless, models that come up with robust results may have particular appeal if the robustness is not obvious. Such models are rare, though. An example of a certain robustness is the unraveling principle in financial disclosure,[22] which states that if a rational user finds that the firm withholds information the user expects it to own, the user does best to assume the information is such that it must be unfavorable to the firm, and react accordingly. Inferring this, the firm is induced to disclose more information than it would otherwise. Another example of a relatively robust result is that residual income is a (and often the only) performance measure that achieves goal congruence between owners and managers who have conflicting interests.[23]

5.2. Empirical tests

Empiricists need a theory to do empirical research and analytical models provide them with a theory. They tell empiricists what variables to collect and relate to the phenomenon they are after, and how to interpret the results. Nonrobustness has the virtue that it helps to develop more refined hypotheses. A prerequisite for being useful for empirical research is that the results are not based on a narrow pathology of a specific model, but instead are sufficiently broad so as to influence observable variables.[24]

However, it is often difficult to test the results of analytical models. The main reason is that many variables that have a substantial influence on the results are not observable. Demski and Sappington (1999) speak of "summarization with errors." Observational difficulties start with utility functions, available sets of actions, beliefs, information endowments, other actions, and contractual agreements. What might be even more important is that realizations of variables may not be observed in equilibrium.

To illustrate, consider the observation that agency relationships include fixed payments, and nevertheless agents exert high effort. Is this a result that casts doubt on incentives and agency models in general? Not necessarily. Suppose that given the agent does not behave as desired, there is the chance that an outcome is realized that cannot obtain if he behaves as agreed (moving support). If the principal were to observe such an outcome, she could infer that the agent deviated, and punish him heavily. In equilibrium, punishment is not observed because the agent can—and will—avoid it, and the (observable part of the) contract specifies a constant salary that shields the agent from output risk (and constitutes optimal risk sharing if the principal is risk neutral).

A characteristic of agency models is the importance of precommitment. An *ex ante* optimal contract usually requires the principal to commit to do something *ex post* inefficient, for example evaluate the agent based on some accounting signal that—given the optimal contract—is *ex post* pure noise. Since only the *ex post* behavior is observed, it might lead to the conclusion that principals act inefficiently—which is not true in an *ex ante* perspective.

In a similar fashion, if contract renegotiation is possible, the principal would design a renegotiation-proof contract, which implies that renegotiation is not observable in equilibrium. Nevertheless, the contract is different from one in which renegotiation were excluded by appealing to some exogenous institution.

In many games, there are a plethora of equilibria; so it would not be surprising to find an infinite number of equilibria. If multiple equilibria occur, it is difficult to draw conclusions as to which equilibrium is the most plausible one.[25] Although there are many refinements of equilibria, they are often not powerful enough to rule out all but one equilibrium. Thus, their predictive ability is somewhat lower.

This discussion indicates that caution is advised if analytical models are tested empirically. An alternative to empirical research may be experimental research. In a laboratory setting, the situation under investigation can be controlled more easily than in real life, and the researcher can manipulate the parameters. However, due to the fact that subjects know the situation is not "real," they may behave differently.

5.3. Policy recommendations

An important characteristic of financial accounting and reporting is that it is governed by detailed accounting standards or rules. Normally, standards are considered exogenous constraints in a model. Analytical models formalize decision problems of parties in such an environment. Many models are on the microeconomic level, particularly those, such as earnings management and disclosure policy research, that analyze incentives. It is less common for analytical models to lend themselves to policy recommendations, because policy-makers must weigh the advantages and disadvantages that particular standards impose on different affected groups, including preparers, users, and intermediaries. Weightings are highly subjective and difficult to defend, and therefore accounting researchers shy away from them.

As mentioned earlier, models search for interesting interaction effects, and do not necessarily capture the main effects. To derive policy implications, the usefulness of results should be based more on major effects rather than on "interesting" effects if these do not coincide.

Another reason that models are not often used by policy-makers is that they want to have conclusive research results, that is, clear and unambiguous answers to their imminent questions.[26] Case-by-case and nonrobust results are perhaps intellectually fascinating, but difficult to translate into advice for standard-setters. They are useful cautions to standard-setters to consider interactions as well as optimal reactions of parties in their deliberations of standards, but they certainly do not give answers to questions such as "Should employee stock options be recognized as expenses in the income statement?" or "Should a performance statement include the disclosure of unrealized fair-value changes of financial instruments in a separate column from other income?" What they can answer is what incentive effects such standards would create.

6. Conclusions

What do we learn from analytical models in financial accounting and reporting? This chapter gives an overview of the advantages and disadvantages of this research methodology and its achievements in the field of financial accounting.

The major advantage of analytical research lies in its precision and the rigor of its analysis, its explicit assumptions, and the logic behind its results. The results can be intersubjectively confirmed. This methodology is particularly useful for gaining insights into situations that are characterized by the strategic interactions of different decision-makers with information asymmetry and potentially diverging interests. The resulting equilibria often include prima facie counterintuitive results, and uncover important conditions that must be present for certain results to hold. The best justification for the use of a model is if the result is surprising relative to the prior knowledge.

The intuitive statements made in the Introduction are: (a) Models tell us that more information is not always better. Besides potential competitive disadvantage, investors may lose because they must consider that the firm acts on superior information. They would change their actions relative to a situation in which the firm has no superior information to avoid being exploited. (b) More disclosure by firms need not be useful, since it does not necessarily increase the amount of information in capital markets. More disclosure may reduce private information acquisition of investors, thereby reducing the total amount of information. (c) Regulators must force firms to disclose information. Otherwise firms might conceal bad news. The unraveling principle tells us that firms will even disclose bad news because of the anticipated skeptical market reaction on nondisclosure. (d) If firms can "lie" in their disclosures without threat of being caught, they will do so. Whether markets must be protected from reacting to such information depends on the sophistication or information efficiency of capital markets. Rational investors could ignore unverified information, thus protecting themselves. Moreover, firms may face countervailing interests and do not lie. (*e*) Earnings management is not necessarily a bad thing because it can convey additional information. (*f*) To provide incentives, management evaluation must be generally based on financial performance measures that contain uncontrollable events. In equilibrium, a contract is designed so that the manager is given the incentives to act as desired. Thus, any variance in the performance measure is necessarily caused by uncontrollable events. (*g*) Effective auditing cannot deter management from making erroneous financial reports. If this were the case, the auditor would not need to invest in auditing, and anticipating this, the manager would have an incentive to make a wrong report.

Many results are idiosyncratic to the particular model in which they are derived, but they caution us not to be too quick to generalize simple arguments. "It depends" results are common. While many results may be seen as a collection of special cases, they are useful for understanding structures and to refine our thinking about such structures.

Some of the examples discussed in this chapter show the difficulties encountered when specific properties of financial accounting are modeled. We still have only a limited understanding of many accounting properties, such as accruals, tidiness, conservatism, realization, fair-value accounting, and the like. Thus, there exists a great potential for future research. Exploiting the rich institutional setting in which accounting is placed is a way to distinguish accounting research from purely applied microeconomics. Moreover, analytical research is internationally applicable, and comparing international institutions gives us further impetus to learn more about accounting. I have noted in this chapter that the set of accepted assumptions changes over time. It may become fashionable to import more assumptions from other methodologies, such as sociology or psychology. Analytical models are open to adopting concepts from other disciplines.

Notes

This chapter is motivated by Dieter Ordelheide's initiative to establish and to support a workshop series on Accounting and Economics within the European Institute for Advanced Studies in Management (EIASM), which has been held every other year since 1994. EIASM has successfully provided a platform for European and international researchers to discuss research mainly under this particular methodology. The chapter is in part based on a presentation given at the Euroconference "Financial reporting and regulatory practices in Europe" in Palermo, Italy, in 2001, and at the EAA Doctoral Colloquium in Seville, Spain, in 2003. Useful comments by Anthony Hopwood, Christian Leuz, and Dieter Pfaff (the editors), John Christensen, Graeme Dean, Ralf Ewert, Barbara Pirchegger, and seminar participants at Nanyang Technological University and The University of Sydney are gratefully acknowledged.

1 There have been several survey papers over time, including for example Verrecchia (1982, 2001), Demski and Kreps (1982), Feltham (1984), Ballwieser (1996), Wagenhofer and Ewert (1997), and Lambert (2001).
2 Lazear (2000: 100) stresses rational behavior, the equilibrium concept, and the concept of efficiency as the fundamental characteristics of economics. These are present in the analytical accounting models, too.
3 See for example Christensen and Demski (2002), part III.
4 There is a different stream of models that has gained attention in recent years. They may be described as representation models. One such model is the Feltham and Ohlson model (Ohlson 1995; Feltham and Ohlson 1995), which links accounting earnings to the market price of the firm. It starts with the identity of the present value of the expected future cash flows and the book value of net assets (equity) plus the present value of the expected future residual incomes, and develops an earnings dynamic that allows for representation of firm value as a simple function of book value of net assets and earnings. There is uncertainty, but no decision-maker involved nor any optimization going on.
5 Contracts can also be used as a precommitment device for parties with whom no contracts are written. For example the strategic transfer pricing literature uses observable management contracts as a means to influence the intensity of price competition on a product market.
6 See also Lambert (2001: 4).
7 This depreciation, while optimal in certain contexts, may become accelerating or even negative in some periods. See Rogerson (1997) and Reichelstein (1997).
8 In managerial accounting, this type of modeling has been used in transfer pricing where alternative transfer pricing mechanisms can be compared to each other. See for example Baldenius et al. (1999).
9 This observation is due to S. Reichelstein who, in his plenary presentation at the Workshop on Accounting and Economics in Madrid 2002, illustrated it by research in auctions. Although there has been much research in optimal auctions, the greatest impact was generated by comparisons of the relative efficiency of different auction types.
10 See Feltham (1984: 180).
11 Taxes may serve as signaling or precommitment devices (e.g. taking into account differential national tax rates) to influence games between the firm and other parties. It may also be interesting to search for ways to undo negative tax consequences on managerial decision-making at the least cost (see e.g. Baldenius and Ziv 2003).
12 See for example Demski and Feltham (1978) and Magee (1980) for budgeting models.
13 For instance, in agency models the agent is usually assumed to accept the contract if it offers the same expected utility than the reservation utility. Assuming instead that the agent must have a strict benefit from accepting the contract may lead to a situation in which, formally speaking, no solution exists, since optimization occurs over an open interval.
14 See Banker and Datar (1989).
15 See Lazear (2000: 112). For a discussion of psychological insights and their economic modeling see Tirole (2002). On the other hand, Christensen and Demski (2002: 437) consider irrational behavior of second-order importance. Kunz and Pfaff (2002) discuss intrinsic motivation and recommend not incorporating it directly into models.

[16] See for example the recent overview in Christensen and Demski (2002, ch. 7). In a series of papers, Ordelheide (1988*a–c*) used a similar framework.

[17] Gigler and Hemmer (2001) model conservatism in a similar fashion to analyze financial reporting strategies.

[18] See in particular Arya et al. (1998).

[19] The same would hold if the auditor's fee is contingent on the reports. For a discussion see Wagenhofer and Ewert (2003: 392–7).

[20] See Ewert (1999), and for an overview of other literature Wagenhofer and Ewert (2003, ch. 10).

[21] See for example Gal-Or (1986).

[22] See for example the recent overviews in Verrecchia (2001: 141–60), and Wagenhofer and Ewert (2003, ch. 7).

[23] See for example Reichelstein (1997) and the subsequent literature.

[24] For an elaboration on this theme see Chapter 3.1 by Verrecchia (2003) in this volume.

[25] Lazear (2000: 114) suggests that models that have multiple equilibria miss out something, for example beliefs and changes of beliefs over time, that should be modeled.

[26] See Schipper (1994: 65–6).

References

Arya, A., Glover, J., and Sunder, S. (1998). "Earnings management and the revelation principle," *Review of Accounting Studies*, 3: 7–34.

Baiman, S., Evans, J. H., and Noel, J. (1987). "Optimal contracts with a utility-maximizing auditor," *Journal of Accounting Research*, 25: 217–44.

Baldenius, T. and Ziv, A. (2003). "Performance evaluation and corporate income taxes in a sequential delegation setting," *Review of Accounting Studies*, 8: 283–309.

—— Reichelstein, S., and Sahay, S. A. (1999). "Negotiated versus cost-based transfer pricing," *Review of Accounting Studies*, 4: 67–91.

Ballwieser, W. (1996). "Ein Überblick über Ansätze zur ökonomischen Analyse des Bilanzrechts," *Betriebswirtschaftliche Forschung und Praxis*, 48: 503–27.

Banker, R. D. and Datar, S. M. (1989). "Sensitivity, precision, and linear aggregation of signals for performance evaluation," *Journal of Accounting Research*, 27: 21–39.

Bushman, R. M. and Indjejikian, R. J. (1993). "Stewardship value of 'distorted' accounting disclosures," *The Accounting Review*, 68: 765–82.

Christensen, J. A. and Demski, J. S. (2002). *Accounting theory—An information content perspective* (Boston, MA: McGraw-Hill, Irwin).

Christensen, P. O., Feltham, G. A., and Sabac, F. (2002). "Correlated performance measures in dynamic incentives with limited commitment." Working paper, University of British Columbia, April.

Demski, J. S. (1998). "Performance measure manipulation," *Contemporary Accounting Research*, 15: 261–85.

—— and Feltham, G. A. (1978). "Economic incentives in budgetary control systems," *The Accounting Review*, 53: 336–58.

—— and Kreps, D. M. (1982). "Models in managerial accounting," *Journal of Accounting Research*, 20(Supplement): 117–48.

—— and Sappington, D. E. M. (1999). "Summarization with errors: A perspective on empirical investigations of agency relationships," *Management Accounting Research*, 10: 21–37.

Dutta, S. and Zhang, X.-J. (2002). "Revenue recognition in a multiperiod agency setting," *Journal of Accounting Research*, 40: 67–83.

Evans, J. H., Hannan, R. L., Krishnan, R., and Moser, D. V. (2001). "Honesty in managerial reporting," *The Accounting Review*, 76: 537–59.

Ewert, R. (1999). "Auditor liability and the precision of auditing standards," *Journal of Institutional and Theoretical Economics*, 155: 181–206.

Feltham, G. A. (1984). "Financial accounting research: Contributions of information economics and agency theory," in R. Mattessich (ed.), *Modern accounting research: History, survey, and guide* (Vancouver: CGA Research Foundation), 179–207.

Feltham, G. and Ohlson, J. A. (1995). "Valuation and clean surplus accounting for operating and financial activities," *Contemporary Accounting Research*, 11: 689–732.

Fischer, P. A. and Verrecchia, R. E. (2000). "Reporting bias," *The Accounting Review*, 75: 229–45.

Gal-Or, E. (1986). "Information transmission—Cournot and Bertrand equilibria," *Review of Economic Studies*, 53: 85–92.

Gigler, F. and Hemmer, T. (2001). "Conservatism, optimal disclosure policy, and the timeliness of financial reports," *The Accounting Review*, 76: 471–93.

Hirshleifer, D. and Teoh, S. H. (2002). "Limited attention, information disclosure, and financial reporting." Working paper, Ohio State University, July.

Hopwood, A. G. (1992). "Accounting calculation and the shifting sphere of the economic," *European Accounting Review*, 1: 125–43.

Indjejikian, R. and Nanda, D. (1999). "Dynamic incentives and responsibility accounting," *Journal of Accounting and Economics*, 27: 177–201.

Klamer, A. and McCloskey, D. (1992). "Accounting as the master metaphor of economics," *European Accounting Review*, 1: 145–60.

Kunz, A. H. and Pfaff, D. (2002). "Agency theory, performance evaluation, and the hypothetical construct of intrinsic motivation," *Accounting, Organizations, and Society*, 27: 275–95.

Kwon, Y. K., Newman, D. P., and Suh, Y. S. (2001). "The demand for accounting conservatism for management control," *Review of Accounting Studies*, 6: 29–51.

Lambert, R. A. (2001). "Contracting theory and accounting," *Journal of Accounting and Economics*, 32: 3–87.

Lazear, E. P. (2000). "Economic imperialism," *Quarterly Journal of Economics*, 115: 99–146.

Magee, R. P. (1980). "Equilibria in budget participation," *Journal of Accounting Research*, 18: 551–73.

Ohlson, J. A. (1995). "Earnings, book values and dividends in security valuation," *Contemporary Accounting Research*, 11: 661–87.

Ordelheide, D. (1988a). "Kaufmännischer Periodengewinn als ökonomischer Gewinn," in M. Domsch, F. Eisenführ, D. Ordelheide, and M. Perlitz (eds.), *Unternehmenserfolg—Planung, Ermittlung und Kontrolle*, in Honor of W. Busse von Colbe (Wiesbaden: Gabler), 275–303.

—— (1988b). "Zu einer neoinstitutionalistischen Theorie der Rechnungslegung," in D. Budäus, E. Gerum, and G. Zimmermann (eds.), *Betriebswirtschaftslehre und Theorie der Verfügungsrechte* (Wiesbaden: Gabler), 269–95.

—— (1988c). "Kapital und Gewinn. Kaufmännische Konvention als kapitaltheoretische Konzeption," in H. Hax, W. Kern, and H.-H. Schröder (eds.), *Zeitaspekte in betriebswirtschaftlicher Theorie und Praxis* (Stuttgart: Poeschel), 21–41.

Reichelstein, S. (1997). "Investment decisions and managerial performance evaluation," *Review of Accounting Studies*, 2: 157–80.

Rogerson, W. P. (1997). "Intertemporal cost allocation and managerial investment incentives: A theory explaining the use of economic value added as a performance measure," *Journal of Political Economy*, 105: 770–95.

Schipper, K. (1994). "Commentary: Academic accounting research and the standard setting process," *Accounting Horizons*, 8(December): 61–73.

Tirole, J. (2002). " 'Rational irrationality': Some economics of self-management," *European Economic Review*, 46: 633–55.

Verrecchia, R. E. (1982). "The use of mathematical models in financial reporting," *Journal of Accounting Research*, 20(Supplement): 1–42.

—— (2001). "Essays on disclosure," *Journal of Accounting and Economics*, 32: 97–180.

—— (2003). "Some policy implications from the theory-based literature on disclosure," Chapter 3.1 in this volume.

Wagenhofer, A. (1996). "Vorsichtsprinzip und Managementanreize," *Zeitschrift für betriebswirtschaftliche Forschung*, 48: 1051–74.

—— and Ewert, R. (1997). "Unternehmensrechnung und ökonomische Theorie," *Homo oeconomicus* XIV(1/2): 31–62.

—— (2003). *Externe Unternehmensrechnung* (Berlin: Springer).

1.2

Aspects of the Future in Accounting: The Use of Market Prices and "Fair Values" in Financial Reports

Michael Bromwich

1. Introduction

This chapter looks at some arguments for incorporating into accounting reports further estimates or predictions of the future and items that embed future cash flows. Addressing this topic may seem to be anachronistic when reactions to the recent corporate scandals, in especially the United States of America, are seeking to reduce the ability of managers to practice fraudulent behavior and accounting manipulation. This has led to a wish for reliable and validated (trustworthy) figures in accounts enforced by new complicated monitoring and inspection processes. However, aspects of the future permeate even conventional accounting and form essential components of the accounting structure. The decision relevancy of accounting, which is generally agreed to be a primary factor giving accounting societal value, may be weakened by the search for trustworthy accounting procedures. The trick is to incorporate aspects of future values without leaving too many degrees of freedom for managerial manipulation. This chapter reviews some suggestions of how far this may be achieved by seeking to use market values in accounting reports.

Existing Generally Accepted Accounting Principles (GAAPs) in a number of countries contain elements of the market values of assets and liabilities. For example, International Accounting Standards (IAS), U.K., and U.S. GAAPs require financial investments that are not long-term investments to be shown at their market values, with unrealized gains/losses on trading and on "held for sale" assets going to income[1] and those from longer-term assets going to equity. Some liabilities are carried at market value. Fair values are to be used in valuing assets and liabilities in acquisitions. Impairment tests that involve comparing asset accounting values and their market values are required on all assets, with the writing down of accounting carrying values to their present values or more usually their market values where these are lower—a nonsymmetrical incorporation of market values.[2]

The Joint Working Group on Financial Instruments and Similar Items (JWG) (comprising standard-setters from a number of countries) have produced proposals that derivatives and other financial instruments should be carried at their fair values and losses and gains on these values should be taken to the income statement (so called "mark to market" accounting).[3]

The International Accounting Standards Board (IASB) has issued an exposure draft requiring insurance companies to mark their assets to market. The Accounting Standards Board (ASB) in the United Kingdom has issued a very controversial standard (Financial Reporting Standard 17, FRS 17) requiring firms to show the market value of the assets of their pension funds and of their liabilities.

Asset market values and revaluations based on them may also be used for physical assets, including property, plant, and equipment in a number of accounting regimes, including that of the IASB and those influenced by the United Kingdom but not, however, under U.S. GAAP, unless the assets were obtained in acquisitions, though here later revaluations are not allowed. Under these regimes, any revaluation gains cannot be included in operating income. Generally, fair valued acquired intangibles and goodwill cannot be revalued. The United Kingdom allows some recognition of internally generated intangibles that may be revalued but only where a clear and well-organized market exists. In the United States, some software-related costs may be recognized but revaluation is not allowed. Present values can also utilized under these regimes, but infrequently, for example in valuing finance leases and in some elements of impairment tests.

The first section of the chapter outlines some of the common concerns of standard-setters with decision-orientated accounting and some of the general arguments for incorporating future-orientated accounting items into accounting reports. There are a vast number of topics that could be discussed but space only allows a look at one of a number of important movements of global significance that strengthen the future perspective in accounting reports. The second section therefore considers the strong movement toward "fair-value" accounting. This mode of accounting bases asset and liability carrying values on the prices that would result from arm's length transactions between well-informed participants, generally, and takes any gains or losses to income. As an example of this approach, some problems with suggestions for accounting for financial instruments are considered in the third section. The fourth section looks more briefly at the use of fair values with nonfinancial assets. The final section gives brief conclusions. Some aspects of the areas to be reviewed have been subject to detailed analytical treatments. Here the emphasis is more general and speculative.

2. Accounting from a decision-making perspective

The conceptual frameworks or statements of principles of the Financial Accounting Standards Board (FASB),[4] the U.K. ASB,[5] and the IASB[6] consider a wide range of users. However, they all seem to give priority to accounting reports that aid reasonably informed investors, usually coupled with creditors, who are willing to study information with sound diligence. The FASB states that financial reporting should aid users in assessing the amounts, timing, and uncertainty of prospective net cash inflows into the enterprise.[7] Many of the recent FASB accounting standards and most standard-setting issues that are being discussed internationally by groups of standard-setters, such as derivatives and related financial instruments, emphasize aiding investor decision-making.

A clear illustration of this common orientation amongst the three standard-setters toward investor decision-making and therefore future-orientated accounting is their very similar definitions of decision relevancy. These generally say that information has the characteristic of relevancy if it has the ability to influence the decisions of users by helping to form or confirm predictions and by altering prior expectations. This is quite a strong definition of relevancy implying that accounting has predictive value concerning elements of the valuation model used by investors but not so strong as the definition which assumes that accounting information "leads" stock prices. Weaker definitions merely require either that accounting information has some "news value" for the market or that accounting information is correlated with, or summarizes, or captures the information used by investors.

A second illustration of this common approach is provided by the very similar definitions of assets and liabilities. The essential characteristics of an asset are stated to be that it had been acquired in the past, is within the control of the firm, and it is expected to provide future economic benefits. Similarly, a liability has the characteristic of involving a future sacrifice to settle a specific and dated obligation incurred in the past.

These definitions are entirely consistent with the view that accounting reports should aid decision-makers in predicting future cash flows. The next section considers what a decision-making approach implies for accounting. The essence of this approach is that accounting items should be measured using their economic values, which are founded on the cash flows they are expected to generate.

2.1. The economic approach to accounting valuation

The first essential characteristic of the economic approach to valuation is that the market value of the firm on a well-organized securities market is assumed to be the present value of expected future dividends to a decision horizon or to infinity. It is the aggregate present value of the dividend flow that matters not its distribution over time. Such valuations would allow for perceived managerial asymmetrical information and the ability of any in-place incentive systems to overcome problems arising from possible managerial behavior. Any valuation applies to a separable quoted entity conditioned by the public information possessed by the market at the time of valuation. Thus, security market prices change over time as the available information alters. A well-organized or well-behaved market is one where all opportunities can be traded (complete markets) and all traders face the same prices for the same items (perfect markets). A well-organized market is also said to be informationally efficient in the sense that the prices generated will be unbiased estimates of market values and will impound all the available public information used in trading in such well-behaved markets.

The expected dividend flow from a company can be estimated directly using a variety of valuation methods (see e.g. Penman 2001).[8] Alternatively, the equity value for a firm can be estimated by adding to the market values of the firm's net assets the value of what is called the "internal goodwill" of the firm or its "organisational efficiency." The use of market values brings the future strongly into accounting reports by utilizing the market view of the future cash flows to be generated by assets. The market values of separable assets in a well-organized market in equilibrium are the market prices of the firm's assets calculated on the basis that each asset will earn a normal return for its risk class. Any valuation of internal goodwill (or organizational efficiency) of the firm is an estimate of the present value of any future super profits over and above any normal returns to be generated by the firm. Super profits are net cash flows over and above the amount required to yield the firm's cost of capital on its net asset value. Here, goodwill refers to internally generated goodwill as distinct from purchased goodwill, which is generally recognized in accounting reports. Expected super profits are generated by, for example:

(a) independent projects having positive net present values;
(b) the benefits from any nonaccounted and nontraded assets, such as the outcomes of research and development; and
(c) the profits flowing from any interrelationships (synergy) between the firm's assets and liabilities and its networks of activities.

In a well-organized market in equilibrium all super profits will have been competed away. Thus, here the market value of a firm's net assets (total assets less liabilities) will equal its value on the securities market.[9] Allowing for temporary super profits in well-organized markets, the accounting equity value of a business obtained using asset and liability market values will equal the present value of future super profits plus the aggregate market value of the business' net assets, where the firm practices clean surplus accounting in which all gains and losses are taken through the income statement. This expression will be equal to the equity value of the firm on the securities market where all markets are well organized and utilize the same information, market participants share common beliefs and objectives, and neither aggressive nor conservative accounting is being practiced.[10,11]

This formulation is similar to Ohlson's residual income approach (see Ohlson 1995; and also Edwards and Bell 1967).[12] This formulation does not especially privilege the market values of assets and liabilities as it can be derived for any clean surplus accounting system. This approach does, however, use values of economic significance as distinct from some other accounting systems. Often market values from well-organized markets measure opportunity costs to the firm. They also measure elements of the firm's endowment, those assets and liabilities that are recognized in the financial report.

With accounting systems that use valuation bases different from market values, the internal goodwill "bridge" between security market value for the firm and the net value of its assets will be wider than the value of super profits defined as the value of profits over and above normal returns. This bridge or "place filler" will always include estimates of the value of assets and liabilities not recognized by the accounting system used, including the values of any interrelationships between assets and liabilities not captured in accounting values and with non-market value systems that will also include estimates of the differences between accounting carrying values and market values of an entity's assets and liabilities. Use of market values reduces need for super profits to be augmented by an adjustment for the difference between market values and accounting carrying values of net assets. Even with a market value accounting system, some further adjustment may be required where the accounting procedures used are conservative or aggressive.

However, critics of value relevance argue that any value-relevant accounting system which seeks to estimate security market value using accounting information is redundant as this merely duplicates security market value that is already available.[13] However, this overstates the role of accounting reports. At least currently, accounting does not report internally generated goodwill. If such estimates were provided by management they would differ from those incorporated in equity values where information and preferences differ. Accounting uses a "bottom up" approach to reporting the values of assets and liabilities and to determining profit (revenue minus the cost of inputs used), which cannot be determined using only information ordinarily available to the market, requiring for example detailed input information and asset lives. Accounting cannot on its own provide a value for the firm (estimates of super profits are also needed and will generally incorporate nonaccounting information). Conventional accounting information, which aids the estimation of super profits, will generally be tied to specific accounting items rather than the entity as a whole. Accounting seeks to provide trustworthy numbers (and some information not otherwise available) for some elements that enter into the valuation model. It therefore seems reasonable that one characteristic of accounting numbers should be their value relevance.

In assessing any argument for market prices the characteristic of these prices should not be forgotten. Market prices reflect only the views of the participants in the marginal transaction. Others may value more highly the traded item because of the cash flows expected to be received from the item in their use. Similarly, suppliers obtain super profits at the transaction price because they would be willing to supply intra marginal units at a lower price. Asset and liability market prices are noisy (incorporate variables not specific to the item being forecast). A firm's cash flows may not reflect, or only partially reflect, changes in the market prices of its assets and liabilities. Market values are more variable over time than management forecasts and traditional historical accounting because they respond to more information signals than either management forecasts or traditional accounting. They may incorporate different information to that possessed by management. They are, however, less likely to be "managed" than accounting numbers. Market prices at a given time may, however, over or undershoot what may be called rational bounds. Even the most ideal markets including those on which financial items are traded may contain a broad range of frictions and imperfections, which mean that prices do not reflect all preferences.[14] It is crucial that such factors are taken into any analysis of accounting using market prices in financial reporting, however this theme is not taken up further here.

2.2. Market values in accounts

The move to market values strongly brings the present in the form of market prices into accounting and therefore the future in the form of future cash flows into accounting. It therefore has to be based on compelling logic. The above reasoning supports the use of market values for assets and liabilities and their revaluations if accounting is meant to aid decision-making by investors insofar as these values can be shown to have economic significance. One approach to showing economic value used by the ASB and to a degree by IASB is to use "value to the business" or "deprival value" reasoning. This seeks to determine the value of assets and liabilities by determining the minimum loss (gain) to the business if the firm were to be deprived of an asset (liability) with sufficient notice so that the firm could compensate for any deprival in its normal markets. Generally, the result of these deliberations will be a market value for the item.

These standard-setters apply this type of argument to less than perfect markets where buying (entry) prices differ from selling (exit prices). Here, looking only at assets, value to the business reasoning involves comparing what is called a separable asset's "value in use" with its entry and exit prices in order to determine the opportunity cost of the asset on deprival. The value in use of an asset owned by a firm is measured by the value of the incremental cash flows contributed to the firm by the asset as estimated by management. This valuation is consistent with the dividend valuation model in that it is based on the asset's contribution to enterprise cash flows. This is not true of either entry prices, which only enter the firm's cash flow plans when replacement is planned, or exit prices, which represent only one strategy available to the firm—selling the asset. Value in use will include any super profits generated by the firm in using the asset and any benefits accruing because of the inter-relationship of this asset with any other existing assets with which it is combined. As this value is based on incremental calculations, net asset value based on value in use may overvalue the firm as each asset value in use imputes to the asset all the super profits to which the asset contributes. Value in use is highly subjective and likely to be highly variable over time and therefore it is argued cannot be used in accounting reports based on trustworthy figures.

Value in to the business reasoning seeks to value an asset at its opportunity cost to the business from a deprival perspective that is determined by the relation between value in use and entry and exit prices.[15] The relation between the value in use of an asset and its market values can take three major forms. One is where the exit price (net realizable value or selling price) of an asset is greater than its value in use and higher than its entry price (generally a temporary situation except when assets are held for sale where value in use has little relevance). The value of such an asset will equal its entry price. The second possibility is that an asset has an entry market value (replacement cost or buying price) equal to or lower than the asset's value in use and higher than its exit value. Here the asset will be valued at entry market price as this measures its opportunity cost to the firm. The third possibility is where value in use is lower than entry value but higher than exit value yielding a value to the business equal to value in use (again a temporary situation).[16]

Value to the business advocates see as the central case where value in use exceeds entry price which exceeds exit price. This is the case where the asset is already possessed and expected to be replaced. Here, its opportunity cost, in the classical sense of the next-best foregone alternative, is its replacement cost (entry price). This opportunity cost can be justified in a number of ways. Possession of the asset saves the cost of buying the asset in the future—possession pushes replacement further into the future. In a firm generating super profits with an asset, its best alternative use is to utilize it to replace another asset of the same type yet to be bought. Thus, in this case the asset's value to the business, its replacement cost, is equal to its opportunity cost defined in the classical way.

However, this reasoning is quite nuanced because this equality requires that the firm must have obtained its optimal capacity, otherwise current or future replacement may not be the optimal act.[17] This is recognized by correct deprival value calculations that involve a valuation based on determining a chain of infinite asset replacements. Where there is surplus capacity the classical opportunity cost will be either the next-best internal use of the asset or its selling price. Selling price will represent opportunity cost only where it exceeds the value of the cash flows from the next-best alternative internal use. The next-best alternative may still be retaining the asset for future use in a period when the firm has obtained its optimal capacity. Here, replacement cost suitably discounted represents opportunity cost. However, the value of the best alternative use of the asset (in, say, producing another unit of the product for sale at a lower price or producing the next-best product) may be below replacement cost. This alternative use value has to be used under opportunity cost reasoning. In these circumstances, classical opportunity cost logic adopts a forward-looking perspective in defining opportunity cost rather than a deprival perspective. Where there is capacity rationing, the classical opportunity cost of the bottleneck asset is the present value of the aggregate contribution (revenue minus incremental direct costs) from the next-best alternative use, which will be to relax the constraint. Using replacement cost, as would value to the business reasoning, implies that any asset constraint will be removed.

Thus economic value to the business reasoning supports the valuation of nonfinancial assets at their market values using entry or exit prices where appropriate, subject to optimal capacity being achieved and providing that these prices are taken from well-organized markets and can thus be audited. Long practice in some accounting regimes allows market prices estimated by professional valuers working in well-organized markets to also be used for specific assets not themselves currently and actually traded in such markets.

Any concern with trustworthiness would, however, rule out both the use of estimates by management of market values and fair values provided for items where well-behaved markets do not exist even if provided by experts. Such estimates cannot be audited and cannot be seen as trustworthy figures. However, ruling out such estimates may be denying the market useful information. Although difficult to test, the sparse empirical evidence suggests that asset and liability market values are found to be useful to investors.[18]

This reasoning, which is more complex than that, used to support exit prices, can be applied to financial liabilities. Generally, financial assets and liabilities traded in well-organized markets will not attract any super profits and therefore their economic values will equal their market prices where entry and exit prices will not be significantly different. The logic becomes more difficult in instances where the liabilities incorporate nonfinancial obligations on the firm, such as payments in advance for later delivery of products and services, for example up-front payments for mobile phones or for pay TV subscriptions and for continuing service. Here attempts have been made to apply the mirror image of the above value to the business reasoning. This has yet to produce fully satisfactory results, but suggests that in at least some circumstances a case can be made for the uses of entry values. Even here, there are differences of opinion as to whether this is measured by the consideration received or other values.[19]

The FASB[20] in the Statement of Financial Concepts No. 7 (SFAC No. 7) and others, such as the JWG, reject value for business reasoning, as they are unable to accept the concept of value in use. They advocate the use of fair values as the valuation base without defining whether entry or exit values are in mind. The arguments provided by the FASB (SFAC No. 7, paras. 17–38) for this rejection of value in use are that present values (necessary for value in use computations) embody managerial intent, and more generally, are entity specific and allow any forecast profits to be realized at the time of recognition. This denial of portraying managerial intent seems strange in any accounting orientated toward aiding decision-making. Any information known about managerial views would be incorporated in the prime dividend decision model suitably adjusted for the uncertainty surrounding such information.

Ideally, fair values embody the market's expectations (strictly those of the marginal traders) concerning assets and liabilities. Thus, FASB wishes to substitute the views of the market for those of the management. They see present value measures as providing an estimate of fair value only where market prices are unavailable. Only when a market price for an asset or liability or for similar assets and liabilities is absent is a present value valuation necessary, as otherwise the marketplace's view of present values of such items is embodied in market prices that are held to capture all elements relevant to asset value.

The FASB's major argument for fair value is that the accounting valuations should, ideally, recognize the amount of asset cash flows and their timing and expectations of changes therein, the time value of money, the price of the risk inherent in assets, and other factors (SFAC No. 7, para. 24). It is argued that it is only fair values that capture just these factors. Using managerial estimates includes additional items to those listed above that reflect differing managerial information and different preferences to the market. Allowing for these in accounting would mean that identical items would be valued differently. The underlying wish is for accounting to state things "as they are", free of any managerial manipulation. Management is thus judged by how well they have taken advantage of past and current opportunities reflected in the market or how far they have foregone such opportunities. All this hardly amounts to a strong theory and ignores other opportunities not reflected in accounting items (such as failure to maintain market share and failure to match product innovation).

Implicit in this movement is a wish to get management to "tell it as it is" and avoid managerial manipulation. Given the subjective nature of many accounting items, there are many different stories that can be told. Using market prices reduces somewhat the scope for storytelling but at the cost of denying investors access to managerial asymmetric information at least in the accounts. This may be a heavy cost to pay and may reduce the value of accounting information to investors. Strictly, an accounting system based only on market prices contains no new information for investors (market prices are available elsewhere) and they could themselves work out the results of such systems for firms, though it would be cheaper for firms to do this. Where only some market prices are used, information on how changes in these items are correlated with or caused by other items not valued at market prices are not made transparent in the financial reports.

The FASB's view regarding the use of market prices may be more restrictive than suggested above. With financial liabilities, it equates fair value only with exit price.[21] The JWG also favors exit values. Similarly, the IASB, in the context of their convergence program with the FASB, in dealing with assets held for disposal, have redefined the recoverable value of an asset (the higher of the two: its value in use and its net selling price).[22] Here, asset fair value, less the cost to sell, is equated to net selling value thereby opting for an exit price as fair value. As far as can be seen, there is no fundamental logic available for this view equivalent to value to business reasoning or, more generally, opportunity cost reasoning as introduced above. Exit prices figures are used as economic models where they represent the best available option to the firm. Using exit values implies that the firm has no better opportunities available to it. This is an empirical question but it implies that financial assets cannot generate super profits. This, as has been seen and will be further analyzed, is a very strong assumption.

The wish to use fair values may be based on a rational expectations view with informationally efficient and well-organized markets. Here, market prices do provide trustworthy numbers that can easily be validated. The reasons for FASB's views may be that the setting envisaged is one involving only financial assets and liabilities in well-organized markets, where the various prices and values are not significantly different and a choice between entry, exit prices, and values in use does not have to be made. Thus, market values can measure some of the cash flows which enter into the dividend valuation model.

However, they will give no indication of the possible overall super profits likely to be obtained by the firm and therefore are not very helpful in decision-making regarding individual entities. In conventional accounting, any *ex post* super profits are part of realized profits that are not specially analyzed and their inclusion in profits is to a degree a matter of managerial choice. Indeed, fair values as seen by standard-setters ideally reflect only the detailed effects on a firm's portfolio of financial items of known market-wide influences. The above arguments in favor of fair value are unlikely to be sufficiently robust to cope with imperfect markets and with nonfinancial assets where there may be a gap between entry and exit prices of assets. Indeed, many current impairment charges have to be, perforce, based on managerial valuations.

Fair-value reasoning cannot deal with accounting items such as internally generated goodwill and many intangibles that do not have a separate market price. From the perspective of business reasoning and economics more generally, if these items are to recognized, they should be shown at their value in use. The only alternative is to use historical cost.

The next section looks at a current attempt to incorporate market values into accounting reports and considers some of the complexities raised in this section.

3. Current issues in using market values in accounting for financial items

The focus on valuation has changed from nonfinancial items to financial assets and liabilities reflecting differing concerns over time. The use of market values for nonfinancial assets and, in some cases, inflation adjustment for monetary items was discussed intensively across the commercially developed world during the mid-1970s and the early 1980s. A number of standard-setting bodies promulgated disclosure requirements or allowed the use of alternative accounting standards in this area under the title "current cost" accounting, which generally required the use of entry prices or their surrogates for non-financial assets but maintained historical cost for financial assets and liabilities with the possibility of some adjustment for general price changes.

These requirements were withdrawn in the mid-1980s in the face of commercial opposition, including the view that current costs were not used in managing the enterprise,[23] empirical evidence that investors seemed not to use current values, an unwillingness to base taxation on current values, which were seen as too subjective to be used, and possibly declining inflation worldwide. This does not mean either that problems earlier associated with nonfinancial assets have gone away or estimates of the value of their future cash flows are not relevant in investment decision-making.

Even though many standard-setters have stated clearly their wish to move over time to market values for all assets and liabilities, there has been no real movement with regard to nonfinancial assets apart from recent concerns with asset impairment and business combinations. Both these concerns have required much of the above theory to be introduced into accounting standards but only in very narrow areas where, perhaps, no other solutions could be found and the theory has been used only in restrictive forms. With impairment, only downward revaluations are allowed and with business combinations any upward revaluation is highly restricted or not allowed. There still seems to be fear concerning the virulent but narrow opposition that is provoked by any statement in this area. As has already been indicated and discussed further below, this leaves a big gap in accounting reports aimed at helping to predict firm values. The switch to fair value seems to have arisen from a need to account for financial instruments.

3.1. Fair values and derivatives

The major current thrust is to seek to use fair (exit market prices) values for valuing financial assets and liabilities.[24] There seems to be a general consensus amongst standard-setters that this is the way to move. Currently, the required treatments of these items differ across standard-setting regimes though there is general agreement on fair values as the valuation base.

Much of the action has focused on derivatives starting with requiring substantial disclosure and currently culminating in recent valuation requirements by the IASB and FASB to use fair values except for some hedges. The JWG has recently published an authoritative consultation document in this area.[25] Their proposals include that derivatives and other financial instruments should be carried at their entry market prices and that losses and gains on these prices should be taken to the income statement (so called "mark to market" accounting but actually requiring much "mark to model" and "mark to estimates") and that generally hedge accounting should not be allowed. Hedge accounting allows gains/losses on a financial item to be delayed so as to match changes in the price of another item. They also suggest major disclosure requirements including a description of major financial risks and their major effects on financial performance, information about balance sheet risks, how all these risks are managed, and information about methods used to estimate fair values.

The JWG bases its argument not on value to the business reasoning but on the attractions of fair-value accounting examined above. Recall that some significant markets for financial assets are often well organized and entry prices will be similar to exit prices, though the JWG and advocates of fair values in general provide no comprehensive evidence of such markets or their pervasiveness. The argument for fair values based on exit prices is that the market price of a financial asset/liability reflects the market's estimate of its present value obtained using the reigning discount rate for the item's risk class, conditional on the information available to the market. (This, however, is equally true of entry prices.) Thus, the income on a financial asset for a period will equal the going interest rate on its opening economic value.[26]

The JWG does not follow either economic or value to the business reasoning. Rather, it says that exit prices of financial items are consistent with the usual definitions of assets and liabilities used by most standard-setters (see JWG 2000, paras. 4.1–4.3) and are consistent with the view that the value of a firm is based on discounted estimates of future dividends (as are entry prices). It is a large step to argue that this supports the view that the market's estimates of the present value of the interest obtained from or paid by financial assets or financial liabilities, should be used to value financial items. This depends on the utility of accounting reports to the user.

Carrying financial assets and liabilities at their entry market values requires the accounts to show how the value of these items change in the face of interest rate changes. One major argument behind the JWG's reasoning is that such reporting will allow investors to appraise management's performance in holding financial assets and liabilities. The accounting report will therefore allow the investor to see what opportunities the management have taken or foregone. This amounts to requiring financial capital maintenance using exit prices and to saying that decisions should be made on this basis at least for financial items. Management may well object to this seeming interference in management decision-making as it did to the capital maintenance concept associated current cost accounting, which required the maintenance of physical capital in decision-making. There are many other forgone opportunities that are not currently reported in accounting reports and which may be more useful to investors, for example the possible benefits from alternative products and different sales plans. The argument for focusing only on the opportunities associated with financial items is that here changes can and should be reacted to instantaneously and at little cost. This implies that all market changes impact on all firms and are not the result of special factors or of government policy. Any easy adaptation is unlikely to be true for many financial items. For example, adjustments to credit lines may take some negotiation and many debt agreements are locked-in for substantial periods of time and trading in them may be difficult. In the latter case, reporting at current exit prices indicates only how well management was able to forecast financial market changes in which it may not have any special expertise. This highlighting of performance in managing financial items may divert managerial efforts from possibly more profitable endeavors. It also suggests that efforts to hedge and to use other methods to avoid possible accounting losses stemming from the use of fair values will increase substantially the number and type of instruments used.

3.2. Hedging

The JWG goes to the heart of the debate between traditional accounting and accounting that takes an economic perspective and rules out hedge accounting. Existing standards still allow this type of accounting. The alternative view basically follows from valuing financial instruments at exit prices. Using market exit prices there is no need to hedge for different accounting treatments of financial instruments as all instruments will be measured the same way and any changes in value between hedged items and the hedge will be counterbalanced. The Group found the widespread practice of hedging the cash flow consequences of risky future transactions permitted by most standard-setters to be more problematic. The JWG wish to rule out hedge accounting for this purpose. They do this for three main reasons. They see financial instruments as independent of other items including nonfinancial items. Therefore they see no reason why gains and losses should be deferred to hedge (insure) other transactions especially as such deferred gains and losses do not qualify as assets or liabilities respectively. Further the expected cash flows from future transactions cannot be treated as either assets or liabilities as defined by most standard-setters. Finally, they do not see management intentions concerning future transactions as relevant to accounts prior to an obligation being created. Thus, the current hedging of items that may occur in the future gives management the ability to manage earnings.

Some critics see a secret agenda here: to reduce the power to match transactions so as to limit the ability to "cherry pick" when to disclose gains and losses. The view here is that matching is an intrinsic and informative part of accounting seeking to bridge between periods (see e.g. Ernst and Young, *The ASB's framework—time for action*).[27] Matching and accruals give some view of the future as management sees it. However, it is important that whatever is done is transparent to accounting users. The primary valuation model, the present value of future dividends, does not speak to this issue as it is only concerned with the present value of the stream of future dividends. However, matching is permissible in present value models providing that allowance is made for any interest accruing from changing the timing of items. Thus, the real debate is about when an accounting item should be recognized. Much of the problem with hedging is that the hedged assets are either not recognized or are not carried in accounts at their economic values.

Other critics of the JWG have made a number of important arguments, some of which are highly technical.[28] Here we just review one or two of these criticisms. One of the major problems with JWG's approach is that well-organized markets for many financial instruments do not exist, for example for much of debt and especially for more exotic instruments. The view is that where a market does not exist for a specific instrument, the value of a similar instrument, with adjustments allowed for any differences, should be used. A generally accepted and tested valuation model to simulate markets should be used in the absence of similar instruments ("mark to model"). Models should be constructed in the absence of an agreed model. Any concern that accounting information should be trustworthy leads to the rejection of marking to models and the use of any substantially adjusted prices of traded similar instruments. However, some financial instruments, such as some swaps, do not have a historical cost and will therefore not appear in the financial report at all if the use of estimates is ruled out. This nondisclosure is a cost of ensuring that auditors are not set impossible tasks. One way around this is to allow the use of such estimates with an auditor's health warning as to the level of assurance.

A second major problem is whether it is possible to unbundle any connections between financial and nonfinancial assets. One example is where unreported super profits accruing from the firm's production or service operations attach to portfolios of financial assets, such as credit cards and prepayments. Examples would be prepaid mobile phones and pay TV channels that offer services to customers for an annual subscription, which is central in attracting and retaining customers. The JWG suggests that attempts must be made to exclude this type of benefit from the prices of financial items using corporate internal models. How such splits can be made in any economically meaningful or auditable way in the face of jointness in the firm's operations is not clear. The problem is again that not all assets are recognized at their economic values (JWG 2000: 216–18).[29] This recommendation is in exact opposition to their recommendations in the face of the major financial jointness faced by a firm—that of creditworthiness.

The problem of creditworthiness arises because the values of a company's liabilities may be affected by the firm's creditworthiness. The degree of creditworthiness of a firm is a function of the perceived risk of its current and future operations, that is of actual and expected super profits of the firm as a whole that are either not analyzed or not recorded in accounts. Standard-setters are divided about the treatment of creditworthiness in the valuation of financial instruments. The JWG suggests that no attempt should be made to separate creditworthiness from other elements of values of financial instruments, which seems to reverse the argument in the previous paragraph concerning gains associated with some liabilities. It also runs counter to the view that market prices are not firm specific.

The argument for incorporating creditworthiness in liability prices is rather complex. Two of the strands of this argument are presented here:

1. Firms that have experienced a decline in creditworthiness will face increasing interest rates and declining liabilities values and therefore

would make a gain if previous arrangements were made at a lower rate of interest and would make a gain on the lower value of its liabilities. These are the same effects as for increases in market interest rates and therefore should be treated the same way.

2. However, these gains will be offset by changes in asset values. Any decline in credit rating will be due to reduced perceptions concerning the existing and future cash flows reflected in reductions in nonfinancial asset values and in the value of expected super profits. Many of these changes may be in intangible assets and in super profits not currently recorded in accounts.

The JWG recognizes the second argument but says that it is outside its remit to suggest changes to accounting for nonfinancial assets and that shortcomings in accounting elsewhere should not comprise what they see as the appropriate accounting for liabilities. This gives a "lopsided" or asymmetric view to accounting and may confuse investors by hiding information. There are no obvious reasons why the market value approach should not be extended to nonfinancial assets where well-organized markets exist. The arguments of the JWG would seem to apply to nonfinancial current assets traded in well-organized markets, though some current assets would be valued at their entry prices. (The revaluation of current assets is currently illegal under EU Directives but the intention is to relax this prohibition.) Downward revaluation of assets is already allowed with impairment tests where asset market values are lower than their carrying values.

This illustrates a more general problem that runs contrary to the views of many standard-setters that financial assets and liabilities are fully separable from each other and from nonfinancial assets. In many of the cases discussed by standard-setters this is true but in other instances there may be a connection. Interest rate changes may reflect market-wide changes in time or risk preferences affecting the cost of debt and of equity. Such changes will affect the cost of equity and therefore the firm's overall cost of capital and will change the (discounted) value of super profits. Alterations in debt cost may therefore also be reflected to a degree in the values of nonfinancial assets. Such interrelationships may be very difficult to recognize without symmetrical accounting. For example, the JWG makes the point that where a firm has fully floating rate debt, where they are required in all time periods to pay the going rate of interest for that period, its value is invariant in the face of what they call a basic interest rate change (JWG 2000, paras. 1.23–1.26). In the case of a rise in this basic rate, they see the firm as being able to meet any additional cash flows required by obtaining a corresponding increased return on its assets; however, this is not guaranteed to many firms. The JWG does not consider how any matching increased return should be reflected in accounting. Thus, changes in the values of financial items may be indicators, sometimes, perhaps, leading indicators, of changes in the values of nonfinancial assets and in accounting profits.

3.3. How far can the use of fair values bring the future into accounting?

The aim of standard-setters with regard to financial items is to show the economic value of each class of assets and liabilities as if they were separable from each other and other entity resources; these values were linearly additive and as far as possible purged of super profits and managerial intent. This view relies on neither a strong theory nor on empirical evidence. It is really based on an economy with all relevant markets being well organized and in perfect equilibrium, which results in markets consistent with the standard-setters' scenario and in market prices that reflect economic values. Stronger theories that can cope with a world of imperfect and incomplete markets have been discussed above and indicate that the market characteristics denied by standard-setters have to be taken into account even with some financial assets and liabilities. However, such approaches require that ideally relevant super profits need to be incorporated into accounting reports where these are to be based on economic values.

Restricting the application of market values to financial items means that any effects of the drivers of such value changes on nonfinancial resources are not recorded. This again produces "lopsided" or asymmetric accounting. It is accounting with, at least, one wheel missing. The first defense against this is that none of the standard-setters has recently considered the valuations of nonfinancial assets—an operation that will require much time and a large amount of resources and one where standard-setters got their fingers severely burnt in the 1970s and 1980s. The second is that recording these effects will increase the subjectivity in accounting reports; but, of course, there is tradeoff between usefulness and reliability, and reliability or trustworthiness have no value on their own. A critic might say that faced with difficult problems, standard-setters have opted for a simple solution, which as a bonus has introduced additional relevant information about the future as seen by the markets into accounting reports for what are pragmatic reasons. Such a critic might also point out that the values of financial items in the setting assumed by standard-setters are not really of central importance to an investor interested in estimating future returns over and above normal returns. If one role of accounting is seen as providing some information about possible super profits then possible valuation bases for nonfinancial assets need further consideration.

4. Nonfinancial assets

Most accounting regimes have moved toward incorporating some values based on the future into accounting for nonfinancial assets. These movements are a long way from the full importation of what usually are called "current" values, to distinguish them from the predominant use of exit values in fair-value accounting, of nonfinancial assets into accounting.

The current treatments are generally not based on any strong theory. The revaluation of fixed assets is really the continuance of long-established practice. To be fair, the ASB's Statement of Principles does imply that this practice could be defended as having value to the business reasoning. This statement does predict the greater use of current values in the future for nonfinancial assets. Even if allowed, this use of current values would only partially aid investors in assessing super profits of the business. Permissible current values are likely to be only those taken from well-organized markets that generally will not manifest super profits. This again suggests that standard-setters are privileging market prices above theory. The contemporary restricted use of current values also does little to help investors to estimate items that are not recognized in conventional accounting.

Two examples from current practice give further instances of lopsided accounting reflecting what are really reactions to pragmatic accounting difficulties. Purchased goodwill has to be valued but this logic does not seem to make it more compelling to standard-setters to value internally created goodwill. To freeze the values of acquired assets at the time of purchase, as does U.S. GAAP, seems to have no obvious theoretical backing nor does the view that all such prices can be deemed to be fair values.[30] Many of these prices will not be taken from well-behaved markets necessary for fair values to have economic significance. If fair values are useful at the time of purchase, they surely should be of value at other times. The U.S. practice seems to suggest that market prices, and estimates based on them, are not really of sufficient quality for continual use in accounting reports for nonfinancial items (an empirical question).

Impairment adjustments generate lopsided accounting in a different way. If management is aware that the market value of an asset has declined, they have to test that this change has not resulted in the carrying value of the asset exceeding its net realizable value unless its value in use still exceeds its carrying value. In most regimes, the symmetrical treatments for market value increases is not allowed or not used for many assets. This is especially true under U.S. GAAP.

In order to determine whether impairment has occurred, management has to look at the value drivers of an asset very widely defined. Indeed, the lists of possible indicators of impairment amount to a list of major business problems of which investors would like to be informed but these are not required to be published. Some indicators of the presence of super profits do appear implicitly in impairment tests where value in use is operative. Impairments of corporate assets that will generally contribute to super profits (goodwill) are, in the U.K. regime, either to be allocated to cash generating units of the enterprise or they have to be tested separately for impairment. This test amounts to checking the firm as a whole or each separable cash-generating unit for impairment. This is also true for tests of impairment of acquired goodwill. Details of such tests would be useful to investors, however, only the results of these tests are declared to investors. Perforce such calculations cannot be based only on market values and managerial estimates and intentions have to play a part in them. It seems lopsided to only allow this for reductions in values especially as the information required is deemed of sufficiently good quality to allow impairment losses to be rewritten when values increase. Opposition to revaluation is based on a wish to avoid managerial manipulation. This suggests that some special mechanisms are available to avoid such distortions with regard to impairments and to reduce incentives to cherry pick when to opt for impairment disclosure. Firms with similar assets do not necessarily follow the same impairment policy or the same timing for such policy.

In summary, market prices of nonfinancial assets do have economic values but the current approaches reflect only sporadically any effects they may have on the firm generally. This leaves a "black hole" in accounting reports, which investors have to fill as best they can. Permissible current valuations of nonfinancial assets do little to remedy this even though market values may be available. Nor do allowable current values (except for the revaluation of mainly property assets) give much indication of any super profits available to the firm even though this information can be used in circumstances where impairment is considered.

The use of market prices for all accounting items will not fully solve the problem that GAAPs do not generally recognize most intangibles and super profits and their potential values, because they are deemed too subjective for trustworthy accounting.

5. Conclusions

Using purely a decision-making perspective this chapter looked at one aspect of incorporating more of the future in accounting reports by incorporating further market values of assets and liabilities into accounting reports. The main analysis focused on contemporary suggestions that all financial items should be carried in the balance sheet at their fair values, and gains and losses in these fair values should be included in enterprise profits. It argued further that the logic supporting such attempts also would apply to many nonfinancial assets and allows their revaluation. Using purely a decision-making perspective, it was argued that attempts should be made to incorporate valuations of super profits into accounts thereby helping to fill an important gap in accounting information for investors.

Value to business reasoning was shown to have been rejected by influential standard-setters, notably the FASB because this reasoning uses estimates of value in use that are firm specific being based on managerial intent. From the decision-making perspective of this chapter, it seems strange to attempt to sterilize accounting figures from managerial intent, which may provide important information for investor decision-making.

With regard to conventional financial items, standard-setters who advocated the use of fair values have succeeded in incorporating additional future in accounting in well-organized markets without allowing additional possibilities for managerial manipulation of accounting figures. Indeed, the use of market prices is held to reduce this possibility relative to that available to existing GAAPs. However, the possibility for substantial managerial manipulation arises where estimates of fair values are permitted (as in mark to estimate and in a different area—acquisitions).

A lack of theory becomes apparent in more complex situations, such as whether hedging should be allowed, which itself incorporates the future as seen by management. Another complex area is where liabilities incorporate effects on nonfinancial items.

This chapter suggests that some of these problems can only be solved by accounting for super profits or for internally generated goodwill, but this raises the major problem that at least some of the available figures for this are likely to be regarded as untrustworthy and unauditable under current conventions. This raises major problems for standard-setters who wish to aid decision-making. Given the possibility of managerial manipulation and the need to use objective information in ensuring accountability, the use of market prices may be the best we can do. However, this only makes informational sense if applied to all accounting items and this extends contemporary accounting considerably. Not reporting super profits means that accounting neglects information valuable to investors and forces them to use other sources that cannot be reconciled with the financial report.

One possibility is for standard-setters to release value in use from the impairment closet and to consider the effects of using the value to business reasoning for the upward revaluation of nonfinancial assets where relevant, perhaps as supplementary information with a clear indication of the degree of audit assurance. Recall that accounting as currently practiced only deals with individual assets (or groups of assets), any revaluation would therefore be confined to these and under the current accounting framework would deal only with any internal goodwill linked specifically to an asset or asset group or to a liability or groups of liabilities. A variant on this approach would be to allow super profits clearly attaching to specific assets to be reported. An example might be the valuation of a film library owned by a pay TV distributor where the type of films attract a specific clientele whose potential size can be reasonably estimated as can their likelihood of remaining with the distributor. Another example would be to allow a valuation to be attached to customer acquisition costs. These are problems that regulators are dealing with and regulations are beginning to be more liberal than current GAAPs because of the economic significance of these items. The conditions for such recognition are usually highly restrictive. This approach cannot be applied to overall goodwill. The general internal goodwill resulting from jointness between the firm's assets and from any network effects would generally go unreported (except where value in use was used as the relevant asset valuation). This would avoid the very difficult task of dealing with corporate assets that cause difficulty in impairment decisions concerning acquired goodwill.

Within the existing mind frames of standard-setters, one way forward is to encourage the publication of information supplementary to accounting reports and of the degree of audit associated with each type of information. A radical solution would be to allow firms to experiment in accounting for super profits, again indicating the audit quality associated with each piece of information. Such approaches should, as far as possible, stay within the framework of the relevant GAAP and explain the reason for any deviation from GAAP and its quantitative significance. Any of these approaches are still far removed from seeking to account for the whole of a firm's internal goodwill, which may well be beyond the scope of accounting.

Notes

[1] In the United Kingdom and EU current financial assets are being carried at historical cost.

[2] IASB has just issued a detailed exposure draft revising its approach to impairment. See ASB (2002), IASB on business combinations, impairment and intangible assets, consultation paper (London: Accounting Standards Board, December), 171–332.

[3] The Joint Working Group (JWG) (2000), Financial instruments and similar items (London: Accounting Standards Board). The Working Group comprised representatives or members of accounting setters in Australia, Canada, France, Germany, Japan, the Nordic countries, the United Kingdom, the United States of America, and the International Accounting Standards Committee (now Board).

[4] FASB (1978), Statement of Financial Accounting Concepts No. 1, Objectives of financial reporting by business enterprises (SFAC No. 1) (Stamford, CT: Financial Accounting Standards Board).

[5] ASB (1999), Statement of Principles for Financial Reporting (London: Accounting Standards Board).

[6] IASC (1989), Framework for the preparation and presentation of financial statements contained in the annual collection of International Financial Reporting Standards (London: International Accounting Standards Board).

[7] See FASB (1978), Statement of Financial Accounting Concepts No. 1, Objectives of financial reporting by business enterprises (SFAC No. 1) (Stamford, CT: Financial Accounting Standards Board), viii.

[8] Penman, S. H. (2001), *Financial statement analysis and security valuation* (Boston: McGraw-Hill Irwin), parts II and III.

[9] Revsine, L. (1973), *Replacement cost accounting* (Englewood Cliffs: Prentice Hall).

[10] Aggressive accounting generates accounting results for a period greater than those using economic values (income and/or asset values being higher than economically justified). Conservative accounting results are lower than is economically justified (income and/or net asset values being lower than the equivalent economic concepts). In practice, aggressive and conservative accounting practices are defined as more liberal or less liberal than GAAP, which itself may contain aggressive or conservative elements relative to the economic results of the firm.

[11] This approach can be expressed as an income amount by deducting the opening value of the endowment from the closing endowment. It can be shown that this income calculation yields an income for a period (called economic income) equal to the going interest rate for the firm on the opening endowment.

[12] Ohlsen, J. A. (1995), "Earnings, book values and dividends in equity valuation," *Contemporary Accounting Research*, Spring: 661–87. Edwards, E. O. and Bell, P. (1967). *The theory and measurement of business income* (Los Angeles: University of California Press).

[13] Holthausen, R. W. and Watts, R. L. (2000), "The relevance of the value relevance literature for financial accounting standard setting." Working paper, The Wharton School, University of Pennsylvania.

[14] Allen, F. and Gale, D. (2000), *Comparing financial systems* (Cambridge, MA: The MIT Press), 127–48.

[15] Solomons, D. (1966), "Economic and accounting concepts of cost and value," in M. Backer (ed.), *Modern Accounting Theory* (Englewood Cliffs: Prentice Hall). This framework is used by ASB in their Statement of Principles when presenting current value accounting (ASB (1999), *Statement of Principles for Financial Reporting* (London: Accounting Standards Board), paras. 6.6–6.9).

[16] Formally, the general rule for the value to the business or deprival value of an asset is min:{RC,max:PV,NRV} where RC is replacement cost, PV is present value or value in use, and NRV is net realizable value. The other three cases are: NRV > RC > PV yielding RC; PV > NRV > RC yielding NRV or RC; RC > NRV > PV yielding NRV or PV.

[17] Bromwich, M. (1977), "The general validity of certain 'Current' value asset valuation bases," *Accounting and Business Research*, 28(Autumn): 242–9.

[18] See Barth, Mary E., Beaver, W. H., and Landsman, W. (2001), "The relevance of the value relevance literature for financial accounting standard setting: Another view." Working paper, Stanford University, January, section 2.

[19] Lennard, A. (2002), *Liabilities and how to account for them, an exploratory essay* (London: Accounting Standards Board, October); and Macve, R. (2002), "Contract liabilities and revenue recognition: A comment on 'deprival value' reasoning." LSE Working paper.

[20] FASB (2000), Statement of Financial Accounting Concepts No. 7, Using cash flow information and present value in accounting measurement, Financial Accounting Standards Board, February.

[21] FASB (1999), Preliminary views: Reporting financial instruments and certain related assets and liabilities at fair value, Financial Accounting Standards Board, December.

[22] IASB (2003), Board decisions on international accounting standards: Update, "Assets held for disposal" (London: International Accounting Standards Board), January, 2.

[23] This point has also been made strongly in the debate about the treatment of financial instruments.

[24] For similar comments to this section see: Horton, J. and Macve, R. (2000), " 'Fair value' for financial instruments: How erasing theory is leading to unworkable global accounting standards for performance reporting," *Australian Accounting Review*, July: 26–39; and Bradbury, M. E. (2000). "Issues in the drive to measure liabilities at fair value," *Australian Accounting Review*, July: 19–25.

[25] JWG (2000), *Financial Instruments and Similar Items* (London: Accounting Standards Board).

[26] Horton, J. and Macve, R. (2000), " 'Fair value' for financial instruments: How erasing theory is leading to unworkable global accounting standards for performance reporting," *Australian Accounting Review*, July: 26–39 argue that this is the wrong income concept to use in a setting of expected changes in interest rates where income should be determined by maintaining the level of future cash flows rather than opening capital value.

27 Ernest and Young (1998), *The ASB's Framework—Time for Action* (London: Ernst and Young, March).
28 See for example: Horton, J. and Macve, R. (2000), " 'Fair value' for financial instruments: How erasing theory is leading to unworkable global accounting standards for performance reporting," *Australian Accounting Review*, July: 26–39; and Bradbury, M. E. (2000). "Issues in the drive to measure liabilities at fair value," *Australian Accounting Review*, July: 19–25.
29 JWG (2000), *Financial instruments and similar items* (London: Accounting Standards Board).
30 IASB (2002), ED3. Business Combinations, Basis for Conclusions in IASB, Proposals on Business Combinations, Impairment and Intangible Assets (London: Accounting Standards Board, December), para. BC74.

1.3

The Limitations of Financial Reporting

Wolfgang Ballwieser

1. Introduction

Financial reporting aims to provide information to actual and potential contracting partners of an enterprise and to the public. The information shows the results of management's stewardship and should be seen as supporting well-founded decisions. In some countries, for example Germany, the profit shown in individual accounts is also the measure of what can usually be distributed to shareholders.[1] However, this part of the contracting function of accounting is not discussed in this chapter.

Very often, the concept of decision usefulness is explicitly mentioned in the framework for financial reporting standards. Such a framework typically exists in countries with noncodified law on financial reporting and sets out the concepts that underlie the preparation and presentation of financial statements.[2] It provides important guidelines for the standard-setter who sets financial reporting standards.[3] In the International Financial Reporting Standards (IFRS), paragraph 12 of the Framework states: "The objective of financial statements is to provide information about the financial position, performance and changes in financial position of an enterprise that is useful to a wide range of users in making economic decisions." Similarly, the Statement of Financial Accounting Concepts (SFAC) No. 1, paragraph 16, says: "The function of financial reporting is to provide information that is useful to those who make economic decisions about business enterprises and about investments in or loans to business enterprises."

From a theoretical point of view, it is not clear if and how these objectives can really be achieved by financial reporting. To discuss this topic, it is necessary to explain what decision usefulness means,[4] what the concepts of measuring financial position and performance are, and especially what drawbacks are generally associated with financial reporting.[5] Having established such a reference point, it is then possible to criticize some of the arguments recently put forward, which, in my view, overestimate the possibilities of financial reporting. If those arguments are trusted by some, an expectation gap will be created harming the credibility of financial reporting. Since the problem cannot be discussed on a priori grounds alone, some empirical evidence may help to achieve more valid conclusions.

The chapter is organized as follows: In Section 2 I discuss what the objectives of financial reporting might be with respect to information. I also explain the term decision usefulness as well as ambitious concepts of using financial statements to measure wealth and income. Section 3 discusses some attempts to test decision usefulness empirically and gives a brief overview of some results. Section 4 concludes.

2. The decision-usefulness concept

2.1. The individual decision-model

Contracting partners of an enterprise are constantly making decisions. For example, owners must decide whether to remain owners or exit from ownership, whether to employ new managers or keep the existing ones, and what the remuneration policy will be for managers. To make such decisions, owners need information about the enterprise and the management's performance.

The decision context can be described by a formal decision-model,[6] consisting of actions of the decision-maker, states of nature that cannot be influenced by the decision-maker, state probabilities and payoffs that result from the combination of a particular action by the decision-maker, and a particular state. This one-period model can be enlarged by modeling consecutive decisions over time, with the decisions represented graphically by a decision tree. The problem is to decide on a strategy, defined as a set of state-dependent decisions. To decide, we must use an objective function that might be the maximization of expected utility.

Within this individual decision-model, we can give decision usefulness a precise meaning. In an *ex ante* consideration, information may be useful for decisions if it alters actions, states, state probabilities, functional relationships explaining the payoffs, and/or payoffs. But not all possible changes of the decision field really help the decision-maker: Information is only useful and has (gross) value, for which a decision-maker will pay if it alters the decision that would have been taken without this information.[7] If the information value is positive, the information is also material. In this context, materiality and decision usefulness cannot be separated.

It is apparent that a standard-setter of financial reporting rules cannot know in advance what information is useful in the sense just described, because usefulness depends on individual decision contexts. If he ignores information costs, an individual decision-maker would prefer finer, more accurate information systems to coarser information systems. But the ordering of information systems with respect to fineness is incomplete, and many users with different orderings will run into the choice-paradox of Arrow, as Demski (1973) has shown.[8] The choice paradox means that if decisions follow simple majority rules, even if there are transitive individual preference orderings, the collective preference ordering can be intransitive. The individual decision-model is excellent for explaining the concept of decision usefulness, but it cannot advise a financial reporting standard-setter.[9] Therefore, we need another approach.

2.2. The measurement of economic wealth or income

2.2.1. Wealth measurement

To avoid the problems described above, a standard-setter of financial reporting may be interested in giving information about well-defined events[10] without a precise measurement of wealth or income hoping that the information will be useful for economic decisions. Alternatively the standard-setter may require a measurement of wealth or income.[11] A clear concept of wealth should be the basis for defining assets and liabilities and for any measurement rule. In this section, I discuss only the wealth measurement approach.

For example, it is plausible to assume that as a measurement of their economic wealth, owners are interested in the market value as an approximation of the potential market price of their enterprise.[12]

If management increases the market value by taking actions with a positive net present value, rather than by using accounting gimmicks or cheating owners and others, this is a good sign. Decreasing market value is not. Individual decisions about buying or selling stock, further employment, and remuneration of management can be solidly founded on this information basis.

If the enterprise is listed at a stock exchange, we might assume that the market capitalization indicates the market price of the company. But this assumption ignores the fact that enterprise sales are transacted at prices that usually exceed market capitalization, because there is a control premium or prices are paid for synergies. Using data published in Mergerstat Review 1994 and 2001, Gaughan (2002) shows that this premium averaged about 40 percent of market capitalization in the United States during the years 1982–2000. This average is the result of different averages of different times (which range from 35.4 to 49.1 percent), which also strongly vary within each period.[13] Since there is no good relation between market capitalization and transaction price, we cannot use market capitalization as a proxy for market price.

For companies, the market value of an enterprise must be estimated by using a discounted cash flow figure, where the cash flows received by the owners due to their ownership are relevant.[14] Of course, this calculation gives only a potential market price, since it does not reflect a real transaction. Nevertheless, it is plausible that owners are interested in this information.

However, the book value of equity has little relation to the discounted cash flow figure. Even less attractive for owners, there is no firm relation between discounted cash flow and book value. The reasons for the difference between book and (potential) market value of equity are the accounting principles that govern financial statements:

1. Assets and liabilities are usually measured by a mixture of historical costs and fair values. Fair values are often only used when they are less than the carrying amounts of assets because the anticipation of unrecognized profits is avoided.[15] The lower-of-cost or market rule leads to an asymmetric handling of fair values and of expected losses and profits. Historical costs no longer represent fair value after an asset has been acquired or produced, and they differ from the value in use of an asset.[16]

2. Assets are normally measured by means of an individual valuation, that is an item-by-item approach, which does not take into consideration the synergies between assets.

3. In general, self-produced goodwill must not be recognized, because of the concept of reliability of financial statements.[17] Self-produced goodwill is the difference between the value of the firm, measured by discounting estimated future cash flows to equity, and the book value of equity, where fair values are used to measure assets and liabilities. The estimation of future cash flows is to a great extent subjective, and conflicts with the principle of using reliable data and giving reliable information to the users of financial statements.

4. According to some regulations, for example U.S. Generally Accepted Accounting Principles (GAAP), firms are not allowed to write up an asset in the case that the reasons for impairment no longer exist.

Even though these reasons are well known, recent discussions ignore this knowledge and seem to overestimate the possibilities of financial reporting. This fact can be shown with respect to: (a) recommendations of reporting for intangibles, especially goodwill, and (b) fair-value accounting.

The literature discusses the gap between market value, which is usually taken as market capitalization rather than the market value of a firm,[18] and book value of equity, especially for firms in sectors such as internet, software, media, and entertainment.[19] It is claimed that this gap is due to intangibles,[20] which should either be capitalized[21] or reported, and explained in the notes or other financial reporting statements.[22] However, this gap cannot be closed by capitalizing all intangibles, as is now explained.

First, the difference between market and book values may change, if share prices can be explained by discounting cash flows and if there is a change of costs of capital for the owners, because they have new expectations about risks. If the market value increases by this windfall profit, what intangible is controlled by the enterprise and can be capitalized?

Second, intangibles must be divided into assets that can be identified, separated, and controlled by the firm,[23] and a remaining asset, which is goodwill. If the objective is to capitalize all intangibles, this capitalization can be done for the group of assets that can be identified, separated, and controlled. The identification and measurement might be realized with R&D outlays: Healy et al. (2002) recently used a simulation model to show that successful-efforts accounting might be preferred against full-cost or full-expense accounting, even in the presence of earnings management by managers.[24] Also, the recognition of acquired goodwill is not a problem, at least at the time of acquisition, since the enterprise paid for it. But the recognition of self-produced goodwill requires corporate valuation. Should this be done each year or each quarter? Is it possible to say that the enterprise is able to control its self-produced goodwill?

Third, the recognition of self-produced goodwill is usually not permitted under national or international accounting rules or GAAP, because there are major reservations on the reliability of the existence and measurement of this asset. The new standards on goodwill in the United States (Statements of Financial Accounting Standards, SFAS Nos. 141 and 142), which prohibit amortization and require an impairment test, are the exceptions to this rule. But those standards were heavily influenced by the lobbying of managers and were the price for repealing the pooling-of-interests method in consolidated financial statements. If financial reporting is to be used to mitigate information asymmetries between the insiders and outsiders of an enterprise and to reduce the problem of moral hazard, then the recognition of self-produced goodwill is counterproductive.

Information in the notes or in other statements struggles with the same or with at least comparable reliability problems as the recognition of self-produced intangibles, especially of goodwill. For instance, Lev (2001) created an information system for intangibles. At the heart of this system is a value chain scoreboard with nine information boxes (see Figure 1.3.1). The boxes show the economic process of innovation of an enterprise, distinguishing between discovery and learning (left column), implementation (middle column), and commercialization (right column).

The scoreboard aims to support management and investors in making decisions. Lev does not give rules for the recognition or measurement of intangibles. He only explains some criteria for producing information for the scoreboard. He promotes standardized indicators, which allow comparisons between firms and over time. For example, he mentions the numbers of patents (cf. box no. 4) or clicks of a website (cf. box no. 6).[25] But what consequences shall we draw after getting such information? The number of patents does not say anything about the cash flows that result when the patents are used. The same applies to the number of "hits" on a website.

This problem is characteristic of the discussion about intellectual capital.[26] On the one hand there is a lack of standardized, and therefore analyzable, figures. On the other hand none of the proposals of how to report for intangibles comments on the interpretation of such indicators.[27]

There are also proposals to inform us about separated goodwill factors. A working group of the German Schmalenbach-Gesellschaft

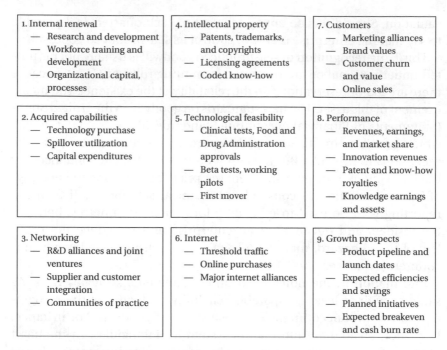

1. Internal renewal — Research and development — Workforce training and development — Organizational capital, processes	4. Intellectual property — Patents, trademarks, and copyrights — Licensing agreements — Coded know-how	7. Customers — Marketing alliances — Brand values — Customer churn and value — Online sales
2. Acquired capabilities — Technology purchase — Spillover utilization — Capital expenditures	5. Technological feasibility — Clinical tests, Food and Drug Administration approvals — Beta tests, working pilots — First mover	8. Performance — Revenues, earnings, and market share — Innovation revenues — Patent and know-how royalties — Knowledge earnings and assets
3. Networking — R&D alliances and joint ventures — Supplier and customer integration — Communities of practice	6. Internet — Threshold traffic — Online purchases — Major internet alliances	9. Growth prospects — Product pipeline and launch dates — Expected efficiencies and savings — Planned initiatives — Expected breakeven and cash burn rate

Fig. 1.3.1. The value chain scoreboard.

Source: Lev (2001: 111, figure 5-1). Reprinted with permission by the Brookings Institute Press.

proposes to provide information about human capital, customer capital, supplier capital, process capital, innovation capital, location capital, and investor capital.[28] Though at first this proposal seems reasonable, we must keep in mind that some categories overlap (e.g. location capital and human capital, if the skills of workers depend on regions) and that the problems of usefulness and reliability of the information are still not solved.

The conclusion is that if economic wealth is measured by discounted cash flows, the measure cannot be shown by a balance sheet, since self-produced goodwill has to be neglected and a discounted cash flow cannot be approximated by an item-by-item valuation, a mode of quantification that governs accounting. It is also impossible to separate and measure certain layers of acquired goodwill. From an agency-theoretic point of view, assuming information asymmetry and different goals of managers and owners, it is highly dysfunctional to mix self-produced and acquired goodwill of reporting units to implement the impairment test set out in the SFAS No. 142. Those who use financial reporting should be skeptical of the reliability of the information.[29]

If these difficulties are known, any standard-setter should explain what an equity number of a balance sheet is saying.[30] Interestingly, there seems to be no clear answer within those frameworks, which argue that they will support information that is useful for decisions.

Turning to my second point, fair-value measurement, there are again simplifications within the debate that might cause expectation gaps. The problems with fair values are as follows:

1. Fair-value measurement aims to provide information about (potential) market prices of assets and liabilities. However, only in a world of perfect and complete markets can the fair value be precisely defined.[31] But in such a world there would be no need for financial reporting,[32] which contains market prices. The information on quantities would be sufficient, since all users could find the relevant prices. In the real world, markets are imperfect and incomplete, and the standard-setter has to decide which market is relevant.[33] Even if he can make this decision, there are differences between a market price and a value in use. Assuming a rational investor, he or she will only invest in an asset if the value in use exceeds the market price. This investment creates a positive net present value. Therefore, the information on market prices can only be a conservative estimate of the value in use at the time of investment, as Dieter Ordelheide (1998) has shown.[34]

2. Selling prices are informative, but only if the enterprise really wants to sell the asset. Selling prices make sense for trading securities, but not for noncurrent assets like property, plant, and equipment, especially for special machinery, or for financial investments.

3. For many assets and liabilities, we cannot find market prices by looking closely at the markets. Instead, we must deduce the market prices by using valuation models. For example, think about financial derivatives[35] or some rental properties. The important questions are, what models are admissible and what are the realistic parameters?

4. Selling and buying prices of individual assets and liabilities are not good proxies for the contribution that such assets and liabilities make to the value of the firm. This value cannot be identified by individual valuation, item by item, and then adding the values. This addition would only be sufficient if the firm had no synergies and self-produced goodwill.

The conclusion is that those who support full fair-value accounting cannot do so with the objective of approximating the market value of the firm. To do so would ignore the reasons why firms exist. Firms exist because they have advantages in combining production factors and in producing and selling goods and services. Doing so leads to lower transaction costs compared to the costs appearing for all transactions done over the markets.[36]

Of course, such arguments are not an attempt to legitimate historical cost accounting. But if we remember the reliability problems of fair-value accounting, then historical cost accounting certainly has some advantages.

2.2.2. Income measurement

Income is a change in wealth. Therefore, it does not make sense to distinguish between wealth and income measurement at first glance. But a second look shows that "good" income measurement can require balance sheet positions that can hardly be interpreted as assets or liabilities.[37]

Let us assume that the financial accounting standard-setter wants users of income statements to be able to extrapolate the actual income figure into the future, which would be a certain kind of predictive ability. Then it would be harmful if formation expenses, expenditure on start-up activities, or costs of raising equity were expensed in the year of formation. This expense would lead to a single, one-year reduction of income that cannot be expected again in the future. But what assets do you create if the relevant costs are capitalized? The Framework of the IFRS defines in paragraph 49: "An asset is a resource controlled by the enterprise as a result of past events and from which future economic benefits are expected to flow to the enterprise." What resource has the enterprise gained by formation? Is it the existence of the enterprise? What is the value of existence? Is it the formation costs? As IAS 38.57 shows, those formation or start-up costs do not represent assets in the IAS sense. They must be expensed, whereas equity costs are deducted from equity capital (Standards Interpretations Committee, SIC-17.6).

There have been concepts developed in accounting theory on what kind of information should be provided by an income figure. For example, the income could be understood as an approximation of the average payments that owners could expect if the sales of the actual year were to be the same for all future periods.[38] But this income could only be shown under very restrictive assumptions,[39] and the duty to show such an income would ignore all the agency problems between owners and management that result from information asymmetry and different goals. What incentives would the management have to give such information truthfully?

2.2.3. Consequences of measurement problems

To avoid the aforementioned problems of informing investors about an ambitious wealth or income figure, other objectives of financial reporting have been formulated. The Framework of the IFRS states in paragraph 15: "The economic decisions that are taken by users of financial statements require an evaluation of the ability of an enterprise to generate cash and cash equivalents and of the timing and certainty of their generation." Similarly, the SFAC (No. 1, para. 25) says: "Potential users of financial information most directly concerned with a particular business enterprise are generally interested in its ability to generate favorable cash flows because their decisions relate to amounts, timing, and uncertainties of expected cash flows."[40] This statement is the result of a shift in accounting literature from the measurement approach, which dominated the first half of the twentieth century, to the information content approach.[41]

There is no explanation on what criteria the measurement of wealth and income—besides reliability, timeliness, and so on—should meet in its content, but there is a hint that users are interested in estimating future cash flows. This concept seems to suit the well-known objective of optimization of consumption streams by individuals in investment theory,[42] especially because this consumption stream also has three dimensions, amount, time structure, and uncertainty.[43]

The problem inherent in a prediction of cash flows using financial statements is that there is no discussion of how we can learn about the timing and uncertainty characteristics of the cash generation. Assets and liabilities contain no explicit information about the time structure of future cash flows. Of course, if the user of financial statements looks at inventories, he or she expects cash inflows that are near to the period of the current financial statements. But does this mean that noncurrent assets do not support cash inflows within the near future? And what about the risk that the inventories cannot be sold at all, or can only be sold with large discounts because the goods of competitors are destroying the market for the company? Uncertainty elements are shown when management has set up a provision for, for example, guarantees, pensions, or taxes. But what about the due dates and the probability distribution of those expected uncertain payments?

It is impossible to develop good information about the three dimensions—amount, timing, uncertainty—of future cash flows. This information is only obtainable through a financial plan that shows expected cash inflows and cash outflows combined with dates and probabilities.[44] This plan is not to be confused with a normal cash flow statement, which is retrospective, covers only one period, and contains amounts that are realized and certain. Such a financial plan is not required, perhaps because of competitive disadvantages and agency problems between the management and contracting partners of the firm, which might otherwise arise.

Thus, the whole burden of estimating future cash flows remains with the users. Those frameworks that use the concept of decision usefulness and mention the support of cash flow estimation leave it to the user as how he or she can overcome this ambitious task. They do not give any serious help.

3. Empirical tests of decision relevance

3.1. Criteria and some results

Even if the decision-usefulness concept cannot be used by standard-setters to prove the decision usefulness *ex ante*, it might be possible to test some form of decision usefulness *ex post*. If we set aside results from interviews and experimental research, we find that tests of decision usefulness often use one of the following forms:[45]

1. Tests of predictive ability of future events or states, for example by multivariate discrimination analysis or artificial neural networks.
2. Event studies, using Beaver's squared and normalized residuals (Beaver's U),[46] the abnormal performance index (API), or the cumulative average residuals (CAR).
3. Tests of value relevance, normally using R^2, the proportion of variance of the dependent variable that is explained by the independent variable.
4. Tests of differences in bid-ask-spreads with respect to different financial reporting systems.

The first kind of tests show that financial reporting can be used to predict the liquidity problems of enterprises, up to liquidation, by means of between three and five ratios.[47] The second kind of tests show that information given with financial reporting leads to, for example, different abnormal performance index (API) curves, depending on good or bad news,[48] and that stock prices are closely related to earnings performance.[49] Though there seems to be a decline in the association between GAAP earnings and stock prices over time,[50] "...there has been a dramatic increase in the association of Street earnings with stock prices."[51] The term "Street earnings" is used for operating or pro forma earnings numbers that exceed the GAAP earnings number, because some income and expenses of the income statement have not been included in calculating earnings. The third kind of tests show the relevance of income figures for (statistically) explaining shareholder returns.[52]

The most significant conclusion from all these tests is that regulated financial reporting provides relevant information to investors.[53] Taking this as given, the relevance of those tests for financial accounting standard-setting is not clear. Holthausen and Watts (2001) show that the assumptions behind most of those tests do not properly describe the objectives of the Financial Accounting Standards Board (FASB).[54] Those tests are based on: (a) the reduction of users of financial reporting to equity investors, which is contrary to the position of the FASB; (b) the use of the aggregate measure of stock price, whereas the FASB is interested in individual investors; and (c) the assumption that verifiability, thus preventing misrepresentation, does not need to be considered.

Even worse, the U.S. GAAP does not follow the assumptions set by the FASB, especially with respect to conservatism: "The degree of conservatism observed in income statements is inconsistent with the FASB's stated views."[55] The direct valuation or inputs to valuation theories that underlie the value-relevance tests offer no explanation for the existence of conservatism. Conservatism can be explained by contracting purposes. If GAAP rules are not constructed for direct equity valuation and are influenced by contracting, litigation, political, and tax considerations, then equity value-relevance tests must fail to help standard-setters.

The fourth kind of tests show that the bid-ask-spreads, for example, seem to be lower when firms commit financial reporting to either IFRS or U.S. GAAP instead of German Handelsgesetzbuch (HGB).[56] Those results show that financial reporting has information content for shareholders, but the precise extent is dependent upon the regulation system.

Nevertheless, there are many disappointing results, which conflict with hypotheses on the advantages of financial reporting. This is shown with respect to segmental reporting.

3.2. The information content of segmental reporting

Segment information should improve the assessments of the return and the risk of the shares of the head of a diversified group. According to portfolio theory, firms diversify to achieve synergies and reduce risk. Since the income of a group is the result of the incomes of segments, which may vary according to the different economic situations faced by the segments, segmentation of the aggregated data will give an insight into the different developments of the segments.

Segmental information is not only supposed to be useful for return and risk assessments, it is also supposed to improve capital-market efficiency and accounting for stewardship. In SFAS No. 131, the objectives of segmental reporting are set forth as follows: "The objective of requiring disclosures about segments of an enterprise and related information is to provide information about the different types of business activities in which an enterprise engages and the different economic environments in which it operates to help users of financial statements:

(a) Better understand the enterprise's performance

(b) Better assess its prospects for future net cash flows

(c) Make more informed judgements about the enterprise as a whole."
    (SFAS 131 para. 3).

There are different approaches to segmental reporting. The FASB follows the management approach (SFAS 131), the IASC prefers the risk and reward approach (IAS 14), and the German standard-setter mixes both (GAS 3). The management approach refers to the internal reporting system of the firm for segment identification. The risk and reward approach identifies segments as being subject to different risks and rewards. The most common segmentation is along product lines and/or geographical areas. The question here is which advantages of segmental reporting can we show empirically?

Many studies on the information content of segmental reporting analyze the predictive ability for sales and earnings and the impact on forecast accuracy.[57] One of the most recent approaches[58] shows that geographic segment information leads to an increased accuracy of predictions of sales and gross profit, but not of earnings. Studies of the return assessment effects of industry segment data are more common than studies of geographic data, especially in earlier publications. Older studies with British and U.S. data confirm both the increased forecast accuracy of sales and earnings.[59]

It is not clear how segment information affects bid-ask-spreads and the liquidity of shares. The study published by Greenstein and Sami (1994) is the only one so far that directly addresses this issue.[60] They find significant, positive results for the reduction of the bid-ask-spreads when segmental reporting is first used. They also show that segmentation of revenues is sufficient for this reduction, and that income segmentation is not superior to segmentation of revenues.[61] Greenstein and Sami show that segment information seems to reduce the bid-ask-spread, but it is not clear whether all influencing factors have been controlled for.[62] Greenstein and Sami themselves argue that the increased analyst following and press coverage for the experimental group might influence their results.[63] Further, they did not control for a self-selection bias resulting from the firms of the control group having previously published segment reports voluntarily. These firms would have done this for a reason, for example because they wanted to signal their superior quality.[64] The effects of this self-selection bias are difficult to predict. Altogether, the results of Greenstein and Sami indicate that segmental reporting can improve capital-market efficiency, but due to their limitations and because there are no other studies confirming their findings, we must interpret their findings with great care.

Givoly et al. (1999) analyze the explanatory power of segment information for share returns compared to nonsegmented data, and the power of earnings in relation to sales in explaining share returns. "The measurement error in segment reporting is assessed based on the association between the segment and its industry's results, with the benchmark being the association exhibited by firms operating in a single line of business within the same industry."[65] They show that the measurement errors in segment information, especially earnings, are larger than those in the financial information provided by single-line-of-business firms.[66] "Further, segment earnings are found to be more prone to measurement error than segment sales."[67] This result can be explained by management intervention, such as allocating common costs and intersegment transfer pricing. "Market tests incorporating segment data show that while both segment sales and segment earnings provide incremental information beyond firm-level sales and earnings, segment sales are more informative than segment earnings. This finding is consistent with segment earnings being more susceptible to measurement errors than firm earnings."[68]

The conclusion is that even in those cases in which the aim of financial reporting is not to show a well-defined and ambitious figure of wealth or income (so-called valuation approach), but where the information content of disaggregated information is central, the results of the empirical tests of decision usefulness are disappointing. Segment information has incremental value, but the highest value is associated with data, which cannot be influenced by management.

4. Conclusions

It is the explicit or implicit objective of financial reporting to be useful in making economic decisions. Even though the decision-usefulness concept is well established throughout the world, it is not clear what the concept really means. It can be explained within a formal decision-model for a single decision-maker, but this model does not help those who are setting standards for financial reporting. Decisions may be supported by information about theoretically sound wealth or income measures. Unfortunately, such measures are not well defined in a world with imperfect and incomplete markets.

If we ignore this and other knowledge, then discussions about the relevance of intangibles and the necessity to recognize them in balance sheets must lead to an expectation gap. All the problems of explaining the difference between market and book values of equity seem to be a question of the recognition of intangibles. This chapter shows that this definitely is not the case, since the market value of a firm is not identical with market capitalization. Further, since accounting principles require that reliable information is given, this requirement contradicts the recognition of self-produced goodwill; requires individual valuation, which does not take into consideration asset synergies; and contrasts with full fair-value accounting.

Those standard-setters that explicitly aim at decision usefulness, especially in helping to make cash flow predictions, give us no ideas on how this objective can be realized by investors or other users of financial reporting.

Nevertheless, many researchers have tried to test the information content of financial statements *ex post*. There have been tests of the predictive ability of financial reporting, event studies, tests of value relevance, and others. This chapter does not give an overview of all such results. I have highlighted only one aspect here, the information content of segment information. Even in this aspect the results are disappointing. Segment information increases the accuracy of forecasts, but the measurement error seems to be higher with segment earnings than with segment sales. This result means that those numbers that might be influenced by management have more noise than sales. This fact is dissatisfying, since only a small part of segment information appears to be of material importance.

Notes

Thanks are due to Martina Bentele, Michael Dobler, Bernd Hacker, and Jörg Hoffmann for stimulating discussions, constructive comments, and some additions. I also thank the editors of this book for helpful comments.

[1] See Ordelheide and Pfaff (1994: 72); Ballwieser (2001: 1242).

[2] See IAS F.1; SFAC No. 1, para. 1.

[3] See SFAC No. 1: 1007.

[4] Also see Staubus (1999) for texts about decision-usefulness and his role in influencing the American regulation.

[5] For an excellent overview of the myths of accounting see Moxter (2000).

[6] See Bromwich (1992: 82–9); Demski (1980: 24–6).

[7] See Demski (1980: 28, 33); Bromwich (1992: 139). This concept is not used, for example, by the FASB, because according to SFAC No. 2, para. 47, "accounting information must be capable of making a difference in a decision by helping users to form predictions about the outcomes of past, present and future events or to confirm or correct expectations." For example, correcting or confirming expectations without triggering decision changes, is not enough to create value in the formerly described sense.

[8] Compare with Demksi (1973).

[9] Compare with Ballwieser (1982: 780–4); Bromwich (1992: 140).

[10] See Sorter (1969).

[11] Staubus (1999: 6–7) mentions that the FASB defined assets, liabilities, and equity instead of profits: "The Board, after bitter debate in the nineteen-seventies, explicitly chose the asset, liability and equity (balance sheet) approach to the conceptual framework rather than the revenue, expense, and income (matching, or income statement) approach that had been popular since 1940." Also see Liang (2001: 230–1).

[12] In the case of certainty, perfect, and complete markets all owners prefer market value maximization, and market value and market price are the same. When there is uncertainty, imperfect, and/or incomplete markets, the desirable characteristics of market prices are void. Valuation is no longer well defined, and it is not clear what properties prices possess. For example compare with Beaver (1998: 68, 38–40). Therefore, market value, measured by discounting cash flows, can only be an approximation of market price, and different individuals estimate different market values.

[13] See Gaughan (2002: 521).

[14] Such cash flows need not be dividends of the acquired enterprise if we take into account synergies for the buyer, which result because of the acquisition, for example cost or tax effects. In other words, the value cannot be measurement by a stand-alone value.

[15] Of course, there are exceptions of the rule, for example for certain securities, derivatives, or in case of long-term construction-type contracts.

[16] Dieter Ordelheide convincingly explained historical cost accounting as an instrument for showing a conservative estimation of values in use for the owners. See Ordelheide (1988: 280–1). The owner will only invest in assets if his/her net present value is non-negative. Therefore, at the time of investment, the present value of future cash flows must be at least as high as acquisition or production costs.

[17] An exemption results from SFAS 142, which will be discussed later on within this section.

[18] See note 13.

[19] Firms in those sectors are very often newly founded, expect high growth rates, have risks above the average, and are listed at the new market segments of a stock exchange.

[20] See Lev and Zarowin (1999: 353–4).

[21] See Arbeitskreis (2001: 991–2); also Lev and Zarowin (1999: 354): "We argue that it is in the accounting for intangibles that the present system fails most seriously to reflect enterprise value and performance, mainly due to the mismatching of costs with revenues."

[22] Compare with Eccles et al. (2001: 57–9).

[23] See IAS, F.49(a), 38.7.

[24] See Healy et al. (2002: especially 678–81).

[25] See Lev (2001: 113).

[26] For further details on intellectual capital see Edvinsson and Malone (1997); Stewart (1998).

[27] Compare with Sveiby (1997); Sullivan (1998: 299).

[28] See Arbeitskreis (2001: 990–1).

[29] I am also skeptical that auditors have the power to support the interests of owners, if those interests conflict with those of the management. However, I cannot discuss this problem here.

[30] SFAC No. 6, para. 49 defines: "Equity or net assets is the residual interest in the assets of an entity that remains after deducting its liabilities." This is not a description of a measurement of wealth.

[31] See Beaver (1998: 77); Bromwich (1992: 102–3).

[32] Compare with Beaver and Demski (1979: 39–40); Barth and Landsman (1995: 100).

[33] There are different preferences in the United States and in the IASB: The IFRS defines fair value uniformly, but the definition according to U.S. GAAP varies. The IFRS prefers the exit price, but according to U.S. GAAP, the fair value can be the exit as well as the entry price.

[34] See Ordelheide (1988: 280–1).

[35] Just compare with the fair values that have been used by Enron in measuring financial derivatives.

[36] Compare with Williamson (1979); Ordelheide (1993, column 1843).

[37] See Moxter (1984: 49–53).

[38] See Moxter (1982: 142–3); Moxter (1984: 124).

[39] See Wagner (1994: 1178–83).

[40] Also SFAC No. 1, para. 39: "Thus, since an enterprise's ability to generate favorable cash flows affects both its ability to pay dividends and interest and the market prices of its securities, expected cash flows to investors and creditors are related to expected cash flows to the enterprise in which they have invested or to which they have loaned funds."

[41] See Liang (2001: 224–31); Beaver (1998: 2–5).

[42] See Fisher (1930: 71); Hirshleifer (1958: 329); Hakansson (1970: 587).

[43] See Moxter (1966: 38).
[44] See Moxter (1966: 45–51).
[45] See for approaches and results for Germany Möller and Hüfner (2002); for Europe Dumontier and Raffournier (2002); for the United States Kothari (2001); Healy and Palepu (2001: 412–14).
[46] See Beaver (1968).
[47] See Baetge (1989: 801–2); for sophisticated approaches cf. Baetge and Heitmann (2000) and Baetge and Krause (1993).
[48] See Bowman (1983: 569–70).
[49] See Ball and Brown (1968).
[50] See for example Francis and Schipper (1999).
[51] Bradshaw and Sloan (2002: 43).
[52] See Kothari (2001: 116).
[53] See Kothari (2001: 116–18); Healy and Palepu (2001: 413).
[54] See Holthausen and Watts (2001: 23–31).
[55] Holthausen and Watts (2001: 38).
[56] See Leuz and Verrecchia (2000: 93).
[57] For an excellent overview see Hacker (2002: 124–40).
[58] See Herrmann (1996: 63–70).
[59] See for example Roberts (1989); Balakrishnan et al. (1990); Swaminathan (1991).
[60] See Greenstein and Sami (1994: 179–99).
[61] See Greenstein and Sami (1994: 193–4).
[62] See Greenstein and Sami (1994: 198).
[63] See Greenstein and Sami (1994: 198).
[64] See Hacker (2002: 145).
[65] Givoly et al. (1999: 16).
[66] See Givoly et al. (1999: 15).
[67] Givoly et al. (1999: 16).
[68] Givoly et al. (1999: 36).

References

Arbeitskreis "Immaterielle Werte im Rechnungswesen" der Schmalenbach-Gesellschaft für Betriebswirtschaft e.V. (2001). "Kategorisierung und bilanzielle Erfassung immaterieller Werte," *Der Betrieb*, 54: 989–95.

Baetge, J. (1989). "Möglichkeiten der Früherkennung negativer Unternehmensentwicklungen mit Hilfe statistischer Jahresabschlußanalysen," *Schmalenbachs Zeitschrift für betriebswirtschaftliche Forschung*, 41: 792–811.

—— and Heitmann, C. (2000). "Creating a fuzzy rule-based indicator for the review of credit standing," *Schmalenbach Business Review*, 52: 318–43.

—— and Krause, C. (1993). "The classification of companies by means of neural networks," *Journal of Information Science and Technology*, 3: 96–112.

Balakrishnan, R., Harris, T. S., and Sen, P. K. (1990). "The predictive ability of geographic segment disclosures," *Journal of Accounting Research*, 28: 305–25.

Ball, R. J. and Brown, P. (1968). "An empirical evaluation of accounting income numbers," *Journal of Accounting Research*, 6: 159–78.

Ballwieser, W. (1982). "Zur Begründbarkeit informationsorientierter Jahresabschlußverbesserungen," *Schmalenbachs Zeitschrift für betriebswirtschaftliche Forschung*, 34: 772–93.

Ballwieser, W. (2001). "Germany—Individual accounts," in D. Ordelheide and KPMG (eds.), *Transnational accounting*, 2nd ed. (Houndmills, Basingstoke: Palgrave), 1217–351.

Barth, M. and Landsman, W. (1995). "Fundamental issues related to using fair value accounting for financial reporting," *Accounting Horizons*, 9: 97–108.

Beaver, W. H. (1968). "The information content of annual earnings announcements," *Journal of Accounting Research*, Supplement: Empirical Research in Accounting: Selected Studies, 6: 67–92.

—— (1998). *Financial reporting. An accounting revolution*, 3rd ed. (Upper Saddle river, NJ: Prentice Hall).

Beaver, W. and Demski, J. (1979). "The nature of income measurement," *The Accounting Review*, 54: 38–46.

Bowman, R. G. (1983). "Understanding and conducting event studies," *Journal of Business Finance and Accounting*, 10: 561–84.

Bradshaw, M. T. and Sloan, R. G. (2002). "GAAP versus The Street: An empirical assessment of two alternative definitions of earnings," *Journal of Accounting Research*, 40: 41–66.

Bromwich, M. (1992). *Financial Reporting, Information and Capital Markets* (London: Pitman).

Demski, J. S. (1973). "The general impossibility of normative accounting standards," *Accounting Review*, 48: 718–23.

—— (1980). *Information Analysis*, 2nd ed. (Reading, MA: Addison-Wesley).

Dumontier, P. and Raffournier, B. (2002). "Accounting and capital markets: A survey of the european evidence," *The European Accounting Review*, 11: 119–51.

Eccles, R. G., Herz, R. H., Keegan, E. M., and Phillips, D. M. H. (2001). *The value reporting revolution* (New York: Wiley).

Edvinsson, L. and Malone, M. (1997). *Intellectual Capital: Realizing Your Company's True Value by Finding its Hidden Brainpower* (New York: HarperBusiness).

Fisher, I. (1930). *The Theory of Interest* (New York: MacMillan).

Francis, J. and Schipper, K. (1999). "Have financial statements lost their relevance?" *Journal of Accounting Research*, 37: 319–52.

Gaughan, P. A. (2002). *Mergers, Acquisitions and Corporate Restructurings* (New York: Wiley).

Givoly, D., Hayn, C., and D'Souza, J. (1999). "Measurement errors and information content of segment reporting," *Review of Accounting Studies*, 4: 15–43.

Greenstein, M. M. and Sami, H. (1994). "The impact of the SEC's segment disclosure requirement on bid-ask spreads," *The Accounting Review*, 69: 179–99.

Hacker, B. (2002). *Segmentberichterstattung—Eine ökonomische Analyse* (Frankfurt am Main: Peter Lang).

Hakansson, N. H. (1970). "Optimal investment and consumption strategies for a class of utility functions," *Econometrica*, 38: 587–607.

Healy, P. M. and Palepu, K. G. (2001). "Information asymmetry, corporate disclosure, and the capital markets: A review of the empirical disclosure literature," *Journal of Accounting and Economics*, 31: 405–40.

—— Myers, S. C., and Howe, C. D. (2002). "R&D accounting and the tradeoff between relevance and objectivity," *Journal of Accounting Research*, 40: 677–710.

Herrmann, D. (1996). "The predictive ability of geographic segment information at the country, continent, and consolidated levels," *Journal of International Financial Management and Accounting*, 7: 50–73.

Hirshleifer, J. (1958). "On the theory of optimal investment decision," *Journal of Political Economy*, 66: 329–52.

Holthausen, R. W. and Watts, R. L. (2001). "The relevance of the value-relevance literature for financial accounting standard setting," *Journal of Accounting and Economics*, 31: 3–75.

Kothari, S. P. (2001). "Capital markets research in accounting," *Journal of Accounting and Economics*, 31: 105–231.

Leuz, C. and Verrecchia, R. (2000). "The economic consequences of increased disclosure," *Journal of Accounting Research*, 38 (Supplement): 91–124.

Lev, B. (2001). *Intangibles. Management, Measurement, and Reporting* (Washington DC: Brookings Institution Press).

—— and Zarowin, P. (1999). "The boundaries of financial reporting and how to extend them," *Journal of Accounting Research*, 37: 353–85.

Liang, P. J. (2001). "Recognition: An information content perspective," *Accounting Horizons*, 15: 223–42.

Möller, H. P. and Hüfner, B. (2002). "Zur Bedeutung der Rechnungslegung für den deutschen Aktienmarkt—Begründung, Messprobleme und Erkenntnisse empirischer Forschung," in G. Seicht (ed.), *Jahrbuch für Controlling und Rechnungswesen 2002* (Wien: LexisNexis Verlag ARD ORAC), 405–62.

Moxter, A. (1966). "Die Grundsätze ordnungsmäßiger Bilanzierung und der Stand der Bilanztheorie," *Schmalenbachs Zeitschrift für betriebswirtschaftliche Forschung*, 18: 28–59.

—— (1982). *Betriebswirtschaftliche Gewinnermittlung* (Tübingen: Mohr).

—— (1984). *Bilanzlehre. Band I: Einführung in die Bilanztheorie*, 3rd ed. (Wiesbaden: Gabler).

—— (2000). "Rechnungslegungsmythen," *Betriebs-Berater*, 55: 2143–9.

Ordelheide, D. (1988). "Kaufmännischer Periodengewinn als ökonomischer Gewinn. Zur Unsicherheitsrepräsentation bei der Konzeption von Erfolgsgrößen," in M. Domsch, F. Eisenführ, D. Ordelheide, and M. Perlitz (eds.), *Unternehmungserfolg. Festschrift für W. Busse von Colbe* (Wiesbaden: Gabler), 275–302.

—— (1993). "Institutionelle Theorie und Unternehmung," in W. Wittmann, W. Kern, R. Köhler, H.-U. Küpper, and K. v. Wysocki (eds.), *Handwörterbuch der Betriebswirtschaft*, 5th ed., vol. 2, columns 1838–55.

Ordelheide, D. and Pfaff, D. (1994). *European financial reporting—Germany* (London: Routledge).

Roberts, C. B. (1989). "Forecasting Earnings using geographical segment data: Some UK evidence," *Journal of International Financial Management and Accounting*, 1: 130–51.

Sorter, G. (1969). "An 'events' approach to basic accounting theory," *The Accounting Review*, 44: 12–19.

Staubus, G. J. (1999). *The Decision-Usefulness Theory of Accounting. A Limited History* (New York and London: Garland).

Stewart, T. (1998). *Intellectual Capital—The New Wealth of Organizations* (New York: Brealy).

Sullivan, P. (1998). "Reporting on intellectual capital," in P. Sullivan (ed.), *Profiting from Intellectual Capital* (New York: Wiley & Sons), 298–304.

Sveiby, K. (1997). *The new organizational wealth: managing & measuring knowledge-based assets* (San Francisco: Berrett-Koehler Publishers).

Swaminathan, S. (1991). "The impact of SEC mandated segment data on price variability and divergence of beliefs," *The Accounting Review*, 66: 23–41.

Wagner, F. W. (1994). "Periodenabgrenzung als Prognoseverfahren—Konzeption und Anwendungsbereich der 'einkommensapproximativen Bilanzierung,'" in W. Ballwieser, H.-J. Böcking, J. Drukarczyk, and R. H. Schmidt (eds.), *Bilanzrecht und Kapitalmarkt. Festschrift für A. Moxter* (Düsseldorf: IDW), 1175–97.

Williamson, O. (1979). "Transaction-cost economics: The governance of contractual relations," *Journal of Law and Economics*, 22: 233–61.

Roles of Financial Accounting: Performance Measurement and Corporate Governance

2.1

Value-Based Management and Performance Measures: Cash Flow versus Accrual Accounting

Dieter Pfaff

1. Introduction

The fundamental idea of value-based management is simple in principle: Since the investors (shareholders) of an enterprise require a sufficient rate of return on their assigned capital, which is oriented toward the alternative investments available, additional value is created only if the enterprise gains more than the capital costs. Therefore, management's aim must basically be to undertake investments with positive net present values, since such investments will increase the value of companies.

But what does this mean for larger firms where, to a large extent, the authority to make investment decisions is delegated? In such a situation, agency problems can arise due to different levels of information, conflicting interests, and the necessity of designing incentive contracts. Controlling decentralized responsibility units with performance measures is a topic that both research and practice have dealt with for decades. Different performance measures for periodically evaluating the performance of companies or their divisions have been analyzed and reanalyzed. This observation is particularly true for profitability measures, such as return on investment (RoI), cash flow return on investment (CFRoI), and for performance measures based on accruals, such as accounting profit and residual income. Past business research has especially favored residual income, which is defined as operating profit after deduction of interest on invested capital.[1]

Residual income has become a popular concept in business.[2] General Motors, in the 1920s, and General Electric, in the 1950s, used variations of this concept.[3] Recently, residual income concepts marketed by the consulting firm Stern Stewart & Co. under the name "economic value added" (EVA®) and other consulting firms with a variety of similar concepts have undergone a strong resurgence.[4] Moreover, the residual income concept is supported by the research of Ohlson and Feltham, which builds on residual income to combine company value and accounting information.[5]

However, when we consider the fact that accruals only develop because cash flows become effective in a period other than the payment period and therefore cannot provide any more information than cash flows per se, the question arises as to why it might be advantageous to use accruals instead of cash flows as a performance measure for controlling incentive problems. Recently, several papers have challenged this concept by showing that accruals may be an essential part of an optimal incentive system.[6] In these models, an advantage of accruals appears when imperfections, such as unobservable expected future cash flows and unknown agent's time preference (problem of the impatient manager), arise.

The objective of this chapter is to reflect on the merits of accrual accounting in light of these imperfections, and to provide some arguments for why we still have only a limited understanding of accruals. The argument is based on a two-period model and attempts to demonstrate the problem of the "impatient manager" as well as how accruals can help solve this problem. In other words, the goal of this chapter is not to develop a model superior to any model devised in the current literature, but rather to lay out the basic rationalization for using both accruals and the underlying assumptions and relationships as clearly and simply as possible. This rationale is then used as the basis for an examination of the question of which direction we might use to develop new models that propose the advantages of using accruals.

The chapter is organized as follows. Section 2 shows the substantial assumptions for the analysis of accruals- and cash-flow-based incentive systems. Section 3 clarifies the connections between compensation functions and performance measures, and shows how performance measures can be designed to induce efficient investment decisions in a two-period model. Section 4 summarizes the results, thereby taking a more general look at the connections between incentive contracts, performance measures, and information structures. Section 5 discusses the problems of analytical research in showing the advantage of using accruals instead of cash flows as a performance measure to control investment decisions. Section 6 concludes the chapter.

2. A simple investment problem

Referring to Rogerson (1997) and Reichelstein (1997; 2000), let us consider a firm with a headquarters and a divisional manager. The company must decide on an investment project. To keep the analysis simple, the model is restricted to only two periods, that is $t \in \{1, 2\}$. The investment generates a cash flow stream of $(-b, c(b))$, where $b \geq 0$ $(b \in B)$ denotes the initial cash investment at the end of period 1 and $c(b)$ the cash flow in period 2. The cash flow in period 2 increases on a diminishing scale along with the absolute level of the initial cash investment b:

$$c'(b) > 0, \quad c''(b) < 0, \quad (b \in B). \tag{1}$$

Because certain advantages of specialization are assumed, headquarters delegates the investment decision in period 1 to the divisional manager. Thus, headquarters has no knowledge of the function $c(b)$.

In addition to the investment activity, the agent chooses the level of short-term activities in period 2. These short-term activities are denoted by e and could be either low (e_L) or high (e_H). They increase the profitability of the investment, that is they complement the basic cash flow $c(b)$ that results from the investment, and include, for example, cost management and marketing activities during the period. Total cash flows in period 2 are $y(\cdot) = c(b) + x(e)$, where e determines the conditional distribution function of $x, f(x|e)$.

It is assumed that control over the investment decision and the motivation for the short-term effort cannot be separated. Thus, the assumption attempts to capture more realistic situations in which there are fewer performance measures used in the incentive contract than the number of activities the agent undertakes. This procedure is compatible with practices in which the common focus is on just a few performance measures and aggregation is a fundamental property of accounting systems.[7]

We also assume that it is in the best interests of headquarters to motivate the manager to exert high effort. Otherwise, there would be no short-term incentive problem. To keep the analysis simple, the manager is assumed to be risk-neutral. Note that since $c(b)$ is not known *ex ante* by headquarters, the firm cannot be easily leased or sold to the manager. The problem that presents itself to headquarters is that of inducing the manager to select the best level of investment possible. Moreover, headquarters must motivate the manager to exert a high level of effort in period 2.

If headquarters were aware of all relevant decision parameters, particularly $c(b)$, it would determine the initial cash investment by the discount factor $p = 1/(1 + r)$ for the evaluation of cash flow in period 2:

$$\max_{b \in B} \text{NPV}(b) = p \cdot c(b) - b. \tag{2}$$

In what follows, we can assume that there is always an internal solution, $b_Z \in B$, for the headquarters decision problem. Due to the concavity assumption, the optimal initial cash investment can be uniquely characterized by the necessary condition:

$$0 = p \cdot \frac{\partial c(b)}{\partial b} - 1 \quad \Leftrightarrow \quad 0 = \frac{\partial c(b)}{\partial b} - (1 + r). \tag{3}$$

Let us consider the case in which headquarters does not have knowledge of the cash flow function $c(b)$. In the context of the incentive contract, in each period $t = 1, 2$ the manager receives compensation contingent on the performance measure. We assume that compensation is a strictly *monotonic* function of the performance measure, so that increased performance by the manager is linked to a higher premium payment.[8]

The stream of future and present compensation levels and effort choices determines the risk-neutral manager's utility. We can assume that his/her preferences can be described by an additively separable utility function of the form:

$$U = s_1(\Pi_1(b)) + \frac{s_2(\Pi_2(b, e)) - v \cdot e}{1 + \tilde{r}} \tag{4}$$

where his/her outside opportunities are represented by a reservation utility $\overline{U} = 0$; s_1 and s_2 denote the compensation in period 1 and period 2; Π_1 and Π_2 represent the respective performance measures.

An essential feature of the models discussed in the literature is that the divisional manager may have strong time preferences, that is he or she discounts future cash flows at a higher interest rate than does headquarters, which is unknown to headquarters ("problem of the impatient manager").[9] One cause for impatience is that the divisional manager may put more intrinsic weight on current consumption, but wealth constraints preclude him or her from borrowing at the interest rate available to the firm (headquarters or owner).[10] A second explanation for different time preferences could be that the firm has been restructured or that the manager will be leaving the firm at some point in the future, which would mean that future cash flows could not be fully distributed to the manager.[11]

To ensure value-based management, headquarters must design suitable control instruments that permit goal-congruent control of the manager by situation-specific variation of the performance measure. To do so, headquarters develops an accounting system that records the cash flows b and $y(b, e)$ *ex post*. However, a fragmentation of $y(\cdot)$ in $c(b)$ and $x(e)$ is not possible, which means that the compensation scheme s_2 must solve the problem of controlling the optimal investment volume in period 1, and the problem of motivating short-term activities in period 2. Therefore, the flexibility provided by controlling both problems separately is strongly reduced.

To allow for incentive systems with high flexibility, we consider the following general class of performance measures $(\alpha \in \Re, \beta \in \Re, \gamma \in \Re, d > 0)$:

$$\Pi_2(b, e) := \alpha \cdot y(b, e) - d \cdot b - \gamma \cdot B_1 \text{ and } \Pi_1(b) := -\beta \cdot b. \quad (5)$$

$\Pi_2(\cdot)$ includes accrual accounting numbers as depreciation $(d \cdot b)$ in period 2 and book value (B_1) at the end of period 1:

$$B_1 := b, \qquad B_2 := B_1 - d \cdot b, \quad (d > 0). \quad (6)$$

If the investment level chosen for the project is depreciated completely over the period, the book value at the end of period 2 will be 0 $(B_2 = 0)$.

By varying the parameters α, β, γ, and d, we can construct an infinite number of performance measures as linear combinations of cash flows, book values, and depreciation. For example, for $\alpha > 0, \beta > 0, \gamma = d = 0$, a performance measure based purely on cash flow results would be:

$$\Pi_2(b, e) = \alpha \cdot y(b, e) \text{ and } \Pi_1(b) = -\beta \cdot b. \quad (7)$$

In addition, we can derive traditional accounting measures such as profits or residual incomes from the system as performance measures. For $\alpha = 1, d > 0$, and $\gamma = \beta = 0$, the following profit measure results:

$$\Pi_2(b, e) = y(b, e) - d \cdot b \text{ and } \Pi_1(b) = 0. \quad (8)$$

Choosing $\gamma = r_c$, we get residual incomes as a performance measure:

$$\Pi_2(b, e) = y(b, e) - d \cdot b - r_c \cdot B_1 \text{ and } \Pi_1(b) = 0. \quad (9)$$

The performance measure according to equation (9) includes r_c, the critical hurdle rate charged to the divisional manager for the capital tied up during period 2. Furthermore, we can create additional measures $\Pi_2(\cdot)$ to these traditional performance measures as linear combinations of cash flow and residual income.[12]

3. Accruals as optimal performance measures

First, we consider the solution to the problem of effort. To induce high effort, the following incentive constraint must be fulfilled:

$$E[s_2(x(e_\mathrm{H}))] - v \cdot e_\mathrm{H} \geq E[s_2(x(e_\mathrm{L}))] - v \cdot e_\mathrm{L}, \tag{10}$$

where E denotes the expected value operator. Thus, the headquarters must offer an acceptable contract that has the important feature of making it in the manager's perceived self-interest to supply the desired high effort. From $e_\mathrm{H} > e_\mathrm{L}$, it follows that the principal should not pay a flat salary that is independent of an observable outcome.

However, contracting on payment by results is only worthwhile from headquarters' point of view if the sum that is eventually paid to the manager, depending on his/her investment decision, is smaller than the advantage gained from the improved operational activity. Otherwise headquarters will prefer a fixed payment, since from headquarters' viewpoint, the manager does not have any incentive to deviate from the optimal investment decision when he or she is being paid a flat salary. In the remainder of the analysis, we can rule out such trivial solutions. Thus, we can examine the problem of optimally controlling the investment decision, which is of special importance for the question of cash flow versus accruals.

If the manager receives compensation contingent on observable measures of $s_1(\Pi_1(b))$, or $s_2(\Pi_2(b,e))$ in each period, then he or she determines the initial cash investment b_B according to:

$$\max_{b \in B} U(b) = s_1(-\beta \cdot b) + \frac{s_2(\alpha \cdot (c(b) + x(e)) - d \cdot b - \gamma \cdot B_1) - v \cdot e}{1 + \tilde{r}} \tag{11}$$

with $B_1 = b$ in the amount of assets tied up at the end of period 1.

Therefore, equation 12,

$$
\begin{aligned}
0 &= \frac{\partial U(b)}{\partial b} \\
&= \frac{1}{1 + \tilde{r}} \cdot \frac{\partial s_2(\alpha \cdot (c(b) + x(e)) - d \cdot b - \gamma \cdot B_1)}{\partial(\alpha \cdot (c(b) + x(e)) - d \cdot b - \gamma \cdot B_1)} \cdot \left(\alpha \cdot \frac{\partial c(b)}{\partial b} - d - \gamma \right) \\
&\quad - \frac{\partial s_1(-\beta \cdot b)}{\partial(-\beta \cdot b)} \cdot \beta,
\end{aligned}
\tag{12}
$$

arises as a necessary condition of the manager's optimization problem. Since, by assumption, headquarters does not know the manager's discount factor, equation (12) must be fulfilled for all $\tilde{r}$ at b_Z, so that the investment decision required by headquarters can be implemented. The necessary condition represents a polynomial of the first degree in $(1 + \tilde{r})$, which can only be identical to 0 as zero-function for all $\tilde{r}$. From this result it follows directly that all coefficients must be 0 $(\alpha(\partial c(b)/\partial b) - d - \gamma = 0$ and $\beta = 0)$. From $\beta = 0$ it follows that $\Pi_1 = 0$. Thus, we can state that the investment volume desired by headquarters can be implemented if, and only if, the basis for calculation is equal to 0 in period 1 $(\Pi_1 = 0)$.

In addition, for *cash-flow-based* compensation systems $(d = \gamma = 0)$, it follows from $\alpha(\partial c(b)/\partial b) - d - \gamma = 0$ that parameter α must equal zero $(\alpha = 0)$. However, this would imply payment of a fixed sum independent of performance, which would not present an incentive to the manager. Instead of making the desired effort, e_H, the manager would limit him- or herself to e_L. To motivate the manager according to e_H, compensation must depend on an observable variable $c(b)$. However, to set the incentives for goal-congruent investment decisions, headquarters must shift the initial cash investment in period 1 to the following period (accrual accounting).

This objective can also be achieved by linking the manager's compensation to the final value of the investment project:

$$s_2(\Pi_2) = s_2(y(b, e) - b \cdot (1 + r)) \text{ and } s_1 = \text{constant.} \tag{13}$$

However, in the two-period model this solution is merely a special case of a more general class of residual income and hence accrual accounting.

If headquarters wants to motivate the manager to implement the required investment volume, then headquarters must pay a fixed compensation in period 1. Then, headquarters must find a suitable performance measure for period 2. The following condition shows what this performance measure should look like:

$$\alpha \frac{\partial c(b)}{\partial b} - d - \gamma = 0. \tag{14}$$

To implement the investment decision that is optimal from headquarters' point of view, we must apply $\partial c(b)/\partial b = 1 + r$ as seen from the first-best solution. If $\partial c(b)/\partial b$ is replaced in equation (14) by $1 + r$, and if the scaling factor α is standardized without restriction of the general validity to the value 1, then d and γ must be selected as follows:

$$d + \gamma = 1 + r. \tag{15}$$

Performance measures that induce an optimal investment volume for headquarters can thus be designed by a linear combination of the parameters d and γ. This result means that they can be constructed by choosing wisely the depreciation and a critical hurdle rate charged to the divisional manager for the capital tied up during the period.

Two cases, which can also be observed in accounting practice, arise:

- depreciation equal to the amount of the initial cash investment b, and
- depreciation that deviates from b.

3.1. Case 1: Depreciation equal to the amount of the initial cash investment ($d = 1$)

If we depreciate the investment fully in period 2, γ must be chosen so that it is exactly equal to the relevant interest rate of headquarters for the calculation of the critical hurdle rate ($r_c = r$). The performance measure for compensation can then be represented as follows:

$$\Pi_2 = c(b) + x(e) - b - r \cdot B_1 = y(b, e) - b \cdot (1 + r). \tag{16}$$

Interpreted in economic terms, this corresponds exactly to residual income or EVA®. The EVA is determined as the difference of net operating profit after taxes (NOPAT) and a capital charge. Here, if taxes are excluded from the analysis, we express NOPAT as $y(b, e) - b$ and the interest rate charged for the capital tied up as $r \cdot B_1$. The interest rate r (by partial outside financing of the project) can also be interpreted as the weighted average cost of capital (WACC) and B_1 as the capital tied up by the initial cash investment. Reports from practice support this finding, showing that many companies increasingly rely on the application of the EVA concept as an internal incentive instrument.[13]

The assessment basis for the case of total depreciation conceals two important principles of accrual accounting, the matching principle and the clean-surplus concept.

According to the *matching principle*, firms record cash outflows, which they can assign directly to certain earnings, in the period as expenses in which the revenues are realized. In the model here, the initial cash investment b is uniquely attributable to the cash inflow $c(b)$ in period 2. Therefore, the capitalization of b in period 1 as asset and its depreciation is necessary in the following period 2, that is when the cash inflows from the investment are realized. In models in which cash inflows occur in more than one period, the sum of depreciation and capital charges must be distributed proportionally to the cash flows.[14]

Following Rogerson (1997) we consider investment projects that generate a cash-flow stream of $(-b, c_1(b), \ldots, c_T(b))$ with the following structure:

$$c_t(b) := \theta_t \cdot c(b) \quad (\theta := (\theta_1, \ldots, \theta_T)) \in \Re_+^T, \quad b \in B. \tag{17}$$

The parameter θ_t is an exogenously given and generally known (relative) productivity or growth parameter for a specific time period. This parameter is completely independent of the level of investment and thus inelastic. In a multiperiod case with inelastic growth parameters, we can use any monotonically increasing compensation scheme. By doing so we can ensure goal congruence if the allocation rule is conditioned on the investment project in the following way:[15]

$$d_t \cdot b + r \cdot B_{t-1} = \frac{\theta_t \cdot b}{\sum_{\tau=1}^{T} \dfrac{\theta_\tau}{(1+r)^\tau}}, \quad t = 1, \ldots, T. \tag{18}$$

Equation (18) shows that we calculate depreciation in such a way that depreciation plus interest reflects the intertemporal distribution of project cash flows (relative benefit depreciation schedule). In the special case of uniform cash flows, the relative benefit depreciation schedule reduces to the annuity depreciation method,[16] which results in identical contributions to residual income in each period.[17]

The idea behind this is as follows: The incentive mechanism using the allocation rule determined by (18) is designed to transform the investment problem to T investment problems that perfectly represent the entire amount of investment for each period. As a result, the divisional manager, even when observing individual periods in isolation, always has the same incentive for each single period to make the best investment decision from the perspective of headquarters. Since both the time period for the incentive coefficient and the manager's discount factors lose their influence on the investment decision, control becomes more flexible.

The *clean-surplus concept* maintains that over the entire life of the enterprise (or project), the sum of cash flows equals the sum of period incomes. All accruals, that is the noncash items in the income statement, must be accounted for as changes on the balance sheet. For our case, this procedure means that profit calculation must obey the accounting identity $(B_t := B_{t-1} - d_t \cdot b)$: all prior-year adjustments, extraordinary items, and asset revaluation surpluses are passed through the profit and loss account.

If the condition of clean surplus is fulfilled, prior research[18] shows that the following identity holds true:

$$\sum_{t=1}^{T} p_t \cdot c_t(b) - b = \sum_{t=1}^{T} p_t \cdot (c_t(b) - d_t b - r_t \cdot B_{t-1}).\qquad(19)$$

This correlation means that residual income measures are compatible with the net present value concept (conservation property). Note that the identity is true for all possible kinds of depreciation methods as long as the sum of depreciation equals b (clean surplus). This identity is also responsible for the fact that the manager has the incentive to determine the appropriate level of investment. However, the optimal investment decision can also be induced by abandoning the clean-surplus concept $(d \neq 1)$. In that case, headquarters must adjust the capital charge, as the next case shows.

3.2. Case 2: Depreciation deviates from the initial cash investment ($d \neq 1$)

If headquarters violates the clean-surplus concept, for example because it would like to integrate the incidental costs, in form of the replacement costs of the assets, into the performance measure $(d > 1)$, then if the investment decision is to be induced as before the capital charge to the manager must be lowered accordingly $(\gamma < r)$. On the other hand if the asset still has a residual value at the end of the lifetime (which may not appear in the manager's performance measure), the critical hurdle rate charged for the capital tied up is $\gamma > r$. Empirical studies show that internal hurdle rates are often very different from the interest rate of the company. Therefore, internal hurdle rates are important control instruments in business operations.[19]

The basic idea behind the skilful selection of both depreciation and capital charges is predicated on the goal-congruent transformation of the investment problem. A crucial point is that the total investment problem is reconstructed for each individual period in a manner that perfectly harmonizes both the interests of headquarters and the manager. To ensure this interrelation, at least two variables are required in the second period (or in any succeeding period in a multiperiod model with $T > 2$). Due to $\alpha > 0$, one of the two variables depends on the cash flow, $y(b, e_1)$ or $c(b)$, respectively, the other depends on the initial investment b. Since, in the case of a more-than-two-period model, this correlation must apply in period 2 as well as in each succeeding period, we can drop out those performance measures in each period that are based only on then-observable cash flows right from the beginning. In contrast to accruals, there is a lack of connection between the initial cash investment b and the later cash flow $c(b)$ for the annuitization of the investment decision. However, accounting that is based on the matching principle ensures such coherence by assigning the investment payments to the periods in which the cash flows occur, for example through depreciation.

4. A more general look at the connections between incentive contracts, performance measures, and information structures

A generalization of the results shown above and a closer look at the formal relation between incentive contracts, performance measures, and information structures yields the following results:

1. If headquarters has no knowledge of future cash flows of an investment project, but if the discount rates of headquarters and manager are identical, the simple solution is to delay the manager's reward to some final date and to pay a fixed salary at all intermediate dates. If this procedure is not feasible and compensation at date t must rely on cash realizations at that date, then goal-congruent compensation schemes are limited to linear structures and the bonus coefficients must remain constant for all dates from date 0 to date T.[20] Incentive schemes based on accruals provide a little more flexibility because the bonus coefficient at date 0 can be selected arbitrarily.

2. If headquarters knows the growth profile of future cash flows, it can enhance the flexibility of incentive schemes based on accruals.[21] Any monotonically increasing compensation scheme can ensure goal congruence if the allocation rule is conditional on the investment project according to the so-called relative benefit depreciation schedule. This procedure is similar to the matching principle, in which firms attempt to record cash outflows as expenses in the period in which the corresponding revenues are realized. Since both the time period for the bonus coefficient and the manager's discount factors lose their influence on the investment decision due to the matching principle, control becomes more flexible. In this way, we can solve the problem of the impatient manager, even though the manager's discount rates

are unknown. If we use the headquarters discount factor for the calculation of the capital charges, the resulting depreciation schedule has to be "tidy," that is the sum of depreciation charges must equal 1.

3. Recent literature on goal congruence and residual income extends the analysis to a number of other representative transactions, such as inventory production,[22] credit sales,[23] long-term construction contracts,[24] asset disposals,[25] research and development projects,[26] provisions,[27] and corporate income taxes.[28] In all cases, goal congruence requires that to avoid intertemporal tradeoffs in the performance measure, the accrual accounting rules achieve proper matching of revenues and expenses.[29] Headquarters uses residual income to create robust incentives for the manager to maximize the present value of future cash flows regardless of the manager's time preferences and the (usually unmodelled) compensation rules.

5. Critical evaluation of recent research approaches to explaining accruals

Recent research on accrual accounting seems to supply reasons for why accrual accounting is of great relevance in the context of managerial performance evaluation and why it is often used there: "In particular, they lend support to the recent emphasis in the practitioner literature on EVA as a managerial performance measure."[30] Nevertheless, the models developed so far are not without their weaknesses and limitations.

5.1. Accruals in models compared to accruals in practice

In the depreciation models showing the correspondence to the matching principle, the coherence applies only to the sum of depreciation and capital charges, which reflects the intertemporal distribution of cash flows. The depreciation itself is distributed differently among the individual periods. Thus, the question arises as to whether previous models can actually explain the procedures observed in practice. For example, why is depreciation often undertaken linearly in both financial and managerial accounting? Even if we assume constant cash flows over time, the resulting depreciation schedule remains complex. Only the entire cost of investment (i.e. depreciation plus capital charges) that is distributed constantly is simple. Therefore, the question arises whether practitioners also make errors in applying linear depreciation or whether there are other well-founded reasons that might explain the use of accruals.

5.2. Rigid information assumptions

To achieve the goal-congruent transformation of the investment problem, headquarters needs certain crucial information. Determining depreciation based on knowledge of the initial cash investment is not problematic. For the calculation of capital charges, headquarters needs its own discount factor and information on the capital that is tied up at the beginning of each period. The knowledge of the capital tied up presupposes information only about the past cash flows; their recording usually does not present a problem. Knowledge of headquarters' own discount factor also does not appear to be restrictive, since it is a prerequisite for the solution of the investment problem even if information is distributed symmetrically. Thus, knowledge of the underlying future contingencies remains crucial. In other words, depreciation and capital charges in the case of the impatient manager must be assigned to cash flows in accordance with the principal's goal.

In the simple model presented here, this information requirement is a trivial problem, since the one-off investment cash outflow b needs only be shifted to the next period. However, if there are more than two periods, due to delegation and the associated asymmetric distribution of information, estimating future cash flows may represent a substantial hurdle. Although headquarters possesses suitable period concepts, in practice it often does not know how to design them in a manner that will satisfactorily solve the problem of the impatient manager. On the other hand, the reader should not overestimate the information claims. These claims are high in the context of financial reporting too, in which, for example if there is a case of multiyear construction, the accountant must be able to make a reliable estimate of total contract revenue, the stage of completion, and the costs to complete the contract (IAS 11.22–24).

5.3. Goal congruence and agency settings

One drawback in the analysis of accrual accounting is the question of how to develop a formal moral hazard problem that will rule out trivial solutions when compensation payments to the agent remain indeterminate. Reichelstein (1997) and Rogerson (1997) do not explicitly model moral hazard, so the reader may overlook this nontrivial cause of performance evaluation. Instead, these authors ask how a manager who is responsible for investments can make the best decision from the perspective of headquarters (goal-congruent investment decisions) regardless of the value of bonus coefficients.

Reichelstein (2000) analyzes moral hazard by assuming that the investment opportunity set depends on the manager's effort. However, the caveat is that the implementation of the investment itself is not subject to moral hazard (as in the simple model presented in this chapter). Therefore, the underlying moral hazard problem and the required bonus coefficients in each period have no bearing on the agent's investment decision.

Wagenhofer (2003) examines a multiperiod, multitask agency model in which a risk-averse agent selects activities with long- and short-term consequences. Given some exogenous contract restrictions, his study shows that accruals may be superior to cash flows.

Dutta and Reichelstein (2002a), as in my model shown above, add moral hazard on one-period actions, but show moral hazard as separable from the investment undertaken. In addition, Dutta and Reichelstein (2002a) assume that the agent possesses private information about the profitability parameter of the investment before the contract is signed (precontract information): "In order for the residual income performance measure to support second-best outcomes, the capital charge rate must not only reflect the principal's cost of capital but also the underlying agency problem. The agent will internalize the principal's investment problem if the capital charge rate is set equal to the hurdle rate, which is the principal's *adjusted* cost of capital after taking into account the agent's expected informational rents. When projects entail additional risk, the capital charge rate must be set below the riskless hurdle rate in order to motivate the risk-averse manager to accept the incremental risk."[31]

Dutta and Reichelstein (1999b) study a multiperiod model in which a risk-averse agent exerts effort that affects only the cash flows of the period in which the effort is exerted. The authors show that residual income and fair-value accounting are superior to a cash-flow-based system because the calculation of residual income shields the agent from bearing the risk of financing activities. In a similar paper, Dutta and Reichelstein (1999a) allow for the effort that affects cash flow in both the current and in the next period. They show that incentive schemes based on residual income give the principal flexibility in setting different incentive provisions over time. The basic assumption is that the principal can use information about future expected cash flows in an incentive system based on residual income.[32]

However, in both papers of Dutta and Reichelstein, as well as in most of the aforementioned papers, it is not really clear why the principal should not use the same information in a cash-flow-based system (Laux,C. 1999). When there are no exogenous contract restrictions, it seems to be difficult to think about accruals in an agency setting in a nontrivial way. Therefore, most current papers on accrual accounting either restrict the incentive function or introduce additional information at the level of the accrual process.

Since agency theory assumes a perfect world (except for the assumptions of asymmetrical information distribution and conflicting interests) and the possibility of being able to write arbitrarily complicated contracts, we must suspect that incompleteness, which the accounting system even distinguishes, cannot be illustrated sufficiently well. Therefore, we might doubt that the analysis of accruals in an agency setting will supply evidence that goes to the heart of the central features of accounting principles.

5.4. Embedded contingencies in accrual-based contracts

From a theoretical point of view, we can interpret the weight placed on outcomes in any incentive contract either as a collection of accounting rules or as a collection of compensation functions.[33] Thus, it is always possible to construct an equivalent cash-flow-based contract that mimics the accrual-based contract.

Leuz (1999) provides a set of conditions under which it is irrelevant whether contracting problems are addressed in the compensation function (with cash-flow-based contracts) or in the performance measure (with contracts based on accruals). One condition is that the set of possible accounting transactions and events (indicators), such as the future cash flow structure in the model above, is available for contracts based on cash flows as well as for those based on accruals.[34]

Granted, this insight at first seems trivial or not useful. Agency theory tells us that we can find an optimal contract $s(y)$ where y denotes the set of contractible primitive variables (here, the history of cash flows up to period t). Since we know the optimal incentive contract, $s(y)$, we can always arbitrarily split it into two (or more) functions such as $s(y) = S(G(y))$ and so on.[35]

However, the message is not that we can arbitrarily split the incentive contract; rather the crucial question is why and how we split it in practice. Why, in practice, are certain contracting problems dealt with by using the performance measure while others are addressed in the compensation function? We know that the optimal incentive contract usually depends on situation-specific variables and on agent-specific variables (such as risk aversion, reservation utility, and so on). In a manner of speaking, we are looking for a separation of $s(y)$ into S (the compensation function) that depends only on agent-specific variables, and G (the performance measure such as accruals) that depends only on situation-specific variables. But why do we do this?

In Leuz (1999), the answer to this question is based on transaction costs and incomplete contracting. Given that in practice, the integration of verifiable transactions and events into accounting rules is used in many different contracts and that writing and verifying contracts is costly and entails certain fixed costs, then separating performance measurement and compensation-function design reduces costs in writing and verifying contingent contracts. Although less contract-specific contingencies such as accounting transactions and events are embedded at the level of performance measures (accruals and the like), more contract- or agent-specific parameters, such as the agent's risk preferences or his/her disutility of effort, are addressed in the compensation function.

This explanation is compatible with the central feature of accrual accounting, the integration of verifiable transactions and events into the accounting rules:[36] "Certain accounting rules apply only if specific transactions or events have occurred. As a result, earnings-based performance measurement is contingent, even if the accounting rules themselves are specified *ex ante* and do not change over the contracting period."[37]

However, one drawback of this kind of explanation of the widespread use of accruals is the introduction of transaction costs, which is somewhat ad hoc. In the end, transaction costs, which are often introduced exogenously and are often not specified in detail, can be used to explain anything and thus diminish the value of the argument. There is also the question of separability: Are the two problems, the optimization of the compensation function and of the performance measure, really separable in practice? Are there really empirically significant situations in which the agent's inclinations and the specifics of the situation in which the decision is made can be separated? It would be useful to examine such questions, as well as those posed earlier, in more depth. In doing so, the agency theory should prove very useful. However, we should take into consideration the fact that agency models generally optimize the incentive contract. Thus, questions of performance measurement and compensation function will always remain linked. However, if we examine the two separately, then the agency theory might prove less useful.

6. Concluding remarks

A better understanding of accruals, which are widely applied in both financial and managerial accounting, is an important and interesting topic. In discussing under what conditions residual income performance measures might be preferable to realized cash flows, recent research shows that by comparison, "residual income economises on the agency cost necessary to provide incentives for the manager. Allocating investment costs over time matches project cash flows with a share of the initial cost, so that residual income reflects the value created by the manager at any given point in time."[38]

Even if recent research results can contribute to a better understanding of accrual accounting and to deriving insightful contracting mechanisms, it cannot really show that accrual-based contracts are preferable to cash-flow-based contracts. The reason is that such studies usually regard either the compensation function or the performance measure as exogenous to the problem. The contracting problems are exogenously shifted into performance measurement and thus lead to an "unfair" comparison. If there were no restrictions on the compensation function and all information was available for performance measurement and compensation-function design, then for incentives and outcomes, cash-flow-based contracts could always be created to be equivalent to accrual-based contracts. Thus, it follows that future research should focus on the separation of performance measures and compensation functions to a greater extent than has been the case up to now. Addressing the question of why, in practice, certain contracting problems are dealt with using the performance measure while others are addressed in the compensation function would seem to be the key to a better understanding of accruals.

Even if the puzzle surrounding the advantageousness of accruals has not yet been solved, important steps have, indeed, been taken in that direction.

Notes

Useful comments by Anthony Hopwood, Christian Leuz, and Alfred Wagenhofer are gratefully acknowledged.

1 See Solomons (1965); Flower (1971); Tomkins (1973; 1975); Emmanuel and Otley (1976); Scapens (1979); Gregory (1987); for some rather skeptical views, on the other hand see Amey (1969a, b) Bromwich (1973); Mepham (1978); Parker (1979); Dearden (1987).

2 See Scapens and Sale (1981); Coates et al. (1992); Drury et al. (1992).

3 See Bromwich and Walker (1998: 392).

4 See Stewart (1991); O'Hanlon and Peasnell (1998).

5 See Ohlson (1995); Feltham and Ohlson (1995; 1996).

6 See Rogerson (1997); Reichelstein (1997; 2000); Laux, H. (1997; 1999; 2001; 2003: 493–521); Pfaff (1998); Pfaff and Bärtl (1999); Dutta and Reichelstein (1999a, b; 2002a; 2003); Pfeiffer (2000a, b); Baldenius et al. (1999); Wagenhofer and Riegler (1999); Wei (2000); Baldenius and Reichelstein (2001); Gillenkirch and Schabel (2001); Pfaff and Pfeiffer (2003); Baldenius and Ziv (2003); Wagenhofer (2003); Dierkes and Hanrath (2002); Diedrich and Dierkes (2003); Dutta and Zhang (2003).

7 For a similar assumption, see Wagenhofer (2003).

8 As we know from theory, such a feature is a necessary condition for optimizing the incentive function, since otherwise, given free disposal, the manager is better off destroying output.

9 See for instance Rogerson (1997); Reichelstein (1997; 2000); Laux, H. (1997); Pfaff (1998); Pfeiffer (2000a, b); Wagenhofer and Riegler (1999); Gillenkirch and Schabel (2001); Wagenhofer (2003). Notice that earlier academic publications implicitly discussed those conflicts of interest between headquarters and division management when managers did not have the same time preferences or time horizons as headquarters. Appropriate depreciation schedules were developed as a part of the asset base debate, to design goal-congruent residual incomes so that *ex ante* (a) residual incomes from projects with the maximum net present value in each period would be greater than the residual incomes of other projects and/or (b) residual incomes in earlier years would not exceed those in later years. Two of these procedures are of primary importance: (a) earned economic income (EEI), proposed by Grinyer (1985), and (b) maintainable residual income (MRI), proposed by Egginton (1995). EEI is the residual cash flow after scaling down the cash flow for every period by the proportion of the investment at that time compared to its present value. MRI selects depreciation so that the residual income in each period is the same. See also Bromwich and Walker (1998: 401); O'Hanlon and Peasnell (1998: 433).

10 See for example Reichelstein (2000: 244, 247).

11 See for example Reichelstein (2000: 244, 247).

12 For details concerning such mixed performance measures, see Pfaff and Pfeiffer (2003).

13 See Stewart (1991) for general implementation experiences of the consulting firm Stern Stewart & Co. See also Young and O'Byrne (2001); Stern and Shiely (2001). For practical evidence in Germany see Ruhwedel and Schultze (2002).

14 See Rogerson (1997); Reichelstein (1997); Pfaff and Pfeiffer (2003).

15 For details see Rogerson (1997); Reichelstein (1997); Pfaff and Pfeiffer (2003).

16 See Reichelstein (2000).

17 See for example Solomons (1965).

18 Preinreich (1938); Hicks (1946); Lücke (1955); Edwards and Bell (1961); Scapens (1979); Peasnell (1981; 1982).

19 See for example Ross (1986); Stewart (1991); Copeland et al. (1996). See also Dutta and Reichelstein (2002a), who show, in an agency setting with moral hazard on one-period

actions, that the hurdle rate must not only reflect the principal's cost of capital but also the underlying agency problem.
20 For details see Pfaff and Pfeiffer (2003).
21 For details see Pfaff and Pfeiffer (2003).
22 See Baldenius and Reichelstein (2001); Dutta and Zhang (2003); Diedrich and Dierkes (2003); Dutta and Reichelstein (2003).
23 See Dutta and Reichelstein (1999*b*; 2003).
24 See Dutta and Reichelstein (2003).
25 See Dutta and Reichelstein (2003).
26 See Dutta and Reichelstein (2003).
27 See Pfaff (1998).
28 See Baldenius and Ziv (2003).
29 Dutta and Reichelstein (2003).
30 Dutta and Reichelstein (1999*a*: 172).
31 Dutta and Reichelstein (2002*a*: 271).
32 In a recently published working paper, Dutta and Reichelstein (2002*b*), develop a two-period agency model to study the use of leading indicator variables in managerial performance measures. In addition to a standard moral hazard problem, the principal wants to motivate the manager not to undertake the directly contractible "soft" investments such as product or process improvements. The authors analyze the role of leading indicator variables in the duration of the agent's incentive contract. Among other results, they show that with long-term contracts, the leading indicator variables may be an instrument for matching future investment return with the current investment expenditure, given that the manager's compensation schemes are not stationary over time. Thus, in this model, the matching is provided by nonfinancial leading indicators and not by residual income measures. However, the key idea of using information about future "cash flows" is the same.
33 See Leuz (1999).
34 Violating this condition yields the straightforward result that the performance measure with access to a (strictly) larger set of verifiable indicators is chosen.
35 This, of course, requires sufficiently rich S and G functions (as s too). See also Banker and Datar (1989).
36 See Ijiri (1967); Butterworth et al. (1982); Ordelheide (1988; 1992); Beaver (1991); Leuz (1998).
37 Leuz (1999: 10). The argumentation is also in the tradition of Ordelheide (1988; 1991; 1992), to whom this chapter is dedicated. Ordelheide's "prospective accounting theory" is based on neo-institutional economics with a special focus on transaction cost economics. Ordelheide argues that the transaction- and event-based representation of uncertainty in accrual accounting can only be understood in a world of information asymmetry and incentive problems. He views nonmonetary assets as (qualitative) risk indicators and their use in accrual accounting as a way to indicate changes in the underlying probability distribution of future cash flows. He shows that historical cost accounting, the realization principle, and the lower-of-cost-or-market rule can be reconstructed in a world of incomplete information and markets.
38 Reichelstein (2000: 261).

References

Amey, L. R. (1969*a*). "Divisional performance measurement and interest on capital," *Journal of Business Finance*, 1: 2–7.
—— (1969*b*). *The efficiency of business enterprise* (London: George Allen and Unwin).

Baldenius, T. and Reichelstein, S. (2001). "Incentives for efficient inventory management: The role of historical cost." Mimeo, Columbia University.

—— and Ziv, A. (2003). "Performance evaluation and corporate income taxes in a sequential delegation setting," *Review of Accounting Studies*, 8: 283–309.

——, Fuhrmann, G., and Reichelstein, S. (1999). "Zurück zu EVA," *Betriebswirtschaftliche Forschung und Praxis*, 51: 53–69.

Banker, R. D. and Datar, S. M. (1989). "Sensitivity, precision, and linear aggregation of signals for performance evaluation," *Journal of Accounting Research*, 27: 21–39.

Beaver, W. H. (1991). "Problems and paradoxes in the financial reporting of future events," *Accounting Horizons*, 75: 122–34.

Bromwich, M. (1973). "Measurement of divisional performance: A comment and an extension," *Accounting and Business Research*, Spring: 123–32.

—— and Walker, M. (1998). "Residual income past and future," *Management Accounting Research*, 9: 391–419.

Butterworth, J. E., Gibbins, M., and King, R. D. (1982). "The structure of accounting theory: Some basic conceptual and methodological issues," reprinted in R. Mattessich (ed.). *Modern accounting research: history, survey, and guide* (Vancouver: Certified General Accountants' Research Foundation), 209–50.

Coates, J. B., Davis, E. W., Emmanuel, C. R., Longden, S. G., and Stacey, R. J. (1992). "Multi-national companies performance measurement systems: International perspectives," *Management Accounting Research*, 3: 133–50.

Copeland, T., Koller, T., and Murrin, J. (1996). Valuation: Measuring and managing the value of companies, 2nd ed. (New York, Chichester, Weinheim, Brisbane, Singapore, Toronto: John Wiley).

Dearden, J. (1987). "Measuring profit center managers," *Harvard Business Review*, 65: 84–8.

Diedrich, R. and Dierkes, St. (2003). "Residualgewinnbasierte Steuerung von Profit Centern unter Berücksichtigung von Verbrauchsfolgefiktionen und außerplanmäßigen Wertkorrekturen," *Zeitschrift für Betriebswirtschaft Ergänzungshe*, 73: 47–69.

Dierkes, St. and Hanrath, St. (2002). "Steuerung dezentraler Investitionsentscheidungen auf Basis eines modifizierten Residualgewinns," *Zeitschrift für betriebswirtschaftliche Forschung*, 54: 246–67.

Drury, C., Braund, S., Osborne, P., and Tayles, M. (1992). *A survey of management accounting practices in UK manufacturing companies* (London: Chartered Association of Certified Accountants).

Dutta, S. and Reichelstein, S. (1999a). "Performance measurement in multi-period agencies," *Journal of Institutional and Theoretical Economics*, 155: 158–75.

—— (1999b). "Asset valuation and performance measurement in a dynamic agency setting," *Review of Accounting Studies*, 4: 235–58.

—— (2002a). "Controlling investment decisions: Depreciation- and capital charges," *Review of Accounting Studies*, 7: 253–81.

—— (2002b). "Leading indicator variables, performance measurement and long-term versus short-term contracts." Mimeo, Haas School of Business, University of California, Berkeley, and Graduate School of Business, Stanford University.

—— (2003). "Accrual accounting for performance evaluation: A synthesis of recent proposals." Mimeo, Haas School of Business, University of California, Berkeley, and Graduate School of Business, Stanford University.

—— and Zhang, X.-J. (2003). "Revenue recognition in a multiperiod agency setting," *Journal of Accounting Research*, 40: 67–83.

Edwards, E. O. and Bell, P. W. (1961). *The theory and measurement of business income* (Berkeley: University of California Press).

Egginton, D. (1995). "Divisional performance measurement: Residual income and the asset base," *Management Accounting Research*, 6: 201–22.

Emmanuel, C. R. and Otley, D. T. (1976). "The usefulness of residual income," *Journal of Business Finance and Accounting*, 3: 43–51.

Feltham, G. and Ohlson, J. (1995). "Valuation and clean surplus accounting for operating and financial activities," *Contemporary Accounting Research*, 11: 689–731.

—— (1996). "Uncertainty resolution and the theory of depreciation measurement," *Journal of Accounting Research*, 34: 209–34.

Flower, J. F. (1971). "Measurement of divisional performance," *Accounting and Business Research*, Summer: 205–14.

Gillenkirch, R. M. and Schabel, M. M. (2001). "Investitionssteuerung, Motivation und Periodenerfolgsrechnung bei ungleichen Zeitpräferenzen," *Zeitschrift für betriebswirtschaftliche Forschung*, 53: 216–45.

Gregory, A. (1987). "Divisional performance measurement with divisions as lessees of Head Office Assets," *Accounting and Business Research*, Summer: 241–46.

Grinyer, J. R. (1985). "Earned economic income: A theory of matching," *Abacus*, 21: 130–48.

Hicks, J. R. (1946). *Value and Capital* (Oxford: Clarendon Press).

Ijiri, Y. (1967). *The foundations of accounting measurement* (Englewood Cliffs, NJ: Prentice Hall).

Laux, C. (1999). "Performance measurement in multi-period agencies: Comment," *Journal of Institutional and Theoretical Economics*, 155: 176–80.

Laux, H. (1997). "Individualisierung und Periodenerfolgsrechnung," in Ch. Scholz (ed.), *Individualisierung als Paradigma* (Stuttgart: Kohlhammer), 101–33.

—— (1999). *Unternehmensrechnung, Anreiz und Kontrolle*, 2nd ed. (Berlin, Heidelberg, New York, London, Paris, Tokyo: Springer).

—— (2001). "Anreize, organisatorische Gestaltung und Führung," in U. Wagner (ed.), *Zum Erkenntnisstand der Betriebswirtschaftslehre am Beginn des 21. Jahrhundert* (Berlin: Duncker & Humblot), 177–97.

—— (2003). *Wertorientierte Unternehmensführung und Kapitalmarkt: Fundierung von Unternehmenszielen und Anreize für ihre Umsetzung* (Berlin, Heidelberg, New York, London, Paris, Tokyo: Springer).

Leuz, C. (1998). "The role of accrual accounting in restricting dividends to the shareholders," *The European Accounting Review*, 7: 579–604.

—— (1999). "Embedded contingencies in earnings-based contracts: A note on the role of accruals in contracting." Discussion paper, University of Frankfurt.

Lücke, W. (1955). "Investitionsrechnung auf der Grundlage von Ausgaben oder Kosten?" *Zeitschrift für handelswissenschaftliche Forschung*, 7: 310–24.

Mepham, M. J. (1978). "A reinstatement of the accounting rate of return," *Accounting and Business Research*, Summer: 178–90.

O'Hanlon, J. and Peasnell, K. (1998). "Wall Street's contribution to management accounting: The Stern Stewart EVA® Financial Management System," *Management Accounting Research*, 9: 421–44.

Ohlson, J. (1995). "Earnings, book values, and dividends in equity valuation," *Contemporary Accounting Research*, 11: 661–87.

Ordelheide, D. (1988). "Zu einer neoinstitutionalistischen Theorie der Rechnungslegung," in D. Budäus, E. Gerum, and G. Zimmermann (eds.), *Betriebswirtschaftslehre und Theorien der Verfügungsrechte* (Wiesbaden: Gabler), 324–49.

—— (1991). "Bilanzen in der Investitionsplanung und -kontrolle: Zur Berücksichtigung von Kommunikationsrisiken und -kosten bei der Entwicklung der finanziellen Zielfunktion der Unternehmung", in D. Rückle (ed.), *Aktuelle Fragen der Finanzwirtschaft und der Unternehmensbesteuerung* (Wien: Linde), 507–34.

—— (1992). "Economic versus accounting values: A reconsideration with respect to uncertainty representation," Discussion paper presented at the London School of Economics, University of Frankfurt.

Parker, L. D. (1979). "Divisional performance measurement: Beyond an exclusive profit test," *Accounting and Business Research*, Autumn: 305–19.

Peasnell, K. V. (1981). "On capital budgeting and income measurement," *Abacus*, 17: 52–67.

Peasnell, K. V. (1982). "Some formal connections between economic values and yields and accounting numbers," *Journal of Business Finance and Accounting*, 9: 361–81.

Pfaff, D. (1998). "Wertorientierte Unternehmenssteuerung, Investitionsentscheidungen und Anreizprobleme," *Betriebswirtschaftliche Forschung und Praxis*, 50: 491–516.

—— and Bärtl, O. (1999). "Wertorientierte Unternehmenssteuerung: Ein kritischer Vergleich ausgewählter Konzepte," in G. Gebhardt and B. Pellens (eds.), *Rechnungswesen und Kapitalmarkt. Sonderheft 41/99 der Zeitschrift für betriebswirtschaftliche Forschung* (Düsseldorf and Frankfurt: Handelsblatt), 85–115.

—— and Pfeiffer, Th. (2003). "Some formal connections between incentive contracts, performance measures and information structures." *Die Unternehmung*, 57: 311–29.

Pfeiffer, T. (2000a). "Investment decisions and managerial performance evaluation," in M. Bonilla, T. Casasus, and R. Sala (eds.), *Financial Modelling* (Heidelberg, New York: Physica), 467–78.

—— (2000b). "Good and bad news for the implementation of shareholder-value concepts in decentralized organizations," *Schmalenbach Business Review*, 52: 68–91.

Preinreich, G. A. D. (1938). "Annual study of economic theory: The theory of depreciation," *Econometrica*, 6: 219–41.

Reichelstein, S. (1997). "Investment decisions and managerial performance evaluation," *Review of Accounting Studies*, 2: 157–80.

—— (2000). "Providing managerial incentives: Cash flows versus accrual accounting," *Journal of Accounting Research*, 38: 243–69.

Rogerson, W. P. (1997). "Intertemporal cost allocation and managerial investment incentives: A theory explaining the use of economic value added as a performance measure," *Journal of Political Economy*, 105: 770–95.

Ross, M. (1986). "Capital budgeting practices of twelve large manufacturers," *Financial Management*, Winter: 15–22.

Ruhwedel, F. and Schultze, W. (2002). "Value-reporting: Theoretische Konzeption und Umsetzung bei den DAX 100-Unternehmen," *Zeitschrift für betriebswirtschaftliche Forschung*, 54: 602–32.

Scapens, R. W. (1979). "Profit measurement in divisionalised companies," *Journal of Business Finance and Accounting*, 6: 281–305.

—— and Sale, J. T. (1981). "Performance measurement and formal capital expenditure controls in divisionalised companies," *Journal of Business Finance and Accounting*, 8: 389–421.

Solomons, D. (1965). *Divisional performance: Measurement and control.* (Homewood, IL: Irwin).

Stern, J. M. and Shiely, J. S. (2001). *The EVA challenge: Implementing value added change in an organization* (New York, Chichester, Weinheim, Brisbane, Singapore, Toronto: John Wiley).

Stewart, G. B. (1991). *The Quest for Value* (New York: HarperBusiness).

Tomkins, C. R. (1973). *Financial planning in divisionalised companies.* (London: Accountancy Age Books).

—— (1975). 'Another look at residual income," *Journal of Business Finance and Accounting*, 2: 39–53.

Wagenhofer, A. (2003). "Accrual-based compensation, depreciation and investment decisions," *European Accounting Review*, 12: 287–309.

—— and Riegler, Ch. (1999). "Gewinnabhängige Managemententlohnung und Investitionsanreize," *Betriebswirtschaftliche Forschung und Praxis*, 51: 70–90.

Wei, D. (2000). "Interdepartmental cost allocation and investment incentives." Mimeo, INSEAD, Fontainebleau, France.

Young, D. S. and O'Byrne, St. F. (2001). *EVA® and value-based management: A practical guide to implementation* (New York: McGraw-Hill Press).

2.2

Corporate Governance and Financial Reporting at Daimler-Benz (DaimlerChrysler) AG: From a "Stakeholder" toward a "Shareholder Value" Model

Ray Ball

1. Introduction

During the last decade of the twentieth century, Daimler-Benz AG radically transformed its approach to corporate governance and financial reporting. The company's governance traditionally had conformed closely to the German "stakeholder" model, with representation on its Supervisory Board by labor, by closely affiliated banks, and directly and indirectly by government. Its financial reporting reflected German-style balance sheet conservatism, with low book values of assets, overstated liabilities, and "hidden reserves" of equity. Balance sheet conservatism allows the companies to "smooth" earnings and allows managers to hide both the amount of assets under their control and any losses they are making from public accountability. This in turn allows the company to make stable dividend, bonus, and tax payments, and to avoid or defer the pain to labor and other parties resulting from actions necessary to stem losses, such as plant closings. Daimler's financial reporting certainly did not reflect U.S.-style income statement conservatism with more timely recognition of economic losses and hence high volatility and skewness of reported earnings.

This all changed with astonishing rapidity. By mid-decade, the company's management was openly espousing a variant of the U.S.

"shareholder value" governance model, had implemented a stock option scheme for executives, had reduced its dependence on a single bank for capital, was reporting under U.S. Generally Accepted Accounting Principles (GAAP) and, by listing its stock on the New York Stock Exchange (NYSE), had bonded itself henceforth to publicly report its economic losses in a timely fashion. Not by coincidence, it had drastically reduced its workforce and closed several plants. By the end of the decade, it had ruthlessly discarded several loss-making businesses, had focused its efforts more closely on its core businesses, and had executed a stunning acquisition (billed as a merger) of the U.S.-based Chrysler Corporation.

The case illustrates many important principles. For example, the changes Daimler made to its corporate governance and financial reporting appear to have been driven primarily by market forces, and certainly were not due to changes in regulation. Daimler faced substantial problems in its core businesses, automobiles and aerospace. Resolving those problems required plant closings, headcount reduction in part through involuntary redundancy, and closure or divestiture of perennial loss-making businesses. The enthusiasm of labor, banks, and the German government for such actions most likely would have been lower than that of shareholders in competing auto and aerospace companies operating under a shareholder value model. In this respect, the case illustrates an important general proposition: that an inefficient corporate governance and financial reporting model is a competitive disadvantage. Competition in global product markets creates pressure on firms to adopt globally efficient corporate governance and financial reporting practices, regardless of the regulatory framework and accepted practice in their home countries. Even if individual firms find it too costly to adapt, global competition creates a competitive survival mechanism for governance and reporting systems. Thus, to the extent that international homogenization of corporate governance and financial reporting practice is efficient, some convergence will evolve as a consequence of international product market competition. Conversely, to the extent that heterogeneity is efficient, market pressures will tend to generate multiple models. The strength and speed of market forces operating on corporate governance and financial reporting is unclear, but in Daimler's case the pressure is clear: it was losing ground quickly in its core automobile business.

Lest the case be misconstrued as supporting the naïve idea of a universally efficient system of corporate governance or financial reporting, three clarifying observations are in order. First, Daimler did not fully embrace the shareholder value model: it remained a German corporation, complying with German governance rules, and grafted elements of the shareholder value model onto its governance and reporting system. Second, complementarity among institutional variables makes fundamental organizational change a costly process, with no guarantee that the net outcome is positive. Third, adopting elements of the shareholder value model might be efficient during a transitional period requiring workforce reductions, plant closings, and disposing noncore businesses, but the efficient solution for a German company in the long term could well be closer to the traditional stakeholder model.

The shareholder value model has obvious attractions for a company that needs to drastically reduce its workforce, close several plants, and dispose of or liquidate several businesses. Nevertheless, changing from one system to the other is fraught with difficulties. How the shareholder value philosophy would catch on in a German context was unclear, particularly in view of the legal requirement that half of the Supervisory Board be elected by labor. The merger imposed additional complications due to the substantial cultural differences between German and U.S. managers. For example, German Chief Executive Officers(CEOs) historically have acted to develop and implement a consensus among members of their managerial boards, whereas U.S. CEOs are accustomed to acting more as decision-makers. After the merger, the compensation of U.S. executives was found to exceed that of their German counterparts by a considerable margin. Some indication of cross-cultural difficulties is apparent in the composition of DaimlerChrysler's management board, which immediately after the merger had approximately half German and half U.S. managers, but which soon lost most of its U.S. members. In general, the complementary nature of institutional variables makes fundamental organizational change a complex, difficult, and risky—and thus, in economic terms, costly—process. There was no guarantee that the net outcome would be positive, that the benefits of change would exceed the substantial costs.

Even if Daimler management were correct in assessing the shareholder value model to be more efficient for the company at the time, and even if the benefits of changing to it were to exceed the costs, it would not follow that this would be the most efficient model for the long term. Assigning to shareholders the primary rights to appoint managers is particularly appealing in times of strategic transition and rapid change, as was the case in Daimler's core businesses at the time it made the governance and reporting changes. However, if the company's businesses were to return to a more stable, steady-state condition, then it might be efficient to return more closely to the stakeholder model. That model certainly served the company well during more stable times. If the relative efficiencies of the various governance models do turn out to be state-dependent, then the current worldwide interest in the shareholder value model, with increased transparency in reporting and disclosure, could be merely transitory. It seems difficult to avoid one of two conclusions: that one system is globally optimal; or that the most efficient outcome is to eschew worldwide homogeneity and allow companies a choice of governance and financial reporting systems. Either way, imposing worldwide homogenization of standards by fiat would have the undesirable effect of removing valuable options for companies to adapt their governance and reporting systems in response to changes in state variables. For Daimler, grafting elements of the shareholder value model onto its governance and reporting might only be efficient during a transitional period requiring workforce reductions, plant closings, and focusing on core businesses.

Moving its country of domicile allows a company to transform its governance system. More intriguingly, the ability to cross-list its securities gives a company valuable options to graft elements of one governance system onto another. By listing its shares in New York, Daimler bonded itself to publicly report its economic losses in a timely fashion, an important ingredient in monitoring and disciplining the actions of its managers (Ball 2001; Ball, Kothari, and Robin 2000; Ball, Robin, and Wu 2001). During 1973, Daimler had padded its earnings to disguise its loss that year, by "booking" two separate gains totalling DM 4.3 billions (US$ 2.6 billions), without informing the German public. NYSE listing required the company to disclose its loss-making for the first time. More importantly, it bonded the company not to repeat such an act, by exposing the company—and its managers and auditors—to stockholder litigation as well as Securities Exchange Commission (SEC) action. Stockholder litigation rights are largely suppressed in most code-law environments, Germany included, so there is less incentive to publicize one's failures. Any changes in governance or accounting standards that are not accompanied by listing in an environment with significant stockholder litigation rights have low credibility (Ball 2001; Ball, Robin, and Wu 2000, 2001). By cross-listing its securities in New York, Daimler grafted substantial elements of the shareholder value governance model onto its stakeholder system, thereby creating an intriguing and instructive hybrid.

The case also illustrates the proposition that financial reporting is an integral property of corporate governance. The comparative transparency of external reporting under U.S. GAAP was seen as an essential ingredient of a shareholder value perspective, presumably by enhancing the capital market's monitoring of managers (Daimler-Benz 1997: 44; Gentz 1999: 6–8). Furthermore, as Daimler-Benz management made clear at the time, it adopted U.S. GAAP for internal reporting purposes as well, apparently to enhance corporate managers' monitoring of individual business-unit managers (Daimler-Benz 1997: 45). The implication is that the discretion that German accounting has traditionally given managers over recorded earnings was being used by business-unit managers to disguise their performance from their superiors, and it would have to change if faster and more decisive attention to loss-making businesses was required. The complexity of all the changes made by Daimler (which included internal accounting, public reporting, stock listing, and espousal of the shareholder value model) illustrates the complementary nature of institutional variables.

Initially, Daimler's radical moves were not well received in the German corporate world, but over time they were understood, and emulated. They were a precursor to widespread change in Western European corporate governance and financial reporting practices, though the extent and permanence of the changes is not yet clear.

2. Background to the events of the case

To understand why Daimler-Benz's management saw a need for such fundamental and thorough change in the corporation's governance, and to form a view on whether the shareholder governance model was thought to be superior in a period of rapid change or whether it was deemed more universally efficient, it is necessary to review the corporation and the position in which it found itself during late 1993.

2.1. The company

Daimler-Benz Aktiengesellschaft (AG) was one of the pioneers of the automobile industry and one of the great corporations of the twentieth century. Daimler-Motoren-Gesellschaft was incorporated in Stuttgart in 1890. Benz & Co. Rheinische Gasmotoren-Fabrik, Mannheim was founded as a partnership by Karl Benz in 1883. In 1910, Daimler shares commenced trading on the Stuttgart exchange and Benz was the world's largest automobile manufacturer, with sales of 603 automobiles. Daimler and Benz merged in 1924, and during the following seven decades the company grew almost continually.

In 1993, almost 40 percent of Daimler-Benz's revenues were derived from aircraft, space, defense, rail systems, microelectronics, and financial services. Nevertheless, passenger cars and commercial vehicles continued to provide the bulk of its revenues and were the primary source of the company's fame. Mercedes Benz had become one of the best-known brand names in the world, and the company's products had a long-standing and well-earned reputation for quality engineering, reliability, refinement, and luxury.

On May 7, 1998, Daimler-Benz and the Detroit-based Chrysler Corporation agreed to merge. Chrysler, the number three U.S. auto company, dated from Walter Chrysler's first model in 1924. By the mid-1990s, it was selling 2.5 million cars and trucks annually. The merger transaction, which was completed on November 12 that year, created DaimlerChrysler AG. At the time, it was the largest cross-border merger in history.

DaimlerChrysler AG currently is the largest manufacturing corporation in Germany. Its revenues for the year 2001 totalled €152,873 million ($136,072 million), making it the seventh largest corporation in the world, in terms of sales. At the end of 2001, it reported total assets of €207,410 million ($184,616 million) and stockholders' equity of €39,004 million ($34,717 million). On December 31, 2001, the market capitalization of DaimlerChrysler on the Frankfurt Stock Exchange was €48.5 billion ($43.2 billion), 6.8 percent of the widely cited *Deutsche Aktienindex* (DAX). Its principal trading markets were Frankfurt and New York, but it also traded in Germany on Berlin, Bremen, Düsseldorf, Hamburg, Hanover, Munich, and Stuttgart, in the United States on the Chicago Stock Exchange, the Pacific Stock Exchange, and the Philadelphia Stock Exchange, and elsewhere on Paris, Tokyo, Toronto, and Zurich.

2.2. Problems in Stuttgart

In contrast with its remarkable history, by late 1993 Daimler-Benz faced significant challenges. While its automobile products continued to live up to their vaunted reputation, a variety of economic and political changes threatened the company's viability as an independent auto manufacturer. Compounding matters, recent diversification moves had turned sour. Daimler-Benz management was struggling to address these problems, but was shackled by a system of corporate governance that was better suited for steering corporate growth and for dividing its spoils among stakeholders, than for confronting strategic decisions with painful consequences for some stakeholders.

The problems facing Daimler-Benz management in late 1993 included:

1. Automobiles:
   - Increasing competition in the luxury passenger-car market (including Toyota's stunning entry with its Lexus brand and BMW's resurgence in top-end models) threatened the company's market niche.
   - Weakening sales of passenger cars throughout Europe had caused Daimler-Benz to revise its 1993 sales plans and production schedules downward.
   - Increasing fixed costs of developing models, platforms, and engines were causing increasing scale economies and therefore problems for lower-volume manufacturers.
   - Platform development costs increasingly were being shared by its competitors across a range of models, creating substantial cost disadvantages for companies that operated with a limited product range. Daimler-Benz production was concentrated in high-end luxury cars, and companies that were trapped in that segment of the market alone were disappearing one by one through merger and acquisition. Sharing platform costs across models was what had allowed Toyota to sell the superbly engineered and produced Lexus at such a low price—a price that Daimler was unable to match with a comparable Mercedes. On the other hand, management was concerned that extending its product range down-market to achieve cross-model economies would dilute the Mercedes brand's cachet.
   - The market had recently moved toward sports utility vehicles (SUVs) and light trucks, generating an urgent need to revamp and extend the company's product line.
   - High German labor costs (hourly rates approximately double those in the United States) made it crucial that production be moved to other countries.
   - Daimler had a substantially unhedged income statement, with a strategic imbalance between costs (incurred largely in Deutsche Marks) and revenues (received in a variety of currencies, including U.S. dollars). This exposed the company to considerable foreign exchange risk over the long term. Recent strength in the Deutsche Marks had eroded profit margins, convincing management of the

need to source more costs offshore. This required closing several German plants and reducing German employment.

- The European auto industry had a glut of capacity. Several Daimler-Benz plant closures were needed, but were politically difficult to implement.

2. Aerospace:
- A downturn in defense expenditure by European and worldwide governments, arising from the so-called "peace dividend," together with a fall in space expenditures, had severely impacted the company's Deutsche Aerospace business. Aerospace accounted for 18 percent of Daimler's 1993 revenues.

- Losses were running unstemmed in the Fokker aircraft corporation acquired during 1993. The acquisition had become an immediate drain on both cash flow and earnings. It was like a voluntary tax on Daimler's core automobile business.

Many of these problems were large and urgent. Their resolution quite possibly could adversely affect employees in several plants as well as companies with which Daimler had close ties. A key question was whether the company's system of corporate governance allowed it to confront such a daunting list of problems within the necessary time frame.

3. Code-law and common-law models of corporate governance, financial reporting, and disclosure

The extent and nature of political influence on corporate governance, financial reporting, and disclosure vary substantially across countries. A simple but helpful proxy for political influence is a dichotomous classification of countries as predominantly code law (high political influence on governance, reporting, and disclosure practices) or common law (governance, reporting, and disclosure practices are determined primarily in the private sector). Furthermore, this simple dichotomy captures important differences in how information asymmetry between managers and parties contracting with the firm is ameliorated (Ball, Kothari, and Robin 2000).

As always, the code- and common-law classes overlap in practice, so caution must be exercised when interpreting such broad categorization. For example, no country follows a purely market or planning system. The U.K. Companies Acts imposed codification on a predominantly common-law system, as did the U.S. Securities and Exchange Acts that created the SEC. Nevertheless, the distinction between code- and common-law countries does reflect the extent of political relative to market influences on corporate governance, financial reporting, and disclosure, and captures important differences in how information asymmetry is ameliorated, so it is employed here as a useful organizing vehicle.

3.1. The code-law model

Most Continental European countries—Germany included—operate 'code law' systems of corporate governance, financial reporting, and disclosure. The origin of law codification normally is attributed to the Roman system of *jus civile* developed under the Emperor Justinian in the sixth century A.D. Government codification was "exported" to most of Continental Europe during Roman occupation.

Code law is established and enforced by governments and their agencies—that is in the public sector not in the private sector. A government agency, such as the French *Conseil national de la comptabilité*, typically is responsible for recommending rules to a legislature for formal approval, or it might even be delegated direct rule-making authority. Either way, code-law systems of corporate governance, financial reporting, and disclosure are written as formal rules (the "code"). Code-law rule enforcement, which requires detection, investigation, and prosecution, also is a public sector activity. By definition, violating code law is a criminal act, subject to the penalties provided by legislation, which typically include fines, incarceration, and exclusion from practice, as well as adverse publicity.

In comparison with common-law countries, code-law countries typically exhibit powerful economic intermediaries. These organizations represent large classes of economic actors (notably labor, capital, and management). There are both economic and political reasons for this.

On grounds of economic efficiency alone, one would expect a greater amount of intermediation in code-law countries. All the economic actors who actually are—or potentially could be—affected by provisions of the code (e.g. millions of shareholders throughout the country) cannot be involved individually in writing and enforcing the code. This would be extremely inefficient and essentially impossible. Hence, codification increases the economic demand for intermediation, such as a single, national body representing all labor unions and hence all unionized employees. The intermediaries act as economic agents for their members, representing them in code writing and enforcement decisions. The usual economics of agency relations presumably apply.

Furthermore, there are political reasons for greater intermediation in code-law countries. Because code writing and enforcement is undertaken by governments or their agencies, it is a politicized process. Even if they have no direct economic interest in an issue, all organized political groups can influence the political process. This in turn increases the rewards to powerful intermediaries, which act as political agents for their members, representing them in code writing and enforcement decisions. The politics of class representation thus are more likely to emerge in code-law countries.

The code-writing authority itself typically is composed of class representatives. In the case of the financial reporting code, these will include top industrialists, bank representatives, labour representatives, and government treasury officials. Representatives of professions, religions, and other interest groups might be involved, depending on the country's politics. Assistance usually is given by nonrepresentative expert members (e.g. academics).

Major politically organized groups frequently are described as stakeholders, a term whose usage in the context of corporate governance appears to have originated, ironically, in the United States, at the Stanford Research Institute during 1963 (Gregg 2001: 21). The origin of their "stake" can be purely political, not economic, in nature. Thus, a group can gain from exercising its political influence, even in an area of economic activity in which it has no direct interest or expertise.

Typically there is a widely accepted hierarchical system of intermediating institutions in code-law countries. The members of each class are represented by those institutions. Thus, we typically observe:

- strong, cohesive nationwide labor organizations;
- strong national-level banks, central banks, and pension and insurance regulatory bodies; and
- strong nationwide business/employer organizations.

Because the national code requires constant enforcement and adaptation to changes in events, these organizations must be able to both: (a) speak for their membership; and (b) work effectively with other national-level organizations.

In code-law countries, the stakeholder model also predominates at the level of the individual corporation. The stakeholders with political power in a given country are in a position to demand representation in corporate governance. This contrasts with the common-law model in which typically shareholders alone are represented.

The political influence of particular groups varies internationally, and consequently there are many variants of the stakeholder model. In Asia, the Japanese *keiretsu* and South Korean *chaebol* systems of investing and trading largely within internally informed corporate groups, and the Chinese system of family-controlled businesses and *guanxi* (connections) networks, are prime examples. Labor unions have little say in code-law writing or enforcement decisions in most Asian countries, because labor is not a strong political force in those countries. Similarly, there is no formal labor representation in corporate governance.

Japanese culture traditionally has emphasized group consciousness. Japan's emergence from a feudal structure therefore did not evolve along the Anglo-Saxon model of arm's length transacting (described below). Japan's emergence from a feudalism naturally evolved into the *keiretsu* system of related-party transacting, reinforced by cross-shareholdings. For securities trading and accounting rules, Japan most naturally provided a strong role for government codification. The most suitable role models were found in Continental Europe, so the German Commercial Code was adopted toward the end of the nineteenth century, during the *Meiji* Restoration. At the corporate level, the "President's Council" (similar to the German Supervisory Board) typically meets frequently (e.g. monthly) and is consensus-oriented. The inclusion of related corporations (major customers, suppliers, banks), as a consequence of cross-holding, is an extension and refinement of the German system, described below.

3.2. The common-law model

Common law emerged in post-Conquest England, approximately a millennium ago. It too was "exported," primarily to former English colonies, and thus it is the basis for much law in Australia, Canada, India, Ireland, and New Zealand, as well as U.S. federal (and much state) law. Common law originates in private practice, not in the public sector. In common law, principles arise largely from accepted practice. After a practice has become widely accepted as being reasonable, it achieves the legal status of being assumed by any reasonable person to have been followed in subsequent instances.

An accounting example is the widespread application of the conservatism principle. If accountants consistently prepare conservative balance sheets over an extended period of time, then that practice would be found to be generally accepted, and any reasonable user of any subsequently prepared balance sheet is entitled to assume it has been followed. Failure to prepare a company's balance sheet on a conservative basis then violates a (lower-case) generally accepted accounting principle.

A more detailed accounting example concerns noncancellable long-term lease agreements. If managers and accounting and financial practitioners almost universally come to view such leases as a nonequity method of financing assets, then a reasonable user of balance sheets would be entitled to assume they were counted as long-term debt. Failure to record them as such would expose the company's managers and accountants to the charge that they failed to record all the long-term debts that any reasonable person would assume had been recorded.

In a pure common-law (private sector) system, the consequence of a failure to comply with the rules—whether they are formally agreed to or implicit in an agreement because a "reasonable person" would expect them to be—is the risk that one is sued by the offended party or parties. If one loses, the penalty is a monetary award of damages to the plaintiff(s).

Judicial and quasi-judicial (e.g. arbitration) processes are central to the creation and implementation of common law. The standard to which parties' conduct is held in common law is that of a reasonable person. A reasonable person would assume that the other party to a contract (including a company disclosing information) is following normal or generally followed practice. When there is disagreement as to what that is, resolution is via arbitration, court proceedings, or some other independent review. In common-law countries, independent accountants and an independent accounting profession play an important and quasi-judicial role in the economy. Adjudicators must take into account a truthful version of all facts and must make judgments that are fair as among parties affected by their decisions—hence the term "true and fair view."

Some decisions have widespread application and thus are implemented as principles or rules. In a private sector system, these are most efficiently decided on a centralized basis by the independent accounting profession as a whole, for two reasons: (a) efficiency due to scale effects, as in a franchise system; and (b) rules allow individual accounting firms to be more independent when negotiating with managers. Examples of profession-wide accounting decisions are counting long-term noncancellable leases as debt, or requiring amortization of purchased goodwill. Economically, mandating central-ized accounting rules is akin to McDonald's Corporation requiring all franchisees to meet strict standards on food preparation and service as a condition of using its corporate trademarks.

Some decisions have only company-specific application. These are left to the individual independent accountant to make. Examples are the number of transactions to be sampled during the audit, or the application of the revenue recognition rule in a complex sales transaction that is unique to the client. Again, this is similar to McDonald's Corporation decentralizing decisions that are most efficiently made on the basis of local knowledge by franchisees.

Precedent plays an important role in a common-law system. It is an efficient way of conveying information. If prior cases have decided as a matter of fact that a practice is generally acceptable, then there is no need to regather and reevaluate all that evidence. In subsequent cases, it is sufficient to impose the principle that was established in the precedent case. Hence the U.S. audit report certifies the accounts are "in accord-ance with generally-accepted accounting principles" (GAAP, in upper case).

The common-law function of the Financial Accounting Standards Board (FASB) in the United States is not widely appreciated. It is more likely that there would be a standard-setting process in the absence of political interference—that is, without Congress, the Securities Acts, and the SEC. Professions voluntarily establish standards to which their members must comply. While the FASB is a lightning rod for political influence, its common-law market function is to discern the accounting principles that are generally accepted as appropriate in U.S. commercial affairs. In economic terms, its market role is to increase the efficiency of contracting with the firm.

There are many variants of the basic common-law system, and the political realities are that in most common-law countries there is par-allel legislative code-law operating. For example, relative to the United Kingdom the United States has tended to formally record its precedents in the form of written statements of the FASB. This does not in itself mean that the United States is a code-law country, because GAAP nevertheless originates in the private sector. However, the political process and the SEC have been moving U.S. accounting toward a public sector code-law system since 1933–4.* U.S. accountants still need to exercise considerable

---

*Subsequent to writing, the U.S. has accelerated this process, creating the Public Company Accounting Oversight Board under the Sarbanes-Oxley Act of 2002.

judicial-style discretion at a decentralized level, because no set of central rules can anticipate all contingencies. Hence, there remains an element of certification of "truthfulness and fairness" in the U.S. audit report.

Formal written statements of accounting principles in the United Kingdom are fewer in number and shorter in length, thus leaving more guidance to the individual accountant. Consequently, there is an element of certification of "compliance with GAAP" in the U.K. audit report. While the U.K. notion of "true and fair" initially appears to apply to a purely judicial approach, common law gives a special role to precedent (including precedent that has been formalized in written rules). Formal statements of the Accounting Standards Board (ASB) in the United Kingdom inevitably play a special role as strongly persuasive precedent.

The shareholder value model of corporate governance tends to dominate in common-law countries. Unlike the stakeholder model, the explanation is economic rather than political. Alchian and Demsetz (1972) argue that, from an economic efficiency viewpoint, stockholders have the greatest incentive to monitor managers, because they are the residual claimants to the value of the company (all other parties are paid-off first), and hence they have the most to gain or lose from actions by managers that affect value. If governance is not politicized, then economic efficiency should prevail, and stockholders or their elected representatives are the most efficient monitoring party. So it is not surprising that the shareholder model is dominant in common-law corporate governance, with shareholders alone having voting rights in appointing the governing board and in establishing the rules governing its conduct.

3.3. Financial reporting and disclosure under code law versus common law

The hierarchical nature of code-law institutional structure has one particularly important implication for corporate governance, financial reporting, and disclosure. Code-law systems typically assume that firms transact with stakeholder representatives, who by dint of their representation in governance are privately informed about relevant events. They are not presumed to rely on information that has been publicly disclosed; the presumption is that they have "insider" access to information. Code-law systems therefore tend to require a lower standard of financial reporting and public disclosure, and thus generate less public information.

Even in large, listed 'public' companies, representatives of all major groups are privately informed. The typical supervisory board thus will have representation from management, employees, banks (and other major suppliers of capital, such as pension or insurance trusts), major suppliers of materials or components, and major customers. Information asymmetry is more likely to be reduced by direct or insider communication between managers and the Supervisory Board representatives of intermediaries (banks and employee organizations). Investment and lending decisions, as well as decisions in relation to the election, re-appointment, and compensation of managers, are more likely to be made as a consequence of information that is directly acquired through representation on the Supervisory Board.

In sharp contrast, common-law systems typically assume that transactions are conducted "at arm's length"—that is by parties who do not know each other. This is not surprising in the light of common-law market, as opposed to, political origins. Common law therefore presumes that economic actors have a right to information and rely upon the information disclosed to them. Conversely, it is not assumed that they have access to private information. The demand for intermediaries (banks, insurance companies, and other institutional shareholders) is lower than under code law, and disclosure to individual shareholders and lenders is a cornerstone of the financial markets.

High standards of public disclosure apply particularly to public corporations. These companies deal with a wide range of the public. For example, when shares are listed on a stock exchange (particularly national or international), then the number of potential shareholders is very large and the identities of all potential shareholders are essentially unknowable. Similar observations can be made about potential lenders, creditors, employees, suppliers, and customers. The practice thus has emerged of reporting to the "public at large." Common-law systems therefore tend to require a higher standard of public financial reporting and disclosure by corporations, and thus generate more public information.

Common-law systems support large public markets. For example, a corporation can raise debt capital directly from the public by selling debt securities in comparatively small amounts (e.g. US$ 1000 bonds) to the general public. None of the individual investors need have access to private information about the corporation's risks; they presume these have been publicly disclosed.

Enhanced public disclosure allows individual investors and analysts to make informed investing and lending decisions. But public disclosure also plays an important role in monitoring managers, including both executives and the nonexecutive members of the Board of Directors. Shareholders vote on the appointment and reappointment of Directors, and approve the schemes that determine management compensation. Public disclosures also influence share prices (Ball and Brown 1968), and therefore affect the stock-based component of executive compensation. Informed stockholders, security analysts, and lenders thus play an important role in common-law corporate governance.

4. Some properties of the German institutional structure

Daimler's actions during the period of this case are best understood against the background of German institutional structure. Those selected are: corporate governance; accounting standards under the German commercial code; incentives to reduce volatility and hide losses in German financial reporting; influence of taxation on German financial reporting; and differences in views on the ownership of corporate earnings.

4.1. Corporate governance

The governance structure of the German stock corporation (*Aktiengesellschaft*, or AG) is prescribed by law, the principal provisions of which are surveyed by Roe (1994). The Supervisory Board (*Aufsichtsrat*) comprises entirely nonexecutive members. It appoints and monitors the Management Board (*Vorstand*), which comprises entirely executives, and thus has ultimate responsibility for the company's strategy. As part of its monitoring function, the Supervisory Board receives and approves the company's financial statements. Reflecting the German stakeholder view of corporate governance, half the Supervisory Board membership of a large corporation is elected by employees and half is elected by shareholders. While shareholders also elect a Chair, and thus can maintain a controlling edge, labor representation in corporate governance is substantial. Despite some occasional experiments with labor or consumer representation, the United States has never seriously embraced the stakeholder view of the corporation. In most public U.S. corporations, shareholders alone appoint the Board of Directors.

The *Vorstand* traditionally is a consensus-oriented structure. Its head has a radically different role than the U.S.-style CEO. The German head does not sit on the Supervisory Board, and functions more as the distiller of the Management Board's consensus, and frequently is referred to as its "speaker." The U.S. equivalent to this board typically is an Executive Committee that is handpicked by the CEO. It comprises the key executives who advise the CEO and implement his or her decisions. The greater emphasis on consensus in the *Vorstand* is not surprising, given that it ultimately is accountable to the pluralistic *Aufsichtsrat* and that it functions in the context of a stakeholder governance system and a "social contract" environment generally.

German banks are the dominant suppliers of equity capital and have a monopoly over the stock broking industry. In addition, they tend to hold individual shareholders' shares in trust and to vote them in a block. Consequently, a few large German banks dominate the representation of shareholders on the Supervisory Boards of German stock corporations. In 1993, Deutsche Bank had representatives on the Supervisory Board of approximately 25 percent of German public corporations (AGs), including Daimler-Benz. In addition, banks are a dominant supplier of credit to German corporations. In the United States, the suppliers of debt and equity capital to a particular firm are considerably more disperse, individuals own relatively more shares and financial intermediaries (banks, insurance companies, and institutional shareholders) typically do not dominate corporate boards.

More than in common-law countries such as the United States, code-law governments and politics influence corporate decision-making. Because taxes generally are paid on essentially the same amount of earnings that is reported in the public financial statements (further described below), government is one of the direct stakeholders in the corporation. A less direct but powerful influence is the close working relation between governments and large corporations that is a characteristic of code-law countries. Some notion of a social contract tends to exert a strong influence on corporate decision-making.

Daimler-Benz's twenty-person Supervisory Board at the end of 1993 included ten elected labor representatives, as required by law. The remainder were bank, corporate, or government representatives. It was chaired by Hilmar Kopper of Deutsche Bank, which has owned almost 30 percent of Daimler-Benz stock.

4.2. Accounting standards under the German commercial code

The *Handelsgesetzbuch* (HGB, or "commercial code") codifies most German rules governing both financial reporting and disclosure. The HGB is legislative in origin; while the situation has changed somewhat in recent years, the German accounting profession historically played little role in standard-setting. Despite popular conception, it is written in relatively abstract terms and is not nearly as detailed as the formal accounting standards governing financial reporting in the United States (GAAP). GAAP are established by the FASB, a private sector body comprising full-time members, who must sever previous connections with accounting firms and corporations, and an extensive staff. It is financed by a wide range of private sector organizations. FASB standards are numerous and detailed. They are recognized by the SEC as authoritative, giving them a quasi-code status.

Perhaps the greatest axiomatic difference between U.S. and German accounting standards lies in accrual accounting. The FASB's Statement of Financial Accounting Concepts No. 6 makes it clear that (para. 145, emphasis added) "the goal of accrual accounting is to account *in the periods in which they occur* for the effects on an entity of transactions and other events and circumstances." In contrast, German rules allow firms to accrue *future* expenses, and in some cases require them to do so. For example, firms are required to accrue estimated repairs and maintenance expenses for the first three months of the following year, as a charge against current-period earnings, and are allowed to accrue as much as the estimated expenses for the entire following year (Nobes and Parker 1995: 277). Other charges, including additional depreciation, can be taken against income but transferred to a tax-deferred stockholders' equity account (Nobes and Parker 1995: 277).

The greater flexibility allowed by German accounting standards is no accident. It provides ample opportunity for German managers to bend financial reporting in order to meet a variety of corporate and personal objectives, such as minimizing corporate taxes, smoothing earnings, underreporting the assets at their disposal, and hiding losses.

In explaining its decision to change to reporting under U.S. accounting standards, the Daimler-Benz management described the difference in these terms:

German and U.S. accounting principles are based on fundamentally different perspectives. While accounting under the German HGB emphasizes the principle of caution and creditor protection, the availability of relevant information for shareholder decision-making is the chief objective of U.S. accounting. The comparability of financial statements—both from year to year and from company to company—and the determination of performance on an accrual basis therefore rank higher under U.S. GAAP than under the HGB. (Daimler-Benz 1997: 44)

Earlier, they had noted wryly: "U.S. accounting principles by far do not allow provisions and reserves to the extent as the German Commercial Code." (Daimler-Benz 1995: 96).

The company's decision to change to U.S. GAAP is tantamount to bonding itself to forego the flexibility in financial reporting that is permitted and encouraged under HGB rules.

4.3. Incentives to reduce volatility (hide losses) in German HGB reporting

There are universal incentives for managers to smooth reported income, that is to reduce earnings volatility. Managers generally have poorly diversified human capital portfolios, and much of their wealth and prestige is tied to the performance of the firm, so volatility avoidance is natural. Typical compensation schemes place a ceiling on earnings-based bonuses, thus causing a managerial preference to defer recognition of very large profits (Healey 1985). Managers also prefer to hide very large losses, to retain their positions (think Enron). Managers therefore generally have incentives to avoid both large profits and large losses, and to reduce earnings volatility. Employees are in a similar position, accentuated by company-wide bonus schemes based on profits. Earnings volatility impacts debt agreements, which explicitly or implicitly monitor income-based or balance-sheet-based ratios). Thus there are widespread incentives to reduce earnings volatility.

Several German institutional variables combine to accentuate the universal desire to reduce earnings volatility. They include:

1. The *Vorsicht* (literally foresight) principle pervades German accounting and leads to conservative reserves of equity as a prudent buffer for the protection of creditors. This implies reducing earnings in good years to the level needed to pay "prudent" dividends and bonuses, creating reserves that can be drawn on to pad earnings in bad years.

2. In code-law countries, Germany included, the incentives to reduce earnings volatility—and, in particular, to hide very large losses—are

unusually strong. They arise from a diverse but consistent set of institutional factors, many of which are outlined below.

3. Stock options and other stock-related compensation schemes are not common in code-law countries, Germany included. Under the stakeholder governance model, rewarding mangers on the basis of outcomes to one stakeholder alone—shareholders—would not be as well received by other parties as it is under the shareholder value model. Consequently, code-law managers are evaluated and incented to a lesser degree on the basis of shareholder value, and more on the basis of reported profits. Risk aversion among managers implies a greater preference to reduce earnings volatility.

4. Employee bonuses and stockholder dividends also are closely linked to reported earnings, creating incentives to reduce earnings volatility. Reporting a loss could eliminate both dividends and bonuses. Earnings therefore are underreported in "good" years and overreported in "bad" (especially loss-making) years.

5. The incentive to reduce earnings volatility is compounded by agency issues that are superimposed. For example, employee representatives on code-law corporate governing bodies usually are annually reelected agents for employees, which gives them additional incentives to avoid reporting losses (and hence omitting bonuses) or even to avoid decreases in earnings (and bonuses).

6. Bank, pension fund, and insurance company shareholders are regulated on the basis of capital adequacy, and hence are harmed by volatility in their own earnings. If they own 20 percent or more of the company's stock they must "equity account" their investment, and hence earnings volatility in their client companies flows directly into volatility of their own earnings and capital adequacy (leverage) ratios. If they do not own enough stock to equity account they show dividends in their own earnings (and retained earnings), so they have an incentive to reduce dividends volatility. Given the typically close dividends–earnings linkage in code-law countries, this translates to reducing the volatility of the earnings of companies in which they hold equity investments.

7. Additional taxes on undistributed earnings create strong incentives to reduce earnings in typical years (other things equal, to not report earnings in excess of those needed to pay the desired dividends and bonuses). This creates reserves to draw on in bad years.

8. Under code law, income calculations for tax and financial reporting are almost identical (the German case is described below). Tax

considerations therefore distort reported earnings. Nonlinearities in the tax rate penalize earnings volatility.

9. Governments also prefer low earning volatility to plan tax collections, and thus reward predictability (in particular they do not want tax revenues to fall in recessions).

Collectively, these institutional factors in code-law countries, Germany included, create strong incentives to reduce earnings volatility—and, in particular, to hide very large losses. Correspondingly, public financial reporting and disclosure—including timely recognition of large losses— play a lesser role, and consequently there is less litigation-risk arising from failure to report or disclose losses in a timely fashion.

Large-sample academic studies confirm these tendencies. Ball, Kothari, and Robin (2000) report that earnings reported in code-law countries exhibit lower volatility, lower left-skewness (reflecting a lower frequency of timely loss recognition), lower timeliness in general, lower sensitivity to economic losses, and lower incremental timeliness relative to dividends.

4.4. Influence of taxation on German financial reporting

Code-law systems tend to generate similar or even identical rules for determining taxable income and "book" income for financial reporting purposes. In Germany, the *Maßgeblichkeitsprinzip* ("authoritative principle") requires tax accounting to be based on the firm's *Handelsbilanz* ("commercial balance sheet"). While this principle is applied at the individual-company level, not the consolidated group level that is relevant to financial reporting, it exerts a subtle but powerful influence. The effect is that for an expense to be deductible for tax, it must also be deducted on the firm's books. The law in France, Japan, and most other code-law countries is similar.

There are two principal reasons for the similarity between accounting and tax in code-law countries:

1. Government is heavily involved in writing the accounting code as well as being responsible for taxation, so it tends to prefer a single set of rules for convenience sake; and

2. Code-law countries develop a "culture" of all stakeholders, including government, "sharing in the same pie," described more fully below.

There is pressure for all distributions, including taxes as well as dividends, labor bonuses, and management bonuses, to be based on the
same income number—that is to be the shares of various stakeholders
in the company's profits.

In contrast, common-law countries typically operate two parallel systems for calculating the incomes of public corporations: income for
financial reporting purposes (book income), calculated under largely
private sector accounting standards (e.g. U.S. GAAP); and income for tax
reporting purposes ("taxable" income), calculated under public sector
rules (e.g. the U.S. Tax Code and IRS regulations).

The effects of the code-law linkage of book and tax incomes include:

1. In addition to its roles in disclosure to external parties (chiefly
   shareholders and lenders) and in incenting and monitoring the performance of managers (a corporate governance function), reported
   earnings must also bear the burden of the firm's and the government's
   taxation policies (including tax minimization and smoothing).
2. Reported income also is influenced by the government's taxation policies. For example, Japan historically has required its accounting rules
   and practices to conform to national macroeconomic objectives. The
   long-deferred loan loss recognition practices of Japanese banks are a
   prime example.
3. Firms have a tax-induced incentive to minimize reported income to
   minimize tax. This leads to conservative balance sheets (due to heavy
   past write-offs of assets against income, heavy past provisions for
   future expenses or losses against income, and underrecognition of
   past gains).

Paradoxically, tax-induced pressure to "manage" reported earnings does
not necessarily lead to understatement of income in every year, for two
reasons. First, all accounting adjustments are a matter of timing. Equivalently, accounting revenue and expense "accruals" tend to reverse over
time. Thus, a firm with high tax deductions in the past has lower deductions in the present and the future. For some accounting accruals, it
is only possible to reduce reported earnings over an extended period of
time by generating uninterrupted growth. In other words, it is possible to
be consistently conservative in the balance sheet, but it is difficult to be
consistently conservative in reporting profits. Second, nonlinearity in tax
rates (e.g. imperfect carry-forward of losses) gives an incentive to reduce
volatility of taxable income, in all countries. In code-law countries, this

translates to reducing the volatility of reported income, which means that income tends to be overstated in bad years.

The connection between taxation and volatility of reported earnings is subtler than the above analysis suggests. Taxation in code-law countries generally (and Germany in particular) is based on company-level taxable income, not consolidated group income. This gives companies the option to uncouple tax and book income by reporting consolidated financials that are not based on the tax records. Few companies choose to do so, presumably because the tax system gives them greater reporting flexibility, including the capacity to hide losses. Taxation and other incentives to reduce the volatility of reported earnings therefore interact in a subtle fashion.

4.5. Who owns earnings: Shareholders or stakeholders?

In common-law countries, the earnings of a corporation are viewed as the property of shareholders. The amount of earnings certainly influences other parties' decisions, including lending decisions, labor negotiations, and political intervention in the company's affairs (Watts and Zimmerman 1986), but the primary ownership of earnings lies unequivocally with shareholders.

The stakeholder model substantially alters the economic role of earnings. In Germany, reported income is more analogous to an annually baked pie, to be divided among the important stakeholders, (government, employees, shareholders and managers alike). Consequently, the size of the pie each year is of direct interest to all stakeholders. Under the *Vorsicht* principle, the amount of earnings is determined with prudential regard for the financial stability of the corporation. This principle legitimizes generally conservative book values as a buffer for the protection of creditors, but it also legitimizes a German earnings variable that is low in volatility and late in incorporating economic gains and losses.

The primary accounting tool available to reduce earnings volatility is to fail to recognize economic gains and losses in a timely fashion; that is to base earnings more on current-period realizations of cash flows, and less on accounting accruals that capitalize changes in present values of future cash flows (Basu 1997; Ball, Kothari, and Robin 2000; Ball, Robin, and Wu 2001). Reported earnings then is a smoothed moving average of past economic income, and thus is less timely in incorporating information about the economic value of the firm.

One justification offered for prudence is the stakeholders' mutual interest in the company's financial stability. This is consistent with conservative book values. A more skeptical view is that stability in the size of the pie also is valued by the agents for intermediaries who gather around the Supervisory Board table, because earnings volatility translates directly into unwanted bonus, dividend, and tax volatility. This interpretation is consistent with the low sensitivity of German corporations' earnings to economic losses (Ball, Kothari, and Robin 2000). It also is consistent with Daimler's reporting behavior in 1993, when it reported a profit even though it was making losses.

5. Daimler's 1993 events: Disclosing a loss, hidden reserves, NYSE listing, U.S. GAAP reporting, plant closings and employee layoffs

The sequence of events that unfolded around Daimler in 1993 was without precedent. It started with Daimler reporting a profit under HGB rules and ended with announcements of plant closings and involuntary employee layoffs. In between, Daimler announced it would list its stock on the NYSE, reported key financial information calculated under U.S. GAAP, revealed it actually was making a loss, and revealed it had substantial hidden reserves.

5.1. Listing in New York

On October 5, 1993, Daimler-Benz stock commenced trading as American Depositary Receipts (ADRs) on the NYSE. No German company had previously listed on a U.S. national exchange, in large part due to the various costs and consequences of meeting the SEC's financial reporting and disclosure requirements. Subsequent events at Daimler revealed how substantial the consequences can be.

In recent years, Germany had been lobbying U.S. authorities for a "mutual recognition" arrangement, under which each would accept reports prepared under the other's rules, but the United States would have none of it. Lawrence Malkin (1992) described the situation as follows:

Germany's biggest companies have hit a brick wall in their drive to list their stocks directly on Wall Street because their accounting system, with its hidden cash reserves, runs directly against the American tradition of disclosing to small investors.

Whether the impasse is the fault of the insularity of the Germans in sticking by the ways or the Americans in insisting on their more transparent standards is moot.

Approximately 200 German companies were registered for trading in the illiquid over-the-counter market, which exempted them from U.S. reporting and disclosure rules. Daimler was the first German company to "break ranks" and apply for full listing.

5.2. U.S. GAAP reporting

On September 17, 1993, in preparation for NYSE listing, Daimler-Benz publicly announced half-yearly earnings that had been calculated under U.S. GAAP. This was the first time that any German public company had done so. The disclosure had widespread and long-lasting effects on Daimler-Benz and other German public companies.

The company's release of earnings calculated under U.S. GAAP was required under Rule 20-F of the Securities Exchange Commission Act of 1934, which regulates U.S. securities markets. Rule 20-F reporting requirements apply to all firms issuing or listing securities on national markets in the United States. The rule requires a reconciliation of the company's home-country financials to those that would be reported under U.S. GAAP. Daimler reported the major effects of differences between U.S. and German accounting rules on Consolidated Net Income and Stockholders' Equity.

5.3. Loss announcement

Another "first" was the company's first-ever reported loss. When calculated according to U.S. GAAP, the loss for the first-half ended June 30, 1993 was DM949 (U.S.$575) million. This surprising outcome was due largely to a 16 percent fall in sales relative to the comparable period in the previous year, an unusual fall for such a stable auto company.

The reported loss was all the more surprising because the company previously had reported a *profit*—DM168 (US$102) million—for precisely the same half-year period. This earlier profit figure had been computed under German accounting standards and had been reviewed and certified by the company's auditors. Many international observers were left

shaking their heads about how the announced profit of a major international corporation could, when merely recalculated under U.S. GAAP,
turn into such a substantial loss. Daimler-Benz later announced a U.S.
GAAP loss of DM1839 million for the full year 1993, compared with a
German-standard profit of DM615 million. The stark difference between
the numbers—approximately DM2.5 (US$1.6) billion—quickly attracted
the attention of analysts, regulators, and accounting standard-setters
worldwide. It drew considerable attention to the radically different
German and U.S. models of financial reporting, disclosure, and corporate
governance generally.

The largest source of difference between the 1993 U.S. and German
earnings disclosed in the 20-F reconciliation is a DM4262 millions reduction described as "Provisions, Reserves and Valuation Differences." The
precise nature of this enormous item was not made entirely clear by
Daimler at the time, but the more astute analysts observed that DM4262
millions equals the sum of two amounts reported in the company's 1993
Consolidated Statement of Cash Flows, "Extraordinary Results" of DM
2603 millions and "Gain on Sale of Securities" of DM1659 millions. The
next-largest item in the reconciliation is the effect of these same items
on income tax expensed under U.S. GAAP. All other differences between
1993 HGB and U.S. GAAP profits essentially netted out. The company's
motives for including the pre-tax gains of DM4262 millions in its 1993
HGB-rule earnings are discussed below. Whatever its motives, the effect
was to turn a loss into a profit.

5.4. Hidden reserves

To have hidden reserves, a company must have reduced earnings during
better times in prior years by strictly accounting means, underreporting both earnings and book values. Creating hidden reserves requires
(in accounting terms) an excessive debit charge against earnings. The
corresponding accounting credit entry can take one or more of three
forms:

1. *Provisions*: creating a notional liability for a specific or even a vague,
   general contingency such as "Provision for Future Losses";
2. *Reserves*: crediting (essentially hiding the profits in) a Shareholders
   Equity reserve account; and
3. *Asset Valuation*: writing-down the book values of assets.

These are strictly bookkeeping adjustments, and (apart from their indirect effect on taxes and other payments based on earnings) do not create new reserves of real funds, because they do not require the company to invest in cash or any other real asset. They simply are book entries. However, they are reserves in two equivalent accounting senses. First, hidden reserves correspond to a deliberate underreporting of the real net assets of the company. For example, it might have deliberately undervalued its inventories, marketable securities, or accounts receivable. Second, hidden reserves are stores of future book profits. For example, under-valued inventory can be used to reduce the cost of inventory usage that is charged against earnings in subsequent years. To increase reported earnings at a later date—usually to cover up losses in a bad year—the company simply has its accountants reverse the entries that created the hidden reserves, debiting any combination of these accounts and using the corresponding credit to increase book income.

Daimler's 1993 20-F reconciliation shows Shareholders Equity under U.S. GAAP as DM26,281 millions, some 50 percent higher than the equivalent HGB number of DM17,584 millions. The largest component of the difference was DM5770 described as "Provisions, Reserves and Valuation Differences." This description is not very informative, but it does imply that in past years the company had made each of the above three types of journal entry to reduce book values and reported earnings.

5.5. Drawing on hidden reserves to cover losses in code-law and common-law countries

Subsequently, earnings can be inflated quite simply by transferring amounts out of the hidden reserves. A credit to earnings is accompanied by a debit entry—to reduce prior provisions for liabilities, or to reduce Shareholders Equity reserve accounts, or to increase the book values of assets. Daimler's DM4262 millions of "Extraordinary Results" and "Gain on Sale of Securities" appear to fall into the second category, a transfer out of Shareholders Equity into the Income Statement for the year. Under U.S. GAAP, these items would have been included in earnings in prior years, but their inclusion was deferred until 1973. As previously noted, it seems no coincidence that they were not included in earnings during good years, that they were included in a year that otherwise would have shown a loss, and that the German public was not informed about either fact.

Conservative balance sheets and underreporting of earnings in good times is consistent with the important German *Vorsicht* principle, which allegedly is for the protection of creditors. A skeptical alternative view, discussed more fully below, is that it protects managers and stake-holders' agent representatives. Companies and their creditors can be expected to "contract around" (i.e. effectively undo) balance sheet conservatism. "Prudent" earnings numbers allow managers to smooth earnings and reduce the volatility of bonuses and dividends tied to earnings. In addition, transfers *out* of hidden reserves allow managers to hide losses.

Managers' ability to create and (more importantly) draw down on hidden reserves is severely constrained in common-law countries. The practice of drawing on hidden reserves to conceal losses was common in England in the nineteenth century (Yamey 1962), but was extinguished effectively in common-law countries as a consequence of the 1932 Royal Mail case, *Rex v. Lord Kylsant* (1932 1 KB 442). This case law was cod-ified in the 1948 U.K. Companies Act, which required companies to distinguish reserves from provisions, consequently "making the creation of secret reserves more difficult" (Nobes and Parker 1995: 103). In the United States, the accounting rule Statement of Financial Accounting Standards (SFAS) No. 5 does not allow reserves to be created by gen-eral charges for unspecified losses. It allows an accrued loss contingency against earnings only when it is *probable* that an asset is impaired or a liability is incurred and an amount of the loss can be estimated. SFAS No. 5 (para. 15) also prohibits transfers out of appropriated reserves into Net Income in any way whatsoever. In addition, the common-law obligation to disclose losses was codified in the U.S. Code of Federal Regulations, Title 17, Section 240.10b-5 (widely known as Rule 10b-5), which makes it unlawful "to omit to state a material fact necessary in order to make the statements made, in light of the circumstances in which they were made, not misleading." This rule has provided the basis for private litigation as well as civil action against U.S. corporations for losses allegedly incurred due to misleading disclosures, including earnings disclosures.

Had Daimler been a U.S. company and reported a profit of DM615 millions, and then subsequently revealed that it had made a loss of DM 1839 millions, there would have been an accounting scandal of major proportions. While it would have been eclipsed in magnitude by some subsequent accounting scandals (such as Worldcom and Enron), this would have ranked among the largest earnings restatements in history, and was an extremely large amount at the time. If Daimler had been traded in New York at the time, possible consequences would have included:

(a) a barrage of litigation from stockholders, lenders, creditors, employees, employee pension plans, and other parties, seeking substantial damages from the company, its managers, and its auditors;

(b) SEC prosecution of the company, managers, and auditors under Rule 10b-5;

(c) damage to the company's reputation from extensive, adverse press coverage, resulting in defection of customers, employees and other parties, and possibly severe political consequences;

(d) damage to the reputation of the company's auditors.

As we see below, the reaction in Germany was precisely the opposite. The problem in the German system was not that Daimler initially failed to report a "bottom line" loss. The problem in Germany was that it subsequently *reported* the loss.

5.6. Initial German reaction

Public reaction was swift and furious. Protesters carried black coffins in the streets of Frankfurt, and the tabloids referred to management board chairman Schrempp as "Neutron Jürgen," a reference to General Electric's ruthless CEO "Neutron Jack" Welch (Vlasic and Stertz 2001: 129).

Among the company's most savage initial critics were managers at other large German industrial companies, including Bayer AG and Siemens AG. German accounting is an integral part of the stakeholder system of corporate governance. For decades the reported earnings of German corporations had directly determined a smoothly rising stream of employee and manager bonuses, dividends, and taxes, like a steadily growing pie in which all parties shared. In many ways, the earnings of a company like Daimler were a microcosm of the postwar German economy, which had experienced steadily growing wealth that was distributed among political stakeholders under a pervasive social contract. Daimler's abrupt departure from traditional German accounting practices therefore challenged a corporate and social governance system that seemingly had served all parties well, and of which Germans were understandably proud. This pride manifested itself in a type of competitiveness with (and suspicion of) the U.S. system, and Daimler management was seen as breaking ranks in that competition.

A related complaint was that, in agreeing to comply with the SEC's insistence on U.S. GAAP information, Daimler-Benz had undermined Germany's prospects for negotiating mutual recognition of accounting standards with U.S. authorities. Mutual recognition was strongly advocated by the German authorities, for example Biener (1994). The concern was valid: Germany subsequently legislated to allow consolidated financial reporting under U.S. GAAP, but the United States has never recognized HGB rules.

The Daimler-Benz move also was seen as reducing the status of an accounting system that is rooted in the philosophy of *Vorsicht*, with its underreporting of book value and heightened creditor protection. How excessive balance-sheet conservatism is in the interest of either creditors or corporations is not obvious to the skeptical observer. The typical justification assumes that reducing credit risk is desirable per se. Dieter Ordelheide frequently made this argument, for example as a member of the Working Group on External Financial reporting (1995). The argument makes no sense in terms of the economics of debt finance. Both borrowers and lenders would be aware of any reduction in credit risk, especially considering the insider access of lending banks. Thus, credit would be priced at an appropriately reduced cost, with no overall gain to creditors. Further, given the firm's investment policy, the reduction in credit risk would be associated with more risk being borne by shareholders and a correspondingly increased cost of equity capital. There would be no net gain ignoring contracting costs, merely a reassignment of risk; this is merely an application of the well-known irrelevance theorem of Modigliani and Miller (1958). The dual to this theorem holds that any preference for particular provisions in financing agreements, including methods of accounting, must be due to reducing contracting costs. Viewed in this light, *Vorsicht* could well increase contracting costs and thereby generate economically inefficient financial reporting, by adding some uncertainty as to the amount of security being offered to lenders, who need to estimate the exact extent of the underreporting in order to price debt correctly. This conclusion is not altered by insider access to information by a closely affiliated bank, which merely displaces the inefficiency by limiting the company to one source of finance. How distorting reported earnings and book values is a more efficient way of contracting to raise credit and equity has never been made clear. I am unaware of any rigorous proof that it does.

Another claimed consequence of German companies adopting U.S. disclosure standards was the adoption of a shorter horizon by managers. Secret reserves were said to provide a buffer against reactions to short-term swings in German companies' performance. A skeptical view here is that secret reserves serve the interests of insiders, not investors, by reducing the volatility of payouts to managers, employees, banks, and the government and by protecting managers from the immediate consequences of bad decisions (Ball, Kothari, and Robin 2000). For example, employee representatives are subject to annual reelection, and thus might care more about short-term bonuses paid to their constituents (and hence emphasize short-term profits) than about long-term firm value and bonus-generating capacity. By giving managers an accounting tool for disguising losses, secret reserves might well allow mangers to delay taking painful decisions about their long-term loss-making investments and strategies, in the vain hope they will return to profitability or that the consequences of their decisions will be passed on to future managers (Ball, Robin, and Wu 2001). Furthermore, *Vorsicht* allows managers to disguise the extent of the resources they have invested in the firm, making them less accountable for their investments and more prone to size maximization, which is not necessarily in the long-term interest of the firm. Stock prices, on the other hand, look to the long term (hence the high price/earnings ratios of growth companies, and the sensitivity of share indices to changes in economic growth). While stock prices look to the long term with obvious error, there is no evidence that managers and stakeholders' agent representatives do better.

Overall, the initial reaction in Germany to the Daimler moves was quite hostile. To an observer of these events from a common-law country, the surprising thing was the object of the adverse German reaction to Daimler's disclosures. The problem was not that it had failed to disclose that it would not have made a profit except for some imaginative accounting, but that it subsequently confessed the deception. A series of simultaneous events helps explain why the confession—not the act—was the problem.

5.7. Plant closings, payroll reductions, and business divestitures

On September 17, 1993, the very day that it released the U.S. GAAP reports, the company announced it would abandon investments that were not central to its core competence, focus its product line, close factories in Germany, and slash its payroll. The immediately announced payroll cuts were 35,000 jobs in Germany by the end of 1994, plus another 8000 jobs in other countries, and included some involuntary terminations. The company thereby revoked fifty years of postwar labor practices. Between the beginning of 1993 and the end of 1996, the number of Daimler-Benz employees in Germany was reduced from 302,464 to 222,821, during which time the total assets of the group increased by over 30 percent (Daimler-Benz 1997: 88). Managers were not spared: 50 percent of the jobs at the company's Stuttgart headquarters were eliminated (Vlasic and Stertz 2001: 129).

In three years of *Unternehmenskonzept*, Daimler streamlined its operations, reinvigorated its product line, and disengaged from businesses that were taxing its core businesses by losing money and distracting management. It dismantled AEG, its century-old and much revered electronics business. It spun off its Energy Systems Division and Automation Division, requiring a DM1600 million charge against 1995 earnings, with an additional DM300 million in 1996. It discontinued financial support for Fokker, which then filed for bankruptcy under Netherlands law, causing a DM2158 million loss to be recorded against Daimler's 1996 earnings. During 2001–2, it sold its stake in the Debis Systemhaus information-technology joint venture to Deutsche Telekom, and part of its U.S. commercial-financing portfolio to GE Capital. In total, eleven of the company's thirty-five businesses were eliminated (Vlasic and Stertz 2001: 129).

Within five years Daimler had merged with Chrysler, the number three U.S. auto manufacturer. Startlingly, within three years it was reporting financial statements prepared "from the ground up" under U.S. GAAP, and was openly espousing a modified shareholder value model.

6. Daimler-Benz's motives

6.1. NYSE listing, U.S. GAAP, corporate governance, and bonding to transparency

The sequence of events raised many questions about the company's motives. For example, why did they fail to disclose that they had used two "one-time" gains to make up operating loss, and then reverse their position by filing in the United States? Indeed, why did they list in New York? Were any parties "fooled" by the German HGB-accounting profit? Did the company intend to deceive anyone when it covered up its loss-making status in its HGB report? The company's problems in its core markets were widely known. Parties with insider access to information are unlikely to have been misled, including banks (as lenders, shareholders, and shareholders' representatives), institutional investors, and employees' elected representatives. Astute readers of the accounts most likely could have discerned that Daimler was making a loss. On the other hand, small investors, international lenders and investors, individual voting employees, and the German government might not have been aware of the full extent of Daimler's actual losses. The German voting public—an important party due to the politics of job cuts and plant closings—was likely to have been misled by the company reporting a profit under HGB rules. Disclosure of the U.S. GAAP loss in its 20-F reconciliation attracted widespread public attention in Germany (and elsewhere) to the company's problems, and made it politically less costly to undertake employment reduction and plant closing decisions.

From a disclosure perspective, it is tempting to conclude that the only reason for Daimler to report under U.S. GAAP was to inform the German voting public about its real losses. But this would ignore the fact that it had the option to report a loss under HGB rules. If the two one-time gains totalling DM4262 had not been booked in 1993, the company would have reported a loss of approximately DM1516 millions, calculated as $DM[615 - (1 - 0.5) * 4262]$ millions. The amount is adjusted for tax, assuming the loss could be carried forward under German tax rules and assuming a 50 percent corporate income tax rate on undistributed profits. This is very close to the U.S. GAAP loss of DM 1839 millions, reported later. If the gains had been included in income but labelled as special nonrecurring items, the company would have been able to report an operating loss to the press. In my opinion, the disclosure perspective (in which the objective of financial reporting is entirely to inform external decision-makers and hence reduce the cost of capital) is much overrated in the accounting literature. Conversely, an underrated objective of financial reporting is its effect on managers' decisions, including the effect of timely loss recognition on the propensity of managers to undertake new loss-making investments and to continue operating their existing loss-making investments (Ball 2001).

6.2. Listing in New York: Bonding to report losses in a timely fashion

Listing on NYSE involved costs and benefits to Daimler (see Radebaugh et al. 1995). One-time costs included legal and other fees for registration with the SEC, NYSE listing fees, the cost of altering the company's accounting system to produce U.S. GAAP financial information, and the adverse political fallout in Germany. Ongoing costs included periodic accounting, legal and registration fees. Collectively, the costs of NYSE listing were thought to be substantial. Many analysts wondered whether the benefits were as obvious as the costs.

A long-term benefit of NYSE listing is diversification of the company's shareholder base. Daimler-Benz's earnings incorporate a component that involves a net-long position on the U.S. dollar, since the company generates more U.S. dollar-denominated revenues than costs. Another benefit is the enhanced liquidity and lower cost of capital, resulting from equity that is more actively traded. Some analysts thought there were public relations and even marketing advantages of the move.

One benefit of NYSE listing that is overlooked in the literature is the effect on corporate governance of the company binding itself to future transparency.[1] In particular, NYSE listing makes it costly to hide losses, as the company had been able to do under flexible German HGB accounting rules. Under the German governance model, decisions that would adversely affect the workforce are difficult to make, due to 50 percent employee representation on the Supervisory Board and political pressure on the company and on its affiliated bank. Their incentives appeared strong enough to have led Daimler to hide its 1993 losses. But in a common-law country—particularly a litigious country like the United States—failure to disclose materially adverse information opens a company to the risk of stockholder litigation, with potentially severe consequences. Trading on NYSE (versus Frankfurt) is executed under U.S. (not German) law. Hence shareholders buying Daimler-Benz stock on NYSE have the right to litigate if they demonstrate losses due to material nondisclosure, and the SEC has the authority to enforce the disclosure requirements of its Rule 10b-5. The question then is: Did Daimler-Benz list on NYSE to bond itself to henceforth disclose—and take prompt managerial steps to correct—areas in which it is not acting in shareholders' interests?

Untimely loss recognition allows managers to undertake *ex ante* negative-NPV investments, for example to maximize size or to acquire "trophy" companies, and pass the earnings consequences on to sub-sequent generations of managers. Untimely loss recognition also gives managers an incentive to continue operating *ex post* negative cash flow investments and strategies, and avoid booking losses on sale or abandon-ment. Timely loss recognition thus can be viewed as a feature of efficient contracting between firms and managers (Ball 2001: 141).

The behavior of Daimler management is consistent with this hypoth-esis. Its disastrous diversification binge had been the brainchild of CEO Edzard Reuter. His successor, Jürgen Schrempp, had been responsible for the Fokker acquisition, which ended in bankruptcy after incurring several years of high losses. The decision to recognize the losses at Fokker is reported by Vlasic and Stertz (2001: chapter 7, 128) as follows:

Schrempp saw a bigger picture. Fokker was a painful chapter, but a valuable learning experience for Daimler. His predecessor, Edzard Reuter, had never admitted a mistake. Daimler's corporate culture punished mistakes. Schrempp was taking a new path, putting himself on the line, and forcing the biggest com-pany in Europe to look in the mirror when it failed. "This will be a great thing," he said resolutely. "The chief executive made a mistake. He admitted it. . . . This is what must happen in the whole company."

Daimler's survival—in a mature, fiercely competitive industry with much excess capacity—was at stake in 1993. Poor corporate governance encourages poor decisions and discourages unwinding of poor deci-sions. Relative to the shareholder value model, the stakeholder model focuses more on dividing rather than maximizing the pie. It better enables managers and board representatives of labor and capital to hide behind poor public disclosure and avoid accountability for bad stra-tegic decisions. Poor disclosure of losses allows managers to waste more resources, putting the company at a competitive disadvantage. Daimler's motives in listing on NYSE were considerably wider than merely increas-ing liquidity, or reducing capital costs: they were focussed on corporate governance and, in turn, on the company's investment and strategic decision-making and ultimately its ability to generate future cash flows.

7. Embracing shareholder value

In its 1996 annual report, Daimler-Benz (1997: 44–5) disclosed several radical changes to its governance. They were linked together under the intriguing title "Value-based management, U.S. GAAP, and new controlling instruments." Four notable features of these changes are noted below.

7.1. Shareholder value

Under the subheading "Understanding value-based management," it described the version of the shareholder governance model that it had embraced as follows:

The permanent and continuous expansion of our company's value is only possible when the interests of all groups that contribute to our success are given the appropriate degree of consideration. Our economic performance and satisfactory returns for our shareholders depend on motivated employees, satisfied customers, and reliable and innovative suppliers. On the other hand, only a profitable company is in a position to obtain the funds required for securing the future from the capital market at relatively favourable terms and to offer its employees secure and challenging jobs and thus earn their long-term commitment. Management at Daimler-Benz is therefore dedicated to increasing the value of the Company for the benefit of everyone involved.' (Daimler-Benz 1997: 44).

Thus, Daimler management was firmly committed to a shareholder value model of corporate governance.

7.2. No stakeholders

The word stakeholder was conspicuous in its absence. Management was careful to give recognition to major parties, using terms such as "all groups that contribute to our success" and "everyone involved," but these terms do not imply participation by the parties in the decision process, an important ingredient of the stakeholder model. There was not even an indication that shareholder value was one of several objectives, to be balanced against other objectives such as employment security or creditor security. It was stated as *the* objective.

7.3. External transparency

Transparent disclosure to the public, including the use of U.S. GAAP for financial reporting, was seen as central to the process of managing against a criterion of shareholder value. For example, when the Chrysler side of the company was losing money in 2001, the response was a turnaround plan involving workforce reductions, asset write-downs, and supplier contract cancellations. Under GAAP, this required an immediate restructuring charge against earnings of €3.1 billion. Earnings thus incorporated the economic loss more quickly, and the losses were stemmed by managers more quickly. The contrast with covering up the 1993 losses under HGB accounting was stark.

7.4. Internal transparency

Under the heading "New controlling instruments," and the subheading "Internal controlling on the basis of balance sheet values in accordance with U.S. GAAP," Daimler gives the following description of implementing U.S. GAAP for managerial reporting throughout the company:

The U.S. GAAP not only made Daimler-Benz more transparent from an external perspective. Because the earnings figures as derived from American accounting principles reflect the economic performance of the company, we are now able to use figures from our external reporting for the internal controlling of the Company and its individual business units rather than relying on the internal operating profit used in the past. (Daimler-Benz 1997: 45)

There appear to be two reasons for changing to U.S. GAAP for internal reporting:

1. When it stated "we are now able to use figures [derived under U.S. GAAP] ... for the internal controlling of the Company and its individual business units," Daimler implied that its internal performance reporting needed reforming as well. It appears that managers of individual lines of business might have been using the wide discretion in accruing expenses and revenues under HGB accounting to smooth reported line-of-business profits, and possibly to hide operating losses, when reporting to their superiors. Their objective would have been to reduce the volatility of their unit's performance, and hence the riskiness of their own human capital. One consequence would be disguising the true profitability of individual lines of business from Daimler's corporate-level management.

2. Transparent disclosure to capital markets certainly changes the incentives of corporate-level managers. But incenting lower-level managers

to act in a manner consistent with the new incentives of corporate-level managers is another issue. One advantage of accounting earnings, relative to share prices in particular, is that total corporate earnings can be decomposed into the earnings of individual business units. Thus, earnings can be used as a company-wide and consistent measure for evaluating and compensating business unit managers. Daimler makes it clear that it has pushed U.S. GAAP earnings down through the corporation, so that business unit managers as well as the corporate office are better incented to focus on shareholder value. This in turn is assisted by the "new controlling instruments," under which the U.S. GAAP earnings of business units are evaluated against the cost of capital for the assets they utilize. The linkage to shareholder value is described in these terms (Daimler-Benz 1997: 45): "The activities that exceed the minimum investment requirement of 12 percent increase the value of the Company because their income exceeds the costs for the capital employed." Conversely, activities that fail to achieve the minimum over the long term decrease the value of Daimler-Benz.

The company therefore saw U.S. GAAP and the shareholder value perspective as being a "managerial" as much as a "financial" accounting issue. Lack of *internal transparency* was a corporate governance liability, reducing unit managers' incentives to deliver profits, allowing loss-making activities to be tolerated longer, and reducing the ability of corporate managers to evaluate unit managers' performances and allocate resources among them. It was a competitive disadvantage. Within three years, the Chief Financial Officer (Gentz 1999) was able to report "significantly risen transparency within the group."

The company moved toward the shareholder value model in other ways as well. For example, in 1996 Daimler-Benz AG instituted a stockholder approved stock option plan for Management Board members and other senior executives. The plan was renewed in 2000.

8. Limitations, outcomes, and risks

While Daimler very clearly adopted elements of a shareholder value model, it equally clearly did not embrace it in its entirety. After the Chrysler merger, it chose to remain a German corporation and thus chose not to totally shed the consequential legal, economic, and other cultural influences on its governance and reporting. For example, its Supervisory Board continued to contain 50 percent labor representation. In his report on "Value-based controlling at DaimlerChrysler," CFO Gentz (1999: 6) described a company trying to evolve a more hybrid governance model than it had described in 1996, incorporating elements of both the U.S. and German systems. He now saw the need to merge the "common philosophies" of "shareholder value management at Chrysler" and "value-based management at Daimler-Benz."

Subsequent indications reveal that merging the two governance models into a viable hybrid could be more difficult than initially envisaged. For example, there were substantial differences in management compensation structures: in 1997, Chrysler CEO Robert Eaton was compensated with $11.5 million, whereas Daimler-Benz CEO Schrempp received only $2 million. German CEOs spend more time developing and implementing consensus among members of their managerial boards, and less time acting as decision-makers, than their U.S. counterparts. The clash in management styles had almost immediate consequences: By 2002, only two of the thirteen members of the company-wide Management Board were from the Chrysler side of the business.

Initially, Daimler's radical moves were not well received in the German corporate world, but over time they became understood as well as emulated. The reaction of Siemens AG is a notorious example. In 1993, its management bitterly criticized Daimler for listing on the NYSE and for reporting under U.S. GAAP, but by 2001 it had followed suit, and its CEO had been quoted in the *Wall Street Journal* (February 2, 2001) as saying: "My predecessor was a magnificent man, but I don't think he knew the share price every day. The first thing we talked about when I came in this morning was the share price." In July 2002, there were forty-six German companies listed on U.S. exchanges. Daimler was the first.

Notes

First version: October 1996. Dieter Ordelheide and I discussed this case, and the principles underlying it, many times over the years, typically when we co-taught on the European Accounting Association's Doctoral Colloquium in Accounting. I like to think we both went away wiser on each occasion. Many valuable comments on prior drafts were given by students in my classes at London Business School, University of Chicago, and University of Rochester, by seminar participants at Melbourne Business School and University of New South Wales, and by conference participants at the 1999 Financial Accounting and Auditing Conference of the Institute of Chartered Accountants in England and Wales. I am indebted to Dieter Pfaff and especially Christian Leuz for extensive editorial and substantive suggestions.

[1] Exceptions are Coffee (1999) and Stulz (1999), which postdate earlier versions of this chapter.

References

Alchian, A. and Demsetz, H. (1972). "Production, information costs, and economic organization," *American Economic Review*, 62/5: 777–95.

Ball, R. (2001). "Infrastructure requirements for an economically efficient system of public financial reporting and disclosure," *Brookings-Wharton Papers on Financial Services*, 127–69.

—— and Brown, P. (1968). "An empirical evaluation of accounting income numbers," *Journal of Accounting Research*, 6: 159–78.

——, Kothari, S. P., and Robin, A. (2000). "The effect of international institutional factors on properties of accounting earnings," *Journal of Accounting & Economics*, 29: 1–51.

——, Robin, A., and Wu, J. S. (2000). "Accounting standards, the institutional environment and issuer incentives: Effect on timely loss recognition in China," *Asia Pacific Journal of Accounting & Economics*, 7: 71–96.

—— —— —— (2001). "Incentives versus standards: Properties of accounting income in four East Asian countries and implications for acceptance of IAS." Working paper, University of Chicago.

Basu, S. (1997). "The conservatism principle and asymmetric timeliness of earnings," *Journal of Accounting & Economics*, 24: 3–37.

Biener, H. (1994). "What is the future of mutual recognition of financial statements and is comparability really necessary?" *European Accounting Review*, 3: 335–42.

Coffee, J. (1999). "The future as history: The prospects for global convergence in corporate governance and its implications," 93 *Northwestern University Law Review*, 641.

Daimler-Benz AG (1995). *Annual Report* 1994 (English-language version) (Stuttgart: Daimler-Benz AG).

—— (1997). *Annual Report* 1996 (English-language version) (Stuttgart: Daimler-Benz AG).

Gentz, M. (1999). "Value-based controlling at DaimlerChrysler," (Stuttgart: Daimler-Chrysler AG), March 15.

Gregg, S. (2001). "The art of corporate governance." *CIS Policy Monograph* 51 (Sydney, Australia: Centre for Independent Studies).

Healy, P. (1985). "The effect of bonus schemes on accounting decisions," *Journal of Accounting and Economics*, 7: 85–107.

Malkin, L. (1992). "A glacial U.S. response to German listing plea," *International Herald Tribune*, April 28.

Modigliani, F. and Miller, M. H. (1958). "The cost of capital, corporation finance, and the theory of investment," *American Economic Review*, 48: 261–97.

Nobes, C. and Parker, R. (1995). *Comparative international accounting*, 4th ed. (Englewood Cliffs, NJ: Prentice-Hall).

Radebaugh, L. H., Gebhardt, G., and Gray, S. J. (1995). "Foreign stock exchange listings: A case study of Daimler-Benz," *Journal of International Financial Management and Accounting*, 6: 158–92.

Roe, M. J. (1994). "Some differences in corporate governance in Germany, Japan and America," in T. Baums, R. M. Buxbaum, and K. J. Hopt (eds.), *Institutional Investors and Corporate Governance* (Berlin: Walter de Gruyter).

Stulz, R. (1999). "Globalization, corporate finance, and the cost of capital," *Journal of Applied Corporate Finance*, 12(Fall): 8–25.

Vlasic, B. and Stertz, B. A. (2001). *Taken For a Ride*. (New York, NY: HarperCollins Publishers).

Watts, R. L. and Zimmerman, J. L. (1986). *Positive Accounting Theory* (Englewood Cliffs, NJ: Prentice-Hall).

Working Group on External Financial Reporting of the Schmalenbach-Gesellschaft-Deutsche Gesellschaft für Betriebswirtschaft (1995). "German accounting principles: An institutionalized framework," *Accounting Horizons*, 9: 92–9.

Yamey, B. S. (1962). "Some topics in the history of financial accounting in England, 1500–1900," in W. T. Baxter and Sidney Davidson (eds.), *Studies in Accounting Theory* (London: Sweet & Maxwell).

On the Regulation and Enforcement of Accounting

Disclosure Regulation

3.1

Policy Implications from the Theory-Based Literature on Disclosure

Robert E. Verrecchia

1. Introduction

What are the policy implications of either more disclosure or more rigorous disclosure standards that arise from the extant theoretical literature in accounting? It seems fair to suggest that many benefits of more disclosure are already well understood and widely accepted. For example, allusions to the fact that more disclosure improves liquidity, reduces costs of capital, and makes markets more efficient are commonplace among regulators and standard setters (Levitt 1998). But in addition to these commonly cited benefits, the burgeoning literature on disclosure has spawned a variety of other implications that, if not entirely overlooked, seem more obscure. Some of these implications concern additional benefits, while others concern unintended negative consequences. In this chapter I review some of these additional implications, and discuss the extent to which these more obscure implications merit greater attention.[1]

To briefly digress, there are a variety of reasons why applications of theory-based research are overlooked. Much of the theory-based work is couched in formal (and complex) mathematical/economic modeling, and thus is inaccessible to the casual reader. Inaccessibility typically limits insights to a small cadre of academic researchers who consume this literature, as well as, perhaps, a few intrepid empiricists who incorporate results from theory-based work into archival data investigations. Inaccessibility is further exacerbated by the fact that policy implications are discussed only peripherally in most U.S. academic accounting journals. This occurs because U.S. academic accounting journals, by tradition, discourage broad policy claims from highly stylized, theory-based models. A justification for this tradition is that theory-based work predicates its analyses on a complex array of assumptions that abstract from many (perhaps most) institutional conventions or norms, and this seems inconsistent with trumpeting sweeping policy implications. Whether justified or not, this tradition typically limits most papers to a few cryptic comments in their conclusions about the efficacy of the paper's results to policy-making in real-world institutional settings.

But in an attempt to be provocative, in this chapter I suggest that an additional inhibitor is that the theory-based literature fails to distinguish adequately between analyses concerned primarily with narrow pathologies versus work with results that are sufficiently general as to extend naturally to broad policy issues. No one should read this chapter as an indictment of the former. Pathologies may describe interesting, if perhaps not commonplace, economic phenomena and provide poignant insights into seemingly perverse economic behaviors and motivations. By the same token, pathologies are an unlikely springboard for arriving at sweeping policy implications involving entire financial markets. To address this issue, I debate the utility of various theories based on the existence of real-world phenomena that comport with the theory. That is, I attempt to point out notions and ideas that originate from the theory-based disclosure literature that are supported by casual empiricism. Alternatively, I point out results that, while meriting some attention, should be relegated appropriately to the category of "interesting pathologies." If one goal of theory-based research is to offer guidance for disclosure policy, care must be taken to distinguish between these two types of research.

In the context of this discussion, I explore two themes. First, what insights does theory-based accounting research bring to the attention of policy-makers, as they relate to the decision to mandate increased disclosure? In addition, how well do these insights comport with casual empiricism? That is, how easily can one relate these insights to phenomena commonly observed in market settings? Casual empiricism is no substitute for a scientific investigation using archival data and formal, empirical methodologies. Rather, my notion of casual empiricism is a story that seems prima facie to comport with the extant theory.

Second, what insights does theory-based research bring to the problem of firms deciding whether to disclose voluntarily: That is disclose in the absence of any mandates? Disclosure mandates provide a threshold level of disclosure. In principle, however, there are no prohibitions on firms disclosing to the fullest possible extent, regardless of mandates. This motivates the following question. Why do firms not gravitate naturally to the highest level of disclosure, thereby rendering mandated disclosure requirements, and, for that matter, disclosure policy choice, irrelevant? As with mandated disclosure, I discuss theories of voluntary disclosure from the perspective of distinguishing between pathologies versus ideas that are more likely to motivate disclosure choice.

2. Public disclosure and private information gathering

To address the theme that concerns applications of theory-based work to mandated disclosure, I start with a paper that is perhaps the genesis of much of the disclosure work in the accounting literature, Hirshleifer (1971). An implication of Hirshleifer that had great resonance with accounting researchers was the notion that secondary capital markets motivate investors to acquire costly private information to compete in what are in effect zero-sum games of trade (i.e. secondary markets). Consequently, any investment in private information-gathering creates deadweight losses for society as a whole. The interesting nature of Hirshleifer's insight was that there exists in economics some conventional wisdom that incentives to invest in "discovery" are insufficient. In the context of secondary markets, however, Hirshleifer's point was that the incentives to discover financial results in advance of their inevitably being reported were too great!

The provocative feature of the post-Hirshleifer theoretical literature on disclosure is its emphasis on proscribing private information-acquisition as a primary policy goal. At one level, this seems a difficult policy to reconcile with unregulated markets and the free flow of goods, services, and information commonly touted in free markets and democratic societies. It is difficult to imagine, for example, promulgating a public policy on disclosure that is predicated on curbing the information-gathering activities of financial institutions whose primary fiduciary responsibility is to protect their clients' investments.

Nonetheless, the suggestion that there may exist too much incentive to acquire private information raises the question of how to proscribe this.

While there may exist no *direct* mechanism to curb investors' appetite for more information, one *indirect* mechanism is to substitute public disclosure for private information-gathering. That is, one indirect way to discourage information gathering is to flood markets with a veritable cornucopia of disclosure. Central to this idea, of course, is the notion that public disclosure has fewer costs, either directly with regard to its preparation and/or dissemination or indirectly with regard to its consequences, than private information-acquisition.

Here, the link to accounting is transparent. To the extent to which financial disclosure substitutes for the private acquisition of financial data, society benefits through the elimination of deadweight losses that arise from information-gathering (Verrecchia 1982). Indeed, to the extent to which investors expend no resources on information-gathering unless the benefits exceed some fixed cost (i.e. the acquisition of private information is a discontinuous process), public disclosure may thwart information-gathering altogether (Diamond 1985).

All of this having been said, does more disclosure lead to fewer resources being invested in private information-gathering? Does the theory comport with casual empiricism? To the extent to which one believes that more disclosure is associated with less information-gathering, it is difficult to reconcile the high disclosure standards in the United States with all the analysts, financial institutions, and financial intermediaries that are U.S.-based. This suggests the following inter-country study: Associate some proxy for a country's financial disclosure standards with some proxy for private information-investment, and determine the sign of the association. Scientific studies aside, casual empiricism suggests that disclosure standards and private information-gathering are positively associated, not negatively.

Fundamental to this study is the following question: What constitutes good proxies? Let us allow for the fact that there exists some measure of cross-country variation in the quantity or quality of a country's required disclosure. What constitutes a good proxy for information investment? The existence of an extensive network of financial analysts and institutions may be one way to associate disclosure standards with information-gathering activities. But consider the following alternative: Investment strategies based on no information-gathering. Recently the *Wall Street Journal* (*WSJ*) reported that Vanguard's Standard & Poor's 500-stock index fund, a popular, passive investment fund that attempts to replicate the performance of the 500 largest U.S.-listed companies, outperformed 84 percent of all mutual funds over the twenty years through year-end 1998 on an after-tax adjusted basis (*WSJ*, January 22,

2002: C1). This performance accounts in large part for the popularity of indexed investment vehicles. In addition, this performance seems compelling evidence that if a high disclosure standard does not entirely vanquish information-gathering as an activity, it at least renders the activity impotent.

The only anecdote that suggests caution in using index fund activity as a measure of the futility of information-gathering is a separate *WSJ* report on emerging markets (*WSJ*, February 12, 2002: C1). Typically one associates emerging markets with settings that are sufficiently inefficient so as to *reward* information-gathering activities. The *WSJ*, however, reported that Vanguard's Emerging Markets Stock Index Fund, also a passive investment vehicle that attempts to replicate the performance of emerging markets, was fourth-best among twenty-one funds having a comparable objective and in existence for a comparable period. In other words, evidence from the performance of index funds may speak more to the superiority of the low-cost nature of that investment strategy than the relation between disclosure and information gathering, per se.

To conclude, early theory-based research in accounting suggested that a primary goal of disclosure policy is to eliminate deadweight losses that arise from private information-gathering. To the extent to which public disclosure degrades private information-gathering, society benefits. Perhaps the only controversy is how one goes about testing this theory. In a formal, scientific empirical investigation, what is an appropriate way to associate more disclosure with fewer deadweight losses that arise from information-gathering? In the absence of any formal investigation, the link between disclosure and private information-investment remains a "theory" whose policy implications are largely in doubt.

3. Unintended consequences of public disclosure

In this section let us allow for that fact that a benefit of public disclosure is that it thwarts information-gathering. Let us also allow for the fact that public disclosure is a costless activity for firms. In this event, why would policy-makers not rally around the highest disclosure standards? Does theory-based work suggest that more disclosure has unintended consequences that should be in the forefront of disclosure policy choice?

One unintended consequence widely discussed in the theory-based literature in accounting concerns the fact that public disclosure reduces investors' *ex ante* expected utility by inhibiting risk-sharing among investors. The theory-based literature's fixation with adverse risk-sharing as a rationale for less mandated disclosure cannot be overstated. Papers that allude to this feature include Demski (1974), Verrecchia (1982), Diamond (1985), Bushman (1991), Indjejikian (1991), Lundholm (1991), Alles and Lundholm (1993), and Kim (1993). But it seems fair to question whether adverse risk-sharing is more plainly a mathematical artifact, and hence something that should not elicit profound concern among policy-makers. To briefly explain the adverse risk-sharing phenomenon, risk-averse investors use markets to share risks. Anything that disrupts optimal risk sharing is potentially hazardous to investors' economic well-being. In theory, disclosure may disrupt risk-sharing. The reason why is that disclosure creates winners and losers. Firms with good financial results will see their shares bid up, while firms with poor financial results will see their shares bid down. If those investors who hold shares in firms that will announce poor financial results are unable to diversify into shares of firms that will announce good financial results, they also will lose. Now it is also true that those investors who hold shares in firms that will announce good financial results will gain. But to the extent to which each investor views "winning" and "losing" as equally likely propositions and is risk averse, in expected utility each investor "loses." That is, in expectation a risk-averse investor values a gamble with equally likely outcomes of winning and losing as worse than no gamble at all. Consequently, disclosure potentially lowers the expected utility of *all* investors.

Of course, the subtle assumption that underlies this conclusion is that investors are unable to trade and diversify in advance of a disclosure. To the extent to which investors *can* trade, disclosure per se has no effect on risk-sharing. Thus, the casual empiricist asks the following question. Is there any evidence that supports the notion that disclosure disrupts optimal risk-sharing? I am at a loss to cite any evidence, at least in U.S. financial markets. Most financial disclosures of firm performance (e.g. annual or quarterly results) are routine events that are widely anticipated. In an attempt to reach for some evidence, one might cite the recent Enron debacle in which employees were unable to trade and diversify their Enron holdings in 401 (k) plans in advance of announcements of Enron's demise. But this speaks more to deficiencies in rules that govern 401 (k) plans than disclosure per se. Perhaps the important policy implication here is that with regard to regulation, the proverbial right hand needs to know what the left hand is doing. As regulatory agencies promote greater disclosure, at the same time some recognition must be given to investors having easy access to diversification strategies, whether they involve 401 (k) plans, lock-ups subsequent to an initial public offering, requirements by firms that top management hold a substantial equity position in firms they control, and the like. In other words, here the important policy implication may be that greater disclosure is incompatible with inadequate portfolio diversification.

In summary, adverse risk-sharing is a feature of markets in which investors are unable to trade in advance of a disclosure. To the extent to which most financial accounting disclosure is anticipated (e.g. quarterly and annual financial statements), as well as most macroeconomic announcements such as shifts in interest rate policy, this concern seems misplaced. After a flurry of papers on this topic, this particular research skein seems to have reached a dead end. I am prepared to offer last rites.

4. Other externalities of disclosure

If adverse risk-sharing is not a negative externality of disclosure, what else might thwart full disclosure? As alluded to above, the positive association between high U.S. disclosure standards and pervasive investment in information-gathering in the United States suggests that public disclosure and private information-gathering are complements and not substitutes. That is, the existence of *some* basis upon which to evaluate a firm through mandated financial statement information may motivate *more* information-gathering. This, in turn, undermines a chief societal benefit of disclosure: The elimination or reduction of the use of real resources in information-gathering.

The notion that public disclosure and private information are complements has been promulgated in the theory-based literature (Kim and Verrecchia 1994; Bushman et al. 1997). When public disclosure of firm performance is combined with private information about firm potential, investors who have knowledge of the latter may be able to realize excess profits. In support of a positive association, the casual empiricist might point to the heightened state of information asymmetry surrounding the brief window of certain financial disclosures, such as earnings announcements (Lee et al. 1994). But other than as a short-window phenomenon, no example comes to mind of more disclosure providing an incentive to acquire more costly private information over longer windows. In view of this, perhaps it is best to suggest that this is a theory worthy of some additional empirical investigation.

However, depending upon whether disclosure is positively or negatively associated with information-gathering activity, this would only serve to highlight another issue. Private information-gathering, even when it results in deadweight losses, increases the amount of information impounded in price. In effect, investors' knowledge about the firm and its activities increases the efficiency of price as a statistic of firm value. Otherwise uninformed investors can condition their expectations on firm share price, which provides them with a costless mechanism to monitor the firm.

In other words, one positive externality of more information-gathering is that it reduces uncertainty over firm value. This is sometimes referred to as "estimation risk": That is, the risk associated with estimating the true, economic value of the firm based on firm share price. From a policy perspective, this raises the following interesting questions: Could public disclosure so thoroughly inhibit private information-gathering as to render markets less efficient? Is it possible that public disclosure and the *total* amount of information are negatively associated? For convenience, I dub the phenomenon in which more public disclosure results in less total information as public disclosure "crowding out" private information.

In theory, examples of public disclosure crowding out private information are not difficult to come by (Morris and Shin 2001). These examples, however, typically rely on some discontinuous relation between public disclosure and private information-gathering, or other, similar-type behavior that some may regard as potentially anomalous. In the absence of discontinuities, theory is more likely to predict that more public disclosure results in more (not less) information *in toto*. So the casual empiricist asks the following question. Do phenomena exist in which public disclosure systematically crowds out private information?

Here, one possible avenue to go down is to suggest that investors may react heuristically to information (Fischer and Verrecchia 1999). That is, suppose that investors systematically overreact to public announcements. This behavior, in turn, may serve to crowd out valuable, private information about firm performance. The casual empiricist has no problem finding support for this idea in the many media references to "exuberant markets." Whether support exists through more formal investigation remains an open question. In a spirit of compromise, let me suggest that investors overreacting to disclosure disseminations is potentially casual evidence that disclosure may generate negative externalities.

5. Disclosure standards aside, what thwarts firms from disclosing voluntarily?

To this point I have limited the discussion to one of the policy implications of more disclosure. But even in the absence of disclosure mandates or standards, all conventional wisdom holds that firms benefit from more disclosure by reducing information asymmetry between firm managers and/or firm insiders, and firm shareholders (Verrecchia 2001). As most policy-makers are aware, the benefits of reduced information asymmetry include: more liquid markets, easier access to capital, lower monitoring costs, and so on. These benefits are widely touted, to the point of their taking on the tenor of a "mantra." As firms cannot be oblivious to these benefits, the interesting question in the theory-based literature is the following: Why is it not the case that firms naturally gravitate toward the highest disclosure standards independent of mandated standards?

The significance of this question in the context of this chapter is that if all firms gravitate toward the highest disclosure standards, disclosure regulation would be superfluous. In other words, the policy implication of full disclosure is that it obviates a need for a "policy."

As with other issues already discussed, the theory-based literature appears to be infatuated with this question. In part, the infatuation arises from casual empiricism that firms do withhold some information. The interesting question is: How can firms sustain the withholding of information when all good commonsense suggests that withheld information triggers an adverse selection problem? Perhaps stated differently, all commonsense suggests that withheld information can only be interpreted rationally as "bad news." Thus, theory would seem to predict that firms that withhold information would be punished severely in the pricing of their shares.

A nonexhaustive list of theory-based rationales that sustain the withholding of information include: proprietary costs, the possible nonexistence of the information, agency costs, and litigation costs. What are the policy implications of each, and how would the casual empiricist sort among them?

Proprietary costs are perhaps the most common rationale proffered for withholding information (Verrecchia 1983; Lanen and Verrecchia 1987; Scott 1994; Clarkson et al. 1994; Bens 2002). That is, firms can sustain the withholding of information by falling back on the notion that information either assists existing competition, or fosters new competition through entry. The problem with a proprietary cost-type argument, however, is that it can be employed to rationalize any element of information-withholding. In other words, it may explain everything, which is to suggest that it explains nothing.

Let me cite a handful of examples of potential deficiencies in the implementation of a proprietary cost argument. For example, consider first a firm with a high gross margin. One interpretation of a high gross margin is that it arises from the fact that the firm has some proprietary business model, technology, management expertise, and the like. As more disclosure might reveal information that might jeopardize its margin, a proprietary cost argument might be invoked to predict low disclosure. An alternative interpretation of a high gross margin, however, is that the firm is tantamount to a monopolist, and thus has little to fear from competitors. In *this* interpretation high gross margins in conjunction with a proprietary cost argument predict high disclosure.

The relation between gross margin and proprietary costs is further complicated by the fact that barriers to entry may be correlated with margins, and some have argued that firms disclose to thwart entry into product markets with low barriers to entry (Darrough and Stoughton 1990). For example, suppose that a high gross margin firm dominates a particular industry and discloses frequently. Is it disclosing frequently because it has few competitive concerns (i.e. proprietary costs are low), or is it disclosing frequently because it has significant competitive concerns (i.e. barriers to entry are low)?

Finally, many theory-based models are predicated on the notion that the benefits of disclosure increase as a disclosure's effect on firm valuation increases, while the cost remains fixed (Verrecchia 1983). As much as anything, this approach is designed to ensure the existence of a disclosure "equilibrium": that is, a disclosure threshold above which the firm discloses and below which it withholds. But suppose that the costs and benefits of disclosure move in parallel. For example, suppose that the announcement of a new, revolutionary product benefits firm valuation. Suppose, however, that by alerting competitors the announcement also entails a proprietary cost that is proportional to the product's revolutionary nature. At least in theory, any manner or pattern of disclosure may arise when costs and benefits are positively associated, thus thoroughly confounding any empiricism, casual or otherwise.

In other words, the downside of providing a facile rationale for disclosing/withholding any information in any circumstance is that it rationalizes all behavior: It may be possible to invoke a proprietary cost-type argument to rationalize any level of information disclosure/withholding. To the extent to which a proprietary cost-type argument is employed by firms as a device to rationalize less disclosure, with some justification policy-makers may view proprietary costs as the *bête noire* of public policy. As for suggestions for studying the existence of proprietary costs in formal, empirical investigations, recent work on segmental reporting seems promising (Harris 1998; Leuz 2004; Berger and Hann 2002).

Another device to sustain the withholding of information is the possibility that, in the minds of investors, the information may not exist (Dye 1985; Jung and Kwon 1988). As a story about the withholding of information in general, a notion premised on uncertainty as to whether information exists seems valid. Against the backdrop of narrowly financial and institutional data, the story seems less compelling. For example, most contemporary controversies involving firms and inadequate disclosure in financial markets revolve around elements of off-balance sheet financing: operating leases, partnerships, special purpose entities, and the like. In other words, most controversies involve situations where information is known to exist, but simply withheld. Now it is true that some firms may have knowledge of their future prospects and others may not, and some firms may have knowledge of their future revenues and others may not, and so forth, and this is consistent with an unavailability-of-information story. But once again the withholding of information premised on its unavailability seems a less compelling story about summary financial data of transactions and/or events that have occurred already (e.g. data generated by historical cost accounting systems).

An additional malaise peculiar to the unavailability-of-information story is that absent a situation in which it can be demonstrated conclusively *ex post* that some firms had knowledge and others did not, how does one ascertain its merit as a story about the withholding of information? Perhaps for this reason, suggestions for testing this theory remain elusive.

At first blush, litigation as a rationale to sustain the withholding or promote the promulgation, of certain types of information would seem to have considerable merit (Ajinkya and Gift 1984; Skinner 1994). For example, securities law in the United States requires that any comments by managers about material events that could affect stock prices be truthful. Hence, the threat of litigation seems a valid deterrent to disclosure. To the casual empiricist, however, the problem with litigation is that it fails to account for variations in firm disclosure "cultures." For example, if litigation deters (promotes) disclosure, why might some firms disclose less (more) while others disclose (withhold) the same type of information? In other words, the litigation story is a useful rationale for withholding information, but only to the extent to which one can reconcile it with observable variations in the frequency and/or quality of firms' disclosures.

Agency costs arise as a consequence of monitoring the possibly unobservable activities of firm managers: For example, managers' efforts, their ability to select projects, their inclination to enrich themselves by trading on inside information, and so on. Agency costs as a rationale to sustain the withholding of information relies on a subtle notion of increased monitoring costs. A very rough rendition of that argument would go as follows. Firm share price aggregates or impounds information about the firm, its prospects, and its managers. The primary purpose of firm share price, however, is to value the firm as an asset, not necessarily the efforts of its managers. To the extent to which more public disclosure about firm performance "crowds out" indirect information about the efforts of its managers, firm share price may be a more efficient statistic about firm value, but a less useful statistic about the noncontractible behavior of managers. Hence monitoring costs and increased disclosure may be positively associated (Baiman and Verrecchia 1996; Nagar et al. 2002).

Here, as well, the question must be asked. Is this result a mathematical artifact, or a compelling story of real institutional phenomena? Allow me to equivocate: I am unsure. On the one hand, an agency cost story requires that the direct effect of more information about the firm in general militates against specific information about a manager's noncontractible level of effort that arises, perhaps, from the fact that the market observes how hard the manager works and impounds that information into price. Prima facie this proposition seems tenuous. On the other hand, a casual empiricist might point to numerous instances where rosy financial statistics have elevated firm share price to the point that investors have overlooked managerial malfeasance and/or incompetence. Suffice it to say that in the absence of more compelling empirical evidence it is difficult to claim that this result has broad policy implications.

As a final story about why firms may withhold information, it may be worth revisiting the notion of heuristic behavior. As I discussed above, if investors overreact to disclosures, increased disclosure may increase share price volatility, lead to the suboptimal allocation of resources, induce all manner of financial turmoil, and so on. As a rationale for withholding information, the casual empiricist might rank heuristic behavior only slightly below proprietary costs. In withholding certain financial data, managers seem to *behave* as if they expect investors to react heuristically. In other words, it may not be so much that investors are heuristic in their use of disclosure as it is that *managers* are heuristic in how they believe the disclosure will be used in market settings! This suggests a variety of empirical studies along the lines of demonstrating that managers appear to make disclosure-choice decisions based on some heuristic perception as to how the market and/or investors use the information (Schrand and Walther 2000).

6. Conclusion

In this chapter I argue that one impediment to employing theory-based research on disclosure is that the work itself often fails to distinguish adequately between work that, while interesting, concerns primarily pathologies versus work that is sufficiently broad in scope as to have compelling policy implications. Obviously, there is some element of self-serving behavior on the part of theory-based researchers not to label their results "pathologies." But this chapter is not an indictment against studying pathological phenomena per se but rather a cautionary tale that pathologies are unlikely to provide a viable springboard for policy choice. A casual or nontechnical consumer of theory-based disclosure research needs to understand this distinction.

Toward that goal, in this discussion I have attempted to point out notions and ideas that originate from the theory-based literature in accounting that comport with casual empiricism. Alternatively, I have attempted to point out results that, while very interesting and worthy of study, should be relegated more appropriately to the category of "interesting pathologies." My sincerest hope is that readers of this chapter will find many of my ideas and comments provocative and controversial, and make every attempt to overturn them through careful, scientific empirical investigation.

Notes

I gratefully acknowledge the comments and suggestions of Philip Berger, Anthony Hopwood, and Christian Leuz in the preparation of this manuscript. The opinions expressed, however, remain exclusively mine.

[1] For a discussion of other insights from the theory-based literature, such as those related to contracting, see Wagenhofer (2004).

References

Ajinkya, B. B. and Gift, M. J. (1984). "Corporate managers' earnings forecasts and symmetrical adjustments of market expectations," *Journal of Accounting Research*, 22: 425–44.

Alles, M. and Lundholm, R. J. (1993). "On the optimality of public signals in the presence of private information," *The Accounting Review*, 68: 93–112.

Baiman, S. and Verrecchia, R. E. (1996). "The relation among capital markets, financial disclosure, production efficiency, and insider trading," *Journal of Accounting Research*, 34: 1–22.

Bens, D. (2002). "The determinants of the amount of information disclosed about corporate restructurings," *Journal of Accounting Research*, 40: 1–20.

Berger, P. G. and Hann, R. (2002). "Segment disclosures, proprietary costs, and the market for corporate control." Working paper, UCLA.

Bushman, R. M. (1991). "Public disclosure and the structure of private information markets," *Journal of Accounting Research*, 29: 261–76.

——, Gigler, F., and Indjejikian, R. (1996). "A model of two-tiered financial reporting," *Journal of Accounting Research*, 34(Supplement): 51–74.

Clarkson, P. M., Kao, J. L., and Richardson, Gordon D. (1994). "The voluntary inclusion of forecasts in the MD&A section of annual reports," *Contemporary Accounting Research*, 11: 423–50.

Darrough, M. N. and Stoughton, N. (1990). "Financial disclosure policy in an entry game," *Journal of Accounting and Economics*, 12: 219–43.

Demski, J. S. (1974). "Choice among financial reporting alternatives," *The Accounting Review*, 49: 221–32.

Diamond, D. W. (1985). "Optimal release of information by firms," *Journal of Finance*, 40: 1071–94.

Dye, R. A. (1985). "Disclosure of nonproprietary information," *Journal of Accounting Research*, 23: 123–45.

Fischer, P. E. and Verrecchia, R. E. (1999). "Public information and heuristic trade," *Journal of Accounting & Economics*, 27: 89–124.

Harris, M. S. (1998). "The association between competition and managers' business segment reporting decisions," *Journal of Accounting Research*, 36: 111–28.

Hirshleifer, J. (1971). "The private and social value of information and the reward to inventive activity," *The American Economic Review*, 61: 561–74.

Indjejikian, R. (1991). "The impact of costly information interpretation on firm disclosure decisions," *Journal of Accounting Research*, 29: 277–301.

Jung, W. O. and Kwon, Y. K. (1988). "Disclosure when the market is unsure of information endowment of managers," *Journal of Accounting Research*, 26: 146–53.

Kim, O. (1993). "Disagreements among shareholders over a firm's disclosure policy," *Journal of Finance*, 48: 747–60.

—— and Verrecchia, R. E. (1994). "Market liquidity and volume around earnings announcements," *Journal of Accounting & Economics*, 17: 41–67.

Lanen, W. N. and Verrecchia, R. E.(1987). "Operating decisions and the disclosure of management accounting information," *Journal of Accounting Research*, 25 (Supplement): 165–89.

Lee, C., Muclow, B., and Ready, M. (1994). "Spreads, depths and the impact of earnings information: An intraday analysis," *Review of Financial Studies*, 6: 345–74.

Leuz, C. (2004). "Proprietary versus nonproprietary disclosures: Evidence from Germany," Chapter 3.2 in this volume.

Levitt, A. (1998). "The importance of high quality accounting standards," *Accounting Horizons*, 12: 79–82.

Lundholm, R. J. (1991). "Public signals and the equilibrium allocation of private information," *Journal of Accounting Research*, 29: 322–49.

Morris, S. and Shin, H. S. (2001). "The NBC effect: Welfare effects of public disclosure." Working paper, Yale University and London School of Economics.

Nagar, V., Nanda, D., and Wysocki, P. (2002). "Discretionary disclosure and stock-based incentives," *Journal of Accounting & Economics*, 34: 283–309.

Schrand, C. M. and Walther, B. R. (2000). "Strategic benchmarks in earnings announcements: The selective disclosure of prior-period earnings components," *The Accounting Review*, 75: 151–77.

Scott, T. (1994). "Incentives and disincentives for financial disclosure: Voluntary disclosure of defined pension plan information by Canadian firms," *Accounting Review*, 69(1): 26–43.

Skinner, D. J. (1994). "Why firms voluntarily disclose bad news," *Journal of Accounting Research*, 32: 38–60.

Verrecchia, R. E. (1982). "The use of mathematical models in financial accounting," *Journal of Accounting Research*, 20(Supplement): 1–42.

—— (1983). "Discretionary disclosure," *Journal of Accounting & Economics*, 5: 179–94.

—— (2001). "Essays on disclosure," *Journal of Accounting & Economics*, 32: 97–180.

Wagenhofer, A. (2004). "Accounting and economics: What we learn from analytical models in financial accounting and reporting," Chapter 1.1 in this volume.

3.2

Proprietary versus Nonproprietary Disclosures: Evidence from Germany

Christian Leuz

1. Introduction

Studying voluntary disclosures provides valuable insights to standard-setters and regulators. First, in deciding whether to impose mandatory requirements, standard-setters need to be aware of situations in which full disclosure is unlikely to arise voluntarily. Second, standard-setters and regulators need to be informed about the costs of mandating disclosure in these situations, which will allow them to weigh the costs against the social benefits of disclosure regulation.

Proprietary costs have been suggested as an important cost of disclosure regulation and are often cited by firms in opposition to proposed disclosure requirements (e.g. Ettredge et al. 2002). They also provide a theoretical rationale for why full disclosure does not prevail in equilibrium, even though firms have incentives to disclose information voluntarily to reduce information asymmetries, preempt costly private information-acquisition, and lower their cost of raising capital (e.g. Diamond 1985; Diamond and Verrecchia 1990; Verrecchia 1983; 1990; Wagenhofer 1990*a*). However, there is little empirical evidence on the existence of proprietary costs and their importance in explaining firms' disclosure choices.

The German institutional setting provides an opportunity to analyze whether competitive concerns govern firms' voluntary disclosures, because until recently firms did not have to disclose complete business segment reports, which are generally viewed as competitively sensitive. I exploit this special feature in my analysis. First, I examine whether, prior to the introduction of mandatory reports in 1999, voluntary segment disclosures were more likely when proprietary costs were small. Second, since cash flow statements were also voluntary prior to 1999, I analyze the determinants of voluntary cash flow statements. Although investors view cash flow statements as informative, such statements are generally less competitively sensitive than segment reports. Thus, I expect proprietary-cost considerations to be less important for voluntary cash flow statement disclosures. This comparison provides a way to benchmark and validate my findings for the determinants of voluntary segment reports. Finally, because Germany now requires segment reporting by all listed firms, I examine *ex post* whether segment reporting would have been more revealing from a competitive point of view for those firms that did not provide voluntary segment reports.

The results generally support the proprietary cost hypothesis. Using binary and ordered probit models, I find that German firms voluntarily provide business segment data when the proprietary costs are low, that is when entry barriers are relatively high, segment information is highly aggregated and firm profitability is low. In contrast, cash flow statement disclosures are primarily associated with proxies that capture capital-market considerations such as cost savings in private information acquisition and high analyst following. However, the results also indicate that the proxies used to capture proprietary costs are not completely irrelevant for cash flow statement disclosures, indicating the difficulty to disentangle capital-market incentive and proprietary-cost concerns.

Regardless of the type of disclosure, I find that firms with lower ownership concentration and higher foreign sales are more likely to disclose voluntarily. Moreover, German firms voluntarily provide both cash flow statements and segment reports whenever they are listed at a foreign exchange where domestic (but not German) firms are required to provide such disclosures (e.g. the London Stock Exchange, LSE). Thus, peer pressures in international capital markets appear to be sufficient to induce both disclosures.

I also find that firms having more heterogeneous segment profits in their mandatory segment reports in 1999 are less likely to provide segment reports when they are still voluntary. For these firms, the average profitability reported in the income statement is less informative about segment profitability, making segment reports more revealing and competitively sensitive. This finding supports the proprietary-cost hypothesis and shows that firms' disclosures are not governed by capital-market considerations alone. If motivated primarily by the desire to inform capital markets, firms with heterogeneous segment profitability should be more likely to provide voluntary segment disclosures, and not less likely as the tests show.

This chapter contributes to the extant literature on financial disclosures in several ways. First, the findings suggest that proprietary costs can be an important reason why full disclosure does not always prevail, despite substantial capital-market benefits of disclosure. The evidence on the determinants of proprietary disclosures shows when such a situation is most likely to arise. This evidence could be informative to standard-setters who consider mandatory disclosure requirements. It also highlights that mandating disclosures can impose costs on firms. These costs should be weighed against the social benefits of the desired disclosures (see also Bushee and Leuz 2003, for evidence on the cost of U.S. disclosure regulation).

This chapter also provides evidence that the determinants of discretionary disclosures can vary across disclosure types. Prior to my chapter, others have suggested that determinants may vary across different types of disclosures (see e.g. Diamond 1985; Dye 1986). Prior work examining subcategories of broad disclosure indices and analyst ratings provides some evidence to this effect (e.g. Lang and Lundholm 1993; Botosan 1997). Meek et al. (1995) explicitly examine this issue constructing different disclosure scores for strategic financial and nonfinancial information. They find that the factors influencing voluntary disclosures by multinational corporations differ across the different types of information. This chapter complements my prior work in analyzing disclosure types along the proprietary-cost dimension.

The chapter is organized as follows. In Section 2, I review the prior literature and describe the German institutional setting. In Section 3, I derive the main hypotheses, lay out my research design, and describe the sample selection and variable construction. Sections 4–6 present the results. In Section 7, I discuss the findings and conclude the chapter.

2. Background

2.1. Literature review

Saudagaran and Meek (1997) note that "proprietary costs have been modeled analytically, but empirical research on their effects on disclosure [...] is notably absent." Healy and Palepu (2001) come to a similar conclusion in their recent survey of disclosure literature. This paucity of empirical research can be largely attributed to the elusive nature of proprietary costs and the difficulty of finding settings where firms' disclosure choices of potentially proprietary information can be observed. Although measurement remains to be an issue, the idea of this chapter is to exploit the specifics of the German institutional environment to construct a more powerful test of the proprietary-cost hypothesis than previous studies.

Scott (1994) is one of the first to explicitly test the proprietary-cost hypothesis using voluntary disclosures of pension plan information by Canadian firms. He argues that this information is proprietary with respect to the labor unions. His findings for the determinants of these disclosures are consistent with the proprietary-cost hypothesis. However, since he examines only one disclosure item, we do not know whether nonproprietary disclosures would have produced different results and whether the findings are in fact driven by the proprietary nature of the information. To address this problem, I explicitly compare two types of voluntary disclosures, segment reports and cash flow statements, which differ in their usefulness to competitors, and assess the relative importance of various determinants in determining these disclosures.

Much of the U.S. literature on discretionary disclosures focuses on management forecasts. However, the decision to voluntarily provide a forecast is quite different from the disclosure policy choices considered in this chapter. These one-time decisions can be viewed as a commitment to provide certain information in the future (regardless of the particular realization of the information). Moreover, U.S. research on industry segment data often focuses on its usefulness for predicting future sales and earnings and to investors (e.g. Collins 1976; Pacter 1993; Wysocki 1998).

Harris (1998) examines the relation between competition and industry segment disclosures and finds that profitable operations in less competitive industries are less likely to be reported as industry segments. Her findings are consistent with the idea that firms hide high-margin operations from competition. More recently, Shin (2002) provides evidence that the relation between competition and voluntary disclosure can depend on the type of product market competition.

Another difficulty of analyzing segment disclosures by U.S. firms is that segment reports are mandatory and have been for decades. Thus, firms' disclosure choices and hiding of proprietary segment information have to be inferred from firms' segment disclosures, for example from the level of aggregation or the fineness of the disclosures (see e.g. Piotroski 2002).

This difficulty creates additional measurement problems and reduces the power of the tests.

For this reason, Berger and Hann (2003a) exploit a recent regulatory event in U.S. reporting, the switch from Statement of Financial Accounting Standards (SFAS) 14 to SFAS 131. Under the old standard, firms purportedly had more discretion in defining industry segments and hiding segment information. The new standard eliminates much of this discretion and "forces" firms to provide more informative segment disclosures (Berger and Hann 2003b). Thus, in comparing segment disclosures under the old and new standard for the same fiscal year, Berger and Hann (2003a) can examine the determinants of previously hidden segment information. They find that firms that previously aggregated information under SFAS 14 had higher abnormal profitability and operations with more divergent performance.[1] These findings are consistent with the proprietary-cost hypothesis.

In this chapter, I use a similar approach and examine firms' segment profitability after segment reporting became mandatory in Germany. Although my setting does not allow for a comparison of segment disclosures under different regulatory regimes for the same fiscal year, as in Berger and Hann (2003a, b), it has the advantage that sample firms were previously not required to provide any information about segment profitability, resulting in a potentially more powerful setting.

In addition, there are studies that analyze either the determinants of segment reports or cash flow statements in countries where these statements either are or were not mandatory. For instance, Schneider (1985) and Bauer and Schader (1996) study voluntary cash flow statements of German and Austrian firms, respectively. Voluntary segment data disclosures are analyzed by Bradbury (1992) for New Zealand, McKinnon and Dalimunthe (1993) and Mitchell et al. (1995) for Australia, and Bernards (1994) for Germany. However, as these studies differ in design, samples, and institutional environments, it is difficult to compare the results and determinants across studies.

2.2. Institutional setting

I analyze disclosure practice of German firms for the fiscal year April 1, 1996 to March 31, 1997. During that time, German reporting standards did not require firms to systematically disclose segment or cash flow information. In fact, the lack of compulsory cash flow statements and segment reports was frequently cited as one of the major shortcomings of German reporting standards (e.g. Goebel and Fuchs 1995). In April 1998 new disclosure legislation was enacted. As a consequence, all listed corporations are now required to provide cash flow statements and segment reports in their consolidated financial statements for fiscal years ending on or after December 31, 1999.

I am confident that this new requirement does not unduly affect my results for firms' choices in 1996 because: (a) I study disclosure practice sufficiently prior to its enactment in 1998; (b) the new law applies to both cash flow statements and segment reports; and (c) there is a significant number of firms that did not provide full segment reports until they were forced to do so in 1999.

2.2.1. Segment information

Until fiscal years ending on or after December 31, 1999, corporations that were either large[2] or had publicly traded securities were required to disclose sales information by activities and by geographical markets if the activities and the geographical markets differed significantly from each other (§§285 No. 4 and 314 (3) HGB). There was no requirement to provide any segment information other than a breakdown of total sales. Moreover, the German Commercial Code (HGB) did not clearly define a "segment." Legal commentaries recommended choosing business and geographical segments such that the benefits and risks were homogeneous within a segment and heterogeneous across segments.[3] Thus, unlike firms reporting under U.S. Generally Accepted Accounting Principles (GAAP) or International Accounting Standards (IAS), which were (and are) required to follow specific criteria, German firms had considerable discretion in defining their segments. Furthermore, segment sales could be suppressed if the disclosure was likely to significantly harm the firm or one of its subsidiaries, in which case the firm has to indicate that this protective clause had been applied (§§286 (2) and 314 (2) HGB).[4]

One other requirement to provide subentity data in a German annual report stems from §§286 No. 11 and 313 (2) HGB. These rules stipulate that a corporation that owns more than 50 percent of another firm's capital must disclose its stake as well as shareholders' equity and net earnings of the other firm. These disclosures do not have to be provided if they are deemed immaterial or likely to harm the firm or one of its subsidiaries (§§286 (3) and 313 (3)). Moreover, financial information about the subsidiaries is generally not matched with business segment sales provided elsewhere in the notes.

Most of my sample firms provide only an abbreviated list of their main subsidiaries and investments in the annual report. However, if a firm uses this list as a way to disclose segment data as defined in this chapter, I code the dependent variables accordingly. That is, I capture segment information contained in subsidiary disclosures. Only one sample firm (Moksel AG) invokes the protective clause on subsidiary disclosures.

Each German corporation is required to publish its individual (or parent only) accounts in the local commercial register. However, these (nonconsolidated) statements provide potentially valuable subentity information only if a group's segments are separate legal entities (i.e. corporations) and if the legal and the organizational structures match. And even if these criteria were met, the usefulness of these statements would be severely constrained by the well-known limitations of nonconsolidated statements.[5]

2.2.2. Cash flow information

Until the recent regulatory change, the German Commercial Code stipulated only that the annual report of a corporation had to provide a true and fair view of the firm's financial position (§§ 264 (2) and 297 (2) HGB).[6] However, the rules did not state how this aim was to be achieved. According to the legal commentaries, this requirement did not imply that firms had to furnish a cash flow statement. But compliance may have entailed additional disclosures about a firm's financial position in the notes.[7] However, if a firm voluntarily disclosed a cash flow statement in the annual report, legal commentaries viewed this information as sufficient to satisfy the above requirement.

It is noteworthy that in Germany, auditors commonly prepare a cash flow statement to analyze the firm's financial position as part of the (nonpublic) audit report to the supervisory board (Mansch et al. 1995). For this purpose, the Institute of Chartered Accountants (IdW) and the Schmalenbach Gesellschaft (SG), an influential group of practitioners and academics, jointly issued a professional recommendation (HFA) on cash flow statements (IdW/SG 1995). These guidelines for preparing and auditing cash flow statements were closely aligned with international practice (IdW/SG 1995). Although this recommendation and German audit practice may have encouraged firms to provide cash flow statements in the annual reports, the disclosure remained voluntary (for empirical evidence see Leuz 2000).

3. Hypothesis development and research design

3.1. Main hypotheses

Based on current theories, I hypothesize that firms tradeoff the capital-market benefits and the proprietary costs of voluntary disclosures (e.g. Verrecchia 1983; Hayes and Lundholm 1996). This hypothesis yields two testable predictions. First, *ceteris paribus* firms are more likely to disclose proprietary information when the potential for such disclosures to create competitive harm is low. For instance, firms operating in industries that are protected by significant entry barriers are more likely to provide competitively sensitive information. Conversely, firms are more likely to disclose such information if they operate in industries that are already fiercely competitive (see also Harris 1998). For these reasons, I expect proxies that capture the potential for competitive harm explain firms' voluntary segment disclosures.

Second, holding all else constant, firms are less likely to provide proprietary information than nonproprietary information. In comparing different types of disclosure, I expect nonproprietary disclosures to be primarily governed by capital-market considerations.[8] For instance, cash flow statements are generally less competitively sensitive than segment reports. Thus, I expect proprietary-cost considerations to be relatively less important for voluntary cash flow disclosures.

To elaborate on this hypothesis, investors and analysts generally perceive cash flow and segment information as useful and the corresponding statements as among the most important parts of the annual report (SRI 1987; AIMR 1993). Cash flow information facilitates an assessment of a firm's cash-generating ability or the persistence of its earnings. Segment information is useful to investors because corporate diversification generally reduces the informativeness of consolidated financial statements (e.g. Ijiri 1995). Several empirical studies support the usefulness of both types of information to investors.[9] Thus, voluntarily providing cash flow statements and segment reports can be viewed as a commitment to disclosure, which reduces information asymmetries in capital markets (e.g. Leuz and Verrecchia 2000).

At the same time, cash flow and segment information can be useful to firms' competitors. For instance, in deciding whether to start a price war, competitors may use cash flow information to assess a firm's liquidity. Segment data is competitively sensitive because it may reveal the operating margins and investments in different lines of business (see also Feltham et al. 1992; Hayes and Lundholm 1996). However, an important difference between the two disclosures is that the former is provided at the firm level, while the latter is disaggregated information. For this reason, segment disclosures are generally more proprietary in nature than are cash flow statement disclosures. Clearly, the distinction is more a matter of degree than kind, but the conjecture is supported in three ways.

First, Gray and Roberts (1988) survey disclosure attitudes of British managers and find that segment disclosures are viewed as among the most highly sensitive items. Managers also pointed out that this assessment critically depends on the level of aggregation. Similarly, in a study on entry deterrence, Smiley (1988) finds that "masking a division's profitability" is the most frequently chosen strategy: About 80 percent of the respondents (U.S. product managers) admit that they use this strategy at least occasionally and more than 50 percent express that entry deterrence is at least as important as other strategic decisions.

Second, the conjecture about the relative magnitude of proprietary costs is further supported by anecdotal evidence from standard-setting: In the United States, firms expressed much concern about the proprietary costs of mandatory segment disclosures. Similar concerns were not raised with respect to mandatory cash flow statements. On the contrary, Australian firms even supported the change from compulsory funds flow statements to more informative cash flow statements (Jones et al. 1995).

Third, the proprietary costs, and also the capital-market benefits of specific disclosures, depend on what information is available elsewhere. For instance, the usefulness of cash flow information does not imply that cash flow statements are incrementally informative, because investors can use the income statement and successive balance sheets to derive a proxy for the firm's cash flow. For this reason, the incremental information content and hence the competitive harm of cash flow statements are likely to be low. But disclosing cash flow statements can nevertheless generate capital-market benefits. It avoids the duplication of efforts thereby creating cost savings to investors and financial analysts (e.g. Diamond 1985).[10] Moreover, it reduces the concerns of uninformed investors that more sophisticated investors know better how to derive a proxy for the firm's cash flow, which should improve market liquidity (see also Diamond and Verrecchia 1990).

In the same way, the usefulness of voluntary segment reports to investors and competitors hinges on the availability of subentity and segment data elsewhere. However, as I noted earlier, there are no close substitutes for a segment report—that is, information on segment profit-ability and segment assets is not readily available elsewhere. However, the extant requirement to provide segment sales likely reduces incremental usefulness of voluntary segment reports to investors. Several U.S. studies find that, in the presence of segment sales, the ability to forecast firms' earnings improves only marginally if additional segment information is available (e.g. Collins 1976; Balakrishnan et al. 1990). But even if additional segment information is of little value to investors, for example in forecasting (aggregate) earnings, it can still be useful to competitors revealing (disaggregated) information about operating margins and investments in particular lines of business.

In summary, the maintained hypothesis that cash flow statements are less competitively sensitive than segment reports seems reasonable. However, capital-market and proprietary-cost considerations are likely to matter to some degree for both voluntary disclosures.[11] Therefore, proxies capturing these considerations are generally not expected to have opposite associations with the two disclosures. Rather, I expect the relative importance of the proxies, that is their marginal effects on firms' disclosure choices, to differ. It is in this sense that I hypothesize that proprietary-cost considerations are more important for segment reports than for cash flow statements.

3.2. Disclosure model

Based on the hypothesis development in the previous section, I examine the determinants of voluntary segment disclosures by German firms. To benchmark and validate my findings, I perform a determinant analysis for voluntary cash flow statements and then compare the marginal effects of the key variables across the two types of disclosures. Because capital-market considerations and proprietary-cost concerns may be difficult to disentangle, I conduct an alternative test that does not rely on a comparison across different types of disclosures and which provides opposite predictions for capital-market and proprietary-cost motives.

Since recent regulation forces German firms to provide segment disclosures for fiscal years ending on or after December 31, 1999, I can analyze the segment data of those firms that chose not to provide voluntary segment reports in 1996. Based on the proprietary-cost hypothesis, I expect that firms that show more heterogeneity in profitability across segments to be less likely to provide voluntary segment reports. For these firms, the average or aggregate profitability reported in the income state-ment is less informative about segment profitability allowing firms to hide competitively sensitive information. From a capital-market and information perspective, these firms should be more likely to provide segment information.

The analysis of determinants is based on the disclosure literature. Prior work in this area suggests firm size, financing needs, profitability, lever-age, and foreign listings as the main determinants of voluntary corporate disclosures (e.g. Lang and Lundholm 1993; Saudagaran and Meek 1997; Healy and Palepu 2001). I include proxies for each of these determinants in my probit analysis of firms' disclosure choices. The first three variables are meant to capture the magnitude of firms' capital-market benefits and proprietary costs. They are the focus of my analysis. All other variables are considered control variables.

3.2.1. Trading volume

I use trading volume to capture firms' benefits from providing voluntary disclosures to the capital market. Similarly, Scott (1994) argues that trad-ing volume is a proxy for cost savings in private information-acquisition generated by voluntary disclosures. Thus, I expect trading volume to be positively associated with firms' voluntary disclosures.[12] Moreover, based on the previous hypothesis development, I expect trading vol-ume to be more important in predicting voluntary cash flow statements than voluntary segment reports. I measure trading volume as log of the total number of shares traded in one year scaled by the firm's market capitalization.

3.2.2. Profitability

From a capital-market perspective, I expect highly profitable firms to voluntarily provide information in order to distinguish themselves from less profitable firms. However, competitors can also use this informa-tion, which can dampen firms' disclosure incentives (Verrecchia 1983; Wagenhofer 1990a).[13] Analytical models and recent empirical work show that the relationship between voluntary disclosures and (realized) profitability is complex and depends on the type of competition (e.g. Verrecchia 1990; Ewert and Wagenhofer 1992; Feltham et al. 1992; Shin 2002).

However, cash flow statements and segment reports are long-run disclosure policy choices. That is, firms commit to provide cash flow or segment information regardless of future profit realizations. This perspective suggests a negative association between profitability and voluntary disclosures, provided that proprietary costs are in fact a concern (see also Harris 1998). Based on the hypothesis that cash flow statements are less proprietary than are segment reports, I predict that the negative relation is more pronounced for the latter. Prior and concurrent studies provide mixed evidence on the association between segment reporting and profitability (see Bernards 1994; Prencipe 2002; Piotroski 2002; Berger and Hann 2003*a*). I measure profitability as the industry-adjusted return on assets.

3.2.3. Capital intensity

The firm's capital intensity is a proxy for entry barriers. As the threat of entry decreases, firms are more likely to make voluntary disclosures to the capital market (Darrough and Stoughton 1990; Wagenhofer 1990*b*). Thus, I hypothesize that both voluntary disclosures are positively associated with capital intensity. Again, based on previous hypothesis development, I expect this variable to be more important for segment reports than for cash flow statements.

However, capital intensity may also capture firms' financing incentives, in which case capital-market benefits and proprietary costs are difficult to disentangle. I address this concern in the robustness checks. I measure capital intensity as the ratio of net property, plant, and equipment divided by total assets.

3.2.4. Control variables

In addition, I control for firm size, leverage, free float, corporate diversification, foreign business, and listings, all of which are likely to be associated with firms' disclosure choices.

I expect firm size to be positively associated with voluntary disclosures for several reasons. First, the costs of producing and disseminating information are likely to be decreasing per unit of firm size due to some fixed component. Second, larger firms typically have a larger investor and analyst following. Thus, firm size is also a proxy for potential cost savings in private information-acquisition generated by voluntary disclosure. Third, large firms are in a better position to "hide" proprietary information, that is profitable segments (see also Smiley 1988; AIMR 1993). They also provide more highly aggregated information for a given number of segments, which should reduce proprietary costs (see also Gray and Roberts 1988). I measure size as the log of total assets.

As agency problems associated with debt are likely to increase with leverage, voluntary disclosures are often hypothesized to be positively associated with leverage. The idea is that voluntary disclosures enhance monitoring (e.g. Leftwich et al. 1981). However, in Germany, public debt agreements are rare. In bank debt agreements, which are widespread, monitoring information can be furnished by other means than the annual report (e.g. Schneider 1985). Furthermore, leverage may also be inversely related to cost savings in private information-acquisition since a higher leverage implies *ceteris paribus* less (outside) equity, implying a negative association. Thus, it is a priori not clear how leverage is associated with either of the two disclosures. Prior studies on cash flow statements or segment reports provide mixed results. While some studies find a positive association (e.g. Bradbury 1992; Mitchell et al. 1995), many report an insignificant effect of leverage (e.g. Schneider 1985; Chow and Wong-Boren 1987; McKinnon and Dalimunthe 1993; Bernards 1994). I measure financial leverage as the ratio of total liabilities including contingencies and total assets.

Jensen and Meckling (1976) argue that agency costs increase as the level of outside equity rises. Moreover, firms with dispersed ownership structures are more likely to use public disclosures to communicate information, but firms with concentrated ownership structures can use other information channels, such as the board of directors. Thus, I expect both cash flow and segment disclosures to be positively associated with the free float, which I define as the percentage of shares that are widely held and known to be available for trading. The existing evidence generally supports this hypothesis for firms' ownership structures (e.g. Schneider 1985; McKinnon and Dalimunthe 1993; Scott 1994; Leuz 2000).

Firms with unrelated lines of business are presumably under more capital-market pressure to provide segment information than are firms with closely related lines of business, because segment reports are relatively more informative and hence more important to investors for firms with unrelated activities (see also Ijiri 1995; Wysocki 1998; Piotroski 2002). But for the same reason, segment reports are likely to have higher proprietary costs for firms with unrelated activities (e.g. Hayes and Lundholm 1996). Consequently, the association between voluntary segment disclosures and the degree of unrelated corporate diversification is a priori indeterminate.[14]

Because this variable is specific to segment reporting, I do not have a prediction for cash flow disclosures. I construct a measure of unrelated diversification by using Standards Interpretations Committee (SIC) codes that indicate firms' activities. For each firm, the Worldscope database provides up to eight SIC codes, on the basis of which I compute the sum of unique one-, two-, and three-digit SIC codes. Adding in this fashion exploits the lexicographic structure of SIC codes and assigns higher numbers to less related diversification.

A foreign stock exchange listing is likely to result in additional demand for voluntary disclosures (Meek and Gray 1989). I expect these pressures to be particularly strong if the domestic firms in this market generally provide this information. Such a situation arises at the LSE and in the U.S. over-the-counter (OTC) market, where cash flow statements and segment reports are mandatory for domestic firms but not required for foreign firms. Therefore, I predict that German firms with a listing at the LSE or American Depository Receipts (ADR) in the U.S. OTC market are more likely to provide voluntary segment reports and cash flow statements. I construct a binary indicator variable to control for this effect. Prior work generally supports this hypothesis (e.g. Cooke 1989; Meek et al. 1995; Saudagaran and Meek 1997).

Multinational firms may face greater demands for disclosures than firms that generate most of their business domestically (e.g. Gray and Radebaugh 1984; Meek et al. 1995). Firms with significant foreign business presumably have a substantial number of foreign stakeholders, resulting in greater pressures to conform to internationally accepted disclosure practices. Therefore, I hypothesize that foreign business and both voluntary disclosures are positively related.

In summary, I estimate the following multivariate binary or ordered probit model:

$$\text{Disclosure} = \beta_0 + \beta_1 \text{ Log (Volume)} + \beta_2 \text{ ROA} + \beta_3 \text{ Capital intensity}$$
$$+ \beta_4 \text{ Log (Size)} + \beta_5 \text{ Leverage} + \beta_6 \text{ Free float}$$
$$+ \beta_7 \text{ Diversification} + \beta_8 \text{ Foreign listing}$$
$$+ \beta_9 \text{ Foreign business} + \varepsilon,$$

where Disclosure $\in$ {Voluntary Segment Reports; Voluntary Cash Flow Statements}.

3.3. Sample selection and construction of disclosure variables

To obtain a comprehensive sample, I choose all industrial firms in the DAX 100 stock index and in the Welt 500 list. The latter comprises the

553 largest German nonfinancial firms ranked by total revenues. I double-check the Welt 500 list against the Worldscope database. This check shows five firms with total revenues of approximately one billion or more that were missing from the Welt 500 list. I add these firms to the sample. From this sample, I eliminate all firms that were not listed at a German stock exchange prior to October 30, 1996, because disclosure incentives of these firms may be different.

I also eliminate all firms that are either a subsidiary of a foreign firm or of a German parent included in the sample. In both cases, the subsidiary's decision to disclose (or not) cash flow statements and segment reports may not be "independent" of the parent, and hence could bias my results.[15] For instance, a subsidiary's disclosure policy may be decided by the parent, in which case including both firms in the sample would result in double-counting. Similarly, the disclosure policy of a subsidiary with a foreign parent may be determined by the parent's foreign disclosure standards.

I also eliminate three firms that were listed at the New York Stock Exchange (NYSE) in 1996 and as a result were required to provide cash flow statements and segment reports. I also exclude two outliers.[16] The final sample contains 109 nonfinancial firms and comprises more than 75 percent of the total market capitalization of German industrials. Table 3.2.1 provides data descriptions and summary statistics for the sample.

Next, I describe the construction of the dependent variables. As the magnitude of the capital-market benefits and the proprietary costs depends on the precision of the information provided, I construct several dependent variables accounting for qualitative differences in the disclosures. Due to the lack of German accounting standards for both disclosures, it is not clear what disclosure constitutes a cash flow statement or a segment report. Thus, in creating several variables, I check the sensitivity of my results to a particular classification. I code all dependent variables based on hard copies of the annual reports for the fiscal year April 1, 1996 to March 30, 1997.

The variables that capture firms' voluntary business segment disclosures are constructed by using the international standards on segment reporting that prevailed in 1996, that is SFAS 14 and IAS 14, as a guide. For all variables, "no voluntary disclosure" equals 0 and indicates that the firm provides segment sales only; disclosure of segment sales is mandatory for publicly traded German firms.

The first binary variable, BDISC1, indicates voluntary disclosure of at least one of the following four items for each segment in addition

Table 3.2.1. Data description and summary statistics

Panel A: Binary variables

	Foreign listing	Listing at LSE or ADR in U.S. OTC market	"Big 6" auditor
Number of firms	27	7	69
Percentage	24.8	6.4	63.3

Panel B: Continuous variables

	Trading volume	Firm size	Profitability (ROA)	Capital intensity	Financial leverage	Free float	Unrelated diversification	Foreign sales
Mean	1.645	9046.7	0.053	0.334	0.706	0.391	9.404	0.382
Median	1.472	2144.7	0.049	0.318	0.723	0.373	9.000	0.433
Maximum	5.035	94568.0	0.270	0.779	0.957	1.000	18.000	0.862
Minimum	0.004	288.8	−0.155	0.022	0.343	0.000	4.000	0.000
Std. dev.	1.246	17978.2	0.064	0.156	0.129	0.282	2.749	0.276

Notes: The sample comprises 109 nonfinancial firms that are listed at a German stock exchange on October 30, 1996 and not a subsidiary of a foreign or another sample firm. Panel A shows the number and percentage of firms cross-listed at a foreign exchange (column 1), cross-listed at the LSE or in the U.S. OTC market (column 2) and having a Big 6 auditor (column 3). Panel B provides descriptive statistics on the continuous control variables. Trading volume is measured as share turnover, that is the number of shares traded in 1996 in all market segments of the main exchange divided by total number of all voting and nonvoting shares outstanding and registered for trading. Firm size is the book value of total assets in million Deutsche Marks for the firm's fiscal year April 1, 1996 to March 31, 1997. Profitability is measured as return on assets, that is operating income before interest, taxes, and extraordinary items divided by total assets. In the probit models, ROA is adjusted by the average ROA of all sample firms with the same industry classification. Capital intensity is measured as net plant, property, and equipment divided by total assets. Leverage is total liabilities including contingencies divided by total liabilities. Free float is the percentage of voting shares that are widely held and available for trading. Unrelated diversification is measured as the sum of the *different* one-digit, two-digit, three-digit SIC codes assigned to a firm's operations. There is a maximum of eight SIC codes. Foreign sales are expressed as the percentage of revenues generated outside Germany.

to sales: operating income, identifiable assets, capital expenditures, or depreciation. SFAS 14 required disclosure of all five items. However, I do not require all five items in the classification, because under IAS 14 prior to its revision, only sales, operating income, and identifiable assets had to be reported.

The second binary variable, BDISC2, uses a more restrictive definition. It requires the firm to disclose at least the operating income for each segment, in addition to the mandatory sales information. This classification is based on the notion that operating income for a segment is a particularly sensitive piece of information, allowing competitors to determine the operating margin.[17]

To distinguish between full and partial segment reports, I create an ordinal variable, BDISC3, with three levels: The highest level (2) indicates a "full segment report" that discloses all five items. The middle level indicates a "partial segment report" reporting at least one, but less than four, items in addition to sales. For comparative purposes only, I code analogous variables for firms' geographic segment disclosures.

I construct three binary variables to capture firms' voluntary cash flow disclosures. The first variable, CFS1, is based on a very broad definition and uses the numeral 1 to indicate any kind of separate cash flow statement, even simple re-expressions of balance sheet changes as sources and uses of cash.

Following previous studies that view "separating out" of a funds change at the bottom of the statement as a distinguishing feature (e.g. Haller and Jakoby 1994; Bauer and Schader 1996), the second variable, CFS2, indicates cash flow statements with a funds change as separate line item. This classification is based purely on form. Presumably, however, form is less important to investors than whether the cash flow statement actually provides additional information.

Based on the idea of "substance over form" the third variable, CFS3, assigns a 1 if the cash flow statement separately provides a funds change (not necessarily at the bottom), and if there is at least one line item, which (a) typically is not provided elsewhere in the annual report and (b) helps to determine the firm's cash flows more precisely.[18] However, this rather strict binary classification has the drawback that the category "CFS3 = 0" comprises firms that publish cash flow statements but fail the information criterion, and firms that do not disclose a cash flow statement at all.

Addressing this issue, I construct an ordinal variable, CFS4, with three levels where the highest level (=2) indicates a cash flow statement that satisfies the criteria used for CFS3, the middle level (=1) stands for any other cash flow statement, and the lowest level ($=0$) indicates no disclosure.

4. Empirical results

4.1. Description of disclosure behavior

Table 3.2.2 (p. 182) reports the frequencies of the different voluntary disclosures. Panel A, which pertains to segment disclosures, shows that over 50 percent of the firms do not provide any additional segment data. The low level of voluntary segment disclosures is in line with previous studies (e.g. Bernards 1994).

Geographic segment disclosures are particularly rare. Previous studies make similar observations in other countries and suggest that geographic segment disclosures can create substantial political costs in addition to any proprietary costs (e.g. Herrmann and Thomas 1997). For instance, tax authorities may use these disclosures in transfer pricing disputes. Since geographic segment disclosures appear to be governed by considerations beyond those discussed in the second section, I do not consider them further in this chapter.

However, having information on both types of segment disclosures, I can check whether it is appropriate to focus on business segment disclosures alone. For instance, firms that are organized geographically might provide primarily geographic segment information. I find that there are only six sample firms where GDISC3 exceeds BDISC3. Dropping these firms from the sample does not materially alter the results or inferences.

Panel B of Table 3.2.2 presents the frequencies for the different cash flow variables. The reported frequencies are in line with those of previous studies on German firms (e.g. Haller and Jakoby 1994; Stahn 1997). Over 80 percent of the firms provide a cash flow statement with a separate funds change. But only 63 percent of the firms provide a cash flow statement that satisfies the more restrictive information criterion, where CFS3 $=1$.

Comparing panels A and B shows that voluntary cash flow statements are far more frequent than voluntary segment reports. Although the majority of the German firms presents a cash flow statement (of any kind), less than 50 percent of the firms provide any business segment data (beyond sales). Moreover, there is no firm that provides both segment profits and segment sales, but not a cash flow statement

Table 3.2.2. Voluntary disclosure policies of German firms

Panel A: Frequencies of voluntary business and geographic segment data

	BDISC1		BDISC2		BDISC3			GDISC1		GDISC3		
	0	1	0	1	0	1	2	0	1	0	1	2
Number	59	50	66	43	59	37	13	89	20	89	15	5
Percentage	54.1	45.9	60.6	39.4	54.1	33.9	11.9	81.7	18.3	81.7	13.8	4.5

Panel B: Frequencies of voluntary cash flow statement disclosures by German firms

	CFS1		CFS2		CFS3		CFS4		
	0	1	0	1	0	1	0	1	2
Number	12	97	20	89	40	69	12	28	69
Percentage	11	89	18.3	81.7	36.7	63.3	11	25.7	63.3

Notes: The sample comprises 109 nonfinancial firms that are listed at a German stock exchange before October 30, 1996 and are not a subsidiary of a foreign or another sample firm. The variables for voluntary segment disclosures in Panel A are constructed using U.S. GAAP and IAS segment reporting standards prevailing in 1996 as a guide. For all variables, "no *voluntary* disclosure" (=0) implies that the firms report segment sales only; the latter is mandatory for all German firms with publicly traded shares. BDISC1 as binary variable indicates whether the firm provides for each segment at least one additional item out of the following four: operating income, identifiable assets, capital expenditures, or depreciation. BDISC2 indicates that, for each segment, the firm discloses operating income in addition to sales. BDISC3 is an ordinal variable with three levels, which distinguishes between full and partial segment reports: "full segment report" (=2) refers to disclosing all five items whereas a "partial segment report" (=1) refers to reporting sales plus at least one but less than four items. In Panel B, CFS1 is a binary variable indicating whether the annual report provides a "cash flow statement" of any, even the simplest, kind. CFS2 is binary and refers to cash flow statements with a funds change provided at the bottom as a separate line item. It is purely based on format. CFS3 is binary indicating cash flow statements that provide a funds change (not necessarily at the bottom) *and* at least one line item that typically is not provided elsewhere in the annual report *and* that helps to determine a firm's cash flow. These items can be noncash line items that are useful in "backing out" the firm's cash flow in a retrograde fashion. CFS4 is an ordinal variable with three levels: full disclosure (=2) indicates a cash flow statement that satisfies the criteria used for CFS3, partial disclosure (=1) refers to any other cash flow statement, and no disclosure (=0) indicates lack thereof.

of some sort. This comparison alone suggests that the two disclosures are quite different in nature. The relative frequencies support the view that segment reports are more proprietary in nature than are cash flow statements. However, it may also reflect differences in information content. Thus, it is important to examine the associations of firms' disclosures with various firm characteristics to disentangle the two explanations.

4.2. Determinants of voluntary segment reports

Before estimating the probit model, I examine the pairwise correlations among the independent variables and run the collinearity diagnostics suggested by Belsley et al. (1980). The statistics indicate a mild collinearity between foreign listings and firm size, which is to be expected. For all other variables, condition indices and variance inflation factors are well below commonly suggested critical values.

On further inspection, I find that all firms with a listing at the LSE or an ADR in the U.S. OTC market voluntarily provide additional segment disclosures. This result suggests that peer pressures in (foreign) capital markets can be sufficient to induce voluntary segment reports (see also Leuz 2000). The finding also implies that the binary variable has to be dropped in the probit analysis as it perfectly predicts one category.

Table 3.2.3 (p. 184) presents three probit models for the determinants of voluntary business segment disclosures.[19] All models have significant explanatory power. Of the three key variables of interest, trading volume shows the lowest significance levels, being only marginally significant in two of the models. In contrast, profitability and capital intensity are highly significant in all models. The only exception is profitability in the second model, where its coefficient has the predicted sign but exhibits only a two-sided p-value $= 0.22$.

Overall, I find that firms with above-industry profitability are less likely to reveal segment data and firms where capital intensity affords entry barriers are more likely to provide segment disclosures. The capital-market benefits captured by trading volume seem to play a lesser role in determining segment reports. These findings are consistent with the hypothesis that proprietary-cost considerations play a major role for segment reporting.

Of the control variables, firm size and free float exhibit a significantly positive association in all models. Unrelated diversification and foreign sales are positively, but only weakly, related to voluntary segment reports. Financial leverage has a negative sign but it is only significant in the ordered probit model. The significant and positive association of free float and the (albeit weakly) negative association of leverage suggest that widely held equity and equity financing play a role in determining voluntary segment reports. Thus, the evidence is consistent with firms trading off proprietary costs and capital-market benefits.

Table 3.2.3. Determinants of voluntary segment data disclosures by German firms (probit models)

	BDISC1 (binary)	BDISC2 (binary)	BDISC3 (ordered)
Trading volume (+)	0.187*	0.103	0.183*
	(1.70)	(0.91)	(1.93)
Profitability (−)	−8.041***	−3.758	−6.993***
	(−2.71)	(−1.23)	(−2.66)
Capital intensity (+)	2.903***	2.890***	2.699***
	(2.82)	(2.94)	(2.98)
Firm size (+)	0.340**	0.390***	0.465***
	(2.56)	(3.07)	(4.03)
Leverage (?)	−1.886	−1.136	−2.506**
	(−1.37)	(−0.81)	(−1.98)
Free float (+)	1.429**	1.497***	1.342**
	(2.33)	(2.60)	(2.43)
Diversification (?)	0.119*	0.123**	0.062
	(1.84)	(2.00)	(1.27)
Foreign sales (+)	0.707	0.943*	0.994*
	(1.23)	(1.63)	(1.93)
Intercept	−7.021***	−7.16***	—
	(−3.43)	(−3.18)	
Log likelihood (prob.)	49.51	47.75	68.75
	(0.000)	(0.000)	(0.000)
Pseudo R^2	0.342	0.347	0.338

Notes: Sample comprises 109 nonfinancial firms that are listed at a German stock exchange on October 30, 1996 and not a subsidiary of a foreign or another sample firm. Predicted signs for the independent variables are in the first column in parentheses. The next two columns report binary probit models estimated with quasi-maximum likelihood procedures. Z-statistics are in parentheses and standard errors are robust to misspecifications of the underlying distribution (see White 1982). The last column reports an ordered probit model with two intercept terms, which are significant at 1 percent level but not presented. BDISC1 is a binary indicating whether the firm provides at least one segment data item in addition to sales. BDISC2 indicates that the firm discloses operating income per segment. BDISC3 is an ordinal variable with three levels, where a "2" refers to disclosing all five items, a "1" indicates at least one item in addition to sales but less than four items. See Table 3.2.2 for details. Trading volume is measured as share turnover, that is the number of shares traded divided by total number of all voting and nonvoting shares outstanding and registered for trading. Profitability is measured as operating income divided by total assets and adjusted by the average ROA of all sample firms with the same industry code. Capital intensity is measured as net plant, property, and equipment divided by total assets. Firm size is the log of total assets in million Deutsche Marks. Leverage is total liabilities including contingencies divided by total liabilities. Free float is the percentage of voting shares that are widely held and available for trading. Unrelated diversification is measured as the sum of the *different* one-digit, two-digit, three-digit SIC codes assigned to a firm's operations. Foreign sales are expressed as the percentage of revenues generated outside Germany. All financial data is measured for the fiscal year April 1, 1996 to March 31, 1997. For all models two-tailed significance levels are indicated by asterisks: *p <0.10; **p <0.05; ***p <0.01.

4.3. Robustness checks

The results are similar across the different segment reporting variables and thus do not seem sensitive to a particular coding scheme. However, there are several other concerns. First, although the models control for a broad spectrum of firm characteristics, there is always the question of whether correlated omitted variables are responsible for the findings. To address this concern, I add analyst following and an indicator variable for Big Six auditors to the models. The introduction of the additional control variables does not materially alter the results or inferences.

Another way to control for additional, potentially unobserved, firm characteristics is to introduce industry fixed effects, as firms in the same industry typically exhibit similar firm characteristics and as competitive pressures vary across industries. Furthermore, firms may imitate disclosure practices of other firms in the industry (Dye and Sridhar 1995). Therefore, I include five industry dummies based on the CDAX industry classification provided by the Frankfurt Stock Exchange. When I reestimate all models, I find that the results reported in Table 3.2.3 are robust to the inclusion of industry dummies.

A second concern is whether a firm's capital intensity primarily captures entry barriers or is also a proxy for its financing needs. The problem is that I expect both constructs to be positively associated with firms' voluntary disclosures. For instance, Shin (2002) argues that capacity competition and the resulting financing needs to motivate firms to disclosure more. Thus, it may therefore be difficult to disentangle capital-market motives and proprietary-cost considerations. To address this issue, I augment the model with other variables related to firms' financing needs and examine the effects on the capital intensity variable. To the extent that these variables pick up cross-sectional variation in firms' financing needs, any remaining association of the capital intensity variable is more likely to reflect entry barriers and proprietary-cost considerations. I use three alternative proxies: the average sales growth computed from 1994 to 1996, the market-to-book ratio, and a forward-looking binary variable indicating equity offerings between 1997 and 1999. I expect all three variables to be positively associated with firms' voluntary disclosures (e.g. Lang and Lundholm 1993). However, only the average sales growth turns out to be significant in some models. More important, the coefficients on capital intensity and their significance levels are very much like those reported in Table 3.2.3. This result supports the proprietary-cost interpretation of the variable.

My final concern is that the sample contains firms that operate in only one industry and thus do not have several segments to report. To address this issue, I note that the sample does not contain any firms for which the Worldscope database provides only one SIC code. However, there are seven sample firms that do not provide the mandatory disaggregation of segment sales, which might indicate that they are single-segment firms. But, as explained in the second section, German firms have considerable discretion in defining their segments. Thus, it is not clear whether firms that report only one segment are in fact single-segment firms and should be excluded from the sample. As a robustness check, I nevertheless drop these seven firms and find that the results and inferences are unaffected.

5. Comparison of segment and cash flow disclosures

An alternative way to test whether proprietary-cost considerations govern firms' voluntary segment disclosures is to compare the findings in Table 3.2.3 with those obtained from disclosures that are not or at least less competitively sensitive. As explained in the second section, cash flow statements provide a reasonable benchmark for this comparison. Thus, I expect that proprietary-cost concerns are less important and that capital-market considerations dominate the disclosure of voluntary cash flow statements, which should also be reflected in the respective proxies for these considerations.

Again, I find that all firms with an LSE listing or an ADR in the U.S. OTC market disclose cash flow statements, so that the indicator variable must be dropped from the model. Table 3.2.4 presents the resulting probit models for the determinants of firms' voluntary cash flow statements. All models have significant explanatory power. The results for CFS1 are not reported but they are similar.

Trading volume is highly significant in all three models and positively associated with firms' cash flow statements, as hypothesized. In contrast, profitability is not significant. Capital intensity exhibits a positive sign in all three models, but is only significant in the last two models in which the cash flow statement may reveal additional information. The significance of capital intensity suggests either that proprietary-cost considerations are not completely irrelevant for cash flow disclosures or that the variable partially reflects firms' financing needs.

Of the other control variables, firm size and free float again exhibit significant and positive associations, as hypothesized. The coefficient on

Table 3.2.4. Determinants of voluntary cash flow statements by German firms (probit models)

	CFS2 (binary)	CFS3 (binary)	CFS4 (ordered)
Trading volume (+)	0.312***	0.324***	0.268***
	(2.82)	(3.14)	(3.20)
Profitability (−/0)	−1.772	1.341	−0.281
	(−0.61)	(0.50)	(−0.13)
Capital intensity (+/0)	1.280	2.138**	2.113**
	(1.32)	(2.37)	(3.06)
Firm size (+)	0.312*	0.394**	0.346**
	(1.94)	(2.37)	(2.36)
Leverage (?)	1.149	2.574	1.876
	(0.79)	(1.64)	(1.55)
Free float (+)	2.241***	1.592**	1.720***
	(2.62)	(2.37)	(2.75)
Diversification (?)	−0.003	−0.016	0.011
	(−0.05)	(−0.33)	(0.22)
Foreign sales (+)	−0.504	−1.191**	−1.061*
	(−0.74)	(−2.04)	(−1.88)
Intercept	−7.332***	−9.578***	—
	(−3.35)	(−4.65)	
Log likelihood (prob.)	36.58	48.13	71.60
	(0.000)	(0.000)	(0.000)
Pseudo R^2	0.296	0.328	0.255

Notes: Sample comprises 109 nonfinancial firms that are listed at a German stock exchange on October 30, 1996 and not a subsidiary of a foreign or another sample firm. Predicted signs for the independent variables are in the first column in parentheses. The next two columns report binary probit models estimated with quasi-maximum likelihood procedures. Z-statistics are in parentheses and standard errors are robust to misspecifications of the underlying distribution (see White 1982). The last column reports an ordered probit model with two intercept terms that are significant at 1 percent level but are not presented. CFS2 is a binary variable equal to 1 if the firm discloses a cash flow statement with a funds change as separate line item. CFS3 is a binary variable equal to 1 if the firm discloses a cash flow statement with a funds change (not necessarily at the bottom-line) *and* at least one line item, which typically is not provided elsewhere in the annual report *and* would be useful in determining the firm's cash flow in a retrograde fashion. CFS4 is an ordinal variable with three levels where a "2" indicates a cash flow statement that satisfies the criteria used for CFS3, a "1" refers to any other cash flow statement, and a "0" to nondisclosure. See Table 3.2.2 for details. Trading volume is measured as share turnover, that is the number of shares traded divided by total number of all voting and nonvoting shares outstanding and registered for trading. Profitability is measured as operating income divided by total assets and adjusted by the average ROA of all sample firms with the same industry code. Capital intensity is measured as net plant, property, and equipment divided by total assets. Firm size is the log of total assets in million Deutsche Marks. Leverage is total liabilities including contingencies divided by total liabilities. Free float is the percentage of voting shares that are widely held and available for trading. Unrelated diversification is measured as the sum of the *different* one-digit, two-digit, three-digit SIC codes assigned to a firm's operations. Foreign sales are expressed as the percentage of revenues generated outside Germany. All financial data is measured for the fiscal year April 1, 1996 to March 31, 1997. For all models, two-tailed significance levels are indicated by asterisks: *p <0.10; **p <0.05; ***p <0.01.

leverage is positive but not significant. Diversification is not significant, which is not surprising in the cash flow models. The significant, negative coefficient on foreign sales in two of the models is puzzling and inconsistent with my expectations.

Clearly, the strong association of trading volume and the insignificance of profitability are contrary to the findings for firms' segment reports. This contrast is consistent with my main hypothesis that proprietary-cost considerations are more important for firms' segment disclosures and that cash flow disclosures are governed primarily by capital-market considerations. However, direct comparisons of coefficients across probit models, even for the same sample, can be misleading. Therefore, I compute the marginal effects of the three key variables for each binary probit model. The marginal effects are expressed as (partial) elasticities, that is the change in disclosure probability for a small percentage change in the respective independent variable, to allow for proper comparisons. I evaluate all marginal effects at the sample mean.

Table 3.2.5 presents the marginal effects of the three key variables: trading volume, profitability, and capital intensity. Based on the hypotheses developed in the second section, I expect the marginal effects of trading

Table 3.2.5. Comparison of the marginal effects across segment and cash flow models

	CFS2	CFS3	Prediction	BDISC1	BDISC2
Trading volume	0.673	2.324	>	0.561	0.262
Profitability	−0.170	0.025	>	−0.193	−0.088
Capital intensity	0.068	0.217	<	0.505	0.423

	Chi squared	p-value
CFS2 vs. BDISC1	8.65	0.03
CFS3 vs. BDISC1	11.59	0.01
CFS2 vs. BDISC2	6.67	0.08
CFS3 vs. BDISC2	11.35	0.01

Notes: The table reports marginal effects of the respective independent variables on the probability of voluntary disclosure for each binary probit model. The marginal effects are expressed as (partial) elasticities, that is the change in disclosure probability for small percentage changes in the independent variable, to allow for proper comparisons. All marginal effects are evaluated at the sample mean. The predictions are based on the notion that segment disclosures are more proprietary in nature than cash flow disclosures and the arguments presented in the second section. The second half of the table reports Chi-squared statistics and *p*-values from a test that the coefficients of the segment and cash flow disclosure model are statistically different for the three variables. They are obtained from a bivariate probit model, where all the coefficients are jointly estimated.

volume to be larger; those of profitability to be less negative, that is larger; and those of capital intensity to be smaller for the cash flow disclosures compared to the segment reports.

Comparing across cash flow and business segment models, I find that the marginal effect of trading volume is always larger in the former. Conversely, the marginal effect of capital intensity is always larger in the segment data model. For profitability the marginal effect is larger, that is less negative, in the cash flow models in three out of four possible comparisons. Thus, the differences in the coefficients are as expected.

To evaluate the statistical significance of these differences, I compute a bivariate probit, which jointly estimates the coefficients of the segment and cash flow disclosure model, and explicitly test whether the coefficients of the three variables are statistically different across models. Table 3.2.5 reports the Chi-squared statistics and p-values, and shows that the coefficients are indeed statistically significant across models. The results are particularly strong when I use "informative" cash flow statements (i.e. CFS3) in the comparison. This observation is consistent with my conjecture in the second section that controlling for information content of the disclosures accentuates differences in proprietary costs. Overall, the findings for the marginal effects are consistent with my hypotheses and suggest that segment data disclosures are more competitively sensitive than are cash flow disclosures.

6. *Ex post* segment disclosures

A different way to disentangle capital-market considerations and proprietary-cost concerns is to examine whether the "nondisclosing" firms are in fact hiding valuable information, as the proprietary-cost hypothesis suggests. But the obvious problem is to obtain the segment information from nondisclosing firms. If such information were readily available to the researcher, it would also be available to competitors, which would cast obvious doubts on the maintained hypothesis that the information is indeed proprietary in nature. However, as explained in the second section, substitutes for segment data are not readily available in Germany.[20]

As noted before, Germany now requires segment reporting by all listed firms for fiscal years ending on or after December 31, 1999. This requirement provides an opportunity to examine segment reports *ex post*. That is, I can analyze whether the segment reports of those firms that did not disclose voluntarily in 1996 are competitively more sensitive or revealing than are the reports of those that chose to disclose.

Based on the proprietary-cost hypothesis, I expect that firms that show more heterogeneity in segment profitability are less likely to provide voluntary segment reports. For these firms, the average or aggregate profitability reported in the income statement is less informative on the profitability of the individual segments, essentially allowing firms to hide competitively sensitive information (see also Hayes and Lundholm 1996). However, if firms' disclosure choices are motivated primarily by the desire to inform capital-market participants, it is precisely these firms that should be more likely to provide segment information. Thus, the test allows me to disentangle proprietary-cost considerations and capital-market motives.

To conduct the test, I collect information on segment profits and assets from the 1999 annual reports and compute the ROA for each disclosed segment.[21] I lose twenty five sample firms either because they have been merged with another firm or ceased operations, or because I am unable to obtain an annual report in Global Access. An assumption of my test is that firms' segment structures in 1999 are representative of those in 1996. To check the plausibility of this assumption, I compare the average number of segments in both years. They are both close to four and not statistically different from each other. Moreover, both numbers are highly correlated on a firm-by-firm basis. Of course, it is possible that firms took measures to obfuscate or hide proprietary segment data in response to the new disclosure requirement. However, such measures are likely to work against my tests.

Table 3.2.6 presents the three previous probit models with the standard deviation of segment ROA in 1999 as an additional control variable.[22] The coefficient on this proxy for segment heterogeneity is negative and highly significant. Thus, firms with more heterogeneous segments in 1999 were less likely to provide segment reports when they were still voluntary. For these firms, the average profitability reported in the income statement is less informative on the profitability in the individual segments, which makes segment reports more revealing and competitively sensitive. This finding is consistent with the proprietary-cost hypothesis and shows that firms' disclosures are not governed by capital-market considerations alone. If motivated primarily by the desire to inform capital markets, firms with heterogeneous segment profitability should be more likely to provide voluntary segment disclosures, not less likely, as borne out by the tests. These results are consistent with recent findings by Berger and Hann (2003b).

Table 3.2.6. Voluntary segment disclosures and *ex post* heterogeneity in segment profitability

	BDISC1 (binary)	BDISC2 (binary)	BDISC3 (ordered)
Ex post segment heterogeneity	−1.823***	−1.210**	−1.994***
(proprietary costs: −/capital market: +)	(−3.50)	(−2.47)	(−4.04)
Trading volume (+)	0.228	0.081	0.234*
	(1.48)	(0.58)	(1.84)
Profitability (−)	−9.550**	−5.477	−6.963**
	(−2.35)	(−1.33)	(−1.98)
Capital intensity (+)	3.855***	3.273**	3.062***
	(2.65)	(2.53)	(2.53)
Firm size (+)	0.364**	0.363**	0.566***
	(2.28)	(2.45)	(4.27)
Leverage (?)	−2.441	−1.588	−2.765**
	(−1.63)	(−1.13)	(−2.11)
Free float (+)	1.718**	1.518**	1.311**
	(2.41)	(2.41)	(2.28)
Diversification (?)	0.211***	0.165**	0.070
	(2.77)	(2.18)	(1.38)
Foreign business (+)	0.907	0.993	1.363*
	(1.19)	(1.40)	(2.02)
Intercept	−8.418***	−6.648**	—
	(−3.07)	(−2.47)	
Log likelihood (prob.)	36.14	38.57	52.47
	(0.000)	(0.000)	(0.000)
Pseudo R^2	0.378	0.333	0.375

Notes: Sample comprises 84 of the 109 nonfinancial firms in the original sample. Predicted signs for the independent variables are in the first column in parentheses. The next two columns report binary probit models estimated with quasi-maximum likelihood procedures. The last column reports an ordered probit model with two intercept terms, which are significant at 1 percent level but not presented. Z-statistics are in parentheses and standard errors are robust to misspecifications of the underlying distribution (see White 1982). BDISC1 is a binary indicating whether the firm provides at least one segment data item in addition to sales. BDISC2 indicates that the firm discloses operating income per segment. BDISC3 is an ordinal variable with three levels, where a "2" refers to disclosing all five items, a "1" indicates at least one item in addition to sales but less than four items. See Table 3.2.2 for details. Segment heterogeneity is measured as the standard deviation of segment ROA. It is measured for the fiscal years ending in 1999 or 2000 after segment reporting became mandatory in Germany. Trading volume is measured as share turnover, that is the number of shares traded divided by total number of all voting and nonvoting shares outstanding and registered for trading. Profitability is measured as operating income divided by total assets and adjusted by the average ROA of all sample firms with the same industry code. Capital intensity is measured as net plant, property, and equipment divided by total assets. Firm size is the log of total assets in million Deutsche Marks. Leverage is total liabilities including contingencies divided by total liabilities. Free float is the percentage of voting shares that are widely held and available for trading. Unrelated diversification is measured as the sum of the *different* one-digit, two-digit, three-digit SIC codes assigned to a firm's operations. Foreign sales are expressed as the percentage of revenues generated outside Germany. All financial data is measured for the fiscal year April 1, 1996 to March 31, 1997. For all models, two-tailed significance levels are indicated by asterisks: *p <0.10; **p <0.05; ***p <0.01.

7. Conclusions

This chapter exploits specific features of the German institutional environment to provide a more complete test of the proprietary-cost hypothesis than previous studies. Until recently, German firms were not required to disclose complete segment reports, which are generally viewed as competitively sensitive.

Analyzing firms' voluntary business segment disclosures, I find evidence consistent with the proprietary-cost hypothesis. German firms voluntarily provide business segment data when the proprietary costs are low. That is, when entry barriers are relatively high, segment information is highly aggregated and firm profitability is low relative to the rest of the industry.

Furthermore, using voluntary and less competitively sensitive cash flow statements as a benchmark, I show that cash flow statement disclosures are strongly associated with proxies for capital-market benefits, while segment disclosures are more strongly associated with proxies for product-market and proprietary-cost considerations. These findings are consistent with the notion that proprietary-costs considerations are more important for the business segment reports, and that cash flow statements are primarily governed by capital-market benefits.

In my final set of tests, I exploit the fact that German firms are now required to provide full segment reports. My tests demonstrate that firms with more heterogeneous segment profitability are less likely to voluntarily provide segment reports. This finding is consistent with the proprietary-cost hypothesis and shows that segment disclosures are not governed by capital-market benefits alone.

Overall, the evidence supports the hypothesis that firms trade off capital-market benefits and proprietary costs in their disclosure choices. Another interesting finding is that German firms that are cross-listed at the LSE or in the U.S. OTC market voluntarily provide both cash flow statements and segment reports. In these markets, domestic (but not foreign) firms regularly provide such disclosures. Thus, peer pressures in international capital markets can be strong enough to induce even proprietary disclosures.

This chapter has several important implications. First, the findings caution us to aggregate different types of information into a single disclosure index, as it is frequently done in recent disclosure studies. If disclosure incentives are distinct across different types of information, as suggested by this chapter, then the different effects may cancel each other and be lost in the index.

A second and more important implication for standard-setters is that proprietary costs can be an important reason why full disclosure does not prevail voluntarily, despite substantial capital-market benefits of disclosure. Thus, proprietary costs can be a reason to mandate disclosures that are deemed desirable by the standard-setters, but would not arise voluntarily. However, it is important to highlight that mandating these disclosures is likely to impose costs on firms.

Finally, the evidence in this chapter should be interpreted with the following caveats in mind. Both proprietary costs and disclosure benefits in the capital market are notoriously difficult to measure. Thus, the inferences and conclusions from this chapter hinge on how well the proxies capture these underlying constructs. Moreover, although this chapter provides evidence that firms "hide" segment information that is competitively sensitive, it is possible that there are other reasons for this behavior. For instance, managers may be reluctant to provide segment information to the extent that it facilitates monitoring by outside shareholders. To explore such possibilities is left for future research.

Notes

This chapter is based on my "Habilitation" (Venia Legendi) at the University of Frankfurt in 2000 and dedicated to the memory of Dieter Ordelheide. Earlier versions of this chapter have benefited from presentation at Goethe University Frankfurt, University of Michigan, the Wharton School, the 1998 annual meeting of the EAA, and the EIASM Workshop on Accounting & Economics at the London School of Economics. I gratefully acknowledge helpful comments from Daniel Bens, Joachim Grammig, Wayne Guay, Robert Holthausen, Laurence van Lent, Peter Pope, Ulrich Rendtel, Claudia Röder, Catherine Schrand, Erik Theissen, Ro Verrecchia, and Peter Wysocki. I would also like to thank Michael Löbig, Aaron Slan, Choon Tat Tan, Bloomberg, Deutsche Börse, and the Deutsche Vereinigung für Finanzanalyse und Anlageberatung (DVFA) for their valuable support in the data collection.

[1] The negative association with profitability is consistent with my findings and those in Harris (1998) and Piotroski (2002). However, there are studies for other countries documenting a positive association. See for example Prencipe (2001).

[2] A corporation is large according to the commercial code (§ 267 HGB) if it exceeds two of the following three size criteria: Total assets > 15.5 million DM, sales > 32 million DM, employees (average over the year) > 250.

[3] See for instance Schülen (1992: § 20), and Adler et al. (1997: § 90).

[4] None of the sample firms invokes this protective clause.

[5] Another source of information may be consolidated statements for *sub*groups (*Teilkonzernabschlüsse*). However, these statements are generally voluntary and rarely provided by German subsidiaries. See Görges and Schulte (1994).

6 Besides the commercial code, § 21 BörsZulV states that firms registering securities for public trading have to provide a cash flow statement in the prospectus. However, neither a publication in the annual report nor a specific format is required. As the case of Fielmann AG illustrates, firms do not necessarily disclose cash flow statements *in their annual report* subsequent to the initial public offering.

7 See Budde and Karig (1990: § 37) and Adler et al. (1997: §§ 70–1).

8 Of course, the direct costs of producing cash flow and segment information could differ. However, it is reasonable to assume that both types of information are produced for internal purposes in any case. Moreover, the marginal costs of disseminating segment or cash flow information are immaterial considering that all firms have to publish an annual report.

9 See for example Livnat and Zarowin (1990) for cash flow information and Pacter (1993), Wysocki (1998), and Piotroski (2002) for segment information.

10 Gebhardt (1984) and AIMR (1993) specifically make this claim for cash flow statements. Similarly, investors and analysts seem to value summaries of historical financial information and fact books, even though the information contained in them is available elsewhere and not new (e.g. SRI 1987).

11 I acknowledge that there may be other considerations in disclosing cash flow statements and segment reports. For instance, the former makes it easier to detect earnings manipulations and the latter facilitates the monitoring of managers' decisions to adapt, expand, or abandon divisions (Wysocki 1998; Berger and Hann 2003a). However, it is not clear that these considerations alter the relative predictions for the two disclosures.

12 Note that the causal relation is not obvious. Voluntary disclosures may reduce informational asymmetries and hence increase trading volume (Leuz and Verrecchia 2000).

13 There can also be proprietary costs in the labor markets. For instance, a highly profitability firm is more likely to encounter pressures from labor unions (Scott 1994). However, in Germany, wage bargaining generally takes place at the industry and not the firm level. Furthermore, labor representatives sit on the board of directors of most large firms (in 106 out of 109 sample firms) and hence may have private access to segment data and cash flow information. Thus, proprietary costs in the labor market are unlikely to affect my results.

14 This reasoning may explain why McKinnon and Dalimunthe (1993) and Mitchell et al. (1995) find that voluntary segment disclosures by Australian firms are not significantly associated with unrelated diversification.

15 The criterion was a stake in the firm's outstanding capital greater or equal to 50%. Note that sample firms may be subsidiaries of nonsample firms, in particular financial firms. But as German financials generally do not consolidate industrial subsidiaries and because accounting practices for financials are quite different, a direct link between the disclosure policies is less likely in these cases.

16 I identified these firms as influential observations distorting some of the cash flow statement regressions. Eliminating both firms is also justified on theoretical grounds, as one is an organization solely set up to promote the business of its owners (1800 independent shoe retailers) and the other was in severe financial distress prior to and at the time of the study. I was not able to identify any further observations whose elimination would materially alter my results.

17 Some firms provide the operating cash flow instead of operating income (e.g. Dyckerhoff AG) because this figure is more appropriate for, or commonly used in, the industry. Since this disclosure also allows competitors to calculate the operating margin, I code it in the same way as the disclosure of operating income.

18 Examples are gains from selling fixed assets or from accounting associates at equity, cash flows from selling fixed assets (and not merely the change in book value), gross cash flows from new loans and repayments, changes in cash and cash equivalents

due to currency translation or valuation changes. Some of these are noncash items. However, knowing these line items helps to compute a firm's cash flow in a retrograde fashion.

[19] The results are virtually unchanged using logit regressions. OLS regressions also produce results similar to those reported.

[20] Even in the United States, Berger and Hann (2003a) find that "hidden" segment data revealed in the switch from SFAS 14 to SFAS 131 is not fully priced in the capital-markets, despite the incentive of capital-market participants to uncover such information. This finding suggests that the information is not readily available via other sources.

[21] Since segment reports are required for fiscal years on or after December 31, 1999 I use either the 1999 annual reports or the data provided for 1999 in the 2000 annual reports.

[22] The results are similar when I use the absolute value of the maximum difference between segment ROAs.

References

Adler, H., Düring, W., and Schmaltz, K. (1997). "Rechnungslegung und Prüfung der Unternehmen." *Kommentar*, 6th ed. (Stuttgart: Teilband 2).

AIMR (1993). "Financial reporting in the 1990s and beyond, position paper prepared by Peter Knutson." Charlottesville, VA.

Balakrishnan, R., Harris, T., and Sen, P. (1990). "The predictive ability of geographic segment disclosures," *Journal of Accounting Research*, 28(Autumn): 305–25.

Bauer, A. and Schader, H. (1996). "Darstellung der Finanzlage im Jahresabschluß—Eine empirische Untersuchung," *Journal für Betriebswirtschaft*, 46: 89–99.

Belsley, D., Kuh, E., and Welsch, R. (1980). *Regression Diagnostics, Identifying Influential Data and Sources of Collinearity* (New York: Wiley & Sons).

Berger, P. and Hann, R. (2003a). "The impact of SFAS 131 on information and monitoring," *Journal of Accounting Research*, 41: 163–223.

——––. (2003b). "Segment profitability and the proprietary costs of discretionary disclosure." Working paper, University of Chicago and USC.

Bernards, O. (1994). *Segmentberichterstattung diversifizierter Unternehmen* (Bergisch Gladbach and Köln: EUL).

Botosan, C. (1997). "Disclosure level and the cost of equity capital," *The Accounting Review*, 72(3): 323–49.

Bradbury, M. E. (1992). "Voluntary disclosure of financial segment data: New Zealand evidence," *Accounting and Finance*, 32(May): 15–26.

Budde, W. and Karig, K. (1990). "Beck'scher Bilanzkommentar." W. Budde et al. (eds.), 2nd ed. (München: Beck).

Bushee, B. and Leuz, C. (2003). "Economic consequences of SEC disclosure regulation." Working paper, University of Pennsylvania.

Chow, C. and Wong-Boren, A. (1987). "Voluntary financial disclosure by Mexican corporations," *Accounting Review*: 533–41.

Collins, D. (1976). "Predicting earnings with sub-entity data: Further evidence," *Journal of Accounting Research*, Spring: 163–7.

Cooke (1989). "Disclosure in the corporate annual reports of Swedish companies," *Accounting and Business Research*, 19: 113–24.

Darrough, M. N. and Stoughton, N. M. (1990). "Financial disclosure policy in an entry game," *Journal of Accounting and Economics*, 12: 219–43.

Diamond, D. (1985). "Optimal release of information by firms," *Journal of Finance*, 40(September): 1071–94.

Diamond, D. and Verrecchia, R. (1990). "Disclosure, liquidity, and the cost of capital," *Journal of Finance*, September 1991: 1325–60.

Dye, R. (1986). "Proprietary and nonproprietary disclosure," *Journal of Business*, 59(2): 331–6.

—— and Sridhar, S. (1995). "Industry-wide disclosure dynamics," *Journal of Accounting Research*, 33(1): 157–74.

Ettredge, M., Kwon, S., and Smith, D. (2000). "The effect of SFAS 131 on numbers of reported business segments." Working paper, Iowa State University.

Ewert, R. and Wagenhofer, A. (1992). "Unternehmenspublizität und Konkurrenzwirkungen." *Zeitschrift für Betriebswirtschaft*, 62(3): 297–324.

Feltham, G., Gigler, F., and Hughes, J. (1992). 'The effects of line-of-business reporting on competition in oligopoly settings," *Contemporary Accounting Research*, 9(Fall): 1–23.

Gebhardt, G. (1984). "Kapitalflußrechnungen als Mittel zur Darstellung der Finanzlage," *Die Wirtschaftsprüfung*, 37(18): 481–91.

Goebel, A. and Fuchs, M. (1995). "Die Anwendung der International Accounting Standards in den Konzernabschlüssen deutscher Kapitalgesellschaften," *Der Betrieb*, 48(31): 1521–7.

Görges, T. and Schulte, J. (1994). "Publizitätspolitik börsennotierter Teilkonzerne—Eine empirische Untersuchung," *Die Wirtschaftsprüfung*, 47(17): 561–74.

Gray, S. and Radebaugh, L. (1984). "International segment disclosures by US and UK multinational enterprises: A descriptive study," *Journal of Accounting Research*, 22(Spring): 351–60.

—— and Roberts, C. (1988). "Voluntary information disclosure and the British multinationals: Corporate perceptions of costs and benefits," in A. G. Hopwood (ed.), *International pressures for accounting change* (London: Prentice Hall).

Haller, A. and Jakoby, S. (1994). "Verbreitung und Entwicklungsstand der Finanzierungsrechnung in Deutschland—Eine empirische Analyse," *Der Betrieb*, 47(13): 641–69.

Harris, M. (1998). "The association between competition and managers' business segment reporting decisions," *Journal of Accounting Research*, 36(Spring): 111–28.

Hayes, R. and Lundholm, R. (1996). "Segment reporting to the capital market in the presence of a competitor," *Journal of Accounting Research*, 34(Autumn): 261–79.

Healy, P. and Palepu, K. (2001). "Information asymmetry, corporate disclosure, and the capital markets: A review of the empirical disclosure literature," *Journal of Accounting and Economics*, 31: 405–40.

Herrmann, D. and Thomas, W. (1997). "Geographic segment disclosures: Theories, findings, and implications," *International Journal of Accounting*, 32(4): 487–501.

IdW/SG (1995). "Die Kapitalflußrechnung als Ergänzung des Jahres- und Konzernabschlusses. Gemeinsame Stellungnahme HFA 1/1995 des Hauptfachausschusses und des Arbeitskreises 'Finanzierungsrechnung' der Schmalenbach-Gesellschaft/ Deutsche Gesellschaft für Betriebswirtschaft e.V.," *Die Wirtschaftsprüfung*, 48(6): 210–13.

Ijiri, Y. (1995). "Segment statements and informativeness measures: Managing capital vs. managing resources," *Accounting Horizons*, 9(3): 55–67.

Jensen, M. and Meckling, W. (1976). "Theory of the firm, managerial behavior, agency costs, and ownership structure," *Journal of Financial Economics*, 3: 305–60.

Jones, S., Romano, C., and Smyrnios, K. (1995). "An evaluation of the decision usefulness of cash flow statements by Australian reporting entities," *Accounting and Business Research*, 25: 115–29.

Lang, M. and Lundholm, R. (1993). "Cross-sectional determinants of analyst ratings of corporate disclosures," *Journal of Accounting Research*, 31(2): 246–71.

Leftwich, R., Watts, R., and Zimmerman, J. (1981). "Voluntary corporate disclosure: The case of interim reporting," *Journal of Accounting Research*, 19 (Supplement): 50–77.

Leuz, C. (2000). "The development of voluntary cash flow statements in Germany and the influence of international reporting standards," *Schmalenbach Business Review*, 52(April): 182–207.

—— and Verrecchia, R. (2000). "The economic consequences of increased disclosure," *Journal of Accounting Research*, 38(Supplement): 91–124.

Livnat, J. and Zarowin, P. (1990). "The incremental information content of cash-flow components," *Journal of Accounting and Economics*, 12: 25–46.

Mansch, H., Stolberg, K., and von Wysocki, K. (1995). "Die Kapitalflußrechnung als Ergänzung des Jahres- und Konzernabschlusses." *Die Wirtschaftsprüfung*, 48(6): 185–203.

McKinnon, J. and Dalimunthe, L. (1993). "Voluntary disclosure of segment information by Australian diversified companies," *Accounting and Finance*, 33 (May): 33–50.

Meek, G. and Gray, S. (1989). "Globalization of stock markets and foreign listing requirements: voluntary disclosures by continental European companies listed on the London Stock Exchange," *Journal of International Business Studies*, 20(2): 315–36.

——, Roberts, C., and Gray, S. (1995). "Factors influencing voluntary annual report disclosures by US, UK and Continental European multinational corporations," *Journal of International Business Studies*, 2(3): 555–72.

Mitchell, J., Chia, C., and Loh, A. (1995). "Voluntary disclosure of segment information: Further Australian evidence," *Accounting and Finance*, November: 1–16.

Pacter, P. (1993). "Reporting disaggregated information." Financial Accounting Series #123-A, Research Report, Financial Accounting Standards Board, Norwalk, CT.

Piotroski, J. (2002). "Segment reporting fineness and the precision of investor beliefs." Working paper, University of Chicago.

Prencipe, A. (2001). "Proprietary costs and voluntary segment disclosures: Evidence from Italian listed companies," Working papers, Bocconi University.

Saudagaran, S. and Meek, G. (1997). "A review of research on the relationship between international capital markets and financial reporting by multinational firms," *Journal of Accounting Literature*, 16: 127–59.

Schneider, P. (1985). *Finanzwirtschaftliche Nebenrechnungen* (Frankfurt: Lang).

Schülen, W. (1992). "Angaben zur Gewinn- und Verlustrechnung," E. Castan et al. (eds.), in *Beck'sches Handbuch der Rechnungslegung* (München: Band I, B 425).

Scott, T. (1994). "Incentives and disincentives for financial disclosure: Voluntary disclosure of defined benefit pension plan information by Canadian firms," *Accounting Review*, 69(1): 26–43.

Shin, Y. (2002). "The effect of product market competition on corporate voluntary disclosure decisions." Working paper, Tulane University.

Smiley, R. (1988). "Empirical evidence on strategic entry deterrence," *Journal of Industrial Organization*, 6: 167–80.

SRI International (1987). *Investor information needs and the Annual Report* (Morristown, NJ: Financial Executive Research Foundation).

Stahn, F. (1997). "Die Kapitalflußrechnung in der aktuellen Berichterstattung deutscher Konzerne," *Betriebsberater*: 1991–6.

Verrecchia, R. (1983). "Discretionary disclosure," *Journal of Accounting and Economics*, 5: 179–94.

—— (1990). "Information quality and discretionary disclosure," *Journal of Accounting and Economics*, 12: 365–80.

Wagenhofer, A. (1990a). "Voluntary disclosure with a strategic opponent," *Journal of Accounting and Economics*, 12: 341–63.

—— (1990b). *Informationspolitik im Jahresabschluß* (Heidelberg: Physica).

White, H. (1982). "Maximum likelihood estimation of misspecified models," *Econometrica*, 50 (January): 1–25.

Wysocki, P. (1998). "Real options and the informativeness of segment disclosures." Working paper, MIT.

Enforcement of Accounting Standards

4.1

New Accounting for Goodwill: Application of American Criteria from a German Perspective

Walther Busse von Colbe

1. The problem

In February 2001, the Financial Accounting Standards Board (FASB) published its revised exposure draft on accounting for business combinations and intangible assets. This proposal was followed, on June 29, 2001, by Statement of Financial Accounting Standards (SFAS) 141 "Business Combinations" and SFAS 142 "Goodwill and other intangible assets." With these new standards, the FASB eliminated the pooling-of-interests method of acquisition accounting and substituted the so-called impairment-only approach to goodwill accounting for the previously mandatory amortization of this intangible asset. The new standards gave rise to an intense debate in Germany on the compatibility of the impairment-only approach to goodwill arising in acquisitions with traditional rules and legal regulations of accounting and on its usefulness for investor decision-making.

About half a year later, the German Accounting Standards Board (GASB), the German standard-setting body, issued its exposure draft No. 1a on the compatibility of SFAS 141 and 142 with accounting directives, issued by the European Economic Community (EEC). The board declared that in spite of the fact that EEC directives require amortization of goodwill within four years following the acquisition or over its useful life, group accounts prepared according to internationally accepted accounting standards, including SFAS 141 and 142, are consistent with the EEC directives. The GASB argued that, according to §292a HGB (Handelsgesetzbuch, the German commercial code that regulates accounting standards), listed corporations following U.S. Generally

Accepted Accounting Principles (GAAP) were exempt from the obligation to set up group accounts in accordance with the regulations of the HGB.

In their comments on exposure draft No. 1a, the majority of accounting academics denied its compatibility with the EEC directives and with German law, and questioned the usefulness of the impairment-only approach. (The comments are publicly available at www.drsc.de.) Although some firms and professional associations approved of the proposals, others doubted its legitimacy and the usefulness of the proposed approach to goodwill accounting. The German Institute of Chartered Accountants (IdW) remained silent, although in its comment on the FASB's revised exposure draft it had expressed "doubts whether the requirement not to amortize purchased goodwill can be based upon the argument that goodwill—in its entirety or to a large extent—is not a wasting asset" (2001: 164).

In the meantime, the GASB's standard No. 1a had been issued and proclaimed by the German Ministry of Justice. Hence, according to § 342 HGB, it can be assumed that standard No. 1a is part of German generally accepted group accounting principles. Some German parent companies, particularly those listed at the NYSE and about half of those listed at the Frankfurt exchange's "Neuer Markt" segment, prepare their group accounts according to U.S. GAAP, in application of § 292a HGB (Pellens and Sellhorn 2001b: 1681–9).

However, it is quite probable that in the near future the International Accounting Standards Board (IASB) and the British ASB will to some extent follow the FASB's lead by banning goodwill amortization. When we observe the frequent changes made to goodwill accounting rules in the United Kingdom (and not only there), we can conclude: "If history is any guide, [the impairment only approach] is likely to last for a few years until its shortcomings are demonstrated by some future accounting scandal. At that point, whoever is setting standards at the time will no doubt revert to one of the previous treatments of goodwill. And so the wheel will continue to turn" (Paterson 2002: 101).

In the following sections, I introduce some economic criteria that lend structure to the ongoing debate on accounting for goodwill (see also Colley and Volkan 1988). These criteria especially address the question of whether the impairment-only approach or the traditional amortization approach is more appropriate for satisfying the investors' information requirements. The following criteria are considered:

- Relevance for the capital markets
- Reliability of the accounting numbers

- Verifiability
- Comparability
- Conservatism
- Consistency with generally accepted accounting principles (compatibility)
- Suitability as a basis for dividend payout.

Except for the two latter criteria, these characteristics are laid down in the FASB's Statement of Financial Accounting Concepts (SFAC) No. 2 "Qualitative characteristics of accounting information." The suitability as a basis for dividend payout is a traditional criterion in Germany and some other Continental European countries. Problems may stem from the fact that these criteria are not considered equally important in different countries, and that some of these characteristics may be in conflict with each other.

2. Relevance for capital markets

In its summary of standard No. 142, the FASB stated, "Financial statement users ... indicated that they did not regard goodwill amortization expense as being useful information in analyzing investments." This assessment is based at least partly on a presentation to FASB on May 31, 2000 by a working group of representatives from Morgan Stanley Dean Witter, Goldman Sachs, Deloitte Touche Tohmatsu, Pricewaterhouse-Coopers, and Arthur Andersen. Trevor Harris of the Columbia Business School and Morgan Stanley Dean Witter led the discussion. The participants compared the goodwill amortization requirement with the impairment-only approach. Based on some empirical evidence and a theoretical model, they argued as follows.

In the sense of SFAC 2, relevance means "helping users to form predictions about outcomes of past, present and future events," especially for future earnings and cash flows. The group measured the relative forecast errors of earnings for two firms in their model over ten years. They found that on average, the error was smaller when purchased goodwill was not amortized but instead was accounted for under the impairment-only approach. Furthermore, the group reported that in the communications sector, analysts usually exclude goodwill when determining the companies' value. Based on these findings the group concluded that the value relevance of accounting earnings for stock returns is greater when goodwill is not amortized because of higher forecast accuracy (Morgan Stanley Dean Witter et al. 2000: 24).

In an empirical study of about 500 publicly traded companies for 1993–8, Jennings et al. (2001: 26), using regressions of share price on per-share earnings before and after goodwill amortization, found the following results: "Even when disaggregated from the remainder of reported earnings, goodwill amortization provides no explanatory power for observed prices beyond that of earnings before goodwill amortization . . . the goodwill amortization component of reported earnings can best be viewed as a source of noise." Thus, the authors concluded that, under the new rules of SFAS 142, banning goodwill amortization from the profit-and-loss statement would not reduce the usefulness of earnings, but might instead improve the information content of financial statements. Brown et al. (1999: 13–15) arrived at a similar conclusion, finding no evidence that stock prices of firms with high goodwill amortization are systematically lower than those of other firms.

Some earlier studies, published in the mid-1990s, are based on U.S. and U.K. data. The results on the association between share returns and differences in goodwill amortization are inconclusive. In his review of this literature, Clinch (1995: 27) concluded, "there is no clear association between reported amortization expense and share returns. It is possible that goodwill amortization is of less importance to investors than other components of net income and any association is difficult to observe through the experimental noise in existing research. Alternatively, goodwill may not be viewed an amortizable asset by investors." (See also Hitz and Kuhner 2002: 284.)

For Germany, hardly any empirical studies of the effects of goodwill amortization or of its exclusion from earnings on share prices exist (Krämling 1998: 153–246). Krämling's (1998: 232) own analysis suggests that different goodwill amortization periods do not affect the extent of association of German firms' equity and earnings with stock price. As early as 1991 the German analysts' association (DVFA/SG 1991: 19) recommended that when computing earnings per share, analysts should eliminate goodwill amortization from reported earnings. However, the DVFA/SG's reason was to improve the comparability of the earnings per share of companies that charged purchased goodwill directly to equity with those companies that capitalized and amortized goodwill. The DVFA/SG did not explicitly address the value relevance issues. When purchased goodwill became more and more important, frequently exceeding firms' equity, it became nearly impossible to charge goodwill directly to equity. In 2000, the DVFA/SG revised its recommendation and argued in favor of goodwill amortization over ten years as the standard procedure. In a recent comment on SFAS 142, DVFA/SG representatives argue that goodwill impairment losses reported in U.S. GAAP statements of German firms are to be regarded as part of operating income.

However, the aforementioned studies, while documenting that investors on average do not feel that goodwill amortization contains relevant information, fail to show directly that an impairment-only approach is superior in that respect. The capital market reactions to goodwill impairment write-offs—and especially the association of goodwill values and earnings numbers generated under an impairment-only approach as contained in SFAS 142—have not yet been tested empirically to an extent sufficient for drawing general conclusions. A discussion of several studies shedding light on this issue follows.

Francis et al. (1996: 133), in an analysis of forty-four goodwill write-off announcements occurring between 1989 and 1992, find "no significant reaction to write-offs of goodwill." This finding is open to different interpretations: The authors point out that managers' incentives "play a substantial role in explaining goodwill write-offs" (1996: 134), suggesting that the high degree of financial reporting discretion associated with these numbers leads to a reduced perception of credibility and information content. Alternatively, the write-offs, while possessing relevance to investors per se, might have been "old news" at the time they were announced, because they were preempted by other information.

The study performed by Henning et al. (2002) is one of the first to analyze empirically goodwill write-offs under SFAS 142. However, while they show that goodwill write-offs appear to be timelier than under the predecessor regime in SFAS 121, they do not explicitly consider the capital market's view of these charges.

Jennings et al. (1996: 530) find "a negative association between equity values and goodwill amortization, after controlling for other components of expected earnings." They stress that this association is weak and exhibits substantial cross-sectional variation, suggesting that "investors may view purchased goodwill as an economic resource that does not decline in value for some firms." They interpret this as support for an impairment-only approach to goodwill accounting that had at the time been under consideration by the Accounting Standards Board (ASB) in the United Kingdom.

Since the capital-market effects of the impairment-only approach have not yet been analyzed to a sufficient extent, we should examine critically the relevance considerations on which the FASB has based its reversal on the traditional goodwill amortization. However, a final judgment on that approach must be contingent on a thorough empirical investigation of the issues involved. The effect of higher volatility of earnings and, possibly, of share prices caused by higher impairment losses should be taken into account.

3. Reliability of the accounting numbers

Reliability is defined in SFAC 2 as "the quality of information that assures that information is reasonably free from error and bias and faithfully represents what it purports to represent." Can anyone be sure that the impairment-only approach meets this definition better than does an improved kind of goodwill amortization?

One of the FASB's arguments for eliminating goodwill amortization is that in most cases the useful life of purchased goodwill cannot be reliably estimated (SFAS 142, para. B79). The useful life is often indefinite. But the FASB's conclusion that assets with indefinite useful lives should be treated like assets with infinite useful lives, that is they should not be systematically amortized or depreciated, respectively, has to be questioned. From a logical point of view there are only two possibilities: the useful life of an asset is either known or unknown. If useful life is known, it is either known to be finite, in which case amortization over that period would be most appropriate, or it is known to be infinite, in which case the impairment-only approach can be justified.

However, if the useful life is unobservable, that is indefinite, it may in reality be either finite or infinite. Due to the uncertainty of future developments, one could argue that a prudent and conservative accounting treatment such as amortization should be adopted in this case. There are both tangible and other intangible assets with indefinite useful lives, for instance some buildings or certain types of machinery. Nevertheless, the need to forecast the useful lives of such assets and to determine the corresponding amount of depreciation has so far not created demands to eliminate depreciation.

The FASB concludes in SFAS 142, "amortization of goodwill was not consistent with the concept of representational faithfulness, as discussed in FASB Concepts Statement No. 2, *Qualitative Characteristics of Accounting Information*" (SFAS 142, summary). This statement, coming more than twenty years after issuing the concept statement, is somewhat surprising and hardly convincing. Obviously, over that twenty-year period the Board changed its point of view. However, nothing forbids the Board from changing its mind if a new situation develops or new ideas arise, but convincing reasons should be given. In this respect, there seems to be a deficiency.

There are other alternatives available to improve the reliability of accounting for purchased goodwill. The Board considered some of them in the September 7, 1999 exposure draft "Business combinations and intangible assets," in which the FASB reduced the maximum amortization period to twenty years, provided guidelines to determining the useful lives of certain elements of goodwill, made mandatory the rule of straight-line amortization, regulated certain disclosure requirements, and so on. Additional disclosure, for instance on the elements of goodwill (Johnson and Petrone 1998; Sellhorn 2000), classification by risk, and periods of useful life (Ordelheide 1997: 588), and reasons for impairment losses, could help analysts in judging the economic value of goodwill and its reduction shown in firms' financial reporting. Because of uncertainties involved in estimating the useful life of goodwill, the fair amount of its reduction through systematic amortization and additional impairment losses can hardly be determined objectively. Therefore, fair and comprehensive disclosures become all the more important.

A number of authors have termed the existing accounting guidance (or during the pre-SFAS 121 period, the lack thereof) pertaining to write-offs of most assets and especially goodwill "discretionary" (see e.g. Francis et al. 1996: 133; Riedl 2002). Others, like Henning et al. (2002) embrace SFAS 142 on the grounds that the impairment-only approach reduces firms' ability to delay write-offs (see also Jennings et al. 1996).

A particular question with regard to SFAS 142 is whether the delimitation of reporting units to assign goodwill and the determination of impairment losses meet the requirements of reliability (Pellens and Sellhorn 2001a: 719). The main problem is measuring the fair value of the reporting unit according to SFAS 142 in test step one, and the fair value of goodwill in test step two, particularly when no share prices for the reporting units are available. The discounted cash flow technique implies the determination of both a risk-adjusted interest rate and future cash flows, but such determination is almost inevitably subjective.

Clearly, reliability and relevance are conflicting objectives in many cases. As the FASB stated in SFAC 2 (para. 90): "Reliability may suffer when an accounting method is changed to gain relevance and vice versa." The debate surrounding the impairment-only approach particularly illustrates this conflict: While its proponents argue that it is conceptually superior to the sometimes arbitrary approach of amortizing goodwill over some prespecified period of time, its opponents criticize the high degree of discretion involved in the write-off decision. In such a conflict, a fundamental change in accounting requirements must be carefully justified. Other qualitative characteristics of accounting information must also be taken into account.

4. Verifiability

According to the definition in SFAC 2, verifiability is "the ability through consensus among measurers to ensure, that information represents what it purports to represent or that the chosen method of measurement has been used without error or bias," meaning that different people are likely to obtain the same measure (para. 89).

Thus, the question arises as to whether the impairment-only approach meets the requirement of verifiability to a greater extent than does the amortization of goodwill. It is likely that the procedure to determine impairment losses as laid down in SFAS 142 makes it easier for management to influence the accounting numbers without the auditors being able to control it than does the amortization of goodwill, especially if the latter had been improved as intended in the FASB's 1999 exposure draft. If management uses these discretionary parameters, it will be more difficult to verify accounting numbers pertaining to goodwill and enforce the regulations in SFAS 142 than it has been in the past. The Enron scandal has shown that enforcement of accounting rules is a critical point that should be carefully considered in the process of developing a standard.

5. Comparability

A further qualitative characteristic of accounting information is comparability. This characteristic means that information about an enterprise can be compared with similar information about other enterprises and with similar information about the same enterprise for some other period (SFAC 2, para. 111). In this context, we must ask if the impairment-only approach will improve or reduce the extent of comparability. The following example may be considered.

There are two identical firms, both of which endeavor to expand their market share. Firm 1 increases the cost of advertising and hires new sales staff, Firm 2 purchases a firm that has an appropriate market share, paying for it a corresponding amount of goodwill. Firm 1 must report the incurred cost in the income statement, thus lowering its profit. Firm 2 shows no expense as long as goodwill is not amortized or impaired. In fact, both firms have the same cash flows, but for Firm 1 the profit shown is less than for Firm 2. If goodwill were amortized over its useful life, the profits of both firms would be approximately equal.

It appears that the impairment-only approach reduces comparability between firms that plan to grow internally and those that adopt an external growth strategy. It has been argued that the profit would be charged twice, first by the amortization of goodwill and second by the ongoing expenses required to preserve the value of purchased goodwill (SFAS 142, B 85; Hitz and Kuhner 2002: 282). However, this argument is not convincing: Amortizing purchased goodwill is the compensation for purchased future profits or avoided cost. Expenditures for maintenance are actually investments in new profit potentials.

Another dimension of comparability involves international comparisons. While the IASB is expected to adopt an approach to goodwill accounting similar to the FASB's in the near future, several years are likely to pass before extensive international convergence occurs in this important area of accounting.

6. Conservatism

"Conservatism is a prudent reaction to uncertainty to try to ensure that uncertainties and risks inherent in business situations are adequately considered. Thus, if two estimates of amounts to be received or paid in the future are about equally likely, conservatism dictates using the less optimistic one" (SFAC 2, para. 82). This principle of prudence should be applied to all balance sheet accounts, at least from a German point of view. For instance, if uncertainty is related to the useful life of an asset and to any value declines of the asset during that time, the principle may require choosing accelerated instead of straight-line depreciation. To prevent any misunderstanding, conservatism does not mean deliberate understatement of assets or overstatement of liabilities, although that has been known to occur in Germany in the past.

However, abandoning goodwill amortization might on the one hand involve the danger of overstating capitalized goodwill because management may be reluctant to show an impairment loss of a recently purchased subsidiary. On the other hand, there might also exist motivations to adopt a big bath strategy, for example after a change in top management has occurred. In the case of goodwill amortization, the amount of goodwill declines automatically. Furthermore, the need to report an impairment loss might only occur in a period when the situation is already bad for the company or for the reporting unit for other reasons. In this case, the principle of conservatism might have been violated in the periods preceding the impairment. An impairment test that only triggers an impairment loss when some threshold of economic decline has been exceeded tends to foster volatility in the time series of earnings.

7. Consistency with GAAP (compatibility)

In SFAC 2, consistency implies uniform accounting policies and procedures from period to period as well as from firm to firm within a single period. Another aspect of consistency is the compatibility of a single accounting procedure with other established accounting methods, and with underlying accounting principles in general. Although we have touched briefly on the aspect of conformance with underlying accounting principles in general, the discussion has only been in relation to the impairment-only approach for goodwill. The compatibility between single accounting methods has not been addressed in SFAC 2 or elsewhere within the FASB's pronouncements. For instance, a lack of compatibility seems to be that part of the purchase price paid for development expenditures can be expensed directly according to FIN 4, although these purchased research and development assets will often fulfill the recognition criteria for intangible assets acquired in a business combination, as laid down in SFAS 141.

In Germany, the lack of contradiction between accounting principles is an important criterion for judging an accounting method, because the fundamental accounting methods are described in the Commercial Code. Therefore, special accounting procedures developed by firms or by the GASB have to correspond to the legal rules. The GASB's standards state explicitly in their preface that a new standard does not contradict either the legal rules or other standards.

We must examine the compatibility of the impairment-only approach with legal rules and with the German GAAP from a German point of view, since this approach may be introduced to group accounting in general. If the International Accounting Standards Board (IASB) follows the procedures in SFAS 142 more or less closely and the June 2002 EEC decree on the application of international accounting principles comes into force, then all groups within the EEC, or at least those that are listed, will be required to prepare their consolidated accounts according to the IASB's International Financial Reporting Standards from 2005 on.

Apart from its contradiction to the present legal requirement to amortize goodwill, the new method has the following problem: The abandonment of goodwill amortization and the determination of an impairment loss, related to a single reporting unit, makes it possible that at least part of purchased goodwill is replaced with internally generated goodwill. But so far, the capitalization of internally generated goodwill contradicts internationally and nationally accepted accounting principles as well as the German legal requirements. Furthermore, the procedures of SFAS 142 result in a more or less arbitrary portion of internally generated goodwill being reported on the balance sheet, which also violates the principle of comparability of financial reporting of different firms.

The issue of whether or not to capitalize internally generated goodwill points to the underlying problem of the asset nature of goodwill. According to SFAC 6 (para. 26), among other criteria, an asset results from a transaction or other event that has already occurred and has created future economic benefits under the entity's control. For purchased goodwill, this past transaction is the purchase of the subsidiary, which gives the firm the control over its future benefits. The FASB has no doubts that the purchased goodwill is an asset (Johnson and Petrone 1998: 296), but in Germany the opinions on this issue are divided. Some activities that create internally generated goodwill have also occurred in the past, but they can hardly be identified and measured. Therefore, if the internally developed goodwill is an asset, it should be capitalized not only to the extent to which it replaces purchased goodwill.

Furthermore, the impairment-only approach violates another, more technical, accounting principle: the requirement that assets should be recognized and valued separately. The replacement of purchased goodwill with internally developed goodwill recognizes a mixture of both. At first, this seems to be of minor importance. However, in principle this solution is the first step to quite a different type of financial reporting: A balance sheet showing the fair values of single assets and liabilities in the sense of the net selling prices or, more important, the fair values of reporting units developed from their future cash flows instead of groups of single assets. Therefore, the income statement would show the cash flow or the turnover of the reporting units and their related cost or their profits only before interests, taxes, and some general overhead or the interest earned on the fair value. The last alternative is well known as "economic profit." But the economic profit is well defined only in the unrealistic world of perfect markets (Hitz and Kuhner 2002: 280, 287).

In part, and as far as the balance sheet is concerned, this concept has been realized implicitly by the FASB's impairment test of goodwill. If the joint project of the FASB and the IASB is to apply the fresh-start method on multiparty business combinations, other new entity formation and joint venture formation would be realized and the original goodwill would become of much greater importance (FASB 2002: 5). According to the fresh-start concept, all firms involved are reported on the balance sheet of the new entity at their fair values, including their internally generated goodwill. Is the FASB aspiring to a fair-value based accounting paradigm? Whatever the FASB has in mind, the impairment-only approach is in sharp contrast to hitherto internationally accepted accounting principles in this respect as well.

8. Suitability as a basis for dividend payouts

In Germany and some other Continental European countries, annual accounts are the basis for decisions concerning dividend payments. According to the German Corporation Act, management must put at the shareholders' disposal at least half of the annual profit reported in the balance sheet. Even though this regulation refers to a firm's individual accounts, in reality the group accounts are the basis for dividend payout decisions. In Germany, creditor protection through conservatism, when there is uncertainty, is an important issue for separate financial statements. The same valuation regulations apply to consolidated accounts. Therefore, only realized profits should be shown in those accounts. After profit distribution, the corresponding assets are withdrawn from creditors' access. Internally developed goodwill is, at its core, the present value of future and unrealized profits. Therefore, its implicit capitalization through the replacement of diminished purchased goodwill could result in unrealized profits being distributed as dividends.

9. Influence on management compensation/ capital budgeting

If the managers of reporting units are responsible for purchasing a subsidiary, they must so far earn at least the cost of capital including interest on goodwill—according to present accounting practice on purchased goodwill only—and goodwill amortization so far. Impairment losses are often unforeseeable and are caused by external events. Making the managers responsible for these losses could lower their motivation, but failing to do so leads to the danger of overpaying for a subsidiary.

Furthermore, if purchased goodwill cannot later be separated from additional goodwill created internally, analysts cannot see whether the purchase of the subsidiary was a success or a failure. However, in view of management's future decisions and of its compensation, it is important to control whether it has made effective investment decisions in the past (Siegel 2002: 750).

10. Closing remarks

In SFAS 142, the FASB stated that purchased goodwill is an asset. The payment given for the subsidiary, be it in cash, cash equivalents, or fair value of marketable securities, is an investment made in the anticipation of earning a return above the market rate on the assets acquired.

Abandoning goodwill amortization is correct, provided that goodwill is the present value of infinite future cash flows, which will be realized exactly as forecast less the purchase price. However, that is a very unrealistic case. Normally, the period over which additional cash from some investment will flow into the entity is limited. Further, actual cash flows almost always differ from forecasts, mostly downwards. Because of this known feature of financial reporting numbers that are based on forecasts, prudent and conservative financial reporting would dictate amortization of purchased goodwill.

In issuing SFAS 142, the FASB departs from this framework, generally abolishing the amortization of goodwill and the depreciation of other intangible assets with indefinite useful lives. SFAS 142 reverts to a treatment of goodwill similar to that which was required before APB Opinion No. 17 was issued in 1970 (Davis 1992: 77).

The FASB argues that goodwill amortization is ignored by analysts and has no influence on share prices. One can admit that goodwill amortization causes no cash outflow, but then the same is true for depreciation. However, in contrast to depreciation, goodwill amortization demands no replacement in the form of purchasing a new enterprise, such as the replacement investment in new machinery after the end of its useful life. In this respect, amortization is different from other costs. Is that the reason investors disregard goodwill amortization? And is their behavior a sufficient argument in favor of eliminating goodwill amortization?

Carrying forward the amount originally paid for goodwill is like having the sword of Damocles hanging over the firm: At some point in time, this goodwill will have lost at least part of its value and will have to be impaired. Admittedly, the balance sheet shows the existence of this sword, but not the strength of the string by which it is hanging. No one can predict when that string will break, sending the sword crashing down to damage the enterprise.

Goodwill, both purchased and internally developed, has its source in market imperfections such as barriers to entry or a firm's competitive advantage. But competition tends to eliminate such advantages in the course of time, for example when a new competitor enters the field or a new technique surfaces (White et al. 2003: 707–8). Then the goodwill is impaired, rather suddenly and profoundly in most cases. We will learn in the future how management will live with this constant threat. Presently, firms appreciate being relieved of the burden of having to make enough profit to cover goodwill amortization.

Even if it were true that goodwill amortization is being ignored by capital markets participants, there is no reason to omit every item in group accounts that is of little interest to analysts. Otherwise, financial reporting would have so many holes that it would lose at least part of its information content. Goodwill amortization would probably not hurt the information content of financial reporting if shown separately on the face of the income statement. On the contrary, retaining goodwill amortization would correspond to the proven qualitative characteristics of accounting information laid down in SFAC 2 and some other criteria, as discussed above.

The preceding discussion suggests that the FASB's abandonment of the traditional treatment of goodwill might not have been exclusively motivated by the perceived improvements to the usefulness of financial reporting, but also by the need to alleviate the effects on companies' earnings of eliminating the pooling-of-interests method of accounting for business combinations.

Prior research has documented that, in most cases, accounting regulation is not only a result of pure academic cognition, but also at least partly the result of political bargaining. For example, McLeay et al. (2000: 79) very impressively demonstrate this fact by their analysis of the transposition of the Fourth European Company Law Directive into German HGB. The parties involved, essentially firms, auditors, and accounting academics lobby for their respective individual interests.

The role of academics is rather weak in this political process (Busse von Colbe 1992: 32). Academics foster a solution that on the one hand enhances the functioning of the capital markets as they understand it, and on the other hand does not contradict other accounting regulations. But such lobbying in favor of public welfare and systematic regulation, it turned out, has only a small chance of success.

The abandonment of goodwill amortization seems to be both unnecessary and unconvincing, unless other reasons can be given. If the FASB had to pay for eliminating the pooling-of-interests method or is contemplating a switch to a fair-value paradigm, then the argument that investors neglect goodwill amortization is only a pretext for abandoning goodwill amortization. The FASB stated in the recently issued SFAC 7, "fair value provides the most complete and representationally faithful measure of the economic characteristics of an asset or a liability" (para. 36). This statement creates the impression that the FASB intends to replace, step by step, the historical cost accounting by fair-value accounting, but without being open and consistent about its true intentions.

Obviously, views on the compatibility of the impairment-only approach for goodwill accounting with the EEC directives are different in Germany and the United Kingdom. According to ASB's FRS 10 paragraph 36–37 "Goodwill and intangible assets" goodwill can generally be amortized. Alternatively, it can be tested for impairment only. From the British point of view, this regulation does not appear to contradict the EEC directives. However, most of the companies in the United Kingdom chose the goodwill amortization to avoid the complexity of the full impairment-only approach (Paterson 2002: 101).

Notes

The author wishes to thank Thorsten Sellhorn for his insightful comments and constructive suggestions.

References

Brown, W. D., Tucker, K. J., and Pfeiffer, R. J. (1999). "A prospective look at the usefulness of separately reporting goodwill charges: An evaluation of 'cash earnings.'" Working paper, University of Massachusetts, December 1999.

216   WALTHER BUSSE VON COLBE

Ordelheide, D. (1997). "Kapitalmarktorientierte Bilanzierungsregeln für den Geschäftswert—HGB—IAS und US-GAAP," in K. H. Forster, B. Grunewald, M. Lutter, and J. Semler (eds.), *Aktien- und Bilanzrecht*, Festschrift für Bruno Kropff (Düsseldorf: IDW-Verlag), 569–89.

Paterson, R. (2002). "Straining goodwill," *Accountancy*, June. 101.

Pellens, B. and Sellhorn, T. (2001*a*). "Neue Goodwill-Bilanzierung nach US-GAAP," *Der Betrieb*, 54: 713–18.

—— —— (2001*b*)."Goodwill-Bilanzierung nach SFAS 141 und 142 für deutsche Unternehmen," *Der Betrieb*, 54: 1681–9.

Riedl, E. J. (2002). "An examination of long-lived asset impairments." Working paper, Pennsylvania State University.

Sellhorn, T. (2000). "Ansätze zur bilanziellen Behandlung des Goodwill im Rahmen einer kapitalmarktorientierten Rechnungslegung," *Der Betrieb*, 53: 885–92.

Siegel, T. (2002). "Zur unsinnigen Bilanzierung eines zufälligen Teils des unbekannten originären Geschäftswertes nach DRS 1a," *Der Betrieb*, 55: 749–51.

White, G. I., Sondhi, A. C., and Fried, D. (2003). *The analysis and use of financial statements* (Hoboken, NJ: John Wiley & Sons, Inc., 3rd ed.).

4.2

Compliance with German and International Accounting Standards in Germany: Evidence from Cash Flow Statements

Günther Gebhardt and Aaron Heilmann

1. Introduction

Financial statements are the result of applying financial accounting standards or legal accounting rules to the transactions of a reporting entity. However, the quality of financial statements depends not only on the quality of the standards, that is their ability to adequately portray the economics of the underlying transactions and events. Even high-quality accounting standards result in high-quality financial statements only if they are properly applied.

Recent accounting scandals such as Enron and Worldcom have focused the attention of the broader public on issues of the quality of accounting standards and the enforcement of accounting standards. Dieter Ordelheide has contributed much to the improvement of German accounting regulation, particularly in the area of consolidated financial statements. He has also been a pioneer in the debate on the enforcement of accounting regulation and has initiated important research in this hitherto neglected area. (See Ordelheide 2001 and Böckem 2000.)

The literature on enforcement predominantly describes or discusses the design of enforcement institutions, either in their national settings or on the basis of international comparisons. Only a few empirical studies try to document and analyze the degree of compliance with accounting standards (see Street et al. 1999; Street and Bryant 2000). Recently,

Glaum and Street (2002) presented the first study on the compliance with International Accounting Standards (IAS) or U.S. Generally Accepted Accounting Principles (GAAP) using German data from companies listed at the New Market ("Neuer Markt").

This chapter presents results on the compliance with German GAAP, IAS, or U.S. GAAP of German companies listed in the DAX, MDAX, SDAX, New Market, and in other market segments. Unlike the earlier studies, we deliberately do not cover the broad range of all accounting rules but concentrate instead on a specific area. We choose to analyze compliance with the rules for cash flow statements, because these rules do not differ much across the systems of accounting regulation and are specific enough to allow statements on the existence of noncompliance without access to internal data.

A second question of interest on compliance is whether the firms follow the German GAAP, IAS, and U.S. GAAP rules to the same extent or differently.

The chapter continues as follows. Section 2 provides the institutional background of the regulations for cash flow statements in Germany. In Section 3 we describe the measurement of compliance and the sample selection. The results of our analysis of a representative sample of cash flow statements published by German companies are presented in Section 4. We present our conclusions in Section 5.

2. Accounting rules for cash flow statements

Listed German corporations are required to present cash flow statements as part of their annual consolidated financial statements, but only for accounting periods ending after December 31, 1998. However, most of the major listed German companies voluntarily published cash flow statements before 1998, following the joint recommendation of the Schmalenbach-Gesellschaft (SG) and the Hauptfachausschuss (HFA) of the Institut der Wirtschaftsprüfer SG-HFA 1/1995 or following IAS 7 or FAS 95 (for a most recent survey see Mayer 2002: 221–2). The regulation in § 297 para. 1 Commercial Code (Handelsgesetzbuch, HGB), introduced in 1998, did not specify details on the form and content of the cash flow statement but left this decision to the then newly created German Accounting Standards Board (GASB), which issued GAS 2 Cash Flow Statements in October 1999—with Dieter Ordelheide serving as the academic member. GAS 2 was published by the

Bundesministerium der Justiz (BMJ) in May 2000 and thus became part of German GAAP.

Also in 1998, the German Parliament introduced an option for German companies in § 292a HGB to apply internationally accepted accounting principles in their consolidated financial statements. Thus, by choosing between German GAAP, IAS, or U.S. GAAP, listed German corporations are able to choose between applying GAS 2, IAS 7, or FAS 95 for their mandatory cash flow statements. GAS 2 was drafted with the intention of being compatible both with IAS 7 and FAS 95 (For a detailed comparative discussion of the standards including also the U.K. Standard FRS 1 see Gebhardt 2001). Therefore, the specific rules in the three standards are similar.

3. Research design

3.1. Measuring compliance

In the most recent study by Glaum and Street (2002) as well as in earlier studies (see Ahmed and Nicholls 1994; Street et al. 1999; Tower et al. 1999; Street and Bryant 2000; Street and Gray 2001), compliance is measured by using checklists of items that must be reported under one or more regimes. The items are represented by zero or one dummy variables that are coded "1" if the item is reported in the annual report and "0" otherwise. The dummy variables are then aggregated by summing up the scores and dividing the sum for each company by the number of items. The result is called the "disclosure compliance index" and serves as a comprehensive measure of compliance.

The earlier studies do not report results for compliance on individual items or on subgroups of items. They only broadly describe the most important areas of noncompliance. Interestingly, the area of cash flow statements is not mentioned as a problem area by Glaum and Street (2002). In this chapter we present results of compliance or noncompliance for individual cash flow statement items and thus can pinpoint the critical areas of noncompliance.

For a comparison across accounting systems, compliance can only be measured by the rules that cover identical problem areas. However, the rules themselves need not be identical. For example, FAS 95 does not accept the inclusion of liabilities in the definition of cash and cash equivalents, but GAS 2.19 and IAS 7.8 allow the inclusion of bank overdrafts repayable on demand. Thus, there is compliance under U.S. GAAP if no liabilities are included and under German GAAP and IAS if either no liabilities or only qualifying bank overdrafts are included.

We also analyze rules for problem areas that are not included in all three standards. For example, the use of formats is prescribed only in GAS 2 but not in IAS 7 or FAS 95. We treat such items as additional quality criteria. We do not include such items in our comparison of compliance, because doing so would introduce a bias against a standard with more detailed rules.

Compliance or quality criteria may not be applicable to all companies. For example, the requirement to display the effects of changes in exchange rates applies only to companies that experience material changes in the value of foreign currency cash or cash equivalents. Thus, the number of companies included in our analysis will vary between items.

3.2. Sample selection

The requirement to present cash flow statements as part of the consolidated financial statements applies to all quoted German companies (see § 297 para. 1 HGB). We use the CDAX database of 740 companies listed on the Frankfurt Stock Exchange as of December 29, 2000 to define the population. We exclude forty-nine companies from the banking and insurance industry because they are required to follow specific rules for cash flow statements under German GAAP (GAS 2–10; GAS 2–20). Cash flow statements are not available for seven companies in liquidation or bankruptcy, and for seventy-one quoted companies that are not parent companies of a group and thus did not prepare consolidated financial statements. We note that under German law, cash flow statements are mandatory only for group financial statements but not for individual financial statements.

We draw a stratified sample from our defined population that is intended to be more representative than a pure random sample for factors that are expected to explain the findings. The factors we choose are the accounting system (HGB, IAS, U.S. GAAP), the type of auditor (Big-5; Non-Big-5), and the stock market segment (DAX, MDAX, SDAX, New Market, other markets). For seven companies, the information needed for classification was not available from the sources of either the Deutsche Börse (2000) or the Hoppenstedt Aktienführer (2000, 2001). Table 4.2.1, panel A, presents the distribution of the remaining population of 606 companies.

Table 4.2.1. Distribution of companies in the population (panel A) and in the stratified sample (panel B)

Accounting system	CPA	Stock market					Total
		DAX	MDAX	SDAX	New market	Other	
Panel A							
GAS	Big-5	6	21	38	10	80	155
	Non-Big-5	1	17	36	7	67	128
IAS	Big-5	6	12	9	60	10	97
	Non-Big-5	3	1	4	77	6	91
U.S. GAAP	Big-5	8	8	1	70	5	92
	Non-Big-5	0	2	1	40	0	43
Total		24	61	89	264	168	606
Panel B							
GAS	Big-5	6	6	5	6	6	29
	Non-Big-5	1	5	7	5	7	25
IAS	Big-5	6	10	9	7	7	39
	Non-Big-5	3	1	3	7	6	20
U.S. GAAP	Big-5	8	8	1	8	3	28
	Non-Big-5	0	2	1	8	0	11
Total		24	32	26	41	29	152

Panel B of Table 4.2.1 presents the distribution of a stratified sample of 152 companies drawn randomly from the cells in panel A. We apply a disproportional selection method that consists of drawing a random sample from each cell of Table 4.2.1, panel A (see Bortz 1999: 86, 88). In relation to the population, the sample size is not equal for all cells. For example, all DAX nonfinancial companies are included and thus the relative sample size is 100 percent. From the SDAX companies that apply to HGB rules, we draw two random samples of five out of thirty-eight companies audited by a Big-5 Auditor and of seven out of thirty-six companies audited by a Non-Big-5 company.

We group the results of our analysis by the different accounting systems. We examine the differences in the distribution of the population for each accounting system and of the corresponding subgroup of our stratified sample by combining the results of each subgroup with the relative weight of the subgroup in the corresponding population. For example, we observe two GAS 2 preparers (out of fifty-four) that do not comply with the minimum requirements of presenting at least some qualitative information about cash and cash equivalents. One company is listed in the MDAX and the other in the Others segment; both are audited by a Non-Big-5 firm. The percentage of noncompliance of 4.6 percent given in the following section is then calculated as (see Cochran 1974: 113):

$$0.0458 = \underbrace{\frac{1}{5}}_{\substack{\text{Noncompliance} \\ \text{in sample}}} \cdot \underbrace{\frac{17}{155 + 128}}_{\substack{\text{Weight in} \\ \text{population of} \\ \text{GAS 2 preparers}}}$$

$$+ \underbrace{\frac{1}{7}}_{\substack{\text{Noncompliance} \\ \text{in sample}}} \cdot \underbrace{\frac{67}{155 + 128}}_{\substack{\text{Weight in} \\ \text{population of} \\ \text{GAS 2 preparers}}}$$

4. Results

4.1. Definitions of cash and cash equivalents

All three standards contain detailed rules on the definition of cash and cash equivalents and require information about the individual components, all of which is given by the vast majority of the sample companies. Figure 4.2.1, panel A indicates that noncompliance can be observed for two (out of fifty-four) companies applying GAS 2 (or 4.6 percent of the population of GAS 2 preparers), for one (out of fifty-nine) IAS 7 preparer (0.76 percent), and for three (out of thirty-nine) FAS 95 preparers (13.79 percent). In most cases firms present the information as a qualitative description of the corresponding line items in the balance sheet.

The standards do not require quantitative information about the components of cash and cash equivalents, but sixty-nine sample companies nevertheless provide this information (GAS 2: twenty; IAS 7: thirty-seven; FAS 95: twelve). Panel B of Figure 4.2.1 demonstrates that the percentage of companies that provide quantitative information on the components of cash and cash equivalents is highest for IAS cash flow statements. Such information can either be derived from the balance sheet or from special note disclosures.

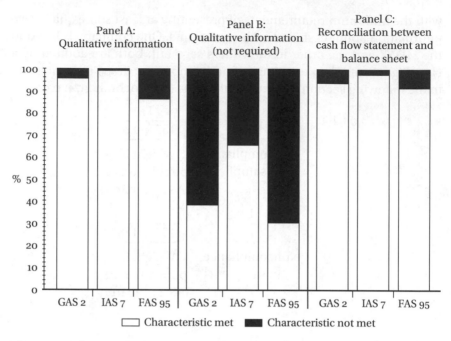

Fig. 4.2.1. Information about cash and cash equivalents.

We also observe a high level of compliance (GAS 2: 93.77 percent; IAS 7: 97.7 percent; FAS 95: 91.42 percent) for the requirements to demonstrate a link between the definition of cash and cash equivalents and the related balance sheet items. Only four GAS 2 preparers, four IAS 7 preparers, and three FAS 95 preparers do not comply.

The quality of the information on the definition of cash and cash equivalents differs considerably. Often, we cannot clearly classify companies as complying or not complying with the rules. Figure 4.2.2 (p. 225) displays different degrees of potential noncompliance. Most companies that are applying FAS 95 clearly state that they include cash equivalents only with maturity of three months or less. Thus, they comply with this important aspect of the definition of cash and cash equivalents.

In contrast, many GAS 2 and IAS 7 preparers include deposits or securities without any information about maturities. Therefore, it is unclear whether all those companies comply with the rules. Based on the information provided, six (out of fifty-four) GAS 2 preparers, eleven (out of fifty-nine) IAS 7 preparers, and one (out of thirty-nine) FAS 95 preparers include securities without stating that they do not include equity securities. Such uncertainty about the definitions of cash and

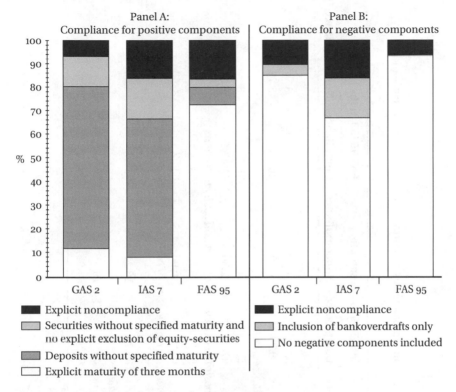

Fig. 4.2.2. Definition of cash and cash equivalents.

cash equivalents is much more relevant for IAS 7 and GAS 2 preparers and should be removed by a clear wording in the notes to financial
statements.

The standards either prohibit (FAS 95) or restrict the inclusion of liabilities in the definition of cash and cash equivalents to bank overdrafts
repayable on demand (GAS 2.19; IAS 7.8). Our sample companies rarely
include liabilities in their definitions of cash and cash equivalents. Such
an inclusion is more popular with IAS preparers (eleven out of fifty-nine),
of which seven companies include even current liabilities with maturities
of up to one year. There are also four GAS 2 preparers and, as an exception, one FAS 95 preparer from the New Market who violate the rules.
Noncompliance in this area is higher for IAS 7 and GAS 2 preparers.

Table 4.2.2 (p. 226) summarizes the results of our analyses of compliance in the area of the definitions of cash and cash equivalents. Even
though we use the least restrictive definitions of noncompliance, ten
GAS 2 preparers (16.91 percent) do not comply with at least one item. Noncompliance appears to be even more prevalent with IAS 7 (34.06 percent)

Table 4.2.2. Percentage of compliance and noncompliance to definition and classification of cash and cash equivalents

	GAS 2 (54 in the sample)		IAS 7 (59 in the sample)		FAS 95 (39 in the sample)	
	Compliance	Noncompliance	Compliance	Noncompliance	Compliance	Noncompliance
General information about cash and cash equivalents						
Absolute	52	2	58	1	36	3
Percent	95.40	4.60	99.24	0.76	86.21	13.79
Link between cash flow statement and balance sheet						
Absolute	50	4	55	4	36	3
Percent	93.77	6.23	97.70	2.30	91.42	8.58
Explicit violations of the compliance for positive components of cash and cash equivalents						
Absolute	49	5	50	9	33	6
Percent	93.49	6.51	83.92	16.08	83.52	16.48
Explicit violations of the compliance for negative components of cash and cash equivalents						
Absolute	50	4	52	7	38	1
Percent	90.88	9.12	83.79	16.21	93.47	6.53
All-over compliance cash and cash equivalents						
Absolute	44	10	40	19	30	9
Percent	83.09	16.91	65.94	34.06	69.64	30.36

and FAS 95 preparers (30.36 percent). However, the quality of the descriptions of cash and cash equivalents differs much across accounting systems. The descriptions of FAS 95 preparers are generally more precise and indicate compliance for thirty (out of thirty-nine) companies.

Whether or not noncompliance in this area differs across accounting systems cannot be inferred clearly from our results. Figure 4.2.2 demonstrates the difficulties of an external judgment on the existence of compliance or noncompliance for forty-four (out of fifty-four) GAS 2 and for forty-five (out of fifty-nine) IAS 7 preparers. These difficulties are due to the imprecise description of the components of cash and cash equivalents tolerated by the auditors.

4.2. Presentation of cash flows from operating activities

The standards offer companies the option to present cash flows from operating activities under either the direct or the indirect method. All companies in our sample use the indirect method, which requires a reconciliation to net cash flows from operating activities that should generally start from either net income (IAS 7.18, FAS 95.29) or from net income before extraordinary items (GAS 2.27). Because the standards require income tax payments and interest payments to be presented either as a special line item in the cash flow statement or in the notes, some companies use net income before interest and/or taxes as the starting point. We classify this as compliance with the standards in Figure 4.2.3, panel A (p. 228).

GAS 2.28 and IAS 7.20 offer the option to start the reconciliation from another income figure. This option is chosen by only one GAS 2 preparer (Kamps 2000: 54; "net income before flotation costs") and also by four IAS 7 preparers who start from operating income (Bayer 2000: 45; AS.Création Tapeten 2000: 55) or an "operating cash flow" (Heidelberger Zement 2000: 65). Metro (2000: 84) starts the reconciliation from gross profit.

GAS 2.27 and FAS 95.29 specify minimum requirements for items that are to be displayed separately in the reconciliation statement. Figure 4.2.3, panel B indicates that the more specific presentation rules of GAS 2 are followed by forty-five (out of fifty-four) of GAS 2 preparers and the rules of FAS 95 by thirty-five (out of thirty-nine) of the U.S. GAAP companies. IAS 7 does not include detailed presentation rules, with the result that many IAS cash flow statements contain significantly

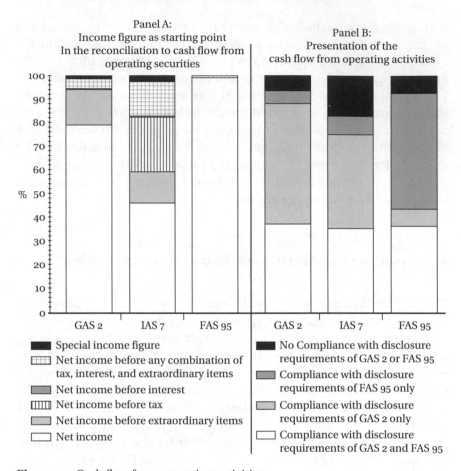

Fig. 4.2.3. Cash flow from operating activities.

less detail. Figure 4.2.3, panel B displays a high rate of compliance with the more specific presentation rules of GAS 2.27. Many IAS preparers seem to follow the presentation rules of GAS 2.

Operating cash flow is defined in the standards as a residual category comprising all cash flows that have not been allocated to investing or financing activities. Noncompliance may result from including cash flows that clearly should be presented as investing or financing cash flows, or from excluding cash flows that should belong to the operating section.

Cash inflows from disposals are to be presented as investing cash flows according to the rules in all three standards. Under the indirect method, net income must be adjusted for gains or losses on disposals in order to present the total cash flow from disposals (equal to book value of disposals plus gains or less losses on disposals) in the investing activities section. Only GAS 2.27 requires that this adjustment be presented separately in the reconciliations from net income. We find that twelve (out of fifty-four) GAS 2 preparers (or 17.11 percent of the population), eleven (out of fifty-nine) IAS 7 preparers (38.32 percent), and twelve (out of thirty-nine) FAS 95 preparers (35.69 percent) have not disclosed this adjustment. This finding does not necessarily imply noncompliance. There may be no gains or losses on disposals in the reporting period, or the gains and losses may be included in other adjustments. However, we find that nine companies clearly include the cash inflows from disposals in the cash flow from operating activities either partly (GAS 2: two, IAS 7: two, FAS 95: four) or fully (Grammer 2000: 21).

4.3. Presentation of cash flows from investing activities

The standards require firms to use the direct method to present cash flows from investing activities. Only for certain short-term investments is it acceptable to net cash inflows and outflows (GAS 2.15a, IAS 7.22–24, FAS 95.12–13).

In our sample, nine (out of fifty-four) GAS 2 preparers (15.28 percent), five (out of fifty-nine) IAS 7 preparers (23.81 percent), and two (out of thirty-nine) FAS 95 preparers (4.41 percent) use the indirect method at least in part. They do so by displaying changes of noncurrent assets, and changes in goodwill or foreign currency adjustments under investing activities. Figure 4.2.4, panel A indicates that the level of such violations is higher for GAS 2 and IAS 7 cash flow statements than it is for those prepared according to FAS 95. We observe many companies that display investing cash flows that are identical with the additions to noncurrent assets in the statement of changes in noncurrent assets ("Anlagespiegel") required of German companies even when they are preparing IAS or U.S. GAAP financial statements.

This result indicates that it is common for companies to derive their consolidated cash flow statements from the consolidated balance sheet and income statement. This method is not outruled by the standards. But by presenting only changes in noncurrent assets, firms do not comply with the standards. Changes in noncurrent assets must be adjusted for changes in the composition of group companies or in exchange rates. Further adjustments are necessary for noncash transactions

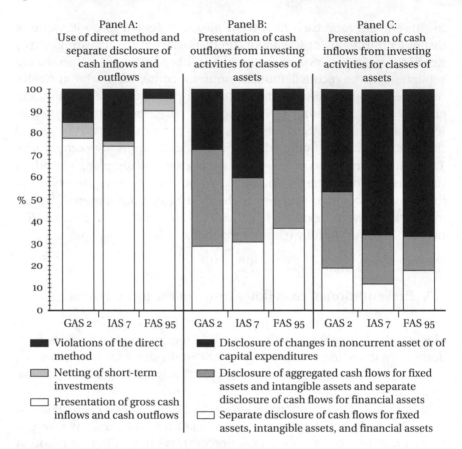

Fig. 4.2.4. Cash flow from investing activities.

(e.g. acquisitions financed by issuing shares) or by transactions involving financial arrangements with suppliers.

We observe that sixteen sample companies present investing cash flows on a net basis. Doing so is acceptable under the standards if applied to short-term investments with quick turnover, high amounts, and short maturities. However, the information given casts doubts on whether these requirements are fully met by all companies. For example, Epcos (2000: 69) presents a "net increase in financial receivables from third parties," which is not easily subsumed under the netting rules of the standards.

Only GAS 2.27 requires minimum presentation rules for investing cash flows. Figure 4.2.4, panel B demonstrates that most GAS 2 preparers (thirty-two out of fifty-four in our sample) do not present cash outflows from investments in intangible assets or property, plant, and equipment, or noncurrent financial assets separately, as required. Panel C indicates that the level of compliance is even lower for the separate presentation of cash inflows. It is interesting to note that the detail of presentation does not differ much across the accounting regimes. Again, the more specific presentation rules of GAS 2 appear to be followed also by IAS 7 and FAS 95 preparers.

4.4. Presentation of cash flows from financing activities

Under all three standards, cash flows from financing activities must also be presented using the direct method. GAS 2.35 explicitly requires that cash flows from both debtholders and shareholders be presented separately. Cash inflows and cash outflows may not be netted except for certain short-term financing activities.

Figure 4.2.5, panel A indicates that the rules are violated by many preparers across all three accounting systems. Thirty (out of fifty-four) GAS 2 preparers (61.97 percent) as well as twenty-eight (out of fifty-nine) IAS 7 preparers (49.52 percent) and fourteen (out of thirty-nine) FAS 95 preparers (31.77 percent) in our sample do not show the cash inflows from issuing new debt and the cash outflows for repayment of debt separately, but instead present the net changes in debt.

These numbers do not include the companies that are netting cash flows from short-term financing activities. We assume that in these cases the exceptions offered by GAS 2.15a, IAS 7.22, or FAS 95.12–13 apply even in the absence of positive information. Only a few companies provide information that netting applies to, for example commercial paper financing or current account liabilities.

Less often we find violations of the rules for presentation of cash flows to or from shareholders (Figure 4.2.5, panel B). However, six (out of fifty-four) GAS 2 preparers (10.32 percent), eleven (out of fifty-nine) IAS 7 (34.07 percent) preparers, and three (out of thirty-nine) FAS 95 preparers (5.64 percent) present only the net change in minority interests. They do not show the cash inflows from issuing new shares to minorities, or the cash outflows from the repurchase of shares from minorities or from dividend payments to minorities.

Often, we find the change of translation adjustments under financing activities (GAS 2: two; IAS 7: four; FAS 95: three). Clearly, such a change is not a cash flow item to be presented there under the direct method,

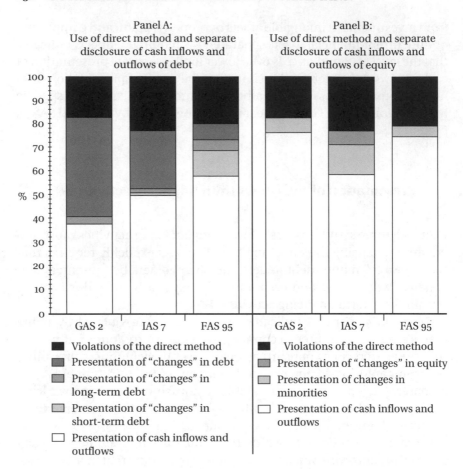

Fig. 4.2.5. Cash flow from financing activities.

as required by the standards. Other items that may not be displayed under the direct method include changes in goodwill directly charged to equity, changes in negative goodwill, and changes in the fair value of available-for-sale financial instruments not included in net income. Again, such lacunae are an indication that many companies derive the financing cash flows from the consolidated balance sheets and income statement, without making the adjustments necessary to arrive at cash inflows and cash outflows.

Some companies include cash flows in the financing section that should be presented as operating cash flows or investing cash flows. Examples are payments to a pension trust (Loewe 2000: 85, 93) better to be classified as payments for employees. P&L transfers ("Ergebnisüber-nahmen"; Metro 2000: 84) should be classified as dividends received and be presented either as operating or investing cash flows.

Table 4.2.3 (p. 234) summarizes the results for the compliance with the requirements to apply the direct method in the investing and financing sections of the cash flow statements. Compliance is highest for FAS 95 preparers (76.07 percent) and lowest for IAS 7 preparers (63.42 percent). The levels of noncompliance are remarkably high—as zero should be the benchmark.

4.5. Additional disclosures

The standards require a comprehensive list of items to be presented either as special line items in the cash flow statement or in the notes (see Gebhardt 2001: 400–16 for an overview). We report results only for selected items that were controversial in the discussions before the standards were adopted.

All the standards require the separate disclosure of interest paid. Such disclosure may be made either as a line item in the cash flow statement or in the notes (GAS 2.36, IAS 7.31, FAS 95.27). Figure 4.2.6 (p. 236), panel A presents evidence that a huge majority (94.04 percent) of GAS 2 prepar-ers (forty-four out of fifty-four) does not disclose interest paid, which is required by the explicit rule of GAS 2.36. The level of compliance is much higher for FAS 95 preparers and highest for IAS 7 cash flow statements. However there are still thirteen (out of fifty-nine) sample IAS compa-nies (31.34 percent) and fourteen (out of thirty-nine) sample U.S. GAAP companies (37.35 percent) that violate a clear rule.

Figure 4.2.6, panel B further demonstrates that again, a huge majority of GAS 2 preparers (forty out of fifty-one companies that are supposed to have paid income taxes) also does not disclose income taxes paid, as required by GAS 2.41. The level of noncompliance again is much lower for FAS 95 preparers and lowest for IAS 7 cash flow statements.

Table 4.2.4 (p. 235) presents the combined results for the additional disclosures of interest paid and taxes paid. An amazing number—forty-five of the GAS 2 preparers or about 95 percent of the population of GAS 2 preparers—fail to provide information that is clearly required by GAS 2. Only nine companies comply fully.

Noncompliance is also very high for IAS 7 and even for FAS 95 pre-parers, where an estimated clear majority of the population fails to provide the information requested by standard-setters.

Table 4.2.3. Combined results for presentation of cash flows from investing and financing activities

	GAS 2 (54 in the sample)		IAS 7 (59 in the sample)		FAS 95 (39 in the sample)	
	Compliance	Noncompliance	Compliance	Noncompliance	Compliance	Noncompliance
Direct method in the presentation of cash flows from investing activities (only explicit violations)						
Absolute	45	9	54	5	37	2
Percent	84.72	15.28	76.19	23.81	95.59	4.41
Direct method in the presentation of cash flows from financing activities (only explicit violations)						
Absolute	45	9	51	8	32	7
Percent	82.72	17.28	76.82	23.18	79.75	20.25
All-over compliance for the use of the direct method in the presentation of cash flows						
Absolute	39	15	46	13	31	8
Percent	69.89	30.11	63.42	36.58	76.07	23.93

Table 4.2.4. Combined results for additional disclosures

	GAS 2 (54 in the sample)		IAS 7 (59 in the sample)		FAS 95 (39 in the sample)	
	Compliance	Noncompliance	Compliance	Noncompliance	Compliance	Noncompliance
Information about interest paid						
Absolute	10	44	46	13	25	14
Percent	5.96	94.04	68.66	31.34	62.65	37.35
Information about tax paid						
Absolute	14	40	41	18	22	17
Percent	12.54	87.46	50.76	49.24	43.21	56.79
All-over compliance for selected additional disclosures						
Absolute	9	45	37	22	20	19
Percent	4.72	95.28	44.32	55.68	38.77	61.32

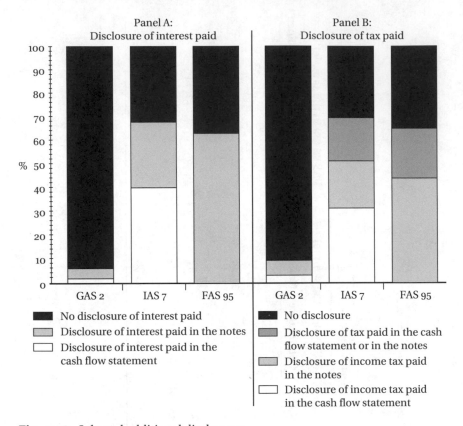

Fig. 4.2.6. Selected additional disclosures.

5. Conclusions

We conclude by noting yet again that our definition of noncompliance is a very forgiving one and thus biased in a friendly direction for the preparers. And yet our study reveals that many German companies do not comply with the rules of the standards for cash flow statements. The extent of noncompliance is remarkably high not only for GAS 2 preparers but also for IAS 7 and FAS 95 preparers.

The major problem areas we identify are the definition of cash and cash equivalents, the presentation of cash inflows and outflows from investing and financing activities where the direct method should be used, and the additional disclosures of interest paid and taxes paid.

Explicit compliance with the definitions of cash and cash equivalents is highest for FAS 95 preparers. Because of an imprecise wording in the notes to the financial statements, there is much uncertainty about the actual definitions used by GAS 2 or IAS 7 preparers. Only if we concentrate on explicit violations, noncompliance is lowest for GAS 2 preparers in this area.

We observe many violations of the rules that require preparers to use the direct method for presenting cash flows from investing and from financing activities. Noncompliance in this area is highest for IAS 7 preparers. Apparently, many companies derive their consolidated cash flow statements from consolidated balance sheets and income statements, but fail to make the necessary adjustments to arrive at the cash inflows and cash outflows as required by all three standards.

The level of noncompliance is extremely high for the additional disclosures that require interest and taxes paid to be presented separately in the cash flow statement or in the notes. Among GAS 2 preparers, compliance is almost nonexistent. As the requirements to provide these numbers were controversial in the discussions before the standards were adopted, it appears that German companies refuse to accept the rules set by GAS 2. Noncompliance here is lower for FAS 95 preparers, but still at a level that is barely acceptable, and surprisingly low for IAS preparers.

Our results raise the question as to which companies fail to comply with the rules of the standards to the extent observed, and why (see Leuz 2000, for a related study of the determinants of voluntary disclosure of cash flow statements). The high level of noncompliance in this special area of cash flow statements might be due to the low weight given to cash flow data by analysts or other users, and the preparers' desire to produce the cash flow statements in a cost-efficient manner.

The role of auditors should be to insist on compliance with the GAAP rules. However, not a single audit opinion on the financial statements of our sample companies included a qualification pointing to noncompliance with the standards on cash flow statements.

In the light of our results, the current discussions aimed at strengthening the institutions for the enforcement of accounting rules appears to be timely and necessary.

References

Ahmed, K. and Nicholls, D. (1994). "The impact of non-financial company characteristics on mandatory disclosure compliance in developing countries: The case of Bangladesh," *The International Journal of Accounting*, 29(3): 62–77.

AS. Création Tapeten AG (2000). AS. Création Tapeten AG, Geschäftsbericht.

Bayer (2000). Bayer AG, Geschäftsbericht 2000, Leverkusen.

Böckem, H. (2000). *Die Durchsetzung von Rechnungslegungsstandards—eine kapitalmarktorientierte Untersuchung* (Frankfurt: Lang).

Bortz, J. (1999). *Statistik für Sozialwissenschaftler* (Berlin, Heidelberg, New York: Springer).

Cochran, W. G. (1974). *Stichprobenverfahren* (Berlin, New York: Walter de Gruyter).

Deutsche Börse (2000). "Statistical market data of 29 November 2000." Frankfurt (www. ip.exchange.de/Internet/IP/ip_stats./nsf/WebIndizesIndesdatenGewichtungCDAX/B71Ca2791714D18141256A86005FAC41/$File/Gewicht_CDAX.xls.openElement; January 25, 2002).

Epcos (2000). Epcos AG, Geschäftsbericht 1999–2000, München.

Gebhardt, G. (2001). "Kapitalflussrechnungen," in E. Castan et al. (eds.), *Beck'sches Handbuch der Rechnungslegung* (München: Beck), C 620.

Glaum, M. and Street, D. L. (2002). "Rechnungslegung der Unternehmen am Neuen Markt—Die Einhaltung der Ausweispflichten nach IAS und US-GAAP," in R. v. Rosen (ed.), *Studien des Deutschen Aktieninstituts*, Frankfurt.

Grammer (2000). Grammer AG, Geschäftsbericht 2000, Amberg.

Heidelberger Zement (2000). Heidelberger Zement AG, Geschäftsbericht, Heidelberg.

Hoppenstedt Financial Information GmbH (2000). *Hoppenstedt Aktienführer* 2001. Darmstadt.

—— (2001). *Hoppenstedt Aktienführer* 2002. Darmstadt.

Kamps (2000). Kamps AG, Geschäftsbericht 2000, Düsseldorf. Gummersbach-Derschlag.

Leuz, C. (2000). "The development of voluntary cash flow statements in Germany and the influence of international reporting standards," *Schmalenbach Business Review*, 55(2): 182–207.

Loewe (2000). Loewe AG, Geschäftsbericht 2000, Kronach.

Mayer, K. (2002). *Gestaltung und Informationsgehalt veröffentlichter Kapitalflußrechnungen börsennotierter deutscher Industrie- und Handelsunternehmen* (Frankfurt: Lang).

Metro (2000). Metro AG, Geschäftsbericht 2000, Düsseldorf.

Ordelheide, D. (2001). "Germany: Group accounts," in D. Ordelheide and KPMG (eds.), *Transnational Accounting*, 2nd ed. (Hampshire and New York: Palgrave), 1353–449.

Street, D. L. and Bryant, S. M. (2000). "Disclosure level and compliance with IASs: A comparison of companies with and without U.S. listings and filings," *The International Journal of Accounting*, 35(3): 305–29.

—— and Gray, S. J. (2001). "Observance of international accounting standards: Factors explaining non-compliance," in The Association of Chartered Certified Accountants (ed.), *ACCA Research Report No.* 74, London.

—— —— and Bryant, S. M. (1999). "Acceptance and observance of international accounting standards: An empirical study of companies claiming to comply with IASs," *The International Journal of Accounting*, 34(1): 11–48.

Tower, G., Hancock, P., and Taplin, R. H. (1999). "A regional study of listed companies' compliance with international accouting standards," *Accounting Forum*, 23(3): 293–305.

4.3

Audit Regulation, Audit Quality, and Audit Research in the Post-Enron Era: An Analysis of Nonaudit Services

Ralf Ewert

1. Introduction

For financial accounting to fairly represent the economic situation of a firm, a combination of high quality accounting standards and a system for enforcing these standards is essential.[1] During the last years, incidences of "creative" and even fraudulent accounting practices have been revealed with an unexpected frequency and order of magnitude. Names like "Enron" and "Worldcom" no longer represent stories of growth and business success. Instead, they have become the most conspicuous symbols of all the accounting shenanigans and accompanying audit failures that have shaken the public's confidence in financial reporting. This situation is, of course, not restricted to the United States. Accounting and audit problems have also been observed in Europe. A noteworthy example is "Comroad," a company that offers soft- and hardware solutions in the mobile telecommunications business and was listed on Germany's "Neuer Markt" Stock Exchange. In the first half of 2002, it was discovered that 98 percent (!) of its reported year 2000 revenues were purely fictitious. (However, the absolute amounts of these misstatements are in no way comparable to those at Enron or Worldcom.)

To restore the financial community's confidence in the financial reporting process, legislators felt they were obliged to take regulatory actions quickly. Perhaps due to the sheer magnitude of the uncovered scandals, the United States is among the first countries in which this process (after a relatively short time of intense discussions) has already led to modified rules for the accounting industry. These modifications were achieved through the Sarbanes-Oxley-Act (SOA), which was signed into law by President Bush on July 30, 2002.

In other countries, the regulatory debate is still going on and its eventual results remain at present an essentially open question. For instance, on May 16, 2002, the Commission of the European Union (EU) has issued the recommendation "Statutory auditor's independence in the EU: A set of fundamental principles." This recommendation is aimed exclusively at aspects of auditing. Although the recommendation is not as comprehensive as the SOA, it deals with the same issues in auditing.[2] However, the recommendation is neither a EU-directive nor an EU-prescription, and therefore it is not obligatory for the EU-members to follow it. Thus, as it stands, it should be viewed as no more than a starting point for a new regulatory debate in the EU (which will clearly be influenced also by the SOA),[3] and its current suggestions (e.g. on the joint offering of audit and nonaudit services (NAS) for the same client) are not as strict as the rules of the SOA.

These regulatory debates display some remarkable features of auditing. The SOA gives the impression that some of the most controversial issues of the last fifty years have now been resolved in just a few months of discussion. The Enron debacle appears to have convinced many parties that audit firms should basically be prohibited from offering both NAS and audit services to the same client.[4]

But what has made such conclusions so compelling? It is true that Andersen (Enron's auditor) received substantial fees from Enron for NAS,[5] but does this imply that these NAS were largely responsible for the accounting failures? After analyzing the Enron case, Benston and Hartgraves (2002: 126) conclude, "US GAAP, as structured and administered by the SEC, the FASB and the AICPA, are substantially responsible for the Enron accounting debacle."[6] Benston and Hartgraves (2002: 127) also stress that the auditors have obviously not been sufficiently attentive and skeptical, but they are extremely cautious about offering quick explanations for the reasons behind this latitude, instead conjecturing several possibilities.

Despite the reservations voiced by the scientific community, the perception that combining NAS and auditing for the same client may be largely responsible for recently observed accounting and audit failures seems to have gained a momentum of its own. Currently, it appears that any auditor offering NAS to her auditees automatically endangers her "independence in appearance" and consequently faces a hard time to convince the public of the quality of her work.

This chapter addresses the question of whether such opinions can be justified by existing research on the issue of combining NAS and auditing. While there are already some reviews of former empirical papers (e.g. Ryan et al. 2001), there is essentially no survey of the related theoretical research and the more recent empirical work. In this chapter, I focus mainly on the theoretical side, which will be critically reviewed and somewhat extended in Section 2. Then, some new empirical work is reviewed in Section 3 and interpreted in the light of the theories presented before. The final section presents conclusions and directions for further research.

2. Theoretical research on NAS and auditing

2.1. Preliminary remarks

Given the importance and regulatory scrutiny of the NAS topic on auditor independence, we would expect to find a large body of theoretical research that analyzes the mechanisms by which NAS may influence auditing activities and auditor reporting. Ideally this research would feature rigorously developed hypotheses that could be tested in empirical studies. In turn, these hypotheses should either provide evidence consistent with the theories or show a need for necessary modifications of the existing conceptual approaches.

Although the number of empirical studies dealing with NAS is indeed large,[7] we rarely find economic models that explicitly address interdependencies between audit and consulting services with regard to possible consequences for auditor independence.[8] In fact, it would be no exaggeration to state that they are at present still in a state of infancy, and Beattie et al. (1999: 71) even go as far as to state that "no formal 'theory' of auditor independence exists." Thus, we see that many empirical studies are based on hypotheses that are either derived completely ad hoc, advanced in the political process, stated in the press, or based on some kind of a priori reasoning, where several possible effects are subjectively weighed by means of personal assessment and/or conviction. Therefore, it comes as no surprise that existing surveys of independence research are mainly based on empirical studies.[9]

Empirical research preceding theoretical developments has also been observed in areas other than just independence and NAS. An example is the early research on informational efficiency of capital markets in which theory largely followed empirical work. However, unlike the case of market efficiency, we are still waiting for a solid theoretical framework of the NAS problem. This lack of theory need not be a severe drawback if the existing empirical results would give a clear-cut picture of the relevant effects, but as will be shown later this is not the case. Conversely, the most recent empirical work on aspects of NAS contains very broad results, or put somewhat differently, if you want to find an entire spectrum of results that ranges from one extreme to the other, you can find it here!

In a situation characterized by a vast number of mixed and often contradictory empirical evidence, it is my sincere conviction that there is now an important role for theory. Theory guides the framing of the issues[10] and provides hypotheses to be tested empirically. Theory gives the structure for the interpretation of empirical results and the framework for a systematic development of knowledge. Concerning NAS, explicit theories would only be superfluous if we could expect that their implications are not essentially different from what can be derived by means of rational argument. However, this is not the case.

In the remainder of this section I critically survey theoretical approaches that are potentially relevant for the NAS issue. Further, I combine some theoretical approaches from the literature in a simple manner and show that a simultaneous offer of auditing and consulting may actually improve the quality of financial statements. Interestingly, this conclusion does not depend on any results of the consulting activities per se (i.e. the information derived from an information system installed by the auditor), but is solely due to incentive considerations in the area of earnings manipulation and auditing. Thus, it differs from the implications of all existing models that are presented in the next sections. After having reviewed (and somewhat supplemented) the theoretical work, I put the result in perspective to recent empirical research in Section 3 where it is shown that many observations are consistent with the above hypothesis.

For my presentation of the theoretical work, I assign existing approaches to two broad categories. Whereas models in the first category rely on arguments of economic bonding between client and auditor, the second category encompasses approaches with an explicit consideration of side payments as a direct representation of collusion between client and auditor. Due to space limitations it is impossible to give an in-depth presentation of all models. Thus, I concentrate on the main thrust of the respective approaches but place somewhat more emphasis on the issue of economic bonding, since these models have received the greatest attention in the independence debate, and it is this area where I intend to provide some new results. Furthermore, I focus exclusively on models that are either directly concerned with the NAS issue or contain variables or relationships that are amenable to a NAS interpretation. Models dealing with other aspects that surely have an additional bearing on auditor behavior (e.g. auditor liability) are not included.[11]

2.2. Models using arguments of economic bonding

2.2.1. Quasirents and auditor reporting decisions

Even a cursory reading of the NAS independence literature published since the mid-1980s reveals that if there is some use of theoretical argument it mainly rests on the quasirent theory, which was first formulated for the context of auditing by DeAngelo (1981*a, b*). This theory explains why an incumbent auditor might receive economic benefits from existing clients even if the audit market is competitive, and even if there are no differences in the capabilities and/or technical competences of auditors competing in the market (i.e. all auditors are capable of performing the required audit work and they incur basically the same costs).

The keys to the argument are the existence of additional start-up costs for performing an initial audit, possible transaction costs for the client in the case of changing the auditor, and the assumption that the incumbent auditor has all the bargaining power for determining the audit fees. Since new auditors will accept a client only if they can expect to recover the start-up costs for the new audit over time, a manager who wishes to change from his existing auditor must incur not only his own transaction costs, but also the additional start-up costs for the new auditor. Thus, the incumbent (having already performed the initial audit) possesses a (virtual) cost advantage *vis-à-vis* a competing auditor. Commanding all the bargaining power over audit fees, she will then transform this advantage into an audit fee that renders the auditee indifferent between the existing auditor and her rivals in the market. Therefore, the incumbent earns fees through her recurring audits that exceed her current audit costs. This surplus generates a stream of economic benefits for auditors who have already performed the initial audit.

However, given a competitive audit market these benefits disappear when auditors compete for the initial audit. At that time, auditors anticipate the benefits they will receive when being the incumbent and set the fee for the first period so as to break even in present value, that is the present value of fees net of audit costs equals "**0**" for any new client. This situation is possible only if the initial audit fee is set below total initial audit costs, a relation that is called "lowballing."

According to this theory, auditors cannot obtain real economic rents from new clients, but they can receive economic benefits from existing clients. These benefits are called "quasirents," since they are competed away in the initial period. The theory only explains the emergence of such benefits despite competition in the audit market. However, there is no formal analysis of possible consequences for auditor reporting decisions in the papers of DeAngelo.[12] Rather, such a link is established by means of an intuitive argument that rests on the observation that in this theory's scenario, an auditor cannot compensate the loss of quasirents by simply acquiring new clients. The quasirents of an existing client yield positive net present values for the audit firm, but new clients just allow the auditor to break even due to competition in the market. Thus, there is economic bonding between a client firm and its auditor. Such bonding can be used by the client's management to exert pressure on the auditor should an accounting conflict occur. Management can threaten to change the auditor if she discloses an unfavorable report. According to this view, the quasirents that an incumbent auditor receives from her existing clients promote biased reporting and a lack of independence.[13]

Given that argument, quasirents may jeopardize an auditor's independence from a specific client. However, at the same time, quasirents from the existing client base of an auditor may act as a safeguard for independence. According to the theory, the auditor is always worse off by losing quasirents. If he discloses a favorable but biased report for a specific auditee, there is a chance that this misreporting may eventually become known to the public. In this case, the auditor's existing clients may conclude that his audits are no longer valuable for the respective firm. For instance, the market may become extremely skeptical of the quality of the financial statements of these firms. This perception may result in higher cost of capital and/or additional bond covenants. To avoid these costs, the management of these firms has incentives to change the auditor, leading to a loss of quasirents from other existing auditees.

Let Q denote the quasirents from a client under consideration, and let S represent the sum of all quasirents from the client base. The probability that a reporting bias will become known to the public is given by p, and d is the percentage of lost quasirents of the sum S. If t denotes the probability of a credible threat to change the auditor in case of an unfavorable audit report, the auditor's expected loss by maintaining his independence is given by $t \cdot Q$. If the auditor's report is not truthful, his expected loss is $p \cdot d \cdot S$. Thus, assuming risk neutrality on the part of the auditor, unbiased reporting is optimal if the following relation holds:

$$p \cdot d \cdot S \geq t \cdot Q \tag{1}$$

Equation (1) shows that, given all other parameters, the larger the existing client base (i.e. the larger the sum S of all quasirents), the more probable is unbiased reporting of the auditor. Rearranging equation (1) yields

$$\frac{p \cdot d}{t} \geq \frac{Q}{S} \tag{2}$$

Inequality (2) illustrates the most prominent implication of DeAngelo's quasirent theory, that is the ratio between the quasirents from a specific auditee to the sum of all quasirents must not exceed a certain level in order for independence to be maintained. This ratio will be smaller for larger audit firms due to the increased magnitude of S implying that larger audit firms should be more independent than smaller ones.

By assuming homogenous clients as a special case (i.e. $S = n \cdot Q$, where n is the number of existing clients), this statement can be most easily demonstrated since in this case inequality (2) becomes

$$\frac{p \cdot d}{t} \geq \frac{Q}{n \cdot Q} = \frac{1}{n} \tag{3}$$

Clearly, given all other parameters, the higher the n the larger the audit firm and the higher the chance that (3) holds. These relationships are the basis for one of the most widely employed proxy for audit quality in empirical studies, namely the size of the audit firm.

2.2.2. NAS and quasirents

DeAngelo's framework was used by Beck et al. (1988) to incorporate NAS. They model the market for NAS as essentially analogous to the audit market. Thus, the market for NAS is competitive and there are transaction costs for the firm if it changes consultants. In the case of recurring consulting services, there are start-up costs for performing the initial consulting work, because the new consultant must become familiar with the client's businesses, structures, and markets. Given these assumptions and the results from the original model, it is not surprising that NAS may give rise to an own-source for quasirents even without possible knowledge spillovers. These spillover effects represent possible economies of scope from offering both auditing and consulting services. In the Beck et al. (1988) model, they are represented by cost reductions for the auditor.

Consider, for instance, a nonrecurring consulting project performed by the auditor. Due to knowledge spillovers this consulting activity may lead to reductions in the costs of performing regular audits.[14] These advantages are not available to competing auditors, thus leaving the upper limit for the incumbent's audit fees unchanged. Therefore, the cost reduction leads to higher future profits from auditing and to higher quasirents for the existing auditor. It generally turns out that by simultaneously offering auditing and consulting services to a specific client, the incumbent auditor's quasirents received from that client increase.

If the magnitude of individual quasirents is viewed as a representation of economic bonding, such bonding thereby increases by the additional NAS activity of auditors. Since the loss of quasirents from an existing auditee may reduce independence, one may be tempted to conclude that independence suffers if auditors are allowed to perform auditing as well as NAS. This conclusion can be found in Beck et al. (1988) and in Ostrowski and Söder (1999). Moreover, it is used in many empirical studies as a theoretical foundation for the respective hypotheses.

However, this conclusion does not automatically follow from simply showing that individual quasirents increase.[15] According to relation (2) above, it is the ratio of individual quasirents to the sum of all quasirents that determines the auditor's decision to report truthfully. If auditors offer both auditing and NAS, they will offer these services not only to one client but basically to their entire client base.

Let QN denote individual quasirents including those from NAS (QN > Q), while the sum of all quasirents is represented by SN > S. Now inequality (2) becomes

$$\frac{p \cdot d}{t} \geq \frac{QN}{SN} \tag{4}$$

Equation (4) implicitly assumes that a firm changing its auditor also terminates the consulting relationship with this auditor. If this does not hold, there cannot be any incremental bonding due to offering auditing and NAS to the same client. However, given that there are knowledge spillovers from bundling auditing and NAS, it seems reasonable to assume that the new client–auditor pair will also try to achieve these synergies, which implies a need for restructuring the consulting assignments.

For illustration purposes, consider the special case with homogenous clients as given by inequality (3). We then have $SN = n \cdot QN > S = n \cdot Q$, and inserting this into (4) yields

$$\frac{p \cdot d}{t} \geq \frac{QN}{SN} = \frac{QN}{n \cdot QN} = \frac{1}{n} \tag{5}$$

Thus, despite higher individual quasirents auditor independence is not affected whatsoever in this special case. Of course, homogenous clients are hardly representative of reality, but this caveat in no way diminishes the thrust of the argument.

Returning to the more general condition (4), the audit firm will almost certainly offer NAS to a large number of its clients, leading to an increase of SN. Even if the relation on the right-hand side of (4) should increase for a given client, logically it must be the case that it decreases for other clients. But this implies that for heterogeneous clients, NAS cannot unequivocally lead to a unidirectional consequence for every auditee. Thus, in this theoretical framework it is almost impossible to derive any systematic effect of NAS for independence. It is not clear to me which hypotheses really follow from this approach for empirical work, let alone what need there may be for a regulatory ban on NAS for auditors.

2.2.3. *Audit effort, NAS, and strategic interdependencies*

One additional drawback of the quasirent framework is its exclusive focus on the auditor's reporting decision. This focus may be due to the definition of independence given by DeAngelo (1981*a*: 116), where "the level of auditor independence is defined as the conditional probability that, *given a breach has been discovered*, the auditor will report the breach" (emphasis added). This concentration on the reporting stage leaves open the mechanisms by which the auditor decides how to use her available audit technologies.

Suppose, for instance, that (1) or (2) do not hold, implying that the auditor will not report truthfully. Knowing this, what incentive should the auditor have to deliver a high-quality audit effort in the first place? Even if she gained knowledge of problems in the firm's accounting system, she would still give in to the pressure of management. But without audit effort, no breach can be discovered, there is nothing to report, and viewed from an *ex post* perspective, the above definition is not applicable.

Even if (1) or (2) are satisfied, there remains the question of audit effort. Providing a high-quality audit level causes the auditor to incur audit costs, which she will then weigh against any potential advantages. In DeAngelo's quasirent framework, due to the competition in the audit market those advantages can hardly come from new clients. However, they may stem from the reduction of potential losses of future quasirents that arise if audit failures become known to the public. In such a case it is not only the ratio Q/S that is relevant for auditor independence but also the absolute magnitude of S and/or Q, since the difference of the values appearing in (1) largely determines the net benefit of more audit effort that has to be compared to the additional audit costs.

Moreover, the relevance of audit failures depends critically on the probability of whether or not the financial accounts are manipulated. From an *ex ante* point of view, the auditor need not fear large losses if she expects only a small probability of errors. However, those errors are largely the result of intentional misrepresentation by the client firm's management. Should the manager expect a low audit effort, he might choose to increase his manipulation efforts in order to receive personal benefits that are somehow connected to the firm's earnings (e.g. bonus payments, lower cost of capital, and so on). Obviously, a game-theoretic situation arises, which is characterized by strategic interdependencies between manager and auditor.

In the remainder of this section I use a simple game-theoretic model to present an idea of how the quasirent framework may be supplemented by incorporating strategic interdependencies[16] and what conclusions can then be derived for an analysis of NAS. My intention here is not to present a complete theory including all possible relationships. Rather the model serves as an illustration to show why it may be worthwhile to broaden the scenario of the existing bonding approaches and what new results might emerge from such an analysis.

The model has two players (manager and auditor), and each player has two actions that are unobservable respectively. The manager's actions are "manipulation" (m) and "admissible accounting" (a). The manager receives a base utility level of U by choosing a. In the case of an undetected manipulation, he reaps an additional bonus of $B > 0$, while he suffers from losses $L > 0$ if action m is revealed.[17]

The auditor's choice is between "high audit effort" (h) and "low audit effort" (l). Action h is essentially a perfect audit technology that puts the auditor in a position to detect any irregularities with certainty, but no errors can be detected if she only uses action l. If the auditor delivers effort l, her net audit fees (i.e. audit fees net of audit costs for level l) are represented by F. The high audit effort h leads to incremental audit costs denoted by C. If the auditor chooses action h and there is an error in the accounting system, the auditor discovers this breach and must decide how to report it. Assuming that relation (1) holds, the auditor will report the breach truthfully, that is the auditor is independent in the sense of the DeAngelo definition given above. If the auditor uses action l, she has no evidence for any possible irregularities and issues an unqualified report.

Given this scenario, the game can be represented as shown in Table 4.3.1.

Table 4.3.1. Payoffs for the auditor–manager game

Auditor–Manager	a	m
l	(F, U)	$(F - p \cdot d \cdot S, U + B)$
h	$(F - C, U)$	$(F - C - t \cdot Q, U - L)$

For each pair of auditor–manager actions, the parentheses in Table 4.3.1 show the values of the respective objective function of the auditor (first expression) and the manager (second expression).[18] Clearly, the assumption that inequality (1) holds is not sufficient to ensure that the auditor may find it profitable to choose effort h. Should it be the case that

$$0 < p \cdot d \cdot S - t \cdot Q < C$$

holds, then Table 4.3.1 shows that the auditor's dominant strategy is to always deliver low audit effort, which would in turn cause the manager to always opt for action m. Thus, to give auditing a chance to improve financial reporting at all, I assume that the following inequality is satisfied:

$$p \cdot d \cdot S - t \cdot Q > C \tag{6}$$

However, it is straightforward to check that with inequality (6) there is no Nash equilibrium in pure strategies. The only remaining equilibrium is one in mixed strategies for both players. For those strategies to be individually rational, each player must be indifferent between his/her pure strategies, which is essentially a condition for the probabilities by which the respective other player takes his/her actions.

Let α denote the probability of the auditor taking high audit effort h in equilibrium (thus $(1 - \alpha)$ is the probability of effort l), and let β depict the equilibrium probability of the manager manipulating the accounts (thus $(1 - \beta)$ is the probability of action a). The mixed-strategy equilibrium of this game is then characterized by:[19]

$$\alpha = \frac{B}{B + L} \tag{7}$$

$$\beta = \frac{C}{p \cdot d \cdot S - t \cdot Q} \tag{8}$$

The quality of the ensuing financial accounts can be represented by the probability Pf that they are free of errors after performing the audit, which is given by:

$$Pf = 1 - \beta \cdot (1 - \alpha) \tag{9}$$

Notice that in equilibrium the arguments of the auditor's decision problem (audit costs, quasirents, and the like) influence the manager's manipulation strategy β. Since NAS modify these arguments, they have consequences for the quality of the final accounts. To illustrate, I again consider the special case of a homogenous client base. Including NAS then leads to the following expression for the manager's policy β_N (CN denotes auditing costs if NAS are also offered and possible spillover effects occur):

$$\beta_N = \frac{CN}{QN \cdot (n \cdot p \cdot d - t)} \tag{10}$$

Equation (10) shows that given any value for CN and QN, the size n of the client base lowers the probability of manipulation implying *ceteris paribus* a higher accounting quality Pf for larger audit firms. This result is consistent with the related result for the original DeAngelo model, but for somewhat different reasons.

However, some new results emerge for NAS. As (5) shows, for the approach taken in Beck et al. (1988) NAS have no direct effect for independence with homogenous clients, since the auditor's tradeoff at the reporting stage remains unchanged. Although this result remains true in the current scenario, the situation changes because NAS exert an influence on the equilibrium strategy of the manager. According to (10), higher quasirents from additional NAS (QN > Q) lead to a lower probability of manipulation. Given all other parameters, this effect has a positive impact on the quality measure Pf. Furthermore, the effects of knowledge spillovers between auditing and NAS will lower the audit costs *vis-à-vis* the case without NAS (CN < C). This effect reinforces the positive influence of higher quasirents and leads to an additional decrease of the manager's probability of manipulation.

Taken together, the inclusion of strategic interdependencies does indeed provide some new insights. In the current independence debate, it therefore seems necessary to go beyond the reporting stage and to extend the analysis by incorporating the preceding actions of auditors and managers. As the above example shows, this approach may obviously lead to unexpected results for the NAS question. The model implies that higher quasirents resulting from additional NAS offers by auditors need not be detrimental for accounting quality. In fact, they may lead to a higher quality of a firm's financial disclosures. This implication is not due to any direct results of consulting services, since the specific details of these services have not been explicitly modeled. It depends entirely on incentive considerations in a strategic audit setting in which the incentives are influenced by quasirents and audit costs, which in turn depend on NAS.[20]

If we assume that a manipulation of accounts may be measured, for instance by discretionary accruals, then we can also derive empirical implications from such an analysis. Given this proxy, the above result implies that higher NAS should be associated with lower discretionary accruals. However, I note that strictly speaking this result holds only under the assumption of homogenous clients. With heterogeneous clients, the denominator of (8) may decrease for some clients, which would give rise to a higher probability of manipulation. However, given the existence of knowledge spillovers, there is now a clear countervailing effect due to lower audit costs (i.e. the nominator of (8)). Although I certainly cannot rule out that this effect is insufficient to compensate for a possible negative influence of quasirents, a resulting net decrease in the quality measure Pf need not be large in those instances. Thus, it is not unreasonable to expect that in a cross-sectional analysis, a negative association between NAS and discretionary accruals can arise.

2.3. Models with explicit side-payments

If we suspect that NAS may enhance collusion between management and auditors, it would be helpful to look for models analyzing direct collusive behavior in auditing. Although several models of this type do indeed exist, they rarely deal with the issue of NAS in an explicit way. The models have their respective origins in very different theoretical frameworks.

2.3.1. Approaches based on principal–agent theory

Models from the principal–agent (PA) framework extend the basic two-person scenario of PA theory by assuming that due to its unobservability the outcome is not available for contracting purposes.[21] Consequently, the principal suffers from contracting restrictions that negatively affect risk sharing and motivation. To overcome this problem, the agent's message regarding the outcome must be audited by an auditor. The auditor is modeled as a rational third party whose effort is also unobservable. The principal designs a contract with both the agent (manager) and the auditor, taking into account the incentives for each party and the need for risk sharing.

As was first shown by Antle (1982, 1984), this contract induces a sub-game between agent and auditor that may give rise to many different equilibria. In the case of implicit collusion both players act noncooperatively. At the same time they recognize that there may exist equilibria with shirking that could lead to higher utilities for both players than the equilibrium preferred by the principal. In this case, there is the danger that agent and auditor somehow coordinate their choices to the principal's detriment.[22] But this coordination only occurs implicitly, that is not via direct communications and/or commitments. Further, it concerns only the auditor's audit effort and her reporting strategy. In this scenario, there is not even a hint of NAS.

The situation becomes slightly different if explicit collusion in the form of side-payments between agent and auditor is allowed. This scenario is studied in Antle (1984) and Baiman et al. (1991). In these studies, to receive a favorable audit report the manager actively offers undercover payments (unobservable for the principal) to the auditor. The principal's problem is to design the contracts in such a way as to prevent explicit collusion between agent and auditor. That NAS may somehow be related to this type of analysis is most clearly expressed by Antle (1984: 16) who states, "the concern over management advisory service contracts may have arisen, at least in part, from the fear that managements could use these contracts as a vehicle for side-payments."

However, from a conceptual point of view this is no genuine theory of NAS. The papers cited above provide theories of how a principal should optimally deal with the danger of side-payments, and it is clear from the outset that this direct collusion can never improve the principal's utility. Thus, invoking NAS is at best a kind of story about one possible mechanism of undercover payments, and the structure of the models definitely rule out any advantages that NAS might have. This procedure is much the same as directly assuming that NAS can only be detrimental. This conclusion is reinforced by observing that the interpretation of NAS as a vehicle for undercover payments implicitly assumes that the fees for NAS are unobservable (since such payments are assumed to be unobservable for the principal). Should this not be the case, then we must assume that any NAS assignments are essentially useless in order to keep the models' structure intact.

2.3.2. Models based on quasirents

The approaches in this category focus again on aspects of quasirents, but within scenarios that differ from DeAngelo's approach. Dye (1991) employs a two-period model in which the manager (not the auditor) has all the bargaining power with respect to audit fees. Should quasirents be observable, investors would be skeptical about the quality of the firm's accounts. To avoid these problems, the manager optimally sets audit fees always equal to audit costs, thus eliminating any quasirents.

This result no longer holds if quasirents are not observable. Dye (1991) shows that at the end of the first period, it may be optimal for the manager to offer unobservable quasirents to the auditor in exchange for a favorable audit report. Here, quasirents are a direct result of collusion between manager and auditor, and they essentially constitute a kind of undercover payment.

Another view on quasirents and side-payments is offered by Lee and Gu (1998). In their model, the owner has the right to engage and fire the auditor. The owner's problem is to motivate the manager to work hard, but again the output is not observable. Thus, an auditor is engaged whose task is to observe the outcome and to report her findings truthfully. However, the manager can offer unobservable side-payments to the auditor for a favorable report.

Lee and Gu (1998) analyze two types of audit contracts. The flat-fee contract consists of a constant fee over time, while a lowballing scheme includes a lower initial fee followed by higher fees in the future. The lowballing contract has the advantage that it increases the minimum side-payment that the manager has to offer in order to make collusion advantageous for the auditor. This lower bound can be set in such a way that it exceeds the maximum amount that the manager is willing to offer as side-payment. In this view, quasirents are actually beneficial for independence, albeit within a special governance structure.

It should be clear from this brief description that for NAS the same objections apply as in the previous section. Again, NAS are not more than a possible story for side-payments, and regarding audit quality the models definitely preclude any positive aspect of NAS because side-payments cannot have any positive effects.

2.3.3. Models considering an optimal level of NAS

Lange (1994) presents a model where the level of NAS is assessed from an owner's point of view. However, the manager is in the position to directly engage the auditor for auditing and NAS. The owner does not know the level of the manager's loyalty. A loyal manager always acts in the owner's interest and demands NAS to an extent compatible with the owner's objective of profit maximization (in this case the model contains synergies for offering auditing as well as NAS). A disloyal manager acts in his own interest, tries to misappropriate assets, and strives to bribe the auditor in exchange for a favorable report. This bribe is accomplished by using a fictitious consulting contract under which the auditor receives a payment but does not provide any real services. Thus, this example exactly reflects the case of useless NAS activities mentioned above, since NAS are essentially a kind of undercover payment to the disloyal manager. The owner's objective function consists of the expected benefits of auditing and consulting, where the expectation is taken over the probability distribution of loyalty. Because the model contains positive as well as negative aspects of NAS, it comes as no surprise that there is some optimal level of NAS.[23]

The model shows that even the extreme interpretation of NAS (as mere undercover payments without tangible economic benefits to the firm) does not rule out advantages for the owner, which is essentially due to the knowledge spillovers that at least in part accrue to the firm in the case of loyalty. However, without such economies of scope, NAS again cannot have any beneficial effects in this model.

A caveat of this model is that all relations are given as exogenous functions. Moreover, it begs the question why even a disloyal manager should not have an interest to demand NAS levels that are advantageous for the firm. Thus, the model cannot address the important case where NAS is actually demanded by the firm's management, but nevertheless there is a danger of manipulated financial accounts.

3. Empirical work

Surveys of empirical research (e.g. Lange 1994: 46–62; Beattie et al. 1999: 71–6; and Ryan et al. 2001: 377–83) on issues of independence and NAS are mostly concerned with the relation between audit and NAS fees as well as with the so-called perception research. These studies use questionnaires and/or behavioral experiments to discern the perceptions of various groups (e.g. auditors, bankers, financial analysts, investors, and so on) on the influence of NAS on auditor independence. Thus, this work essentially covers the aspect of "independence in appearance." The results of this research are inconclusive. Summarizing these studies, Ryan et al. (2001: 380) state that the effects "of consulting services on users' perceptions of independence are mixed, but point toward financial statement users believing that relatively small amounts of consulting services have little effect on auditor independence and actually increase auditor competence."

In the remainder of this section I concentrate on somewhat differ-ent and more recent empirical work that addresses the relationships among NAS, accounting accruals, and auditor opinions, which has (to my knowledge) not been reviewed before.

3.1. NAS and discretionary accruals

Empirical research on the relation between NAS and accruals has been stimulated by the new Securities Exchange Commission (SEC) rules on independence that were issued in November 2000 and became effective in 2001. These rules require the disclosure of NAS fees and thus enable empirical examinations of the relations between NAS and various other variables using U.S. data. In an almost direct response to these rules, several working papers quickly appeared that made use of the first dis-closures of NAS data. At the time of this writing, none of these papers has been published in any journal, but they are available from the SSRN online database. They are almost exclusively concerned with the relation between NAS and total, discretionary, and/or abnormal accruals. How-ever, one paper considers qualified audit opinions (see the next section for this approach). The basic hypothesis in these papers is that more independent auditors should restrict the firms' earnings management, and if NAS compromises auditor independence, then higher NAS should be associated with higher accruals.

The findings of this research are mixed. Although Chung and Kallapur (2001) do not find any significant relationships, Dee et al. (2002) and Frankel et al. (2002) find a positive relation between NAS and discre-tionary accruals. This finding would be consistent with the fear that higher NAS might negatively influence auditor independence.

However, Ashbaugh et al. (2002) raise methodological concerns regarding these results and reexamine the data using a refined methodo-logy. They document a negative relation between NAS and their measure of discretionary accruals, which would contradict a negative influence of NAS on independence.

Antle et al. (2002) raise two further objections. First, the recent U.S. data are all clustered in the year 2001, which may impede more gen-eral conclusions from the data. Second, they stress that in reality, auditing, NAS, and accounting accruals are expected to result from comprehensive and complex optimizations. Therefore, it is necessary to incorporate this simultaneity into an empirical study. To deal with these issues, Antle et al. (2002) concentrate their analysis on U.K. data (where the disclosure of NAS fees has been mandated since 1992) and use a simultaneous-equation approach. For the U.K. data they find a negative relation between NAS and abnormal accruals. Their results also hold in preliminary tests that use U.S. data.

Thus, the results are clearly inconclusive if viewed in total. However, the methodologically most sophisticated studies definitely run counter to the conventional wisdom that NAS may impair auditor independence. In fact, the contrary seems to hold. With the current arguments this finding is hard to explain. Antle et al. (2002: 15) do it best by invoking productive effects for the auditee stemming from auditors' knowledge spillovers. However, as Antle et al. (2002: 8) admit, "there seems no particular reason why economies of scope should be related to abnormal accruals, *ceteris paribus*."

But some explanation can be provided by looking at the game-theoretic extension of the bonding scenario presented above. Considering the strategic interdependencies reveals that it is not unreasonable to expect that NAS may decrease the managers' probability of manipulation, which should in turn be associated with lower abnormal and/or discretionary accruals. This explanatory potential should encourage further development of this approach.

3.2. NAS and auditors' qualification decisions

A second category of empirical papers concentrates on direct outputs of auditing as manifested in the auditors' reports. The hypothesis is that a qualified report may be detrimental for the auditor due to a greater likelihood of the auditee changing its auditor and the resulting loss of quasirents. If NAS impairs independence, the propensity of auditors to issue qualified opinions should decrease. With a few exceptions, the papers in this category use Australian data, where the publication of fees for NAS has been mandatory for several decades. Moreover, the papers often concentrate on qualifications with respect to "critical" situations, that is qualifications relating to the going concern status or for firms that are "financially distressed" (e.g. being measured by losses).

The first papers for the Australian market yielded mixed results. Although Barkess and Simnett (1994) cannot find any significant result,

Wines (1994) detects a negative relation between NAS and qualified opinions, consistent with the hypothesis of impaired independence.

However, Craswell (1999) criticizes Wines's (1994) approach for its methodological deficiencies. Using more control variables and data from almost all listed Australian firms, Craswell (1999) cannot fail to find any significant relations between NAS and qualified reports.

This result has been confirmed by Craswell et al. (2002), who use data from both local and nationwide audit offices. The DeFond et al. (2002) study of the U.S. market finds that NAS do not have any significant impact on going-concern opinions, but that the sum of audit and nonaudit fees is positively associated with the propensity to issue a going-concern qualification.[24] In the abstract of their paper, the authors interpret their findings as indicating that "recent SEC regulations based on concerns that non-audit services impair auditor independence, are unfounded."

One caveat of these papers is that they cannot control for the real situation of the auditee. We can observe qualified or unqualified opinions, but what cannot be observed is whether these opinions conform to what the auditor really knows about the respective situation. An audit failure only arises if the auditor knows that a qualification is actually required, but refrains from doing so.

In order to somehow control for this case, Sharma and Sidhu (2001) consider Australian firms that have gone bankrupt and have been delisted from the market. They study the auditors' going-concern reports in the year immediately preceding bankruptcy and advance the hypothesis that the respective auditors should have been aware of this critical situation. They find a negative relation between NAS and the propensity to qualify. This finding is consistent with a negative impact of NAS on auditor independence. However, their study covers only forty-nine firms. It seems problematic to draw more general conclusions due to the small sample size.

Similar to the accrual studies, this category also shows an entire spectrum of results, which can hardly be explained by current arguments. The lack of a convincing explanation is especially true for the findings of Sharma and Sidhu (2001). If the auditor really knows that the auditee will almost certainly go bankrupt in the near future (which is the stated hypothesis of the authors), what incentive should she have to compromise her independence from an NAS standpoint? The probability that the auditor will receive any benefits from future NAS is only marginal, while there is a high danger of losses in reputation and possible damages from litigation.

In the going-concern case, the game-theoretic model extension presented above is not really applicable. For example, if we interpret the manager's action m as inducing going-concern problems, it is hard to imagine what advantages the manager receives even if this policy should go undetected. Thus, the manager's dominant strategy would be action a, and any strategic interdependencies disappear. In addition, the need to issue a going-concern qualification may arise independently from the manager's policy. This possibility is not included in the model's scenario. Thus, there is clearly a need to extend the analytical approach.[25]

4. Conclusions and implications for future research

This chapter reviews and extends theoretical research on the relation between NAS and auditor independence. In addition, it presents a survey of the most recent empirical papers on these issues.

To summarize, there is no evidence that a simultaneous offering of auditing and NAS to the same client may unequivocally and systematically impair auditor independence. Although there are some results implying that NAS could decrease independence, there is also strong theoretical and empirical evidence that NAS may be beneficial for both the final quality of the audit and the audited financial statements. Thus, the ban on offering NAS given by the SOA cannot be founded on results of current research. For the regulatory discussions that currently take place in Europe, I cannot recommend a simple transfer of the recent U.S. rules.

However, the chapter also shows that the current research on NAS and auditing leaves much to be desired. Despite the importance that has unanimously been attributed to NAS for many decades, there is surprisingly little conceptual knowledge regarding the specific relationships and interdependencies by which NAS, auditing, and reporting are intertwined. As my discussion makes clear, the development of hypotheses and the explanation of empirical results in this area may benefit from more theoretical research. What is needed is a comprehensive conceptual approach that links demand, supply, and incentive effects of auditing and NAS. In addition, results that emerge from such analyses should be combined with other research dealing with auditors' incentives (e.g. research on auditor liability), which would provide a comprehensive picture of relevant effects.

The fact that, despite the regulatory importance worldwide, there is currently a relatively small body of theoretical research on bundling NAS, and auditing is evidence that the difficulties of constructing informative models capable of addressing these issues are larger than they are in other areas. Moreover, should the SOA be viewed as a "final" regulatory solution to the NAS problem in the United States, it seems unlikely that (due to the responsiveness of the recent U.S. research on regulatory discussions) more significant research on NAS issues will come from the U.S. scene. Thus, I suspect that further theoretical developments will have to come from elsewhere. In any case, the incentive problems of combining NAS and auditing are still an open issue, from both the theoretical and the empirical side.

Notes

I would like to thank Christian Ernst and Alfred Wagenhofer for valuable comments. Of course, I am responsible for all remaining errors.

[1] The aspect of enforcement of standards by means of auditing and governance rules has always been emphasized in the work of Dieter Ordelheide. See, for example, his comments with respect to the debate on issues of international accounting in Ordelheide (1996, 1998).

[2] However, the discussions concerning the basic contents of the EU recommendation preceded the Enron case. Modifications with respect to Enron were included only in the final stage before its publication.

[3] Possible implications of the SOA for Germany are, for example, discussed in Lanfermann and Maul 2002.

[4] Revsine (2002: 138–9) even calls it a "benefit" of the Enron case that people could be convinced that "drastic" improvements in auditor independence are necessary, and he welcomes the proposals that later appeared in the SOA. Critical opinions regarding these regulatory actions are relatively rare. In a short comment on the Enron case, Demski (2002: 130) states that one should "not rush to embrace new regulatory structure," because he has doubts that the misstatements represent a "system" problem.

[5] According to Benston and Hartgraves (2002: 107), Andersen received $25 million for auditing and $27 million for NAS in 2000.

[6] Demski (2002: 130) and Largay (2002: 154) make similar points.

[7] The results of many studies that appeared until 2000 are summarized in Ryan et al. (2001).

[8] Of course, there is some analytical research that combines aspects of auditing and consulting. Antle and Demski (1991) present a formal theory of possible contracting advantages by simultaneously offering audit and consulting services, but their model completely neglects aspects of independence. Gigler and Penno (1995) model the consequences of imperfect competition between audit firms for the client's demand for consulting services, but they also are silent on the independence issue.

[9] The papers of Beattie et al. (1999) and Ryan et al. (2001) exclusively deal with empirical work. The report by Antle et al. (1997) considers some theoretical aspects, but the main arguments come from the empirical side.

[10] Antle (1999) also stresses this point with respect to the role of conceptual research for the debate on independence.

[11] A review of related approaches can be found in Ewert (1999: 61–94) and Wagenhofer and Ewert (2003: 425–68).

[12] This fact also holds for some other models of quasirents. Kanodia and Mukherji (1994) analyze the process of fee determination using a mechanism-design approach, where the client has the bargaining power but there is asymmetric information about audit costs. The optimal contract offered to the incumbent entails quasirents with positive probability, which again disappear at the time of the initial audit. Gigler and Penno (1995) consider the basic scenario of DeAngelo, but now there are cost differences between audit firms with respect to current audit costs. The optimal cost-matching between the client and auditors may, however, change stochastically over time. This situation also leads to the existence of economic benefits for incumbent auditors. Both approaches provide alternative explanations for the existence of quasirents, but again, there is no direct consideration of possible consequences for auditor reporting decisions.

[13] This intuitive kind of reasoning has been criticized by Magee and Tseng (1990). They present a more formal analysis of the auditor's incentives for misreporting by identifying the conditions that are necessary to make the manager's threat credible. They qualify DeAngelo's model and show that in many situations, there is actually no problem for auditor independence despite the existence of positive quasirents.

[14] Knowledge spillovers can, of course, go in either direction, see for example Simunic (1984: 688) and for further analysis Ostrowski and Söder (1999).

[15] The following arguments have already been advanced in Ewert (1990: 196–8). See also Arruñada (1999: 84–6) for a similar analysis.

[16] The model is in the spirit of the approaches in Magee (1980), Fellingham and Newman (1985), and Ewert (1993). Surveys of game-theoretic approaches to auditing can be found, for example, in Ewert and Stefani (2001a) and Wagenhofer and Ewert (2003: 399–419).

[17] These arguments may be explained by various factors. See for a detailed discussion of these aspects Ewert (1993).

[18] For the entries for the manager, the assumption of a positive B implies that the manager reaps net benefits from an undetected manipulation of the accounts, that is his advantages outweigh possible disadvantages that may accrue to him if (with probability p) the accounting failures become known in the future.

[19] See for example the derivation in Ewert (1993: 734–6).

[20] Of course, there is no doubt that the model is of a restricted nature due to the assumptions employed. For instance, the only source of accounting failures is from management's manipulation, the auditor's technology is perfect, the entries in the four cells of Table 4.3.1 appear only in a very general manner, etc. However, the purpose of the model is not to fully present a complete approach, but to show a potential avenue for extending current analyses.

[21] Detailed reviews of these models are beyond the scope of this chapter. They can be found in Ewert (1990: 39–165) and Ewert and Stefani (2001b).

[22] See for possible contracting solutions to this problem Sen (1988) and Yost (1995).

[23] This conclusion can also be found in Böcking and Löcke (1997) with somewhat different arguments.

[24] Lennox (1999) obtains similar but only weak evidence for U.K. data.

[25] Matsumura et al. (1997) present a game-theoretic analysis of going-concern problems by including a replacement auditor and considering the manager's decision to possibly switch the auditor. However, this model is not concerned with the issue of NAS.

References

Antle, R. (1982). "The auditor as an economic agent," *Journal of Accounting Research*, 20(2): 503–27.

—— (1984). "Auditor independence," *Journal of Accounting Research*, 22(1): 1–20.

—— (1999). "Accounting firms, the accounting industry, and accounting research," *British Accounting Review*, 31: 1–13.

—— and Demski, J. (1991). "Contracting frictions, regulation, and the structure of CPA firms," *Journal of Accounting Research* 29(Supplement): 1–24.

—— Gordon, E. A., Narayanamoorthy, G., and Zhou, L. (2002). "The joint determination of audit fees, non-audit fees, and abnormal accruals." Yale University. Available from www.ssrn.com.

—— Griffin, P. A., Teece, D. J., and Williamson, O. E. (1997). "'An economic analysis of auditor independence for a multi-client, multi-service public accounting firm.' A report prepared on behalf of the AICPA in connection with the presentation to the Independence Standards Board of 'Serving the public interest: A new conceptual framework for auditor independence.'" Downloadable at http://ftp.aicpa.org/public/download/members/div/secps/isb/0117194.doc.

Ashbaugh, H., LaFond, R., and Mayhew, B. W. (2002). "Do non-audit services compromise auditor independence? Further evidence." University of Wisconsin, Madison. Available from www.ssrn.com.

Arruñada, B. (1999). *The economics of audit quality* (Boston, Dordrecht, London: Kluwer).

Baiman, S., Evans, J. H., and Nagarajan, N. J. (1991). "Collusion in auditing," *Journal of Accounting Research*, 29(1): 1–18.

Barkess, R. and Simnett, L. (1994). "The provision of other services by auditors: Independence and pricing issues," *Accounting and Business Research*, 24: 99–108.

Beattie, V., Brandt, R., and Fearnley, S. (1999). "Perceptions of auditor independence: U.K. evidence," *Journal of International Accounting, Auditing & Taxation*, 8(1): 67–107.

Beck, P. J., Frecka, T. J., and Solomon, I. (1988). "A model of the market for MAS and audit services: Knowledge spillovers and auditor-auditee bonding," *Journal of Accounting Literature*, 7: 50–64.

Benston, G. J. and Hartgraves, A. L. (2002). "Enron: What happened and what we can learn from it," *Journal of Accounting and Public Policy*, 21: 105–27.

Böcking, H. J. and Löcke, J. (1997). "Abschlußprüfung und Beratung," *Die Betriebswirtschaft*, 57: 461–74.

Chung, H. and Kallapur, S. (2001). "Client importance, non-audit services, and abnormal accruals." Purdue University. Available from www.ssrn.com.

Craswell, A. T. (1999). "Does the provision of non-audit services impair auditor independence?" *International Journal of Auditing*, 3: 29–40.

——, Stokes, D. J., and Laughton, J. (2002). "Auditor independence and fee dependence," *Journal of Accounting and Economics*, 33: 253–75.

DeAngelo, L. (1981a). "Auditor independence, 'low balling,' and disclosure regulation," *Journal of Accounting and Economics*, 3: 113–27.

—— (1981b). "Auditor size and audit quality," *Journal of Accounting and Economics*, 3: 183–99.

Dee, C. C., Lulseged, A., and Nowlin, T. S. (2002). "Earnings quality and auditor independence: An examination using non-audit fee data." Virginia Commonwealth University. Available from: www.ssrn.com.

DeFond, M. L., Raghunandan, K., and Subramanyam, K. R. (2002). "Do non-audit service fees impair auditor independence? Evidence from going concern audit opinions." University of Southern California. Available from www.ssrn.com.

262   RALF EWERT

Demski, J. (2002). "Enron et al.—A comment," *Journal of Accounting and Public Policy*, 21: 129–30.

Dye, R. (1991). "Informationally motivated auditor replacement," *Journal of Accounting and Economics*, 14: 347–74.

EU Commission (2002). *Statutory Auditors' Independence in the EU: A Set of Fundamental Principles*. Brussels.

Ewert, R. (1990). *Wirtschaftsprüfung und asymmetrische Information* (Berlin, Heidelberg: Springer).

—— (1993). "Rechnungslegung, Wirtschaftsprüfung, rationale Akteure und Märkte," *Zeitschrift für betriebswirtschaftliche Forschung*, 45: 715–47.

—— (1999). "Wirtschaftsprüfung und ökonomische Theorie—Ein selektiver Überblick," in M. Richter (ed.), *Theorie und Praxis der Wirtschaftsprüfung II* (Berlin: Schmidt), 35–99.

—— and Stefani, U. (2001a). "Wirtschaftsprüfung," in P. J. Jost (ed.), *Die Spieltheorie in der Betriebswirtschaftslehre* (Stuttgart: Schäffer-Poeschel), 175–217.

—— —— (2001b). "Wirtschaftsprüfung," in P. J. Jost (ed.), *Die Prinzipal-Agenten-Theorie in der Betriebswirtschaftslehre* (Stuttgart: Schäffer-Poeschel), 147–82.

Fellingham, J. C. and Newman, D. P. (1985). "Strategic considerations in auditing," *The Accounting Review*, 60(4): 634–50.

Frankel, R. M., Johnson, M. F., and Nelson, K. K. (2002). "The Relation Between Auditors' Fees for Non-Audit Services and Earnings Quality." MIT Sloan School of Management. Available from www.ssrn.com.

Gigler, F. and Penno, M. (1995). "Imperfect competition in audit markets and its effect on the demand for audit-related services," *The Accounting Review*, 70(2): 317–36.

Kanodia, C. and Mukherji, A. (1994). "Audit pricing, lowballing, and auditor turnover: A dynamic analysis," *The Accounting Review*, 69(4): 593–615.

Lanfermann, G. and Maul, S. (2002). "Auswirkungen des Sarbanes-Oxley Acts in Deutschland," *Der Betrieb*, 55(34): 1725–32.

Lange, S. (1994). *Die Kompatibilität von Abschlußprüfung und Beratung* (Frankfurt Lang).

Largay, J. A. III (2002). "Lessons from Enron," *Accounting Horizons*, 16(2): 153–6.

Lee, C.-W. J. and Gu, Z. (1998). "Low balling, legal liability, and auditor independence," *The Accounting Review*, 73(4): 533–55.

Lennox, C. (1999). "Non-audit fees, disclosure, and audit quality," *European Accounting Review*, 8(2): 239–52.

Magee, R. P. (1980). "Regulation and the cost effectiveness of independent audits," in J. W. Buckley and J. F. Weston (eds.), *Regulation and the accounting profession* (Belmont:), 163–77.

—— and Tseng, M.-C. (1990). "Audit pricing and independence," *The Accounting Review*, 65(2): 315–36.

Matsumura, E. M., Subramanyam, K. R., and Tucker, R. R. (1997). "Strategic auditor behavior and going-concern-decisions," *Journal of Business Finance and Accounting*, 24: 727–58.

Ordelheide, D. (1996). "Internationalisierung der Rechnungslegung deutscher Unternehmen," *Die Wirtschaftsprüfung*, 49: 545–52.

—— (1998). "Wettbewerb der Rechnungslegungssysteme IAS, US-GAAP und HGB," in C. Börsig and A. G. Coenenberg (eds.), *Controlling und Rechnungswesen im internationalen Wettbewerb* (Stuttgart: Schäffer-Poeschel), 15–53.

Ostrowski, M. and Söder, B. H. (1999). "Der Einfluß von Beratungsaufträgen auf die Unabhängigkeit des Abschlußprüfers," *Betriebswirtschaftliche Forschung und Praxis*, 51: 554–64.

Revsine, L. (2002). "Enron: Sad but inevitable," *Journal of Accounting and Public Policy*, 21: 137–45.

Ryan, S. G., Herz, R. H., Iannaconi, T. E., Maines, L. A., Palepu, K., Schrand, C., Skinner, D. J., and Vincent, L. (2001). "SEC auditor independence requirements," *Accounting Horizons*, 15(4): 373–86.

Sen, K. (1988). "Using an augmented revelation mechanism to resolve tacit collusion in auditing," *Journal of Accounting, Auditing and Finance*, 13: 99–116.

Sharma, D. S. and Sidhu, J. (2001). "Professionalism vs commercialism: The association between non-audit services and audit independence," *Journal of Business Finance & Accounting*, 28(5): 595–629.

Simunic, D. A. (1984). "Auditing, consulting, and auditor independence," *Journal of Accounting Research*, 22: 679–702.

Wagenhofer, A. and Ewert, R. (2003). *Externe Unternehmensrechnung* (Berlin et al.: Springer).

Wines, G. (1994). "Auditor independence, audit qualifications, and the provision of non-audit services: A note," *Accounting and Finance*, 34: 75–86.

Yost, J. A. (1995). "Auditor independence as a unique equilibrium response," *Journal of Accounting, Auditing and Finance*, 20: 81–102.

On the Politics and Standard-Setting of Accounting

The Role of Accounting in Society and Constituent Lobbying

5.1

The Politics of Accounting: A Framework

Dieter Ordelheide

1. Preliminary remarks

Accounting is a societal institution. Admittedly, when we discuss the purchase method to account for acquisitions, the deferral method to calculate deferred taxes or the accrual method to value pension reserves, accounting techniques tend to supersede any thoughts about the political dimension. However, the political dimension becomes obvious when we jointly consider all the methods that go into the preparation of financial statements. Accounting is concerned with nothing less than the conceptualization of capital, its concrete expression in numbers, as well as its budgeting and monitoring, and thus with a societal institution that is so central to our economic system that it has given it its name. Even though today we speak of the "market economy," it is evident that the rules by which capital or income are determined are among the central institutions of our economic system. These rules are politico-economic because they are means by which societal groups can alter and improve their economic situation.

Those who have devoted themselves to the study of the politics of accounting probably agree with this assertion. But doesn't the antithesis, that accounting is essentially apolitical, have more merit than we are willing to admit? Accounting has served many and varied political systems throughout history. According to the archaeologist, Schmandt-Besserat, clay figures such as spheres, cones, discs, and pyramids that have been excavated in Syria, Turkey, Israel, Iraq, and other countries of the Near East, the oldest of which have been dated to 8000 B.C., were employed in a system of accounting. Mattessich is convinced that they were used in a "prototype" of double-entry bookkeeping as far back as roughly 3200 B.C. But even if you date the origin of accounting to a later period and that of double-entry bookkeeping to Northern Italy in the fourteenth and fifteenth centuries, no one would deny that accounting has a very long history. However, if we speak of "accounting," independently of the historical periods in which accounting was used, this language implies a certain identity or time-invariant concept. That is, there is "something" that has survived the transition from the urban via the national to the global economy; the transition from agriculture via industrialization to the Information Age; the transition from mercantilism via the Manchester School and socialism to a social market economy; and the transition from the clay figures in the Near East via handwritten ledgers to the hard drive of a PC—an essential core remains that we call "accounting."

Can anyone imagine a "politics of the wheel"? Alas it does not exist. Is not our accounting—like the wheel—a human invention that, admittedly, has been slightly adapted over the course of time, but which nevertheless satisfies such fundamental human needs that it is, at its core, basically independent of the political organization of society? But isn't then a political theory of accounting as marginal as the contentious reporting issues for specific transactions with which accounting theory concerns itself?

In the political theory of accounting, the usual model of interaction between politics and accounting is that the political process changes accounting practice. Stakeholders comprise the active and accounting the reactive element—the "politics of accounting," where politics is the subject and accounting the object. One can also think of the relationship between politics and accounting in a different way. Instead of focusing only on the changes, one can choose to see the elements of accounting that always remain the same. Accounting is a big house that has accommodated many political regimes during the several hundred years of its existence without losing its identity—this perspective would result in the politics of accounting where accounting is the subject. Apparently, the same processes that change accounting also preserve its identity. What constitutes this identity and how has it been possible to preserve it over the centuries? I will return to this question in a future lecture.

Since the term "politics of accounting" is a rather vague one, I begin by providing a working definition. I then develop a framework for the politics of accounting. Subsequently, I examine the ontology of accounting and discuss its implications for the politics of accounting as a topic for research.

2. Politics of accounting: Shaping accounting as a societal institution

The politics of accounting unquestionably played an important role in the decision of the American Securities and Exchange Commission (SEC) to demand a particular organizational structure as part of the ongoing reforms of the International Accounting Standards Committee (IASC). But would you also count the depreciation policy of the British cruise operator P&O in the preparation of its financial statements or even this P. D. Leake chapter on the theme of politics of accounting as politics of accounting? These two examples alone make it quite clear that we are dealing with a rather vague phenomenon. Therefore I first explain what I mean by "politics of accounting." My aim is to elucidate in which sense politics of accounting will be the subject of this chapter.

Activities involving accounting have an impact on the welfare of a society and its members. Perhaps the effect is not always direct and is in some cases less pronounced than in others, but nonetheless every activity with which accounting is connected can somehow be seen to have social consequences. If we use this as our criterion, then the term "politics of accounting" would be all-encompassing, and would certainly include both this chapter and the drawing up of financial statements by the cruise operator P&O. Some British authors, for example Tinker, and also Hopwood and Miller as editors of *Accounting as a Social and Institutional Practice* seem to understand the term "politics of accounting" in a similarly broad sense. In contrast, I would like to limit myself to those activities meant to shape accounting as a societal institution; indeed I would limit myself even further by dealing with only those societal institutions that have, or can claim to have, practical significance on a national or international level. *The politics of accounting—as it is understood here—shapes accounting as a national or international institution.*

For example, whenever international organizations such as the European Union (EU) or the International Accounting Standards Board (IASB), or national bodies such as the German Bundestag, the British Accounting Standards Board (ASB), the French Conseil National de la Comptabilité (CNC), or the American Financial Accounting Standards Board (FASB) formulate accounting rules, governmental and quasi-governmental agencies, companies preparing financial statements, financial analysts and investment advisors, auditors and tax advisors, employees' representatives, accounting professors, lawyers, and other affected parties all make their influence felt. They propose changes or defend the status quo, comment on the suggestions of others, wield knowledge, money, and other instruments of power—all this to promote accounting rules that are as favorable to them as possible. Such activities, which people employ to influence national or international standards for the preparation, auditing, and disclosure of accounts, certainly belong to the politics of accounting.

Since I use the term "accounting" in the broad sense of the constitution of accounting, the organization of its regulation is likewise a subject for the politics of accounting. It determines to a large degree to what extent individuals or groups are able to contribute to the political process. Examples include the debates surrounding the establishment of the Review Panel in the United Kingdom, the legal recognition of a privately funded and organized Standards Committee in Germany, the change of FASB voting rules, and the reorganization of the IASC and, in particular, the proposed change in status of its board members.

The politics of accounting ends where the pure application of accounting begins. The politics of accounting shapes accounting as an institution. It tries to effect changes, prevent proposed changes, or subjects current accounting practice to scrutiny. In contrast, the application of accounting does not call current accounting practice into question. It operates within the framework of existing institutions, often without the individual practitioners' even being aware of this fact. It makes use of the existing structure and thus affirms it. In this respect, the application of accounting is the opposite of the politics of accounting. Politics shapes, while application employs and thereby reenforces the status quo.

I realize that the dividing line between politics and application is still a bit fuzzy, but it will suffice for my purposes. Some examples may help to clarify the problems involved. When the cruise operator P&O draws up its annual accounts according to British Accounting Standards, accounting is not shaped as an institution but rather merely applied. Conversely, when Daimler-Benz became the first German company to prepare its annual accounts according to U.S. Generally Accepted Accounting Principles (GAAP), this move involved not only the application of existing standards, but was also politics of accounting because it called the national institutions of accounting into question—successfully as it later turned out. During the hyperinflation of the 1930s in Germany, Fritz Schmidt developed his "Organic Theory" and propagated it in his Frankfurt lectures. This was politics of accounting, as I understand it. On the other hand, my Frankfurt lecture for undergraduates, "Introduction to accounting," is not, because in this lecture I merely present the existing institutions.

3. The ontology of accounting as a societal institution

Now that I have limited the term "politics of accounting," it needs to clarify what I understand by the term "accounting as a societal institution." I will answer this question in several steps. First, I propose that accounting, like other societal institutions, only exists because we think it or conceive of it. To formulate this idea somewhat provocatively, accounting exists because we believe it exists. I invoke this notion to demonstrate that the content of what we conceive of as accounting is determined by the functions that we associate with it. Accounting is an instrument, it is a means to an end, and it is these ends that imbue it with significance. Next, I argue that accounting becomes a societal institution when the parties involved share a common view of its functions, and accounting can only fulfill its functions provided that they are so shared. Moreover, accounting can only fulfill its functions in a complex interplay with other functions (and institutions) surrounding accounting. Finally, I assert that these functions have an implicitly normative character. From all of this it follows that values, desires, and utilities constitute accounting.

3.1. Accounting as a thought construct ("Denkmuster")

When we communicate about accounting, we speak as if there were "something" that existed outside of and apart from us. For example, we might say, "The European true-and-fair-view principle is embodied in Article 2 of the Fourth EU Council Directive"; or "Vodafones's financial statements are available on the Internet"; or "The chief accountant of the SEC is a powerful man in the world of US accounting." Thus, in formulating our comments, we as speakers do not enter into the picture at all. We speak about these and other elements of accounting exactly as we would about Mont Blanc, the Scottish Highlands, the Mississippi River, and all the other things that exist outside of us. We depersonalize. We objectify. Here we are, the ones who prepare the annual reports, the readers of those reports, auditors or university professors, and there is the true-and-fair-view principle, Vodafone's balance sheet, or the chief accountant of the SEC.

I do not intend to discuss why we speak in this way. I would merely like to highlight that this style of communication conceals the fundamental elements that constitute accounting. What we think of as "accounting" includes: companies' accounting systems; concepts such as assets, liabilities, profit, cash flow, balance sheet, profit and loss statement, segment reporting, the principle of the lower of cost or market; and additionally, the statutory or professional standards in which these concepts are articulated and the regulatory agencies along with their supporting organizations. They all exist in us only as "thought constructs" or "thought patterns."[1]

Admittedly, accounting has certain tangible aspects, such as: paper, on which computations and the norms upon which they are based are printed; letters, numbers, and other printed symbols; materials, from which computers are made and on which letters, numbers, and other symbols are stored; sounds, which people produce when they talk about accounting; and, indeed, the people involved in accounting themselves. Such tangible aspects, however, are not in and of themselves elements of accounting. They can only become elements of accounting if we bestow upon them the status of elements of accounting in our minds, as we do with, for example, the true-and-fair-view principle, General Electric's financial statements, and the chief accountant of the SEC.

I do not mean by this that we conceive of accounting in the same way as we form images of Mont Blanc, the Highlands, or the Mississippi River in our mind's eye. What I mean is that only because we mentally assign status to the physical aspects do the "true-and-fair-view principle," "General Electric's balance sheet," and the "chief accountant of the SEC" exist as elements of accounting. They exist within us only as intellectual or thought constructs. Being an element of accounting is not an inherent quality of these physical aspects that is independent of the individuals concerned; rather, this quality arises in the minds of those individuals. In other words, if we did not allocate a particular status to letters, numbers, and symbols as well as to individual instruments, accounting would not exist. It would not be a part of our world. In contrast, Mont Blanc, the Scottish Highlands, and the Mississippi River, like all observable objects in the natural world, exist without our conceptions of them, at least if one does not subscribe to a subjectivism in which the entire world exists only in the minds of individuals.

In the nineteenth century, the statement of sources and applications of funds, segment reporting, and the British ASB did not as yet exist. But why did it not exist? Because, for whatever reasons, the accounting experts of the day had not conceived of them yet, and not because they existed already but lay undiscovered, like for example the sixth moon of Jupiter. Accounting exists only because we conceive of it. A thought construct is a necessary prerequisite for accounting to exist, not the other way round.

As a consequence, the politics of accounting emerges from the thought constructs of those who shape accounting, and it is directed at the thought patterns of all of those who are involved in accounting. It is successful only if it manages to change their thinking. But how thought constructs emerge in peoples' brains is often complex and generally not exposed to view. For instance, for politics to change ways of thinking it is not necessary to directly influence those involved in accounting; it can make use of other institutions. If, for example, codified regulations are generally accepted, it is enough to change them in order to change ways of thinking. Only on the surface is politics directed at codified regulations, standards, organizational structures, and positions. These are but intermediaries affecting the thought patterns of those involved in accounting.

3.2. Meaning through functionality

So far, I have spoken only generally about thought constructs. What meaning do they have? What determines the meaning we ascribe to the instruments of accounting? We lend meaning to the physical instruments as a result of the functions we associate with them. The configuration of letters, numbers, and other symbols, which we call financial statements, are meant to inform us about a company's assets and capital. The investments and capital that a company controls give what we call "the balance sheet" its meaning. This notion applies correspondingly to the statement of cash flows, which is designed to inform us about a firm's payments. Thus, every financial statement has its own function in communicating to us the economic situation of the company. Someone born in the Brazilian rainforest, who has never seen the symbols, which to us constitute a balance sheet, and who, indeed, has never even heard of a balance sheet, could not come up with the idea that it is used to represent the assets and capital of an enterprise. What a balance sheet, a cash flow statement, and all the other statements and numbers mean to us derives, therefore, from the functions that we associate with accounting in our minds. Functionality not only supplies the basis for the financial statements themselves, but also for the organization of accounting and the decision-makers in the field of accounting. The chairman of the ASB, as knowledgeable in the field of accounting as he may be, becomes for us an element of the British accounting system not in his individual capacity, but rather only by virtue of the functions with which we associate him. The role not the individual is an element of accounting.

The meaning or symbolism we thus assign to the elements of accounting can, in turn, be a means to a further end. For example, accounting information provided to a supervisory board regarding the economic situation of the company might help the board members to decide whether to discharge the management. Such information can also be used to help financial analysts to estimate the value of the company. Furthermore, the trade unions should be informed of whether any leeway for wage-increase demands exists without thereby endangering the company's existence and therefore the job security of the unions' members. We can establish similar sequences of functions for every element of accounting, and since these functions are interdependent it is appropriate to speak of a network of functions that imbues the physical instruments of accounting with meaning for us.

I need not go into detail about the many and varied functions of the different elements of accounting. They are sufficiently well known. What I wish to emphasize is that these functions are what constitutes accounting. We can also ascribe functions to Mont Blanc or the Scottish Highlands, mentioned above. Mont Blanc is suitable for mountain climbing while the Highlands are suitable for hiking. Such functions are not, however, constitutive elements of Mont Blanc or the Highlands; they exist independently of any functions. Conversely, accounting would not exist without its functions. If we lived in paradise, where, by definition, economics as an idea would make no sense, an income statement or balance sheet would have no function, and according to my hypothesis, would never be conceived of and so would simply not exist. Thus, its functions are constitutive to accounting in the ontological sense.

3.3. Collective intentionality

How do we proceed from accounting as an individual thought construct to accounting as a societal institution? This step requires something that I, following Searle, would like to term "collective intentionality." Here, collective intentionality means that

(a) the individuals involved are in agreement on which functions they ascribe to accounting within society;

(b) they are aware of the fact that they share a common view of these functions; and

(c) this commonality is a necessary prerequisite for the ability of accounting to fulfill its functions.

Under these conditions, the functions we ascribe to the physical instruments constitute accounting as a societal institution. For example, those who prepare and use financial statements must agree that certain symbols represent a balance sheet and that this balance sheet provides valid information about the assets and capital of the company. Only then can the company publishing these figures convey information about its assets and capital to the readers of its financial statements. There must be general agreement that the chief accountant of the SEC has certain powers that define his role. Only then can s/he act with the authority of the chief accountant and only then will the people involved accept her/his instructions and advice.

3.4. The institutional richness of the accounting environment

Accounting as a societal institution is linked to a large number of other societal institutions in a multitude of ways. In isolation, without these relationships to other institutions, it would not be viable. This institutional richness is demonstrated by such a simple statement as: "The head of the Directorate General XV of the European Commission supports changing EU directives to grant member states the right to vote on whether fair-value reporting of financial instruments should be introduced." In issuing such a statement, the speaker mentions a large number of societal institutions: fair-value reporting and financial instruments as institutions of accounting; and on another level, the European Commission, the Directorate General XV, the head of the Directorate General, the EU directives, and the member states. All of these are societal institutions in the sense outlined above, that is thought constructs founded on collective intentionality. Additionally, the interrelations of the societal institutions among themselves are extremely complex. For instance, the European Commission proposes changes to the EU directives, which are prepared in the Directorate General XV. The head of the Directorate coordinates tasks and maintains personal contact with the relevant commissioner. The member states transform the directives into national law. "Proposing," "preparing," "coordinating," "contacting," and "transforming" are but a few of the large number of relationships that exist among these institutions. Similarly, member states also propose employees for the Commission; they sit on Commission committees such as the Contact Committee; they advise, they finance, they praise, they protest against, and they threaten the Commission. By virtue of the Fourth EU Directive, we have placed accounting into the extremely complex web of relationships with all these other institutions.

I need not demonstrate in detail that this is but a very small fraction of the institutional environment of accounting. Institutions such as language, writing, a numerical system, and a system for measuring goods and money are presently indispensable to accounting.

Moreover, what is represented in accounting, namely the assets and capital of a company, is also itself a societal institution, at least in part. For example, bank deposits that are owned by a company are physically no more than electrical impulses in a computer. Only when we, under certain conditions—that is that the computer belongs to a bank and the bank has confirmed the entry—agree to accept it as a medium of exchange and a store of value, does money become a societal institution. Similarly, patents and trademarks, shares, bonds and other claims, long-term liabilities, short-term liabilities, and equity capital are all thought constructs whose existence as societal institutions presupposes collective intentionality.

In addition, the interdependencies between accounting and the institutions surrounding it are flexible. Accounting does not necessarily require a particular configuration of surrounding institutions in order to fulfil certain functions, but can be similarly effective in its functions with different configurations. For example, accounting rules can be promulgated by parliament or by private standard-setters, such as the ASB or FASB. The democratic legitimacy that private standard-setters lack must then be provided by other societal institutions such as "due process" and governmental supervision of those standard-setting bodies.

When seeking to change accounting practices, politics inevitably gets embroiled in the tangled web of relationships among accounting and its supporting institutions. Thus, change can only succeed if this web is taken into consideration. For this reason, the EU was least successful in harmonizing accounting rules in those member states that have a long tradition of regulating accounting. National traditions conflicted with EU directives. For example, in Germany, France, and the United Kingdom, accounting has long been linked in many and diverse ways with other institutions; for example in Germany, with the tax code and the heritage of Roman law. For instance, the true-and-fair-view principle (Art. 2 of the Fourth EU Directive), which allows an override of specific accounting rules, violates the Roman law principle that *lex specialis* takes precedence. Accounting rules that require, or at least allow, asset valuation above acquisition costs, would have significant tax ramifications in Germany due to the link between financial and tax accounting, established by the authoritativeness principle. In the United Kingdom, the Continental tradition of statutory regulation of accounting was not compatible with the national tradition of regulation by the accounting profession or by a private standard-setting body. Consequently, a particular status had to be bestowed upon the standards of the ASB.

This is, indeed, precisely where the problems inherent in the international regulation of reporting lie. What role will national standard-setting bodies play if conglomerates or company groups are permitted to publish their consolidated financial statements according to International Accounting Standards (IAS)? How, then, will we resolve the discrepancy that groups and conglomerates prepare their financial statements according to international regulations while individual companies prepare theirs according to national rules? Violators of national rules are, as a rule, penalized by national laws, but how are violations of IAS standards to be dealt with? If it is not possible to embed the system of IAS accounting standards into the various national institutional structures, then the success of international standardization of accounting is likely to be as modest as that of European harmonization.

3.5. Normative and causal foundations of the existence of accounting

Let us now delve a little deeper into the conditions under which accounting exists. I have worked out in detail that it is the functions of accounting that lead us to imbue the physical instruments and thus the existence of accounting itself with meaning. The functions of accounting correspond to the effects desired and conceived by those participating in the process. Thus, the functions are based on conceptualizations of causal and normative relationships. Causal relationships are equally intrinsic to the human condition as values and desires. Since societal institutions exist only as mental constructs, causal relationships must also be mental constructs, that is conceived causality.

Accounting is, in general terms, a means to the end of information. Every means–end relationship we conceive of for accounting implies a selection process. Both accounting per se and the purposes it is meant to fulfill are chosen by us. Neither accounting as a means nor the ends to which it is employed are preordained. There are always alternatives to accounting as it has been practised or devised, and there are always additional effects of any particular form of accounting than those we aim to achieve. Thus a company can publish its periodic earnings in the form of either a profit and loss statement or a comparison of balance sheets; a profit and loss statement can be prepared according to the total-cost method or the cost-of-sales method; a balance sheet can be published in account form or columnar form; individual transactions, external assets and capital positions of a company can be classified in various ways in the accounts, and they can be denominated in different ways; and the medium of communicating information can vary. Information about cash flow can be communicated through the original, derivative direct or derivative indirect, statement of sources and applications of funds; entries can be structured according to operational, investment or financial cash flow, or any other conceivable scheme.

Furthermore, each of these published sets of accounting figures has multiple effects. The profit and loss statement, structured according to the fourth EU Council Directive, not only provides information about profits, but also about revenues and expenses. From this it is possible to determine the cash flow indirectly or, in conjunction with information on the number of employees, the employees' average salary. It can provide information of interest to shareholders, creditors, employees, and academics. This information can have far-reaching effects. A shareholder might sell his stock, a creditor might renew a loan, an employee's sense of job security might be enhanced, or an academic might use the figures in his lectures. The number of imaginable forms of accounting that can be enlisted for various purposes and the number of imaginable effects that can result from any particular form of accounting are virtually endless.

If we do not choose certain desired effects as our purposes, we will surely remain adrift in this vast sea of fathomable causes and effects. All other effects must be cast overboard. They are, admittedly, still present, insofar as we are aware of them, but we do not consider them relevant. In addition, we choose particular forms of accounting as a means to achieve our chosen purposes, and alternative forms are not taken into consideration.

This selection of purposes and forms of accounting is dependent upon desires, preferences, and values. Management often *wants* to be able to choose how exactly to present its financial statements. The SEC and FASB *favor* reporting geared toward the principle of "decision usefulness" above all other principles. The chairman of the ASB *rejects* the IASC's draft proposal for the treatment of deferred taxes.

However, the normative basis of accounting is even broader than this. It does not confine itself merely to weighing alternative forms of accounting and their associated effects. Values also influence which forms of accounting and their associated effects we generate in our minds. These are not preordained. Rather, they are mental constructs that we ourselves develop. These developments too are driven by aspirations and values. Inflation accounting originated in Germany in the context of the hyperinflation of the 1930s. "IAS-light" and "GAAP-light" originated when continental enterprises wanted to take advantage of the reputation of both systems in international capital markets without straying too far from national traditions of presenting financial statements. Executives tend to become creative in their accounting when their companies are foundering. On closer examination, we can find values behind all the institutions of accounting. Just as surely as you will get wet if you go into the water, so you will be surrounded by values when you operate within the context of a particular society's culture. Thus as an essential constitutive element, values are to accounting as water is to the sea.

4. Implications of the ontology of accounting for political research

I conclude this chapter with a few general remarks on the implications of this particular ontology of accounting for political research.

If we accept the proposition that accounting exists "only" as a mental construct, then what interests us—namely accounting as a societal institution—remains concealed. We would have to be mind readers to be able to know what the physical instruments of accounting really mean to those who are involved in accounting. Since we are not, in fact, mind readers, we have no way of directly apprehending accounting as a societal institution. This presents not merely an *ex ante* dilemma that can be resolved *ex post*; it presents a fundamental impossibility.

There is, however, one way to gain some understanding of accounting as a societal institution, albeit one that is fraught with uncertainties and risks. Since accounting as a societal institution requires that a common view of its functions is shared within society, and since communication is a pre-condition for this common ground, analyzing such communication is one—in my opinion the only—way to explore accounting as a societal institution. It is only through oral statements made in the context of surveys, debates, and interviews, and through written documents such as statutes, standards, statements made by stakeholders, organizational charts, internal company memoranda, and actual sets of accounting figures that we can gain access to accounting as a societal institution.

We academics are so accustomed to basing our data on such written and oral expressions that we sometimes tend to forget that what we can observe is not necessarily, in the final analysis, what we really want to know. If there were an exact correspondence between thoughts and their written expression, and if the statements of those involved in the field of accounting evoked the same associations in us as academics as in those making the statements, then these statements would be unambiguous indicators of the patterns of thought behind them. Of course, we know that this is not the case and thus, communication can only offer an imperfect indication of accounting as a societal institution. On the other hand, the degree of imperfection varies considerably. What different people understand by "liquid assets," machines, or the chairman of the IASB is relatively unambiguous. Such concepts as "asset," "liability," and "profit" are on the other hand already considerably woollier, while concepts such as "true-and-fair view" and "decision usefulness" probably have as many meanings as there are people.

That the communications of those involved in accounting are even useful as indicators at all results from the fact that the existence of accounting as a societal institution can only be established if and when collective intentionality is present and that, again, presupposes communication among the various parties involved. If people's aims differed fundamentally from what they expressed or if there were merely a coincidental connection between ideas and their written expression, communication and thus accounting as a societal institution could not succeed. Consequently, accounting, as it is expressed, functions in principle as an indicator of accounting as it is conceived.

Let us now consider the written expressions more closely.

1. Accounting as a societal institution finds expression in statutes, standards, contracts, and representations by or of accounting organizations. However, it is difficult to conclude from these written expressions what the existing state of accounting practice is, because statutes and organizational charts do not or only very imperfectly

circumscribe the functions that accounting is supposed to serve and the values and needs that are thus supposed to be served. It is not the function of written expressions such as statutes to elucidate the framework within which accounting exists; they are designed to regulate the application of accounting. Statutes and standards are therefore often formulated in the conditional and use language such as, "If conditions x_1 to x_n are fulfilled, then action y is allowed, required or proscribed." It is not possible to ascertain directly from such language the functions that these norms are supposed to serve, or the values behind them. But we can deduce them, a process that we will examine in more detail shortly.

2. The communications of those directly involved in the political process and the documentation of such communication provide more immediate information. As a rule, those who call for the reform of accounting practice give reasons for doing so. These reasons are indicative of functions and values that their proponents aim to further. But here, too, there is not always perfect accord between what people think and what they say; likewise, peoples' own interpretation of what they say is not necessarily the same as that of researchers acting as observers. The same fundamental qualification applies to all academic exploration of peoples' motives, and the underlying values, needs, aims, etc.

There are different approaches and methods that can be employed to deal with this dilemma.

1. We are accustomed to interpreting texts without being conscious of the actual process of interpreting or understanding them. On the other hand, hermeneutics involves deliberate and methodological understanding. As applied to accounting, hermeneutics—like ontology, a major branch of philosophy—is practised chiefly by jurists interpreting legal texts. We can, however, also import these methods to analyze the influence of political communications and their expression in statutes, regulations, or organizational charts on operational patterns of thought.

2. Another technique involves mitigating the problem of understanding by limiting ourselves to an analysis of the interrelationships between well-defined indicators. This is common practice in empirical research, such as quantitative studies of lobbying or capital markets research. When I analyze correlations between cash flow or profits in a given period and stock market prices, these are relatively

clearly defined, so that one can assume that the results will be understood in a similar manner by many participants in the process.

3. In analytical research, the problem is solved by drawing up a *typology* of the economy being examined. The principal and the agent are archetypes, and so is the information that is exchanged between them in the form of accounting. The problem of understanding is lessened by employing fictional constructs. It is a well-known quandary that statements made within such a framework can only provide very limited information about accounting as a societal practice.

4. Finally, by institutionalizing it, we make conducting research on accounting possible despite this dilemma. Empirical capital-market research and the economic theory of organization are accepted within the academic community as valid approaches because we agree that they are useful ones. Analogously, all the conditions I have detailed above for accounting as a societal institution apply to such institutionalizations. They are mental constructs whose content is determined by the functions we ascribe to them. They become an institutionalized subject of research through the collective acceptance of the functions selected on the basis of aspirations, values, and goals. Academic research in accounting and politics—as well as so-called positive accounting—is thus necessarily normative in the sense that values, aspirations, and utility are constitutive of these approaches.

Notes

This chapter is a draft of a lecture that Dieter Ordelheide intended to give as part of the 2000 P. D. Leake Lecture Series at Oxford University. Sadly, he deceased before he was able to deliver the lectures. This previously unpublished draft has been translated from German and slightly edited for publication in this volume.

[1] The German term Dieter Ordelheide used is "Denkmuster" (editors' remark).

5.2

Constituent Lobbying and Its Impact on the Development of Financial Reporting Regulations: Evidence from Germany

Stuart McLeay, Dieter Ordelheide, and Steven Young

This chapter examines the impact of constituent lobbying activity on accounting regulators during the transformation of the Fourth European Company Law Directive into German accounting law. Using detailed published commentaries prepared by representative organisations on draft accounting legislation, we provide evidence concerning the preferences of the three primary German constituencies—preparers, auditors, and academic experts. Initially, a model that merely distinguishes between the three constituencies suggests that the industry lobby group representing preparers exerts the greatest influence on the decisions of the German legislature. However, when the empirical model is extended to include all two-way interaction effects, the relative power of preparers is seen to be far lower, with the influence exerted by industry depending crucially on the support of at least one of the remaining lobby groups. © 1999 Elsevier Science Ltd. All rights reserved.

1. Introduction

The economic consequences of policy decisions make it impossible for accounting regulators to select non-controversial treatments on any of the issues they face based solely on technical considerations. Instead, the choice of appropriate accounting regulations reflects, at least in part, a social decision whereby regulatory bodies attempt to manage conflict between competing constituencies by selecting the most socially acceptable solution (Horngren, 1972; Sunder, 1988; Zeff, 1978). The political nature of accounting rule-development naturally raises questions concerning both the responsiveness of policy-makers to constituent pressure, and the distribution of power among competing interest groups. One means by which prior research has explored the source and extent of political influence in the context of accounting regulation is through the analysis of constituent lobbying activity. This study builds on extant research by examining public lobbying activity in Germany during the period when the Fourth European Company Law Directive (hereafter Fourth Directive) was transformed into German commercial law, the regulatory regime at the time being fundamentally different to that previously analysed.

Lobbying research in the accounting literature has focused almost exclusively on financial reporting regimes in English-speaking countries, most notably that of the US (Puro, 1984, 1985; Sutton, 1984; Tandy & Wilburn, 1992, 1996), and to a lesser extent those of the UK (Hope & Gray, 1982; Nobes, 1991; Sutton, 1984), Australia (Klumpes, 1994; Walker & Robinson, 1994) and New Zealand (Rahman, Ng & Tower, 1994). While this body of work affords crucial insights into the nature of the standard-setting process, the institutional similarity of these regimes limits the generalisability of reported findings and provides little evidence as to the effect of the organisational form on the lobbying process. Examination of alternative regulatory environments is, therefore, warranted. In this context, the system operating in Germany until recently provided one of the most obvious examples of codified accounting regulation (Nobes & Parker, 1991, p. 12), where the legislature assumed primary responsibility for the development of financial reporting regulations, and where accounting rules were drafted by lawyers and administrators in the Ministries of Justice and Finance.

Implementation of the Fourth Directive represented a landmark in German accounting regulation, codifying as it did certain aspects of financial reporting which were already generally accepted in countries such as the US and UK.[1] On the other hand, as a key element of the European Union's harmonisation programme, the Fourth Directive also contained many aspects of German law which were then implemented elsewhere in Europe, that is the requirements for companies to adopt (i) defined methods of asset valuation, and (ii) compulsory balance sheet and profit and loss formats. In the case of Germany, the provisions of the Fourth Directive were enacted into national law via the Accounting Directives Law (*Bilanzrichtlinien-Gesetz*), forming the legal basis for financial reporting for German companies. To obtain agreement on the provisions of the Fourth Directive at a European level, the document contained a large number of national options, affording member states significant flexibility over the transformation of many of its specific provisions. At a national level, the process of choosing between these various alternatives has provided a powerful setting within which to explore the political nature of accounting regulation.[2]

Using commentaries published by representative organisations during the transformation process, we identify the preferences of the three primary German accounting constituencies (industry, auditors, and academic experts) in relation to 169 separate financial reporting issues spanning aspects of valuation, recognition, disclosure and financial statement format. A striking feature of the approach adopted in Germany when the Fourth Directive was implemented is the manner in which representations made to the legislature reflected the collective view of the members of professional and industrial associations.

The relative influence of each of the lobby groups involved is assessed by examining the extent to which constituents' stated preferences were ultimately reflected in the Accounting Directives Law. The approach used to identify lobbyists' preferences is similar to that employed in extant research whereby lobbyists' publicly available comments are classified as either 'for' or 'against' the associated exposure draft (e.g. Brown, 1981; Francis, 1987; Puro, 1984). Traditionally, such a coding procedure has proved problematic due to the relatively broad nature of both comment letter responses and the exposure drafts to which they pertain, resulting in the need for considerable judgement when reconciling the two (Puro, 1984).[3] In contrast, because the German accounting rules under consideration were similar in structure to US tax code regulations, lobbyists' proposals and the sections of commercial law to which they refer were concise and highly specific in nature. This results in (i) greater objectivity with respect to the identification of lobbyists' preferences, and (ii) a more reliable measure of power (i.e. the extent to which these preferences are now reflected in commercial law).

A generalised linear model is used to assess how the German legislature incorporated constituents' preferences in the regulations it promulgated. In addition to providing an appropriate means of modeling the relative influence of each lobby group in isolation, this approach enables a formal analysis of the way in which constituents' preferences interact to determine policy outcomes. To the extent that the support of all sectors of the financial community is often seen as an essential element in the development of accounting regulations (Horngren, 1972), the potential influence of any particular lobbyist is expected to be conditional, at least in part, on the position adopted by other lobby groups (Benveniste, 1972; Dyckman, 1988). To date, however, this issue remains relatively unexplored in the empirical literature. Initial findings for our main effects models suggest that, conditional on a proposal being made, industry exerted the greatest influence on the decisions of the legislature, while the odds of success associated with an academic proposal were significantly less than one. However, when the model is extended to include all two-way interactions between lobbyists, industry's power is seen to have declined, with the outcome depending crucially on agreement between industry and one or more of the remaining lobby groups. Additional tests confirm that, rather than any single group's preferences consistently dominating the legislature's decisions, it was the existence of agreement among participant groups that ultimately determined the odds of success for a given proposal. As with the US, therefore, the process of accounting-rule development in Germany at the time of the implementation of the Fourth Directive appears to have been characterised by 'power equivalency' and the desire for political consensus.

In addition to empirically examining the politics of accounting rule-development within a fundamentally different and empirically more amenable regime to that previously considered, this study adds to the literature in three further respects. First, several commentators (e.g. Puro, 1984; Sutton, 1984) have suggested that the distribution of power among competing constituencies may vary as a function of the particular accounting issue under consideration. Because this study examines the politics of accounting rule-development across a wide range of accounting issues in relation to a single event, we are able to develop a more comprehensive model of accounting regulation than in prior work, where the focus has been largely restricted to the analysis of single (or small subsets of) accounting issues in isolation. We present results which suggest that power and influence are indeed conditional on the nature of the financial reporting issue: in particular, any relative influence that industry exerted on the legislature appears to have been restricted to disclosure issues.

Secondly, although the standard-setting process in many English-speaking countries has a strong private sector tradition, a degree of state intervention in regulatory initiatives remains a distinct possibility

(Vieten, 1995; Wyatt, 1991).[4] Even in Germany and France, which have seen the recent creation of standard-setting bodies, financial responsibility for accounting regulation remains within the state budget. The precise effect of these differing regulatory structures on the rule-development process remains ambiguous: for example, while Dyckman (1988) raises concerns over the susceptibility of public sector regulators to political pressure from those antagonistic to business, Sutton (1984) contends that the deliberations of private sector institutions are more susceptible to constituent influence due to their lack of legal mandate.[5] To the extent that theoretical arguments alone cannot unambiguously delineate the potential costs and benefits of public sector involvement in the regulatory process, the issue is an empirical question. Comparison of the findings reported in this paper with the evidence documented for the US and similar systems highlights the existence of important commonalities across different institutional settings with respect to the accounting rule-development process.

Finally, the globalisation of business and the expansion of the capital markets has led to increasing pressure for accounting harmonisation and, by implication, a greater understanding of alternative financial reporting regimes. However, while many in the financial reporting community have resisted this pressure, choosing instead to focus attention on US standard-setting activity on the grounds that it is these standards which ultimately form the basis of international harmonisation efforts, the importance of alternative accounting approaches can no longer be denied (Wyatt & Yospe, 1993). Nowhere is this more clearly demonstrated than in the SEC's decision to allow three international accounting standards (or parts thereof) to be accepted in cross border filings without reconciliation to US GAAP,[6] even though the results produced by the application of these standards are substantially different from those produced under US GAAP (Bayless, Cochrane, Harris, Leisenring, McLaughlin & Wirtz, 1996). Evidence concerning both the process by which accounting rules are developed and the way in which these rules reflect constituents' preferences, represents an important step towards understanding the product of alternative financial reporting regimes.

The remainder of the paper is organised as follows. The next section reviews extant lobbying research. We then present an overview of the institutional characteristics of accounting regulation in Germany at the time of the implementation of the Fourth Directive, together with details of the European accounting harmonisation programme. The following sections discuss the data and sample, describe the estimation procedure, and present the results. The paper concludes with a summary and discussion.

2. Literature review

Using Downs' (1957) model of voting, Sutton (1984) identifies the conditions under which rational lobbying will occur. Given a choice between two alternative proposals, lobbying is predicted in those circumstances where the differential wealth effect associated with the two proposals, discounted by the perceived probability of influencing the outcome, exceeds the cost of lobbying. Hence, the propensity for lobbying is hypothesised to be increasing in both (i) the magnitude of the perceived wealth effect, and (ii) the expectation of influencing the final decision. To the extent that the potential economic consequences of securing a favoured proposal are thought to be greater in absolute terms for preparers than for users, evidence reported by Tandy and Wilburn (1992) for the US indicating that preparers are more active lobbyists than users serves to support Sutton's first prediction. Similar lobbying patterns have been documented by Sutton for the UK and Walker and Robinson (1994) for Australia. In addition, the significant financial interest of audit firms in their clients' welfare helps explain the relatively high lobbying propensity observed for large US public accounting firms, while the low levels of lobbying observed for US accounting academics has been partly attributed to the lack of a significant wealth effect (Tandy & Wilburn, 1996). Further, intra-industry studies indicate that the likelihood of an individual firm engaging in lobbying activity is also positively associated with the magnitude of the perceived wealth effects (e.g. Francis, 1987; Griffin, 1983; Kelly, 1982, 1985; Watts & Zimmerman, 1978). Tandy and Wilburn (1996) also document direct evidence in support of Sutton's second prediction. Specifically, they find that one of the main reasons cited by US academics against active participation in the FASB's due process procedures is their perceived low probability of success. However, since prior research has focused almost exclusively on the type of financial reporting system prevalent in English-speaking countries, little evidence exists to support Sutton's additional assertion that these predictions will hold irrespective of the institutional setting within which accounting regulations are developed.

While the benefit term in Sutton's lobbying equation is expected to vary between preparers and users in general, it may also differ across alternative accounting issues for any preparer–user combination (Sutton, 1984), suggesting that constituent lobbying propensity may be affected by the scope and nature of the accounting issue under consideration. For example, Tandy and Wilburn (1992) document greater lobbying activity by the industry and academic constituent groups on substantive standards compared with both industry standards and amendments. Similarly, substantive standards elicited a greater mean number of submissions from public accounting firms than for industry standards. Further, Puro (1984) provides evidence that the extent of preference alignment between preparer and auditor lobby groups may also differ according to the underlying nature of the accounting issue: preparers and auditors are more likely to adopt similar lobbying positions in relation to proposals designed to standardise accounting treatments, whereas they tend to adopt competing positions in relation to issues of disclosure. To the extent that agreement among two or more groups results in a multiplier effect, whereby the combined influence of the coalition is significantly greater than the influence of a single group acting alone (Benveniste, 1972; Dyckman, 1988), Puro's findings suggest that constituent influence may also vary as a function of the nature of the financial reporting issue under debate. To date, however, this issue remains largely unexplored in the empirical literature.

Several studies (e.g. Brown, 1981; Hussein & Ketz, 1980; Newman, 1981; Puro, 1985) have used lobbying data to investigate the impact of pressure groups on the policy decisions taken by standard-setting agencies following allegations in the Metcalf report (US Congress, 1976) that the FASB was unduly influenced in its policy-making process by certain sectors of society (primarily the large audit firms and their clients). However, the evidence reported in these studies suggests that the FASB's policy decisions are not consistently dominated by any single group or coalition of groups. Instead, results suggest the influence of many centers of power. Indeed, Hussein and Ketz (1991) conclude that the FASB's deliberations are characterised by a system of 'power equivalency', whereby the structural and relational contracts make it impossible for any single agent or coalition of agents to dominate the process. Similar conclusions are presented by Hope and Gray (1982) in relation to the UK standard-setting process. While this body of work provides important evidence concerning the political nature of accounting regulation, Hussein and Ketz (1991) argue that power and influence are determined, at least in part, by the prevailing regulatory structure. Consequently, different regulatory structures may be associated with different political outcomes. A broader understanding of the politics of accounting regulation therefore demands the analysis of alternative regulatory systems.

3. Institutional background

Traditionally, decisions on accounting rules have been viewed in Germany not only as a technical matter on which a group of accounting experts should be competent but also as an issue of public policy having a relatively broad social basis (Ordelheide & Pfaff, 1994, p. 82). The resulting law-based system of financial reporting is primarily dependent on commercial law, with strong connections to tax law,[7] and this is still the case following the recent reform which established a body to develop German accounting standards. Until 1985, the Stock Corporation Law (*Aktiengesetz*) of 1965 represented the primary source of accounting requirements for listed companies, supplemented by provisions in the Commercial Code (*Handelsgesetzbuch*) and income tax law.[8] Following the transformation of the Fourth (and Seventh) Directive into German commercial law in 1985, the Accounting Directives Law became the legal basis for financial reporting in Germany. The Accounting Directives Law amended the Commercial Code, the latter containing the general accounting and auditing rules applicable to all companies, together with a special section relating to stock corporations and limited liability companies.

While the Accounting Directives Law codified many important accounting principles and standards, the German legal provisions are not exhaustive. For example, foreign currency translation and accounting for leasing and government grants are not regulated explicitly in the Commercial Code. In the absence of such regulations, companies have resorted to tax law and tax court rulings for authoritative and legally-binding interpretations of the Commercial Code. Additionally, certain non-authoritative legal interpretations are combined with authoritative rulings to form the 'Correct Accounting Principles' (*Grundsätze ordnungsmaßiger Buchführung* or *GoB*) explicitly referred to in the Commercial Code.[9] This combination of legislative rules and legal interpretations provides a distinctive hierarchical structure to accounting regulation in Germany (Ordelheide, 1999), creating two primary mechanisms through which parties have been able to shape financial reporting practice. First, agents have influenced commercial law directly by lobbying the legislative body during the rule-development process. Such participation by representative bodies in law-making has constituted an important part of the due process of accounting regulation in Germany, actively encouraged by the legislature. Second, agents can contribute to the market for legal interpretations. Law commentaries and interpretative articles which seek to clarify legal requirements have been produced regularly by barristers, judges, auditors, experts from business and the public sector, and academics.[10] Until now, the complete system of legal interpretations has been collected together and published in law commentaries and financial accounting handbooks [e.g. *Adler-Düring-Schmaltz* (Forster, 1997)].

Reflecting the codified approach to regulation in Germany, the accounting rule-development process was coordinated until recently by the Ministry of Justice. In contrast with the Anglo–American approach, only a relatively minor role was ascribed to the audit profession, for which the traditional emphasis was concerned with clients' compliance with the law rather than with the development of binding accounting principles and procedures.[11] While accounting in Germany has been influenced by a wide range of other parties, including private research institutes, academic accountants, preparer groups organised by the Confederation of German Industries, and the audit profession, the financial reporting regulations examined in this study were drafted by lawyers and administrators in the Ministries of Finance and Justice.

3.1. European accounting harmonisation and the Fourth Directive

An objective of the European Union is the convergence not only of economic conditions but also of member states' respective national laws to the extent required for the common market to function in an orderly manner. To achieve this aim, a programme of legal harmonisation has been implemented involving the development of a series of Company Law Directives. When the European Commission has obtained agreement on a set of proposals relating to the harmonisation of a particular topic, it places a Draft Directive before the Council of Ministers. If the Directive is adopted, governments of the member states have a specified period in which to enact the legislation and incorporate the Directives' provisions into their national law. To obtain agreement at a European level, it is usual for a Directive to contain a range of national options, affording member states significant flexibility when enacting its provisions into national law. It is the choice among these national options with respect to the Fourth Directive that provides the background to our analysis of accounting regulation in Germany.

Integration of the provisions of the Fourth Directive into German law began with the publication of the legislature's transformation recommendations. Comments on this document were invited from all interested parties in Germany and used by the Ministries of Justice and Finance to produce a pre-draft law. Five subsequent draft laws were published prior to enactment of the Accounting Directives Law in December 1985 and comments were received following each stage. While 27 organisations were officially invited to comment during the drafting stage, only industry, academia and the audit profession engaged in formal lobbying on a material number of accounting issues and on successive drafts of the law. The restriction of lobbying activity to this limited set of financial reporting experts reflects, at least in part, the highly complex nature of German commercial law and the resulting barriers to entry this creates. The absence of formal lobbying activity by user associations may be partially explained by the decision of the German banks (the primary users of financial reporting information) to adopt a preparer position for lobbying purposes. The greater involvement of preparers relative to users in the lobbying process is also consistent with both Sutton's (1984) theoretical model of lobbying activity and with Tandy and Wilburn's (1992) study of constituent lobbying of the FASB.

Lobbying was conducted both publicly in the form of published commentaries and submissions to official hearings, and privately in the form of unpublished letters and informal discussions. Reflecting both the collectivist nature of German society (Power, 1997) and cost efficiencies associated with organised lobbying activity (Sutton, 1984), all formal proposals were issued through representative agencies. The preparer viewpoint was represented by the Association for Finance and Management (*Gesellschaft für Finanzwissenschaft in der Unternehmensführung*) and the Combined Associations of German Industry (*Spitzenverbände der deutschen Wirtschaft*).[12] Proposals from each association were developed by a series of working parties, membership of which was drawn from the corporate sector, and published in the journal *Der Betrieb*.[13] The audit profession's viewpoint was jointly represented by the Institute of Auditors (*Institut der Wirtschaftsprüfer*) and the Chamber of Auditors (*Wirtschaftsprüferkammer*). Proposals were drawn up by working groups, issued as professional opinions, and published at the outset in *Der Betrieb* and later in *Die Wirtschaftsprüfung*.[14] Finally, the academic position was represented by the Accounting Committee of the Association of German Business Studies Academics (*Kommission Rechnungswesen im Verband der Hochschullehrer für Betriebswirtschaft*). Formed in 1977 specifically to facilitate academic participation in the process of transforming European Company Law Directives into German law, the Committee appointed two working groups to debate the draft legislation. The results of these debates were then submitted to the Committee and, after subsequent modification, published as official opinions in *Die Beitriebswirtschaft*.[15]

4. Data and sample

Empirical tests are conducted using commentaries published by the representative bodies identified in Section 3.1 during the draft law stages of the transformation process.[16] For all accounting issues examined, both industry associations made identical proposals. To simplify the empirical analysis and increase model parsimony, we aggregate these two associations to form a single industry group, denoted IND. Similarly, because the Institute of Auditors and the Chamber of Auditors acted in unison throughout the transformation process (Ordelheide, 1999), we aggregate these two parties to form a single auditor group, denoted AUD. Proposals made by the Accounting Committee of the Association of German Business Studies Academics are denoted ACA.

For each lobby group (IND, AUD and ACA), all publicly available comments were surveyed to identify each formal proposal. A total of 169 separate issues covering aspects of valuation, recognition, disclosure and financial statement format were identified on which at least one of the three groups commented formally.[17] The nature of these proposals was such that they clearly indicated (i) the specific legal provision under discussion and (ii) the lobbyist's proposed accounting treatment.

Consistent with much of the extant literature on accounting regulation, we adopt a pluralist model as a means of operationalising the concept of political power.[18] Within this framework, power is assessed by distinguishing those lobbyists whose proposals are ultimately adopted (i.e. successful) from those whose proposals are rejected (i.e. unsuccessful). Lobbyists with the highest proportion of 'successes' are then considered to exhibit the greatest political influence while those with the lowest proportion are assumed to be the least influential. For the 169 issues on which at least one of the three groups proposed a change to the law, the proposals were compared with the legal requirement contained in the final text of the Accounting Directives Law. For each constituent, a recommendation corresponding to the accounting treatment ultimately required by the Accounting Directives Law is categorised as 'successful'. Alternatively, a recommendation which fails to correspond with the treatment required by the Accounting Directives Law is assumed to have been 'unsuccessful'. Finally, in the event that a lobbyist makes no formal (i.e. publicly available) proposal on a particular issue, an absence of lobbying activity is inferred.

The procedure described above provides a relatively objective measure of the extent to which lobbyists' proposals are ultimately realised by the legislature in commercial law. Admittedly, as the approach relies on final outcomes to generate the observable counts of 'successes', it does not allow for a detailed investigation of strategic lobbying behaviour in a multi-period framework where there may be variation in the level of interest with respect to individual points of law. Nevertheless, the database provides a unique setting in which to estimate lobbyist influence and to assess the overall impact on such influence of agreement and disagreement between lobbyists. Indeed, an important aspect of constituent lobbying is that success depends not only on each interest group's own actions but also on the degree of consensus and conflict among the participant groups (Benveniste, 1972). An explicit consideration of the interaction between lobbyists' stated preferences therefore seems appropriate. A limitation of our data, however, is that when two or more parties submit similar proposals, we are unable to distinguish between those cases which arise as a result of an explicit coalition and those cases where it represents two independently determined positions. Consequently, when modeling lobbyists' interactions, we define 'agreement' simply as the stylised fact that two equivalent proposals have been made, while 'disagreement' is defined as the presence of a proposal and a counterproposal. Further, an implication of the participation of three lobby groups in the rule-development process is the occurrence of situations where two of the interest groups make the same proposal while the third makes a counterproposal. We model such situations as a set of two-way interactions comprising one case of agreement (e.g. between IND and AUD) and two separate cases of disagreement (between IND and ACA and between AUD and ACA). Finally, an additional characteristic of the data is that in the case of disagreement, one of the proposals always becomes law. That is, conflict amongst lobby groups always leads to success for one or more of the parties involved. On the other hand, uncontested proposals made by one, two or three parties may fail to become law. Here, the lobbying process in Germany is modelled on the basis of these stylised facts.

Table 5.2.1 (p.298) presents the observed frequencies of success, failure and non-participation, cross-classified by lobby group. The three lobby groups made a total of 269 proposals, 148 of which were successful. The draft law was amended by the regulator with respect to 63% of the issues on which comments were made (i.e. 106 issues out of 169). When only one of the lobbying groups made a proposal, less than half (43 of 97) of the respective regulations were revised. In contrast, the regulator changed the legal text in 63 of the 72 issues which attracted proposals from more than one lobby group. In summary, the conditional probability that a proposal would be successful if made by just one lobbying group was only 0.443, but it was as high as 0.875 if made by more than one lobbying group.

A fuller understanding of these success probabilities requires an approach which controls not only for conditioning factors such as the differences between the parties in the odds of making a proposal in the first place but also for the likelihood of agreement or disagreement over the nature of the proposed amendment to the law. In the latter case, these probabilities can be estimated either for the general case (i.e. that there exists agreement or disagreement, or both, over an issue) or the specific (i.e. that two parties in particular agree or disagree). In this way, an idea can be gained not only of the odds that a proposal will succeed but also of how such odds vary across the parties when they agree or disagree. In this paper, we refer to the odds of making a proposal as θ and to the odds that it will succeed as ω, whilst agreement is denoted by ϕ and disagreement by φ. A more detailed discussion of model development in this context is given below, followed by the empirical results.

5. Model specification

The count in each cell of Table 5.2.1 follows a multinominal frequency distribution with unknown probabilities (Francis, Green & Payne, 1993). A statistical model to estimate the probability structure of this data may be written in the form of a generalised linear model (Nelder & Wedderburn, 1972). For situations in which the response variate is a vector of frequencies from a multi-way contingency table and the explanatory variables are categorical (i.e. no proposal, proposal accepted, or proposal rejected), McCullagh and Nelder (1989) demonstrate that the appropriate formulation is a log-linear model with a log link function and a Poisson distributed error. Under this scheme, the count in a given

Table 5.2.1. Constituent lobbying activity in relation to the transformation of the Fourth Directive into German commercial law, cross-classified by constituent group and lobbying outcome[a,b]

	Auditors	Industry			
		No proposal	Accepted	Rejected	Total
Academics	No proposal	0	22	22	44
= No proposal	Accepted	13	10	0	23
	Rejected	11	3	5	19
	Total	24	35	27	86
Academics	No proposal	8	5	6	19
= Accepted	Accepted	3	6	3	12
	Rejected	0	1	0	1
	Total	11	12	9	32
Academics	No proposal	21	10	0	31
= Rejected	Accepted	0	8	0	8
	Rejected	2	8	2	12
	Total	23	26	2	51
					Total
Academics	No proposal	29	37	28	94
= Total	Accepted	16	24	3	43
	Rejected	12	12	7	32
	Total	58	73	38	169

[a] The sample consists of 169 separate accounting issues on which at least one constituent group (i.e., industry, auditors, or academics) lobbied the German legislature. For each accounting issue, lobbyists' proposals were compared with the ultimate legal requirement contained in the Accounting Directives Law. Proposals corresponding to the Accounting Directives Law requirement were considered successful and coded 'accepted', while proposals which did not correspond with the Accounting Directives Law requirement were considered unsuccessful and coded 'rejected'. In the event that a lobbyist made no formal (i.e., publicly available) proposal on a particular issue, an absence of lobbying activity was inferred.

[b] The industry constituency was represented by two organisations: The Association for Finance and Management and the Combined Associations of German Industry. Since both organisations adopted the same lobbying position for all 169 cases examined, we aggregate these two associations to form a single industry group. The auditor constituency was jointly represented by the Institute of Auditors and the Chamber of Auditors on all 169 cases examined. These two parties are again aggregated to form a single auditor group. Finally, the academic constituency was represented by the Accounting Committee of the Association of German Business Studies Academics.

cell may be expressed as a function of the main effects (subscripted IND, AUD, and ACA) and the associated interactions. As well as this approach representing the most appropriate modeling procedure given the nature of the data, it affords the additional advantage of facilitating an explicit analysis of the way in which individual lobbyists' preferences interact in determining German accounting law.[19]

The standard approach in log-linear modeling assumes that hierarchical models are to be fitted, such that the existence of a higher-order interaction necessarily implies the inclusion of all lower order terms marginal to it (Francis et al., 1993, p. 249). We therefore fit a number of levels of the model to account for the extent of agreement or disagreement, the relative influence of the individual lobbying organisations, the odds of success when such consensus and conflict exists, and finally, the effect on those odds of the mix of parties involved.

5.1. Conditional independence

The lowest order log-linear model is that of complete independence, where the expected value is equal in each cross-classified cell, except for the structural zero in the corner cell where none of the lobbyists makes a proposal. However, since this simplistic model is unlikely to provide any material insights into the structure of our data, we begin by fitting a model where the probabilities of making a proposal are allowed to vary across the constituent groups. We refer to this initial model as the model of conditional independence, since the estimates of expected acceptances and rejections are conditional on a proposal having been made but are independent of the relative influence of the lobbyists and any possible interactions between them. The model of conditional independence therefore represents the null against which each group's relative influence, and the impact of agreement and disagreement, may be assessed. For the model of conditional independence, the log of the observed count may be generalised as

$$\log C' = \sum_i \theta_i, \qquad (1)$$

where:

C' = a vector of observations representing the observed counts, C, in Table 5.2.1, adjusted for the mean effect;

θ_i = the log-odds that lobby group i makes a proposal;

i = the industry (IND), auditor (AUD), or academic (ACA) lobby groups.

For each lobby group i, θ is defined as a two-level factor, taking the value one if i made a proposal and zero otherwise.

5.2. Relative influence

This model evaluates the unconditional odds of success for each of the lobbyists. In this case, the log of the mean-adjusted observed count is

$$\log C' = \sum_i \theta_i + \sum_i \omega_i, \tag{2}$$

where:

ω_i = the log-odds that a proposal made by lobby group i will be accepted.

All other variables are as previously defined and, for each lobby group i, ω_i is defined as a two-level factor, taking the value one if i's proposal was successful and zero if it was rejected.

5.3. Agreement and disagreement

Adding the main effects of agreement and disagreement to model (2) generates the following model:

$$\log C' = \sum_i \theta_i + \sum_i \omega_i + \phi + \varphi \tag{3}$$

where:

ϕ = the overall log-odds that two parties will make the same proposal, defined as a two-level factor taking the value one if any two lobbyists make the same proposal, and zero otherwise;

φ = the overall log-odds that two proposals differ, defined as a two-level factor taking the value one if any two lobbyists make different proposals on a given accounting issue, and zero otherwise.

While model (3) is expressed as a main effects model, interaction terms can also be included to account for those cases where two lobbyists are in agreement while the third seeks a different outcome (i.e. $\phi \cdot \varphi$), and also for the log odds that an identical proposal put forward by more than one party will lead to a change in the law (i.e. $\omega \cdot \phi$). At the general level, the interaction between disagreement and success ($\omega \cdot \varphi$) remains constant in this study, since for each case involving conflicting proposals, one of the proposals always became law.

5.4. Agreement and disagreement with lobby group i

The generalised models presented above can be rewritten to allow for the relative odds of agreement or disagreement with the ith lobby group, as follows:

$$\log C' = \sum_i \theta_i + \sum_i \omega_i + \sum_i \phi_i + \sum_i \varphi_i \qquad (4.1)$$

where:

ϕ_i = a two-level factor taking the value one when a proposal put forward by lobby group i is in agreement with any other proposal, and zero otherwise;

φ_i = a two-level factor taking the value one when a proposal put forward by lobby group i is in disagreement with any other proposal, and zero otherwise.

Model (4.1) may also be extended by including interaction terms to account for the relative odds of success when there is agreement and disagreement. This extended model is written as

$$\log C' = \sum_i \theta_i + \sum_i \omega_i \phi_i + \sum_i \omega_i \varphi_i \qquad (4.2)$$

where:

$\omega_i \phi_i$ = the sum of the main effects that a proposal made by lobbyist i will be successful and that a similar proposal to lobbyist i's will be made by another lobby group, plus the interaction effect on the success of a proposal by lobbyist i when a similar proposal has been made by another lobbyist (i.e. $\omega_i \phi_i = \omega_i + \phi_i + \omega_i \cdot \phi_i$);

$\omega_i \varphi_i$ = the sum of main and interaction effects of a successful counterproposal from lobbyist i (i.e. $\omega_i \varphi_i = \omega_i + \varphi_i + \omega_i \cdot \varphi_i$).

5.5. Agreement and disagreement between lobby groups i and j

The final model allows for each of the possible two-way cases of agreement and disagreement between each pair of lobbyists i and j, where $i \neq j$. This model may be specified as

$$\log C' = \sum_i \theta_i + \sum_i \omega_i + \sum_i \sum_j \phi_{ij} + \sum_i \sum_j \varphi_{ij}, \qquad (5.1)$$

where:

ϕ_{ij} = a two-level factor taking the value one when i and j are in agreement, and zero otherwise;

φ_{ij} = a two-level factor taking the value one when i and j are in disagreement, and zero otherwise.

Finally, the relative odds of succeeding in changing the draft law when there is either agreement or disagreement between i and j may now be added as interactions. The odds of success for lobbyist i are given by $\omega_i \cdot \phi_{ij}$ in the case where the proposals put forward by i and j are the same and by $\omega_i \cdot \varphi_{ij}$ where they differ, giving the following model:

$$\log C' = \sum_i \theta_i + \sum_i \sum_j \omega_i \phi_{ij} + \sum_i \sum_j \omega_i \varphi_{ij} \qquad (5.2)$$

where:

$\omega_i \phi_{ij}$ = the sum of the main effects that a proposal made by lobbyist i will be successful and that a similar proposal to lobbyist i's will be made by lobby group j, plus the interaction effect on the success of a proposal by lobbyist i when groups i and j put forward the same proposal;

$\omega_i \varphi_{ij}$ = the sum of the main effects that a proposal made by lobbyist i will be successful and that a counter proposal to lobbyist i's will be made by lobby group j, plus the interaction effect on the success of a proposal by lobbyist i when groups i and j make conflicting proposals.

Since the relative odds of success when i and j are in agreement are necessarily identical for the two parties involved, the interaction terms $\omega_i \cdot \phi_{ij}$ and $\omega_j \cdot \phi_{ij}$ are equal. In contrast, since the relative odds that lobby group i will win a contest with j are the inverse of the relative odds that lobby group j will win, $\omega_i \cdot \varphi_{ij}$ is equivalent to $-\omega_j \cdot \varphi_{ij}$.

A summary of the hierarchy of main effects models and their associated factor structure is presented in Table 5.2.2.

5.6. Goodness of fit

The appropriate measure of goodness of fit for a log-linear model with a Poisson error is the deviance (D). The deviance compares the maximised log-likelihood for the nth fitted model (m_n) and fully saturated model and provides a general test of the adequacy of the fitted model.[20] Accordingly, the relative goodness of fit of two nested models (m_1 and m_2) is measured as the difference between their associated deviances ($D_1 - D_2$) where m_1 is nested in m_2. $D_1 - D_2$ is asymptotically chi-squared distributed with $d_1 - d_2$, degrees of freedom. A significant value for $D_1 - D_2$ indicates that

Table 5.2.2. The hierarchy of main effects models of the politics of accounting regulation in Germany[a]

Conditional independence[b]	$\log C' = \sum_i \theta_i$	(1)
Relative influence	$\log C' = \sum_i \theta_i + \sum_i \omega_i$	(2)
Agreement and disagreement	$\log C' = \sum_i \theta_i + \sum_i \omega_i + \phi + \varphi$	(3)
Agreement and disagreement with i	$\log C' = \sum_i \theta_i + \sum_i \omega_i + \sum_i \phi_i + \sum_i \varphi_i$	(4.1)
Agreement and disagreement between i and j	$\log C' = \sum_i \theta_i + \sum_i \omega_i + \sum_i \sum_j \phi_{ij} + \sum_i \sum_j \varphi_{ij}$	(5.1)

where:

C' = a vector of observations representing the observed counts in Table 5.2.1, less a constant term;

θ_i = the odds of a proposal being made by lobby group i;

ω_i = the odds of a proposal made by i succeeding;

i = industry (IND), auditors (AUD) or academics (ACA);

ϕ = the odds that, for a given issue, two lobby groups make the same proposal;

φ = the odds that, for a given issue, two lobby groups make different proposals;

ϕ_i = the odds of agreement with i;

φ_i = the odds of disagreement with i;

ϕ_{ij} = the odds that i and j make the same proposal, where $i \neq j$;

φ_{ij} = the odds that i and j make conflicting proposals, where $i \neq j$;

---

[a] The model is a log-linear model with a log link function and a Poisson distributed error. The dependent variable is a vector representing the log of the observed counts in Table 5.2.1, while the explanatory variables are a series of n-level factors. All estimated coefficients are log-odds ratios (i.e., the exponent of the regression coefficient is the relative odds of the count falling into one of the possible categories). A regression coefficient of zero therefore implies odds equal to one, while a positive (negative) coefficient implies odds greater (less) than one.

[b] The model of conditional independence allows the probability of a proposal being made to vary across the three constituent groups while holding constant their relative influence on the decisions of the legislature. The model of relative influence evaluates the odds of success for each of the three lobbyists, conditional on a proposal being made. The model of agreement and disagreement extends the model of relative influence to account for the main effects of agreement and disagreement. Generalising further, model (4.1) accounts for the relative odds of agreement or disagreement with lobby group i. This model is further extended by adding the interaction terms $\omega_i \cdot \phi_i$ and $\omega_i \cdot \varphi_i$ which, respectively, capture i's relative odds of success given agreement or disagreement with either of the remaining constituent groups. Finally, model (5.1) accounts for all possible two-way cases of agreement and disagreement between each pair of lobbyists i and j. This model is extended by adding the interactions $\omega_i \cdot \phi_{ij}$ and $\omega_i \cdot \varphi_{ij}$ which, respectively, capture i's relative odds of success in the event of agreement or disagreement between lobbyists i and j.

m_2 is a better model than m_1 or equivalently, that the terms omitted from m_1 are significant. The appropriate F-ratio compares the mean change in deviance $(D_1 - D_2)/(d_1 - d_2)$ and the mean residual deviance (D_2/d_2), and is distributed $F \sim [(d_1 - d_2), d_2]$.

6. Empirical results

Model (1) reflects the propensity for a particular lobbyist to submit a proposal. The coefficients[21] from the model of conditional independence provide evidence of industry's high submission rate and the low level of public involvement by the German audit profession in the rule-development process: industry submitted proposals on 111 of the 169 issues examined (66% proposal rate) compared with 75 proposals submitted by the audit profession (44% proposal rate). Further, German accounting academics are seen to display a higher propensity for public lobbying than the audit profession, in contrast to the findings documented for the US and similar regimes. While this result may partly reflect the German auditor's traditional concern for the application of financial reporting rules, rather than for the development of these rules (Vieten, 1995), the high level of public lobbying activity observed for German accounting academics may result from the evolution of the legal perspective as the dominant research approach to date in Germany, whereby accounting researchers have been actively involved in a form of jurisprudence, by interpreting existing laws where doubts have arisen.[22]

Table 5.2.3 (pp. 306–7) presents tests of the change in deviance for the hierarchy of models discussed above, along with the estimated coefficients. The change in deviance associated with fitting model (2), which provides evidence as to the relative power of the three lobby groups, is not significant at conventional levels ($p = 0.241$). However, it is notable that the odds of success are significantly greater than one for industry (log-odds = 0.652; odds = 1.92 : 1; $t = 3.27$) and significantly less than one for the academic experts (log-odds = -0.466; odds = 1: 1.59; $t = -2.07$). These findings reflect the fact that industry succeeded in 73 out of 111 proposals submitted (i.e. 63%) whereas the academics succeeded in only 32 of their 83 proposals (i.e. 38%). The insignificant coefficient estimate on the ω_{AUD} term indicates that the odds of success for the audit profession were approximately equal to one. Examination of the results documented in panel B of Table 5.2.3 confirms that, after accounting for the general effects of agreement (ϕ) and disagreement (φ), industry's odds remain significantly greater than one ($t = 3.31$), while the odds of success for the auditor constituency remain equal to one and those for the academic constituency are again significantly less than one. In sum, the findings for models (2) and (3) suggest that German industry exerted most influence over the legislature during the transformation of the Fourth Directive into commercial law. In contrast, the influence of the academic community appears to have been relatively low, despite their active participation.

Extension of model (3) to include the general interaction term $\omega \cdot \phi$, which accounts for the log-odds of success given agreement between any two lobby groups, provides further insights into the politics of accounting rule-development in Germany. The positive and significant coefficient on $\omega \cdot \phi$ ($t = 2.65$) indicates that the overall odds of success are increased by more than $2:1$ when any two groups take similar positions with respect to a particular financial reporting issue, reinforcing the view that the responsiveness of the German legislature is a positive function of consensus among lobby groups. The findings for Germany that agreement among constituent groups has been an important factor influencing the decision of the legislature is consistent with the views expressed with respect to the US by Dyckman (1988) and Horngren (1972), both of whom argue that the search for political consensus underlies many of the financial reporting solutions proposed by the FASB.

Models (4.1) and (4.2) account for the relative odds of agreement or disagreement with the ith lobby group. Panel C of Table 5.2.3 reports a significant and positive estimate of ϕ_{AUD} ($t = 3.14$) under the main effects model (4.1), suggesting a high likelihood that lobbying by auditors would have been accompanied by consensus. This effect alone, however, does not change the measures of relative influence, with industry continuing to appear more successful than the other groups. Model (4.2) extends model (4.1) by including interaction terms which account for the relative odds of success when there is agreement or disagreement with lobbyist i. Consistent with the view that agreement among lobby groups represents an important element in the rule-development process, the relative power of industry is seen to have fallen when the empirical model is extended to include interactions with each lobby group, suggesting the existence of important multiplier effects in relation to industry's perceived influence on the decisions of the legislature. Specifically, the relative odds of industry's preferred accounting treatment being incorporated into commercial law now declines from approximately $2:1$ ($t = 3.27$) in the relative power model to just less than $1:1$ ($t = -0.34$) in

Table 5.2.3. The relative influence of constituent lobby groups in Germany (t-statistics in parentheses)[a]

Panel A: Relative influence

	Relative influence of lobby group i			Deviance	$\Delta Deviance$[b]	F[c]	p-value
	ω_{IND}	ω_{AUD}	ω_{ACA}				
Model (2)	0.652	0.295	−0.466	71.747	17.234(1, 2)	1.521	0.241
	(3.27)	(1.27)	(−2.07)				

Panel B: Agreement and disagreement[d]

	Relative influence of lobby group i			Agreement (ϕ) and disagreement (φ)		Deviance	$\Delta Deviance$	F[c]	p-value
	ω_{IND}	ω_{AUD}	ω_{ACA}	ϕ	φ				
Model (3)	0.665	0.279	−0.518	−1.380	−1.708	53.515	18.232(2, 3)	1.817	0.185
	(3.31)	(1.19)	(−2.25)	(−2.54)	(−3.55)				

Panel C: Agreement and disagreement with each lobby group

	Relative influence of lobby group i			Agreement (ϕ) and disagreement (φ) with i										Deviance	$\Delta Deviance$	F[c]	p-value
				$i=$ IND				$i=$ AUD				$i=$ ACA					
	ω_{IND}	ω_{AUD}	ω_{ACA}	ϕ_i	φ_i	$\omega_i\cdot\phi_i$	$\omega_i\cdot\varphi_i$	ϕ_i	φ_i	$\omega_i\cdot\phi_i$	$\omega_i\cdot\varphi_i$	ϕ_i	φ_i	$\omega_i\cdot\phi_i$	$\omega_i\cdot\varphi_i$				
Model (4.1): Main effects	0.593	0.238	−0.411	0.613	1.129			1.243	−0.675			0.393	0.391			50.991	20.756(2, 4.1)	0.882	0.534
	(2.92)	(0.99)	(−1.78)	(1.57)	(1.75)			(3.14)	(−1.75)			(1.05)	(0.82)						
Model (4.2): Main effects	−0.117	−0.054	−0.632	−0.199	0.795			1.032	−0.745			0.206	0.394			39.943	10.72(4.1, 4.2)	0.323	0.905
	(−0.34)	(−0.13)	(−1.63)	(−0.38)	(1.02)			(1.98)	(−1.38)			(0.46)	(0.67)						
:Interaction effects						0.505	1.242			0.292	0.038			0.390	−0.052				
						(0.75)	(2.55)			(0.53)	(0.50)			(0.75)	(−0.07)				

Panel D: Agreement and disagreement between lobby groups i and j

| | Relative influence of lobby group i | | | Agreement (ϕ) and disagreement (ψ) between i and j | | | | | | | | | |
| | | | | i,j = IND, AUD | | i,j = AUD, ACA | | i,j = ACA, IND | | | | | |
	ω_{IND}	ω_{AUD}	ω_{ACA}	ϕ_i	ψ_i	ϕ_i	ψ_i	ϕ_i	ψ_i	Deviance	ΔDeviance	F^c	p – value
Model (5.1): Main effects	0.548	0.276	−0.398	2.710	1.510	1.971	0.325	1.394	2.686	25.562	$46.185_{(2,\,5.1)}$	3.915	0.019
	(4.29)	(1.09)	(−1.64)	(4.45)	(2.25)	(4.29)	(0.66)	(2.27)	(4.35)				
Model (5.2): Main effects	0.103	0.240	−0.753	2.480	1.920	1.749	0.586	−0.010	2.461	12.899	$12.663_{(5.1,\,5.2)}$	1.145	0.426
	(0.35)	(0.62)	(−1.99)	(3.16)	(2.87)	(2.95)	(0.01)	(0.01)	(3.85)				
:Interaction effects				$\omega_i\cdot\phi_{ij}$	$\omega_i\cdot\psi_{ij}$	$\omega_i\cdot\phi_{ij}$	$\omega_i\cdot\psi_{ij}$	$\omega_i\cdot\phi_{ij}$	$\omega_i\cdot\psi_{ij}$				
				0.166	−1.353	0.150	−1.392	2.095	0.353				
				(0.25)	(−1.53)	(0.21)	(−1.14)	(2.17)	(0.55)				

[a] Reported coefficients are from a log-linear model with a log link function and a Poisson distributed error. The dependent variable is the log of the counts in the cells of Table 5.2.1, adjusted for a mean effect. Coefficient estimates are log-odds ratios: a regression coefficient of zero implies odds equal to one, while a positive (negative) coefficient implies odds greater (less) than one. Subscripts IND, AUD and ACA indicate the industry, auditor and academic lobby groups, respectively. Models are described in Table 5.2.2.

[b] The subscripts in parentheses indicate the nested models for which the change in deviance is reported. The deviance for the model of conditional independence (model 1) is 88.981. Note that the θ_j coefficients in model 1 are also included in all subsequent estimations, but for parsimony are not recorded.

[c] The F-statistic represents a test of the relative goodness of fit of two nested models. The relative goodness of fit is measured as the difference in the associated deviances (ΔDeviance) of two models, x and y, where x is nested in y. The change in deviance is asymptotically F-distributed. A significant F-statistic indicates that y is a better fitting model than x, or equivalently, that the terms omitted from x are significant.

[d] The model of agreement and disagreement may be modified to include interaction terms measuring the general odds of success when there is either consensus ($\omega\cdot\phi$) or conflict ($\omega\cdot\psi$). When these interaction terms are included instead of the separate ω_j effects for the individual lobby groups, the deviance falls from 88.981 for the model of conditional independence to 63.751 ($F = 1.345, p = 0.292$). The relevant coefficient estimates are $\omega\cdot\phi = 0.842(t = 2.65)$ and $\omega\cdot\psi = -0.145$ ($t = -0.75$), again emphasising the positive and significant impact of consensus within the lobbying process.

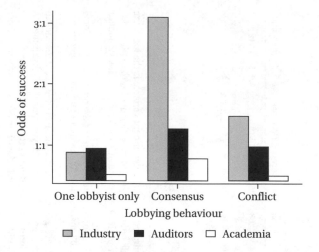

Fig. 5.2.1. The effect of agreement or disagreement between constituent lobby groups in Germany on the likelihood of success of a proposal to amend the draft accounting law.

Notes: the log odds ratios are given in Panel C of Table 5.2.3: as ω_i estimates in the case of one lobbyist alone, $\omega_i\phi_i$ when there is agreement with another party (i.e. consensus) and $\omega_i\varphi_i$ when there is disagreement (i.e. conflict). Agreement with another party increases the odds of success considerably for all lobbyists. On the other hand, when there is disagreement between lobbyists, only industry tends to be more successful.

model (4.2) in those cases where the only proposal to have been made is from industry. However, the positive and significant coefficient for the $\omega_{\text{IND}} \cdot \phi_{\text{IND}}$ interaction term indicates that the relative odds of an industry-submitted proposal being recognised in commercial law were more than three times greater ($t = 2.55$) when industry's preferences were aligned with those of one of the remaining lobbying organisations (see Figure 5.2.1 above). We interpret these findings as evidence that industry's influence on the decisions of the legislative body was crucially dependent on the support of at least one of the remaining lobby groups.

Several factors may help explain these observed multiplier effects. First, Watts and Zimmerman (1986) argue that industry's lobbying position is primarily motivated on opportunistic grounds. This self-interest motive can serve to reduce the credibility of industry-submitted proposals, thereby reducing the likelihood of their acceptance. However, to the extent that industry's position appears more credible when supported by a group of acknowledged financial reporting experts (in this case, either the audit profession or accounting academics), the likelihood of acceptance increases. Secondly, it is widely acknowledged that industry represents a powerful lobby group in Germany. Consequently, for cases in which their position was matched by one or more financial reporting constituencies, a body of opinion may have been created whose political influence was simply too great for the legislature to ignore.

Models (5.1) and (5.2) account for agreement and disagreement between industry and auditors, industry and academics, or auditors and academics. Model (5.1) estimates the main effects for agreement and disagreement between lobbyists i and j and leads to a significant fall in the deviance ($p = 0.019$) with respect to the model of relative influence, as documented in panel D of Table 5.2.3, suggesting that identification of the specific parties involved is an important explanatory factor. The findings confirm the inference drawn previously that the auditors were likely to adopt the position of another group, either industry ($t = 4.45$) or academia ($t = 4.29$), while the latter two were more likely to be in conflict with each other ($t = 4.35$). Model (5.2) extends model (5.1) to account for the odds of success in cases of agreement and disagreement between groups i and j. Results indicate that industry's relative power declined substantially when such interactions were accounted for, again suggesting that the ability of German industry to influence the policy decisions of the legislature may have been largely conditional on the support of at least one of the remaining constituent-groups. In particular, model (5.2) suggests the existence of a significant multiplier effect when there is agreement between industry and academia ($t = 2.17$). Thus, while the academic community appears to have exerted relatively little influence over the decisions of the legislature when considered in isolation, German academics are seen to have derived significant influence through their interaction with industry.

6.1. Partitioning by accounting issue

Extant research by Puro (1984) and Sutton (1984) suggests that the distribution of power among alternative lobby groups may vary as a function of the nature of the financial reporting issue under consideration. To explore this possibility further, we partitioned the 169 separate points of accounting law into two groups, one of which comprised all points of law relating to issues of valuation and recognition ($N = 92$) while the other comprised all points of law relating to issues of disclosure and financial statement format ($N = 77$). While acknowledging the inherently

Table 5.2.4. The relative success of industry, auditors and academics, partitioned by type of accounting issue (t-statistics in parentheses)[a]

Model	Relative influence (Model 2)		Agreement and disagreement between i and j			
			(Main effects model 5.1)		(Interaction effects model 5.2)	
	Valuation and recognition	Format and disclosure	Valuation and recognition	Format and disclosure	Valuation and recognition	Format and disclosure
ω_{IND}	0.251	1.308	0.073	1.206	0.030	0.262
	(1.00)	(3.68)	(0.26)	(3.34)	(0.07)	(0.62)
ω_{AUD}	0.550	0.000	0.576	0.122	0.486	−0.022
	(1.70)	(0.00)	(1.61)	(0.31)	(0.86)	(−0.04)
ω_{ACA}	−0.133	−0.898	−0.234	−0.72	−0.859	−0.730
	(−0.45)	(−2.51)	(−0.72)	(−1.86)	(−1.51)	(−1.41)
Deviance	46.922	50.431	16.034	17.461	9.283	1.674
ΔDeviance[b]	$4.191_{(1,\,2)}$	$23.447_{(1,\,2)}$	$30.888_{(2,\,5.1)}$	$32.970_{(2,\,5.1)}$	$6.751_{(5.1,\,5.2)}$	$15.787_{(5.1,\,5.2)}$
F^{c}	0.566	2.945	4.173	4.091	0.848	11.005
p-value	0.644	0.059	0.014	0.015	0.571	0.003

[a] The initial sample of 169 separate accounting issues has been partitioned into those dealing with valuation and recognition matters ($N = 92$) and those dealing with format and disclosure matters ($N = 77$). Separate generalised linear models were then estimated for each partition. For parsimony, only the relative influence coefficients (ω_i) are reported for all models. The coefficients are from a log-linear model with a log link function and a Poisson distributed error. The dependent variable is the log of the counts from either the valuation and recognition contingency table or format and disclosure contingency table. Coefficient estimates are log-odds ratios: a regression coefficient of zero implies odds equal to one, while a positive (negative) coefficient implies odds greater (less) than one. Subscripts IND, AUD and ACA indicate the industry, auditor and academic lobby groups, respectively.

[b] The subscripts in parentheses indicate the nested models for which the change in deviance is reported.

[c] The F-statistic represents a test of the relative goodness of fit of two nested models. The relative goodness of fit is measured as the difference in the associated deviances (ΔD) of two models, x and y, where x is nested in y. This difference is asymptotically F-distributed. A significant F-statistic indicates that y is a better fitting model than x, or equivalently, that the terms omitted from y are significant.

arbitrary nature of this partitioning scheme, the approach at least partly captures Sutton's characterisation of preparers as more concerned with regulations which affect the measurement of earnings and the valuation of assets and liabilities.[23]

Models (1)–(5) were re-estimated for each sample partition. Table 5.2.4 presents the coefficient estimates and associated deviances for models (2), (5.1) and (5.2). The focus of this table is confined to the ω_i terms as the remaining coefficient estimates were quantitatively similar to those reported in Table 5.2.3. The relative influence attributable to the industry constituency appears to be restricted to issues of disclosure and financial statement formats: in the case of model (2), industry's relative log-odds of success are 1.308 ($t = 3.68$) for format and disclosure issues, compared with only 0.251 ($t = 1.00$) for issues of valuation and recognition. However, consistent with the findings presented in Table 5.2.3, all ω_i coefficient estimates in both sample partitions become insignificant when the effects of agreement or disagreement between lobbyists are accounted for, again emphasising the importance of political consensus with respect to the accounting rule-development process. The differential impact of agreement and disagreement on lobbying success across the various financial reporting issues may be inferred from examination of the reductions in the deviance associated with the estimation of model (5.2) for the two sub-samples: the change in deviance is significant for format and disclosure issues ($p = 0.003$) but not for valuation and recognition issues ($p = 0.571$).

7. Summary and conclusions

This paper presents evidence on the impact of constituent lobbying activity on the policy decisions of the German legislature during the transformation of the Fourth Directive into German commercial law. Three main lobby groups are identified: industry, auditors and academics. With the exception of the levels of lobbying activity observed for the academic constituency, the active groups display a remarkable similarity to those documented for the US and similar regulatory regimes. The high level of participation by German accounting academics, relative to the levels observed in the US, can be partially explained by the active market for legal interpretations in Germany. Together, these results support Sutton's (1984) model of lobbying activity and provide prima facie evidence in support of Sutton's additional conjecture that these patterns will hold irrespective of the institutional setting.

Using publicly available proposals, we identify the preferences of each lobby group with respect to 169 separate accounting issues. These preferences are then reconciled with the eventual accounting treatment required by the Accounting Directives Law as a means of empirically operationalising the concepts of power and influence. Several important findings are documented. First, analysis of the main effects models suggests that the industry lobby group exerted the greatest level of relative power over the legislature, while the proposals issued by the academic community display the least likelihood of success. However, when the empirical model is extended to include interaction terms which account for agreement and disagreement between the lobby-ists, industry's relative power is seen to have declined, suggesting that the influence of preparers on the decision of the legislature depended crucially on the support of at least one of the remaining lobby groups. While the academic community on its own appears to have exerted relat-ively little influence over the decisions of the legislative body, academic experts acting in unison through a formal lobbying group appear to have derived significant influence through their contribution to a process in which agreement between lobbyists was a key feature of account-ing lawmaking. Finally, additional tests indicate that industry's relative power was largely restricted to format and disclosure issues, again depending crucially on the support of either the academic or auditor groups.

Interestingly, German law was amended in May 1998 to mandate a private sector institution to develop accounting standards applicable to group accounts and to advise the Ministry of Justice on changes to accounting law. The *Deutscher Standardisierungsrat* has since been founded and, once published by the Ministry of Justice, the DSR's standards should have the standing of legally-recognised accounting principles.[24] The DSR has been modelled on the FASB, and is staffed by independent experts: three from industry, two auditors, one financial analyst and one academic. Although the DSR will instigate due process for the development of its standards, final decisions will require a two-thirds majority of its board. Therefore, in conclusion, we can say that the consensus between the parties which we have demonstrated in this paper is now being institutionalised within the new framework.

Acknowledgements

The authors gratefully acknowledge the helpful suggestions made by Brian Francis, Pelham Gore, Chris Nobes, Ken Peasnell, and work-shop participants at Frankfurt University, Lancaster University, the University of Wales, Bangor, the 1997 British Accounting Association Conference, the 1997 European Accounting Association Conference and the 1997 Financial Accounting and Auditing Research Confer-ence. Research assistance was provided by Marc Währisch. Financial assistance was provided by the European Union Human Capital and Mobility Programme, Contract ERBCHRXCT.

Notes

1 Notable examples include the 'true and fair view' requirement and the need for increased disclosure.
2 Since this study examines only the transformation of the Fourth Directive into German national law, rather than the development of the Directive at a European level, it is possible that an additional dimension of the political process has been omitted from the analysis. At a national level, the transformation recommendations proposed by any lobby group(s) must have been developed within the framework of the Fourth Directive. Consequently, the framework of the Directive represents a significant external constraint on the regulatory process (Diggle & Nobes, 1994; Hussein & Ketz, 1991).
3 For example, Puro (1984) discusses the coding problems arising from cases in which respondents support one or more parts of an exposure draft while opposing or remaining silent on others.
4 The FASB operates under the continual threat of increased Congressional involvement in the standard-setting process (Kirk, 1988). In the UK, recent changes to the standard-setting structure have resulted in the creation of a direct link between the Financial Reporting Council and the Department of Trade and Industry and while at present the UK government chooses to maintain a relatively passive stance, this position cannot be guaranteed in the future.
5 Further, Chatov (1985) argues that because bodies like the FASB act as agents of the network creating them, they are more likely to accede to the network's wishes, and in the case of conflict are more likely to favour the preferences of the most powerful group.
6 The International Accounting Standards (IASs) permitted by the SEC in cross border filings are IAS 7: Cash Flow Statements, parts of IAS 21: The Effects of Changes in Foreign Exchange Rates and IAS 22: Business Combinations. Further, IASs are now accepted by the London Stock Exchange for cross-border listings.
7 The strong association between financial reporting and tax accounting is the result of the *Maßgeblichkeitsprinzip* which requires that the statutory accounts form the authoritative basis for taxation and the 'reverse authoritativeness principle' (*umgekehrte Maßgeblichkeitsprinzip*), which requires that tax rules must be observed in commercial accounts in order to benefit from tax incentives.
8 No additional specific regulations existed for alternative corporate forms such as limited liability companies or for non-corporations such as partnerships and sole traders.
9 The GoB has been interpreted as meaning 'those principles which are not comprehensively codified but which, by application in specific cases, lead to a correct accounting treatment by reference to the objectives of financial statements. They can be determined deductively by making full use of statute and case law, accounting theory, pronouncements of the Institute of Auditors, as well as accounting practice' (Brooks & Mertin, 1986).
10 For example, the Institute of Auditors (*Institut der Wirtschaftsprüfer*) regularly publishes opinions on legislative pronouncements, laws, and contemporary financial accounting and auditing issues. While these opinions are not legally binding, the risk of an

auditor being accused of professional malpractice is higher if an auditor has certified financial statements that are in conflict with such recommendations (Ordelheide, 1999).

[11] Whereas in the US, performance of the audit function is not a prerequisite for affiliation to the AICPA, membership of the Institute of Auditors is confined to practising auditors only. This distinction reflects fundamental differences in the role attributed to the profession in each country: in the US, the audit profession assumes significant responsibility for the development of accounting standards; by contrast, the German audit profession operates within a more tightly defined jurisdiction, where the emphasis rests firmly on performance of the statutory audit function (Vieten, 1995).

[12] The former is a private organisation of senior accounting and finance managers from the large German corporations, while the latter is an umbrella organisation for various business associations, including representatives from the retail, banking, and small firm sectors. For the purpose of enacting the Fourth Directive, the following groups were involved: the Federation of German Industries; the Association of German Industry and Commerce; the Federation of German Wholesale and Foreign Trade; and the Federation of German Banks (Ordelheide, 1999).

[13] *Der Betrieb* Vol. 31 (1978) pp. 1464–1466; Vol. 32 (1979) pp. 1–8 and 1093–1097; Vol. 33 (1980) pp. 1–12; Vol. 34 (1981) pp. 2448–2462; Vol. 37 (1984) pp. 1–12; Vol. 39 (1986) pp. 1985–1988 and 2553–2556.

[14] *Der Betrieb*: Vol. 32 (1979) pp. 1237–1242 and 1296–1300; *Die Wirtschaftsprüfung*: Vol. 33 (1980) pp. 501–523; Vol. 34 (1981) pp. 609–621; Vol. 37 (1984) pp. 125–140; Vol. 38 (1985) pp. 349–353; Vol. 39 (1986) pp. 537–553.

[15] *Die Betriebswirtschaft*: Vol. 38 (1978) pp. 453–455; Vol. 39 (1979) pp. 1–70; Vol. 40 (1980) pp. 589–597; Vol. 43 (1983) pp. 5–15.

[16] Consistent with prior work, this study focuses on observable lobbying behaviour. To the extent that private lobbying was either more influential than public lobbying, or differed in respect to the nature of the preferences expressed, the results of this study should be interpreted with caution.

[17] Of the 169 points of accounting law identified, 46 related to issues of valuation, 46 to issues of recognition, 36 to issues of financial statement format and 41 to issues of disclosure.

[18] The pluralist model of power has been the subject of significant criticism [see Lukes (1974) and Walker and Robinson (1993) for a discussion]. However, in defence of the pluralist model, Lukes (1974) acknowledges that in many cases it represents the most useful method of operationalizing and analysing power.

[19] Since our interest is restricted to those issues on which at least one of the three lobbyists made a proposal, the corner cell IND = ACA = AUD = 0 is treated as a structural zero (Francis et al., 1993, p. 272).

[20] A significant value for the deviance indicates that a significant term has been omitted from the model. For the Normal model, the deviance is equal to the residual sum of squares, while in the case of the Poisson model it has an interpretation similar to the Pearson goodness of fit statistic (Francis et al., 1993, p. 275).

[21] The θ_i estimates from model (1), representing the log-odds that lobby group i will make a proposal, were as follows: $\theta_{IND} = 3.034$ ($t = 2.98$); $\theta_{AUD} = 2.314$ ($t = 7.62$), $\theta_{ACA} = 2.479$ ($t = 6.61$). T-tests for the significance of individual parameter estimates are based on the assumption of a symmetric likelihood function. Reported t-statistics represent only a guide to the significance of a particular parameter with respect to a null of zero, rather than indicating the relative likelihood, and must therefore be interpreted with caution.

[22] In serving the market for interpretations, some academics will derive support from audit firms or direct from industry. In this respect, they are not necessarily disinterested individuals who serve merely to interpret the law. However, participation in the process

of redrafting the law is through the auspices of an academic body which acts on behalf of the German academic profession as a whole, not individual academics.

[23] Partitioning at a finer level of accounting issue was not possible due to an insufficient number of observations in each partition to allow reliable estimation.

[24] New legislation has also been passed to allow German listed companies the option to use internationally accepted accounting rules in their group accounts as an interim measure until 2004. In turn, the new DSR has been given the task of adapting German accounting principles to international norms by that date.

References

Bayless, R., Cochrane, J., Harris, T., Leisenring, J., McLaughlin, J., & Wirtz, J. P. (1996). International access to US capital markets: an AAA forum on accounting policy. *Accounting Horizons, 10*, 75–94.

Benveniste, G. (1972). *The politics of expertise.* London: Croom Helm.

Brooks, J. P., & Mertin, D. (1986). *Neues Deutsches Bilanzrecht/New German accounting legislation.* Düsseldorf: IDW-Verlag GmbH.

Brown, P. (1981). A descriptive analysis of select input bases of the Financial Accounting Standards Board. *Journal of Accounting Research, 19*, 232–246.

Chatov, R. (1985). The possible new shape of accounting regulation in the United States. *Journal of Accounting and Public Policy, 4*, 161–174.

Diggle, G., & Nobes, C. (1994). European rule-making in accounting: the seventh directive as a case study. *Accounting and Business Research, 24*, 319–334.

Downs, A. (1957). *An economic theory of democracy.* New York: Harper & Row.

Dyckman, T. R. (1988). Credibility and the formulation of accounting standards under the Financial Accounting Standards Board. *Journal of Accounting Literature, 7*, 1–30.

Forster, K. H. (1997). *Adler-During-Schmaltz, Rechnungslegung und Prüfung der Unternehmens.* Stuttgart: Poeschel.

Francis, B., Green, M., & Payne, C. (1993). *GLIM 4.* Oxford: Oxford University Press.

Francis, J. R. (1987). Lobbying against proposed accounting standards. *Journal of Accounting and Public Policy, 6*, 35–57.

Griffin, P. A. (1983). Management's preferences for FASB Statement no. 52: predictive ability results. *Abacus, 19*, 130–138.

Hope, T., & Gray, R. (1982). Power and policy making: the development of an R&D standard. *Journal of Business, Finance, and Accounting, 9*, 531–558.

Horngren, C. T. (1972). Accounting principles: private or public sector? *Journal of Accountancy, 134*, 37–41.

Hussein, M., & Ketz, J. (1980). Ruling elites of the FASB: a study of the big eight. *Journal of Accounting, Auditing and Finance, 3*, 354–367.

———— (1991). Accounting standards-setting in the US: an analysis of power and social exchange. *Journal of Accounting and Public Policy, 10*, 59–81.

Kelly, L. (1982). Corporate lobbying and changes in financing or operating activities in reaction to FAS No. 8. *Journal of Accounting and Public Policy, 2*, 153–173.

—— (1985). Corporate management lobbying on FAS No. 8: some further evidence. *Journal of Accounting Research, 23*, 619–632.

Kirk, D. J. (1988). Looking back on fourteen years at the FASB: the education of a standard setter. *Accounting Horizons, 2*, 8–17.

Klumpes, P. (1994). The politics of accounting rule-making: developing an Australian pension accounting standard. *Abacus, 30*, 159–189.

Lukes, S. (1974). *Power: A radical view*. London: Macmillan.

McCullagh, P., & Nelder, J. A. (1989). *Generalised linear models* (2nd ed.). London: Chapman and Hall.

Nelder, J., & Wedderburn, R. (1972). Generalised linear models. *Journal of the Royal Statistical Society, 135*, 370–384.

Newman, D. P. (1981). An investigation of the distribution of power in the APB and FASB. *Journal of Accounting Research, 19*, 247–262.

Nobes, C. (1991). Cycles in UK standard setting. *Accounting and Business Research, 21*, 265–274.

——, and Parker, R. (1991). *Comparative international accounting*. Hemel Hempstead: Prentice Hall.

Ordelheide, D. (1999). Germany. In S. J. McLeay, *Accounting regulation in Europe*. London: MacMillan.

——, and Pfaff, D. (1994). *European financial reporting: Germany*. London: Routledge.

Power, M. (1997). Academics in the accounting policy process: England and Germany. In J. Flower & C. Lefebvre. *Comparative studies in accounting regulation in Europe*. Leuven: Acco.

Puro, M. (1984). Audit firm lobbying before the Financial Accounting Standards Board: an empirical study. *Journal of Accounting Research, 22*, 624–646.

—— (1985). Do large accounting firms collude in the standards-setting process? *Journal of Accounting, Auditing, and Finance, 8*, 165–177.

Rahman, A. R., Ng, L. W., and Tower, G. D. (1994). Policy choice and standard setting in New Zealand: an exploratory study. *Abacus, 30*, 98–117.

Sunder, S. (1988). Political economy of accounting standards. *Journal of Accounting Literature, 7*, 31–45.

Sutton, T. G. (1984). Lobbying of accounting standard-setting bodies in the UK and the USA: a Downsian analysis. *Accounting, Organisations and Society, 9*, 81–95.

Tandy, P., and Wilburn, N. (1992). Constituent participation in standards-setting: the FASB's first 100 statements. *Accounting Horizons, 6*, 47–58.

—— —— (1996). The academic community's participation in standard setting: submission of comment letters on SFAS Nos. 1–117. *Accounting Horizons, 10*, 92–111.

US Congress. Senate Subcommittee on Reports, Accounting and Management of the Committee on Government Operations (1976). *The accounting establishment: a staff study* (Metcalf Staff Report). 94th Congress, 2nd Session.

Vieten, H. (1995). Auditing in Britain and Germany compared: professions, knowledge, and the state. *European Accounting Review, 4*, 485–511.

Walker, R. G., and Robinson, S. P. (1993). A critical assessment of the literature on political activity and accounting regulation. *Research in Accounting Regulation, 7*, 3–40.

—— —— (1994). Related party transactions: a case study of inter-organisational conflict and the 'development' of disclosure rules. *Abacus, 30*, 18–43.

Watts, R., and Zimmerman, J. (1978). Towards a positive theory of the determination of accounting standards. *The Accounting Review, 53*, 112–134.

—— —— (1986). *Positive accounting theory*. New Jersey: Prentice Hall.

Wyatt. A. (1991). Accounting standards setting at a crossroads. *Accounting Horizons, 5*, 110–114.

——, and Yospe, J. F. (1993). Wake-up call to American business: international accounting standards are on the way. *Journal of Accountancy, 176*, 80–85.

Zeff, S. (1978). The rise of economic consequences. *Journal of Accountancy, 146*, 56–63.

5.3

Drafting Accounting Law: An Analysis of Institutionalized Interest Representation

Stuart McLeay and Doris Merkl

This chapter examines the process through which accounting law was redrafted in Austria in preparation for European Union (EU) membership, paying particular attention to the changes in the legal text of the Financial Reporting Act between the Ministerial and Governmental drafts. The Ministerial draft was the outcome of discussions between representatives of employers, employees, academics, and accountants in an attempt to reach consensus on the legal text in cooperation with the Ministry of Justice. These deliberations took place behind closed doors, but were followed by a process of public consultation. In these circumstances, we are able to identify changes in those aspects of accounting law to which the main parties could not at first agree, and hence to assess the *unconditional* influence of powerful groups that is exercised in circumstances where disagreement between the parties is already apparent.

1. Introduction

This chapter examines the politics of accounting regulation by investigating the process through which accounting law was redrafted in Austria in preparation for EU membership. Particular attention is paid to the opportunities that were provided to interested parties to influence the legal text, as evidenced in this specific case by the changes that took place between the Ministerial and Governmental drafts of the Austrian Financial Reporting Act. The chapter is motivated by Dieter Ordelheide's research on the legal dimensions of accounting regulation (Ordelheide and Pfaff 1994; Ordelheide 1999), and builds directly on the statistical methodology developed in McLeay, Ordelheide, and Young (2000). Together, these two empirical studies, the first in Germany and the second in Austria, provide rare evidence on the processes underlying accounting rule-making in a strictly legal context. This is in contrast to the many published analyses of the procedures adopted by standard-setting agencies, which tend to draw up their own rules of accounting in the shadow of the law rather than within the legal system itself.

In spite of the many connections between Austria and Germany, and the ample scope for transferring legal text in the German language from one jurisdiction to the other, the processes that were adopted by the legislatures in these two member states of the EU, when implementing the accounting directives, were substantially different. In Germany, the lengthy procedure was one of initial public consultation that was followed up by invitations to a large number of representative organizations to comment on each new draft of the law. In Austria, in contrast, the first legal draft was the outcome of deliberations that took place behind closed doors. These discussions, between representatives of employers, employees, academic experts, and practicing accountants, were undertaken in an attempt to allow a small number of key interest groups to reach early consensus on the legal text in cooperation with the Ministry of Justice, and were followed later by a process of public consultation. This chapter describes the background to these events and then focuses attention on those aspects of accounting law to which the main parties could not at first agree, leading to an assessment of the *unconditional* influence of powerful groups that is exercised in circumstances where disagreement between the parties is already apparent.

2. The origins of Austrian accounting legislation

From an international perspective, the case of Austrian law-making warrants detailed examination because the setting is one in which the tensions between jurisdictional autonomy and the processes of globalization have long been evident. This is not a reference to the hegemony of the English-speaking world that is central to much international accounting research, but refers instead to the neighborly relationship between

Austria and Germany.[1] Indeed, the history of Austria has been inter-twined with that of Germany for centuries and, like any two countries sharing a common language and history, they exhibit very similar institu-tional and organizational structures that are usually the result of transfers from the politically more dominant party. Until 1871, when the Second German Empire was established, the flow was from Austria, which had headed the German Empire until 1806 and continued to be a power-ful presence in the form of the Austrian Empire under the Habsburg dynasty.[2] When the Austro-Hungarian Empire ceased to exist and Austria became the small federal republic it is today, this flow reversed.[3]

Because of their geographic proximity and close ties, today Germany is Austria's most important trading partner. It is hardly surprising therefore that Austria often follows Germany's example as far as business matters such as accounting regulation are concerned. This was not the case ini-tially, however, as the first comprehensive legal instrument of accounting regulation in the German language was the Austrian General Commer-cial Code, the *Allgemeines Handelsgesetzbuch*, established in 1863. It remained in place throughout the Austro-Hungarian Empire and the First Republic (see Table 5.3.1).[4] In the course of the twentieth century, the approach to accounting regulation changed.[5] Indeed, a major impe-tus to Austrian financial reporting occurred by means of the introduction of German company law in 1938 in the course of the annexation of Austria by Germany. The *Aktiengesetz*, which had been implemented in Germany in 1937, remained in place when Austria regained its independence and was only replaced in 1965. In contrast to Germany, which carried out a major financial reporting reform in the same year, the 1965 revisions in Austria basically represented no more than an "austrification" (Janschek 1987: 82) of the German prewar company law.[6]

An amendment to these accounting regulations was initiated in June 1982, which led to consensus amongst all political parties to undertake a major reform of financial reporting regulation in Austria.[7] An under-lying motive, however, was the harmonization of Austrian financial reporting practices with European directives in anticipation of joining the European Community. The result was the Financial Reporting Act (*Rechnungslegungsgesetz*) of 1990, which reformed Austrian financial reporting by consolidating the various accounting regulations that previ-ously had been dispersed amongst the Commercial Code, the Company Law, and other legislation.[8] Interestingly, like the 1938 legislation, the law of 1990 also involved a ready-made solution from Germany.

This asymmetric power relationship between the two countries is widely recognized but often remains unquestioned. For instance, the

Table 5.3.1. The historical evolution of accounting legislation in Austria

Legal instrument	Date	Details of legislation
Royal order (*Hofdekret*)	1768	Requirement for all merchants to keep accounts
Austria and Germany become separate states	1806	Development of separate, but interdependent Austrian and German financial reporting regulations
Governmental permission (*Vereinspatent*)	1852	Creation of public share-issuing limited liability companies (AGs) under government permission
General Commercial Code (*Allgemeines Handelsgesetzbuch, AHGB*)	1863	Requirement to retain books and business correspondence for 10 years, prepare a balance sheet and an inventory; ban on capitalization of intangible assets, unless acquired by way of purchase; and obligation to capitalize assets and debts at market value at balance sheet date, to write-off doubtful debts partly and irrecoverable debts completely
Amendment of the General Commercial Code	1874	Requirement of stock companies to establish a reserve fund and a profit and loss account
Regulation concerning stocks (*Aktienregulativ*)	1899	Universal right to official permission for the establishment of stock companies if certain prescriptions are fulfilled
Private Limited Company Law (*Gesetz über Gesellschaften mit beschränkter Haftung, GmbH*)	1906	Private limited company (GmbH) as new corporation structure
Annexation of Austria by Germany	1938	Introduction of German financial reporting regulations to Austria
German Company Law (*Aktiengesetz*)	1938	Formats for balance sheet and profit and loss account, and preparation thereof; requirement to conform to the principles of proper bookkeeping (guidelines concerning accounting, inventory, the balance sheet, etc.; for example prudence in asset valuation, true and correct presentation, consistency, completeness, and clarity); asset valuation at purchase price or manufacturing cost; option to apply either the cost or the attributable value principle for fixed assets, whichever is lower; lower of cost or market principle for securities; historical cost principle for current assets; and definition of production costs; requirements for the AG to install a board of supervisors, to produce a business report, and to audit the accounts
Austria regains its independence	1945	Development of separate, but interdependent Austrian and German financial reporting regulations
Amendment of Company Law (*Aktiengesetz*)	1965	No significant changes
Amendment of private limited company law (*GmbHNov*)	1980	Application of the AG law concerning bookkeeping, auditing, disclosure, and the annual business report to 'large' GmbHs
Company Law Transformation Act (*Gesellschaftsrechtsänderungsgesetz*)	1982	Obligation of auditor to report on impending insolvency or irregularities in annual accounts; abolition of possibility to extend time span for registration of annual accounts at register court; submission of auditor's report to every member of the supervisory board

Continued

Financial Reporting Act (*Rechnungslegungsgesetz*)	1990	New layout of balance sheet and profit and loss account, and requirement to prepare notes on the financial statements; requirement to apply the same methods of valuation consistently from one year to the next, restriction on the creation of hidden reserves, ban on capitalizing administrative and selling expenses, option to capitalize business development costs, which have to be depreciated over 5 years, and requirement to write-off goodwill systematically over a period not exceeding its useful economic life; "true and fair view" as legal objective of financial statements; differences concerning the requirements on auditing and disclosure between "big" and "small" AGs
	1994	Requirement to compile group accounts
Austria joins the EU	1995	Harmonization of Austrian financial reporting regulations with the 4th, 7th and 8th EU Directives
EU-Company Law Transformation *Act (EU-Gesellschaftsrechtsänderungsgesetz, EU-GesRÄG)*	1996	Reclassification of limited liability companies into "small," "medium," and "large"
Ministerial Decree (*Verordnung*)	1997	Concerning the use of forms regarding size-dependent disclosures
Consolidation Act (*Konzernabschlußgesetz*)	1999	Option for listed companies to prepare their consolidated accounts according to IAS or U.S.-GAAP
Amendment of the Commercial Code (*Änderung des Handelsgesetzbuchs*)	2000	Extension of exceptions of joint stock companies of a certain size regarding individual accounts, but removal of these exceptions for consolidated accounts
Amendment of the Commercial Code (*Änderung des Handelsgesetzbuchs*)	2001	Option for companies to electronically transfer annual accounts to the register court and obligation of register courts to publish annual accounts in electronic form

tradition of "borrowing" or "imitation" has been justified by the close economic ties between the two countries, as follows:

The Fourth EC Directive and the German "Bilanzrichtliniengesetz" formed the basis for the new 'Austrian Financial Reporting Act'. Because of the close relationship between Austria and Germany, and the special nature of the Austrian economy, the new Act (RLG) follows fairly closely the German Accounting Directives Law. Germany is Austria's most important economic partner, its dominant role can be seen in the fact that both the Austrian Commercial Code and the Tax Law tend to follow the corresponding German rules. (Mandl 1993: 397)

The last two comprehensive changes to Austrian legislation, the *Rechnungslegungsgesetz* of 1990 and its successor in 1996, reflect the legal tradition as in Germany of referring to general principles, that is "the principles of proper bookkeeping" that form the basis upon which solutions for specific problems are sought (Lukas and Zetter,

1997; Eberhartinger 2000). They may lead to different interpretations, in which case it is the duty of the courts to resolve the conflict by means of a judgment, which then assumes a legally binding character. As the regulations are traditionally broad in scope and open to interpretation, this has also given rise to independent commentaries on the issues surrounding financial reporting. In fact, Ordelheide's observation that in Germany "lawyers, judges, auditors, accounting academics and other experts from the business and public sectors . . . offer interpretations of accounting law" (Ordelheide 1999: 112) is equally applicable in Austria. It follows that another justification for the closeness between the two legal systems is that it enables experts to base their interpretation of Austrian law upon German law, and to use German reference works on the subject as background in commenting on the Austrian rules (Eberhartinger et al. 1999). Nowotny, an academic member of the ministerial working group on Austria's Financial Reporting Act, refers to the economic gains arising from legal transfer whilst emphasizing the preservation of some order of national distinctiveness by avoiding "slavish imitation" of German law, as follows:

The harmonisation of German law with EU accounting regulations held particular interest for Austria because of practical considerations. This does not, however, signify a slavish imitation of the German *Bilanzrichtliniengesetz*. However, as far as company law is concerned, this historical closeness to German commercial law has been advantageous since there is a rich source of jurisprudence and reference works available to deal with numerous problems of interpretation. In a small economic region this resource for problem-solving could only be developed gradually. (Nowotny, 1987: 183f.; translation)[9]

In one of Austria's leading commercial law reviews, *Recht der Wirtschaft (RdW)*, this free-rider advantage is elevated to the level of the law-makers themselves and is mentioned as the main driving force behind the use of German regulations as a model in commercial law-making in Austria:

The Austrian Ministerial Draft concerning the new financial reporting regulations is largely based on the German Accounting Directives Law. This imitation is a deliberate attempt to further utilise German academic accounting research and jurisprudence, thus continuing an established tradition in commercial law. (*RdW* 1988/6b: 278; translation)

Yet the possibility of unanimous, unquestioning acceptance of legal transfers from Germany is surprising if one considers the particularities of Austria's national identity. It is, like that of many countries sharing linguistic, cultural, and economic ties with a dominant neighbor, such as Ireland and Canada, largely derived in contrast to that neighbor, that is as not being German, British, and American. This negative identity involves insisting on a difference, without being able to define it. It is remarkable therefore that Austrians, who allege their national distinctiveness in most other aspects of life, ranging from their language and literature to their political system, might readily encourage and accept German legal transplants as far as corporate activities are concerned.[10] A possible explanation for such a phenomenon could be that all parties involved in the regulation and enactment of accounting rules benefit. That is to say, the Austrian legislature may gain by free-riding on ready-made German regulations, the accounting professionals by utilizing the "rich source of [German] jurisprudence and reference works" mentioned above, and the academic experts by having a wider platform for their publications.

At the same time, the connection between Austrian and German accounting regulation could also be considered to be weakening, as the International Accounting Standards Board (IASB) and the Financial Accounting Standards Board (FASB) have become more important influences (Eberhartinger et al., 1999). But this does not necessarily mean that Germany's influence on Austrian accounting is on the decline. An alternative explanation is that the influence of the IASB and the United States takes place indirectly through Germany. Consequently, the connection between Austrian and German accounting regulation might not be weakening, but just becoming more complex. Indeed, traditionally, German accounting regulations are not just imported into Austria, but are also assigned a higher authority. Whenever individuals and organizations are opposed to a particular Austrian regulation, which happens to differ from its German counterpart, the fact that the latter emanates from Germany is used as a means of justifying their argument. A good example of this phenomenon is a complaint by the Association of Austrian Banks and Bankers that the Austrian draft of the 1990 Act does not grant financial institutions exceptional status, as far as the build-up of hidden reserves is concerned:

In this particular case we should also follow the German legislator's example of allowing German banks in §26/1 dKWG[11] to fall below the valuation limits stated by the HGB[12] in the case of receivables and securities constituting current assets. (Association of Austrian Banks and Bankers 1988; translation)

The consensus opinion seems to be that German regulations are an example that should be followed, and that justification is required when Austrian regulations differ from the German model, and not when they follow it. Consequently, it would appear on the face of it that any interest group that seeks to influence accounting regulations in Austria faces an uphill struggle, having to establish a "difference" and "distance" from German regulations. However, whilst the interrelationship between Germany and Austria constitutes an important aspect of political activity in the Austrian regulatory process, in so far as this tradition of "borrowing" and "imitation" forms an integral part of the wider set of arrangements for rule-making activity, there are two aspects of the political processes surrounding the implementation of EU accounting directives, which differed considerably between these two countries. First, the directives had already been implemented in Germany when Austria began the process, and therefore the legal text was readily available. Second, whilst both legal systems provided for public consultation over the drafting of the instrument that implemented EU accounting directives, the process in Germany was one of initial public consultation followed by repeated soundings of a large number of interest groups over successive legal drafts. In Austria, however, the first legal draft was the outcome of preliminary discussions *in camera* between a small number of representative organizations, followed by public consultation over the unresolved issues. In the next section, this overtly "corporatist" approach in Austria is discussed in greater detail.

3. Austrian corporatism and accounting regulation

If it is assumed that uncovering the power relationships inherent in the regulatory process goes beyond analyzing interest group participation in decision-making and encompasses an understanding of the institutional structure of society, it is necessary to discuss the role of corporatism in the modern Austrian political and socioeconomic landscape, and the link that is provided between civil society and the state. Indeed, this allows us to incorporate an important aspect of accounting regulation into our analysis, namely the political activity occurring in terms of rule-making processes and organizational structures.

The Austrian political system has provided ideal conditions for corporatism to flourish, through the stability of structures and continuity in the formulation and implementation of policies (Karlhofer 1996). This has been achieved by means of concentrating interests in encompassing associations, namely the Chamber of Commerce and the Chamber of Labour.[13] Any laws impacting on social and economic issues, including financial reporting regulations, have required the formal involvement of these associations. It appears that, while representing the particular interests of their members, the chambers have been able to achieve a high level of cooperation and conflict resolution and serve a wider public interest despite the fact that they are also in competition with one another (Tálos and Kittel 1996).

This organizational cooperation is achieved by means of social partnership (*Sozialpartnerschaft*), which constitutes a major element of corporatism, through repeated negotiations (Unger 1999). This not only takes place between the Chamber of Commerce and the Chamber of Labour, but also between them and the state, the third partner in the corporatist framework. Stability is provided by the interplay between three elements, namely the legal framework, the chamber system, and the interlacing between interest organizations and political parties (Karlhofer 1996). Due to their quasi-monopolized position (membership of these organizations is compulsory for employees and employers), the chambers have a powerful and pervasive influence in Austria's political and socioeconomic landscape. Indeed, by formally involving the chambers in social and economic legislation, the social partnership acts as a state-sponsored instrument of privileged, institutionalized lobbying.[14]

A further aspect is the alignment between political parties and these interest groups. These alliances come to bear during the law-making process and thus add complexity to the lobbying process.[15] What is more, apart from the Chamber of Commerce and the Chamber of Labour, two other associations with voluntary membership have rights of participation in the legislative process. The resulting structure of interest

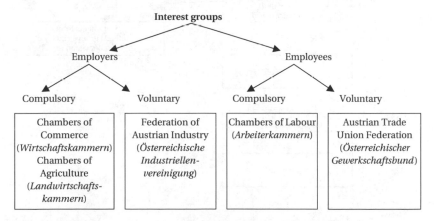

Fig. 5.3.1. The structure of interest representation in Austria.

Note: Interest representation during the drafting of law is either a statutory obligation or a right to participate. Thus, the involvement of designated interest groups in the legislative process is either compulsory or voluntary, as indicated above.

representation in Austria is shown in Figure 5.3.1, suggesting a degree of balance in so far as the power distribution of employers and employees is concerned.

When laws are drawn up, the relevant ministry takes the role of mediator between the interest groups. Often the ministry prepares a list of dissenting opinions after the interest organizations have provided their statements on a draft. Subsequently, the list is discussed by the interest

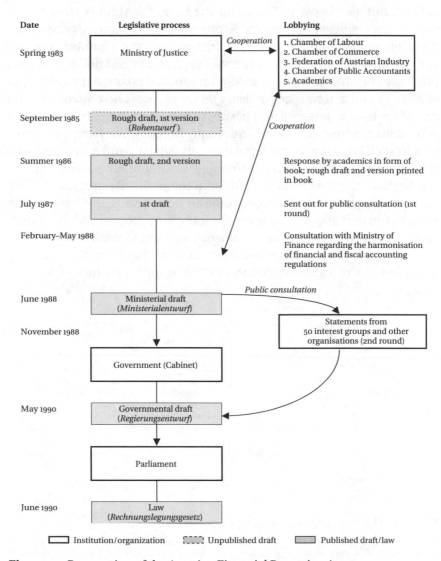

Fig. 5.3.2. Preparation of the Austrian Financial Reporting Act 1990.

group representatives under the mediation of the minister or a ministerial representative (Tálos and Kittel 1996: 38).[16] The law then progresses
further through various stages. At some point during this process, an
"interested public" is invited to submit statements, which are then considered in subsequent drafting stages. Finally, Austria's legislative body,
the Parliament, passes the law.

Figure 5.3.2 shows the development of the Financial Reporting Act
through its various stages together with the regulatory structure inherent in accounting legislation. The Chamber of Commerce and the
Chamber of Labour were involved in the drafting process as statutory participants of the two working groups together with representatives of the
Ministry of Justice, the Federation of Austrian Industry, and additional
technical expertise provided by the Chamber of Public Accountants
and authoritative academics.[17] The law progressed through four draft
stages before it was passed by Parliament in 1990. Table 5.3.2 provides
a summary of the legal drafts, relevant publications and supporting
documentation.

Interest group representation occurred via two channels, namely
(a) the two working groups, one for financial reporting and the other

Table 5.3.2. Drafting stages of the Austrian Financial Reporting Act

	Legal drafts	Relevant publications	Supporting documentation
1985	Rough draft *Rohentwurf*	Not published	Unavailable/nonexistent
1986	Second draft	Egger and Ruppe 1987: 277–319.	Compilation of academic opinion
1988	Ministerial draft *Ministerialentwurf*	*RdW* 1988(6)b.	Deliberations of two ministerial working groups. Formal written submissions by 50 representative organizations and others
1990	Governmental draft *Regierungsentwurf*	*RdW* 1990(5)b.	Transcript of parliamentary debate

Note: The analysis reported in this chapter draws upon the documents relating to the Ministerial draft, as highlighted in the table.

for group accounting, and (*b*) the submission of statements by various interested parties.[18] Although there is little information available regarding the relative influence of the various representative organizations within the working groups, the outcome of the deliberations of the ministerial working groups in Austria is contained in an internal document prepared by the Ministry of Justice, dated May 1988, which lists the issues that remained open or were not resolved and the different views of the various interest groups on these particular issues.[19] The 'interested public" was invited to submit statements on the third draft, the *Ministerialentwurf* (Ministerial draft). Fifty individuals and organizations responded to the call for comments, and these were taken into consideration during the fourth and final draft, the *Regierungsentwurf* (Governmental draft), which was approved by the Cabinet.[20]

4. Analysis of interest representation in accounting regulation

Research concerning the involvement of interest groups in accounting regulation covers a variety of settings, not only the development of financial accounting standards[21] but also the preparation of public sector accounting standards (Ryan et al. 1999, 2000), the preparation of auditing standards (Brennan and Pierce 2001), and the drafting of accounting law (McLeay et al. 2000). Much of the research in this area focuses either on identifying the factors that motivate interested parties to respond to exposure drafts, or on assessing the responsiveness of policy-makers to constituent pressure and understanding the dispersion of power among competing interest groups. The first area has its origins in positive accounting theory and mainly addresses the imbalance between the parties in their participation in regulatory processes. The other strand of research can be traced back to Sutton's emphasis on "the actions which 'interested parties' take to influence the rule-making body" (Sutton 1984: 81). In this respect, however, Walker and Robinson's (1993) criticism concerning the tendency of accounting regulation research to rely on a narrow view of the regulatory process and power relationships is still valid. They argue that research concerned solely with the quantitative analysis of written submissions to the regulatory body has limited validity in that it only captures the final stages of the overall process. The earlier stages, which are concerned with contests over the powers of regulatory bodies, the composition of boards, and the overall structure of regulatory arrangements, also have a considerable impact on regulatory outcomes.

Walker and Robinson also draw attention to the fact that analyses of written submissions are informed by a one-dimensional view of power implicit in pluralism, where the involvement of interest groups in competition with each other is regarded as the single most important feature of organized political life.[22] Within the pluralist model, power is dispersed over a wide range of organized groups and only manifests itself in participation in decision-making. An alternative model, elitism, whereby power is concentrated in the hands of those who occupy commanding positions in large institutionalized hierarchies, results in a focus upon the sources of power, not its exercise. But we may go further still, beyond elitism and pluralism. Rather than seeing power as the result of individual decision-makers, it is collective forces and social arrangements that are held to be important, particularly in setting agendas. Once this is accepted, then it is not enough to point to instances of conflict and claim that they are the only sites of power. Indeed, a particularly effective use of power is to prevent conflict of various sorts from arising in the first place, something which cannot be seen if attention is paid only to observable conflict.[23]

Since previous accounting research in this area has been based predominantly on the pluralist decisional method, its approach to, and assumptions about, power predetermine the findings and results. Weetman (2001) is an exception in this respect. By using a political model that contrasts three alternative interpretations of the concept of power, Weetman goes beyond the issue of the uni-dimensional distribution of power in the lobbying process to explore issues that are not addressed by conventional analysis, such as the ways in which decisions are prevented from being taken (i.e. a two-dimensional view), and the ways in which potential issues are kept out of view altogether by control of the political agenda (a three-dimensional view), thereby shifting the focus from individual issues toward the structural influences that shape accounting standard-setting. Accordingly, Weetman comes to regard the lobbying activity surrounding FRS 3 in the United Kingdom not as evidence of a consensus-based approach to accounting standard-setting, but as "a mechanism for creating a new definition of consensus in which the critical issues are argued out in private before the consultation is brought to the public domain as an exposure draft for a final polish" (Weetman 2000: 105).

This understanding of the politics of accounting regulation lies at the heart of our own analysis of law-making. As discussed earlier, we focus on a distinctive step in the political process that underlies the development of accounting law in Austria whereby, after the initial round of discussion between the principal interest groups and the preparation of a preliminary draft law behind closed doors, the public interest is then addressed by setting down unresolved issues for further comment. Prima facie, the institutional context of Austrian law-making would appear to be quite different from standard-setting by a delegated agency. However, the analysis reported in this study reveals how the forces shaping the socio-political and economic landscape impact on law-making and thus on accounting regulation in a manner that mirrors Weetman's characterization of standard-setting.

In particular, although the detailed proceedings within the two ministerial working groups that were outlined above are not accessible to analysis and our study is restricted to comments on unresolved issues that were submitted at a later stage, the process itself has important implications for the underlying power relationships between the parties involved. As suggested, the type of lobbying analysis that is based on the pluralist decisional method might not be sufficient in this particular regulatory framework, since it is based on a one-dimensional view of power regarding decisions on issues over which there is an observable conflict of interests and where policy preferences are revealed by political participation (see Lukes 1974: 15). In this particular context, the notion of power that focuses on control over the political agenda may be more fitting. Such an approach captures the type of power inherent in the corporatist framework, namely that of preventing conflict from arising in the first place, and which might not be appreciated if attention is paid only to observable conflict. According to Lukes (1974: 24), this is the most effective and insidious use of power, which has its source in the "contradiction between the interests of those exercising power and the real interests of those they exclude."[24] Although the following analysis of submitted statements examines the impact of interest group participation as just part of the process, the evidence that is reported is consistent with the view that public consultation in the final stages could be little more than a symbolic act, as there are no significant asymmetries in the distribution of power. However, the results also tend to show that interest groups with similar proposals are more likely to see changes in the law when they lobby the lawmaker.

Finally, with regard to the research method, it should be noted that lobbying research that is based on written submissions invariably entails the quantification of qualitative data. It is not surprising therefore that major methodological problems in lobbying research revolve around the issues of categorizing the lobbyists and their responses, the scope of the text that is analyzed, the nature of the coding method that is applicd, and the type of modeling that is undertaken. For example, lobbyists are commonly characterized by reference to key groupings, but these may well be defined in the light of the particular set of comments. Moreover, depending on the focus and depth of the analysis, the analysis may be based either on the written submission as a whole (Tandy and Wilburn 1996; Gilfedder and Ó hÓgartaigh 1998) or on individual issues addressed in such submissions (Harding and McKinnon 1996; Weetman et al. 1996; Weetman 2000; Ryan et al. 1999, 2000; McLeay et al. 2000; Brennan and Pierce 2001).[25] Submissions are either coded in binary form, such as "agree/disagree" (McLeay et al. 2000; Brennan and Pierce 2001), or according to a more discriminating scale with several ordered categories (Harding and McKinnon 1997; Weetman et al. 1996; Ryan et al. 1999, 2000; Weetman 2000; Brennan and Pierce 2001). The reported measurements range from descriptive frequencies of occurrence (Harding and McKinnon 1996; Gilfedder and Ó hÓgartaigh 1998) to probabilistic expectations of outcomes (McLeay et al. 2000). The approach taken in this chapter is based on the outcomes of written submissions, which permits some statistical inference even with a relatively small number of cases, as is shown in the analysis that is set out below.

5. Analysis

The analysis is based on an internal ministerial document listing unresolved issues in the Ministerial draft, together with formal written statements concerning this draft submitted by interest groups and individuals.[26] The focus of our analysis will be on changes that have an effect on accounting, excluding a number of comments that concerned minor corrections to the wording of the legal text and including a number of new proposals and suggested clarifications. When these are pooled with comments on unresolved issues identified in the internal ministerial document mentioned above, twenty-three sections of the draft law were candidates for amendment.

Table 5.3.3 (pp. 332–3) lists the respondents and the points of law to which their proposals relate. Altogether, eighty-three comments were made on fifty-four separate issues by twenty-four individuals and organizations. Of the latter, eleven were representatives of associations: six

Table 5.3.3. Proposals to amend Austrian accounting legislation, by point of law

Lobbyist	Reference ($$)																										
	10	189/2	189/4a	189/4b	193/2	195a	195b	195c	195d	195e	195f	198/3a	198/3b	198/3c	198/7a	198/7b	198/8a	198/8b	198/8c	198/8d	198/8e	201/1a	201/1b	201/1c	202	203a	203b
Ministry of Economic Affairs	Y																										
Strommer, Reich-Rohrwig, Karasek			Y	Y								N			Y								Y		Y		Y
Chamber of Public Accountants	N			N			N																		Y		
Association of Austrian Newspaper Publishers	N																										
Federation of Austrian Industry	N											N				Y							Y				
Austrian Chamber of Labour					Y	N																					
Federal Chamber of Commerce	Y	Y											Y		Y	Y					Y		Y				
Federal Chamber of Engineers	N												Y														
Ind1								N																			
Superior Regional Court Vienna						N																N					
Salzburg Kommissionen						N																					
Regional Government Office, Vienna																	Y			N							
Ind2 (Professor)														N					N	N				N			
Regional Government Office Upper Austria									N																		
Ind3 (Professor)										N										N							
Ind4 (Dr.)										N																	
Supreme Administrative Court													N			Y											
Austrian Chamber of Lawyers											Y																
Austrian Trade Union Federation						N														N			Y				
Association of Austrian Banks and Bankers																											
Austrian Raiffeisen Association Austrian Notaries' Chamber																										Y	
Prime Ministers' Office																											
Austrian Central Bank																											

Lobbyist	Reference ($$)																										
	203c	203d	203e	217–220a	217–220b	217–220c	221/1a	221/1b	221/1c	221/1d	222/1a	222/1b	223a	223b	229/1	231	232/4	237/8a	237/8b	Transitional Regulations	244a	244b	244c	246	246/4	277a	277b
Ministry of Economic Affairs																											
Stommer, Reich-Rohrwig, Karasek																											
Chamber of Public Accountants								Y			Y	Y			Y	Y	Y	Y				Y				Y	
Association of Austrian Newspaper Publishers	N																										
Federation of Austrian Industry																								N			N
Austrian Chamber of Labour			Y			Y				N	N	Y		Y			Y	Y		Y	Y	N		N	N		
Federal Chamber of Economics						N				N										N				N	N		
Federal Chamber of Engineers						Y																					
Ind1																											
Superior Regional Court Vienna		Y			Y		Y						Y														
Salzburg Kommissionen		Y						Y																			
Regional Government Office, Vienna																			N	Y							
Ind2 (Professor)																											
Regional Government Office Upper Austria																											
Ind3 (Professor)					Y																						
Ind4 (Dr.)																											
Supreme Administrative Court																											
Austrian Chamber of Lawyers																											
Austrian Trade Union Federation									N																		
Association of Austrian Banks and Bankers																											
Austrian Raiffeisen Association				Y																							
Austrian Notaries' Chamber									N																		
Prime Ministers' Office														Y													
Austrian Central Bank																							N				

Note: Individuals who submitted proposals are not named here, but are indicated as Ind1 to Ind4.

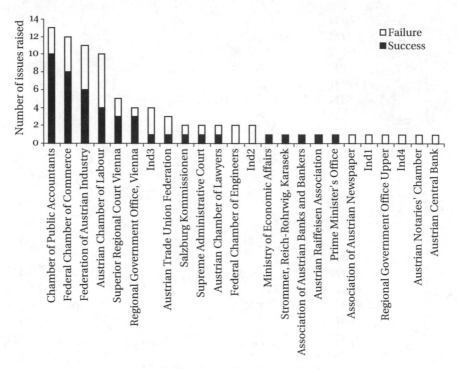

Fig. 5.3.3. Number of proposals to amend accounting law made by respondents.

employer associations, two employee associations, and three representing lawyers and accountants. Four organizations, namely the Chamber of Public Accountants, the Chamber of Commerce, the Federation of Austrian Industry, and the Austrian Chamber of Labour raised 55 percent of all issues. These are the same organizations that were members of the ministerial working groups. Figure 5.3.3 ranks the number of proposals made by respondents, and also indicates the variability in the levels of influence over legal redrafting.

These success rates are reported in descending order in Table 5.3.4. Altogether, forty-three comments by sixteen individuals and organizations led to a change in the legal text, whereas forty comments by nineteen interested parties failed to persuade the law-makers of the need for amendment. The unconditional probability of success is 0.52 overall.

In order to estimate success rates for each of the main constituencies, the respondents were categorized as lobbying on behalf of either (a) employers or (b) employees, or simply as (c) legal or accounting experts. A note of caution must be recorded with regard to such

Table 5.3.4. Ranking of interest groups based on the success rate of proposals to amend the accounting law

Lobbyist		Success	Failure	Total	Success rate
Ministry of Economic Affairs	Expert	1	0	1	1.00
Strommer, Reich-Rohrwig, Karasek	Expert	1	0	1	1.00
Association of Austrian Banks and Bankers	Employer	1	0	1	1.00
Austrian Raiffeisen Association	Employer	1	0	1	1.00
Prime Minister's Office	Expert	1	0	1	1.00
Chamber of Public Accountants	Expert	10	3	13	0.77
Regional Government Office, Vienna	Expert	3	1	4	0.75
Superior Regional Court Vienna	Expert	3	2	5	0.60
Federal Chamber of Commerce	Employer	7	5	12	0.58
Federation of Austrian Industry	Employer	6	5	11	0.55
Salzburg Kommissionen	Expert	1	1	2	0.50
Supreme Administrative Court	Expert	1	1	2	0.50
Austrian Chamber of Lawyers	Expert	1	1	2	0.50
Austrian Chamber of Labour	Employee	4	6	10	0.40
Austrian Trade Union Federation	Employee	1	2	3	0.33
Ind3	Expert	1	3	4	0.25
Federal Chamber of Engineers	Employer	0	2	2	0.00
Ind2	Expert	0	2	2	0.00
Association of Austrian Newspaper Publishers	Employer	0	1	1	0.00
Ind1	Expert	0	1	1	0.00
Regional Government Office Upper Austria	Expert	0	1	1	0.00
Ind4	Expert	0	1	1	0.00
Austrian Notaries' Chamber	Expert	0	1	1	0.00
Austrian Central Bank	Employer	0	1	1	0.00
Total		43	40	83	0.53

Note: The organizations that were consulted during the preparation of the first and second drafts of the legislation are highlighted in the table. Involvement was either as a statutory obligation (Federal Chamber of Commerce and Austrian Chamber of Labour) or as a right to participate (Austrian Chamber of Labour and Federation of Austrian Industry). The Chamber of Public Accountants provided technical expertise. Individuals who submitted proposals are not named here, but are indicated as Ind1 to Ind4.

categories, even though the corporatist framework lends itself to grouping in this way. First, we took the view that comments on behalf of courts and government offices were offered as legal expertise. Second, given the nature of the proposals put forward, we considered the comments made by banks and banking associations to be those of employers and employer associations.[27] Finally, it is possible that practicing lawyers and accountants may well have their clients in mind when engaging in the legal process, but we considered all to be giving expert opinions. Based on this categorization, it was found that the employer representatives' success rate was 54 percent and that of the employees was 38 percent. Grouped together, these lobbyists recorded a success rate of 49 percent, and that of the legal and accounting experts was 57 percent.[28] These unconditional probabilities are consistent with the view that a comment letter submitted to the Austrian authorities is as likely to lead to a change in the law as not, and that legal and accounting expertise is slightly more influential than lobbying on behalf of corporate interests.

One further aspect of the process concerns the effect of agreement or disagreement between the parties on the probability of influencing the law. In Table 5.3.5, which includes a short description of each point of law under discussion, the position taken by each constituency on each issue is compared with the outcome. Of the eighty-three comments on the fifty-four separate points of law, forty-one involved one constituency only.[29] A wider interest was shown in the other thirteen issues, some where the parties were consistent in their views on the change to be made to the law and others where there was disagreement. As summarized in Table 5.3.6 (p. 339), the probability of success for any proposal advocating a change in draft accounting law is 56 percent, but this increases to 65 percent when two or more constituencies are in agreement and decreases to 36 percent if there is disagreement between the parties. The explanatory power of agreement and disagreement is greater than that of lobby group influence.[30]

In the corporatist framework, where there are three principal actors (capital, labor, and the state), this outcome is consistent with an even-handed game.[31] When one lobbyist tries to bring about a change in the draft law, the chances of that happening are roughly in the order of one success from every two proposals. When lobby groups agree on the legal amendment, the odds that the law will change are about two successes from every three proposals. And when lobbyists disagree on the proposed change to the law, the odds are reduced to about one success in every three proposals.

Table 5.3.5. Interactions between interest groups in the lobbying process

§§		Constituencies	Issue	Influential parties
Employer associations				
1	189/2	Employer association	Readability of data in electronic form	Employers
2	198/3	Employer association	Write-off of formation and reorganization expenses for part enterprises to be allowed	—
3	198/8	Employer association	Inclusion of provisions against product liability risks	Employers
4	203	Employer association	Request for exemption	Employers
5	203	Employer association	Option to capitalize in course of tax investigation	—
6	203	Employer association	In context of valuation, "specific circumstances" to be broadly defined	Employers
7	217–220	Employer association	Request for exemption for cooperatives	Employers
8	232/4	Employer association	Option to provide breakdown of profit and loss account entries in the notes	Employers
9	244	Employer association	Obligation to prepare consolidated accounts to be dependent on a minimum of 25% of shares owned by parent company	Employers
10	246/4	Employer association	Ministry of Justice to determine size threshold below which there is exemption from the obligation to compile group accounts	—
Employee associations				
11	193/2	Employee association	Deadline for filing accounts to be shortened	Employees
12	222/1	Employee association	Annual accounts to be presented to members of supervisory board	Employees
13	244	Employee association	Consolidation in case of cooperatives	—
14	277	Employee association	Distribution of annual reports to social partners	—
Legal/Accounting experts				
15	189/4	Expert	Legal requirement to keep books applies when a new company becomes a legal entity, not at the date of registration	Experts
16	189/4	Expert	Extension of accounting regulations to nonregistered traders	Experts
17	195	Expert	"True and fair view" principle leads to a decrease in transparency	—
18	195	Expert	Cash flow statement recommended in order to provide insight into the financial situation	—
19	195	Expert	Change wording I	—
20	195	Expert	Change wording II	—
21	195	Expert	§195 (true and fair) and §196 (content of accounts) to be condensed into one regulation	Experts
22	198/3	Expert	Company reorganization expenses	—
23	198/7	Expert	Change wording, in order to stress obligation to state provisions separately against relevant assets	Experts
24	198/8	Expert	Definition of "provision against future expenditure" required	—

Continued

Table 5.3.5. (Continued)

§§		Constituencies	Issue	Influential parties
25	198/8	Expert	Abolish provisions for uncertain liabilities	Experts
26	198/8	Expert	General definition of "provisions" required	—
27	201/1	Expert	Definition of "prudence principle" required	—
28	201/1	Expert	Clarification required	—
29	202	Expert	Inclusion of withdrawals in valuation obligations required	Experts
30	203	Expert	Limitation of write-ups to special circumstances is inappropriate	Experts
31	203	Expert	Specific circumstances for write-ups need to be defined	Experts
32	217–220	Expert	Clarification required	Experts
33	221/1	Expert	Classifications are unsystematic	Experts
34	221/1	Experts (2)	Regulation is misplaced in this context	Experts
35	221/1	Expert	Clarification required	—
36	223	Expert	Clarification required	Experts
37	229/1	Expert	Outstanding contributions to nominal capital to be shown separately under receivables	Experts
38	231	Expert	Breakdown of income from subsidiaries and associates required in notes to accounts	—
39	237/8	Expert	Current regulation to conform to 4th EU directive	Experts
40	237/8	Expert	Request for less disclosure	—
41	244	Expert	Request for exemption	—
42	277	Expert	Annual accounts to be published with audit report	Experts

Employer associations and employee associations

| 43 | 246 | Employer associations (2) v. Employee | Increase in company size threshold regarding exemption to compile group accounts | — |

Employee associations and legal/accounting experts

44	195	Employee association and experts (2)	Extension of addressees of financial reporting	—
45	198/8	Employee association and experts (2)	More details to be provided in provisions regulations	—
46	223	Employee association and expert	Summarized items to be listed separately in notes	Employees and experts

Employer associations and legal/accounting experts

47	198/7	Employer associations (2) and expert	Extension of capitalized discounts to include all liabilities	Employers and experts
48	222/1	Employer association and expert	Definition of "accounts" to include "notes to the accounts"	Employers and experts
49	198/3	Employer associations (2) and expert	Write-off of company formation expenses to be allowed	Employers
50	10	Employer associations (2) v expert and other employer associations (2)	Number of newspapers in which accounts have to be published	Expert and 2 employer associations

Continued

Table 5.3.5. (Continued)

§§		Constituencies	Issue	Influential parties
Employer associations, employee associations and legal/accounting experts				
51	201/1	Employer associations (2), employee association and expert	Inclusion of separate valuation	Employers, employees, and experts
52	217–220	Employer associations (2) and expert v. employee association	Abolition of audit of "large traders"	Employers and experts
53	221/1	Employer associations (2) v. expert and employee association	Increase company size threshold for general exemption from detailed disclosure	—
54	T	Employer association v. expert and employee association	Extension of period for pensions provisions	Employees and experts

Table 5.3.6. Constituency combinations in the lobbying process

	Number of proposals	Number of legal points involved	Proposal success rate (%)
Relative influence			
Employers	26	17	54
Employees	13	12	46
Experts	<u>44</u>	41	57
Total	83		
Agreement and disagreement			
One lobbyist only	41	41	56
More than one: in agreement	23	8	65
in disagreement	<u>19</u>	<u>5</u>	37
Total	83	54	

6. Conclusions

This chapter provides a detailed study of accounting law-making in Austria. The first part dealt with the regulatory environment, which involved a historical overview of accounting regulation in Austria and an analysis of the interrelationship of the Austrian and the German regulatory systems. The two systems were found to be in an asymmetrical power relationship, with Austria as the dependent party. Legal transfer in the form of reliance on German legal text when formulating Austrian law strongly reflects this relationship. At the same time, each jurisdiction promotes the wider participation of representative organizations in its own legal process, and the corporatist structure in Austria offers well-defined procedures in this respect involving institutionalized representation in addition to public consultation.

The rest of the chapter provides an analysis of constituent lobbying during the drafting of the Austrian Financial Reporting Act of 1990. The analysis, which was carried out by means of investigating the statements issued by various individuals and interest groups and made available by the Ministry of Justice, revealed a low number of conflicting proposals during the initial stage of the legal process that was organized through ministerial working groups. This was taken as evidence for the impact of corporatism on the Austrian regulatory process, resulting in compromises between state-sponsored, centralized organizations during earlier stages of the drafting process by means of resolving controversial issues behind closed doors. Moreover, the opportunity to be able to import a ready-made solution from Germany introduced another factor, that the existing German *Bilanzrichtliniengesetz* already took account of the views of interest groups in Germany.

Consistent with this, the general odds of changing the subsequent draft on the basis of comments from the wider interested public are about 50:50, with a suggestion that legal and accounting experts have slightly more influence in these circumstances. At one level, this suggests that the traditionally strong influence of the corporate lobby may well have been exercised at an earlier stage as suggested above, either in the preparation of the legal drafts imported from Germany or behind closed doors in Austria prior to public consultation. However, the analysis also shows that, when agreement and disagreement between the parties is taken into account, the corporatist framework seems to be consistent with an even-handed approach by the law-maker, with the odds of influence increasing where two or more parties agree, and decreasing where two or more parties disagree. Thus, in spite of the differences in the political processes of accounting regulation in the two countries, these results are consistent with the earlier finding in Germany (McLeay et al. 2000) that the influence of powerful lobby groups may depend crucially on the support of others when the law is involved.

Notes

We thank Sonja Bydlinski and Christian Rauscher of the Austrian Ministry of Justice for access to working papers on the Austrian Financial Reporting Act, and Alfred Wagenhofer, David Neal, Georg Merkl, and Carol Tully for helpful comments, particularly with regard to financial accounting terminology and translation issues. We are also grateful to participants at the European Accounting Association conference in Athens, Greece, in April 2001, and the EIASM Euroconference on Financial Reporting and Regulatory Practices in Europe in Palermo, Italy, in May 2001. The project forms part of the HARMONIA program of research into accounting harmonization and standardization in Europe, and we acknowledge the financial contribution of the European Commission through the Human Potential Programme, Contract HPRN-CT-2000–00062.

[1] In writing this chapter, we have tried to avoid the "cultural blindness" of parochial accounting research that is described by Wallace and Gernon (1991), and which might otherwise have prevented us from seeing what is right under our noses. To quote a contemporary British anthropologist: "Our own culture is like our own nose. We do not see it because it is in front of our very eyes and we are accustomed to look straight through it to see the world. Indeed, if we see it at all, we see it as part of the world." Barley (1989: 3).

[2] Germany spent the first two-thirds of the nineteenth century trying to establish itself as a nation state after existing as a collection of small imperial estates under the leadership of Austria for over 200 years. The abdication of Franz II of Austria as Emperor of the Holy Roman Empire marks the end of the existence of Austria and Germany as one state. The Austro-Hungarian Empire, as a collection of nation states but granting equal status to Austria and Hungary and under the leadership of the Habsburg dynasty, existed from 1867 to 1919.

[3] Since then, Austria has looked toward Germany with a mixture of envy and awe, as a "big brother" whose moves are carefully watched and often imitated.

[4] Two amendments introducing tighter regulations for stock companies were introduced in 1874 and 1899 as a reaction to the collapse of the Vienna stock exchange in 1873, which plunged Austria and Germany into an economic crisis lasting into the 1890s. Further details concerning the history of accounting regulation in Austria can also be found in Nowotny and Gruber (1993, 1995), as well as in Table 5.3.1. One purpose of this initial reflection on the past is given in Walton (1995: 1): "The ensemble of accounting practices and regulations in any country at any given time are not representative of the present, but are rather an accumulation of past decisions which have been modified in response to many different stimuli over a span of time; it follows that anyone wishing to study the current state of financial reporting in a particular country needs to examine how the regulations have developed historically, in order to understand the present."

[5] Nowotny and Gruber (1995: 35) explain that the "development of book-keeping legislation not only for companies but for all kinds of business took place outside of the General Commercial Code, in company law and tax law. As a consequence of this, bookkeeping was no longer seen only as an instrument of documentation and the basis of decision making; other aspects which are typical results of bookkeeping in respect to public corporation—namely its emphasis on shareholders' and creditors' protection—influenced all bookkeeping regulations in Austria."

[6] See also Seicht (1999: 5) who notes that Austria's Company Law of 1965, which was a direct result of the reformation of German Company Law in the same year, did not entail any changes as far as its "substance" was concerned.

[7] The amendment was introduced in the course of a parliamentary debate on the Insolvency Law Transformation Act (Insolvenzrechtsänderungsgesetz), which was passed as a result of a spate of major bankruptcies (Janschek 1987: 82). The bankruptcy of the Österreichische Klimatechnik GmbH caused a political scandal because of the involvement of a state-owned bank, the Länderbank AG, as its main creditor.

[8] The reform process of financial reporting was continued in 1996, when the EU Company Law Transformation Act (EU-Gesellschaftsrechtsänderungsgesetz) was passed as a result of Austria joining the EU in 1995. The EU-GesRÄG was based on the Financial Reporting Act of 1990 and completed the process of harmonization with EU regulations.

[9] Elsewhere, Altenburger takes a similar view in recognizing the need for striking a "balance between conformity and independence" (1995: 245; translation).

[10] On legal transplants see Watson (1974) and Ebbers and McLeay (1997).

[11] Deutsches Kreditwesengesetz (German Banking Institutions Act).

[12] Handelsgesetzbuch (Commercial Code).

[13] There is also a Chamber of Agriculture, which is not relevant in the context of financial reporting. The Chambers have a federal structure, with organizations in each of the nine Austrian states.

[14] Indeed, the Chambers are entitled to evaluate bills before they are passed to Parliament: since they have to be asked anyway, the ministries in charge of preparing new legislation often consult experts from the Chambers in the drafting process (Seidel 1996).

[15] This network of affiliations constitutes the ideal way of direct lobbying by means of private meetings with rule-makers (Sutton 1984).

[16] An internal document of the Ministry of Justice confirms that this was indeed the case during the drafting process of the Austrian Financial Reporting Act. Whenever the parties involved were unable to reach an agreement, the Ministry of Justice stressed its role as a mediator and proposes a compromise.

[17] The presence of all corporatist players in the regulatory process is bound to have an impact on the modus operandi of the two ministerial working groups on financial reporting. In fact, corporatism has already been recognized as a separate mode of regulation in Puxty et al.'s (1987) comparison of accounting regulation in advanced capitalist societies. In their analysis, the corporatist state integrates organized interest groups "into its own centralised, hierarchical system of regulation" (284).

[18] Sutton (1984) points out that the actions that "interested parties" take to influence the rule-making body, collectively referred to as "lobbying," vary widely in nature—from written submissions to the rule-makers to pressure brought to bear on elected representatives or government agencies. A hierarchy of methods, consisting of direct and indirect lobbying, provides a better representation of the true nature of the lobbying process. Sutton also draws attention to the fact that lobbying is an ongoing process, which cannot be pinpointed to certain times or even to a specific period of time. In that respect, the timetable provided for the drafting of the Austrian Financial Reporting Act is simplified in Figure 5.3.2 and Table 5.3.2. For instance, the parliamentary debate following the passing of the Insolvency Law in 1992 can be interpreted as the result of interest group dissatisfaction. The fact that the Ministry of Justice invited interested parties to comment on size thresholds in September 2000, shows that the debate on this issue and thus lobbying on its behalf is still ongoing.

[19] In fact, the academics published their views on the drafting process in the form of a collection of commentaries (Egger and Ruppe 1987). Individual chartered accountants and tax accountants also made their views known by means of publishing articles in various professional journals, but they do not seem to be acting as a collective body during this stage.

[20] Both of these drafts are published in the commercial law journal, *Österreichisches Recht der Wirtschaft* (1988/6b: 217–78 and 1990/5b: 177–239).

[21] Including the Accounting Standards Board in the United Kingdom (Weetman, et al. 1996; Gilfedder and Ó' hÓgartaigh 1998; and Weetman 2001), the ASRB in Australia (Harding and McKinnon 1997), the FASB in the United States (Tandy and Wilburn 1996), and the International Accounting Standards Board (MacArthur 1996).

[22] As such, lobbying research in accounting implicitly follows the procedures suggested to political scientists by Barach and Baratz (1962: 948): "a) select for study a number of 'key' as opposed to 'routine' political decisions, b) identify the people who took an active part in the decision-making process, c) obtain a full account of their actual behaviour while the policy conflict was being resolved, and d) determine and analyse the specific outcome of the conflict."

[23] This "conflict-which-does-not-happen," or latent conflict, has its source in the contradiction between the interests of those exercising power and the real interests of those they exclude (Lukes 1974). Despite postmodernist attempts to reconceptualize power as domination through discipline (Foucault 1977, 1988), Lukes' concept of power is still used by political scientists to define and measure power (Hay 1997, 1999; Doyle 1998; Schaap 2000).

[24] Indeed, in some cases, the parties involved might not even be aware that they are being excluded.

[25] More formally, such data may be subdivided into sampling units, context units, and recording units (see Jones and Shoemaker 1994: 144). In lobbying research, a written submission to a standard-setting body or an interview regarding a particular exposure draft constitutes the sampling unit. Within this, statements and opinions regarding specific issues can be classified as context units, with individual sentences, phrases, or key words constituting recording units.

[26] The total number of formal written statements is fifty, but two are duplicates, which reduces the number to forty-eight. The statements vary substantially in length and detail. They range from one to fifty pages and contain references to up to thirteen specific accounting issues. Some express an overall attitude to the Ministerial draft, some refer only to specific sections in the law, and others do both.

[27] For instance, the Central Bank's proposal regarding consolidation concerned the position of the Mint as a banking subsidiary.

[28] The small, unbalanced sample does not provide sufficient statistical power to reject the hypothesis that the probability of influencing the law is constant across these groups. The F-statistic of a logistic regression of lobbying outcome explained by lobby group influence is 0.504 ($df = 2, 80$; p-value $= 0.606$), with log odds Employers -0.620 (standard error 0.266); Employees -0.955 (0.443); Experts -0.565 (0.199).

[29] In all but one case there was just one respondent involved.

[30] The F-statistic of a logistic regression of lobbying outcome explained by agreement and disagreement is 1.386 ($df = 2, 80$; p-value $= 0.256$). Again, the sample does not provide sufficient statistical power to reject the hypothesis that agreement or disagreement between the parties has no more effect than a single proposal by one lobbyist only. However, an F-statistic greater than 1 does suggest that the explanatory factors (Agreement and Disagreement) account for more than the average contribution to explaining variability in the prediction error, even though the imbalance in the sample is such that the p-value is unconvincing. Nevertheless, it may be noted that the relative effects, expressed as relative log-odds, are Agreement 0.147 (standard error 0.346); and Disagreement -0.433 (0.407), and a weak test (0.95) leads to the conclusion that when there is agreement between lobbyists, the odds of success in influencing the law are significantly higher than when there is disagreement.

[31] The drafting process has been characterized elsewhere as one of cooperation, coordination of interests, and consensus: "The current draft of the Financial Reporting Act

[Governmental draft 1990] is the result of long-term, complex and in-depth discussions involving experts from all interest groups: representatives of the business community, the legal and accounting professions, academia and experts from the Ministry of Justice. The resulting draft is the product of negotiations, which lasted for a number of years, with the aim of reaching a consensus" (Platzer 1988; translation).

References

Altenburger, O. (1995). "Ausgewählte Unterschiede zwischen der neuen österreichischen und der deutschen Rechnungslegung," in C. Djanani, H. Kofter, and R. Steckel (eds.), *Anpassungsprozesse in Wirtschaft und Recht*. Europäische Union Rechnungslegung und Steuern. Festschrift für Hans Leza zum 60. Geburtstag (Vienna: Linde Verlag).

Barach, P. and Baratz, M. S. (1962). "Two faces of power," *The American Political Science Review*, 56(4): 947–52.

Barley, N. (1989). *Native land. The bizarre rituals and curious customs that make the English English* (Harmondsworth: Penguin).

Brennan, N. and Pierce, A. (2001)."Constituent lobbying in an auditing context: Evidence from Ireland." Working paper presented at the 24th Annual Congress of the European Accounting Association in Athens, April 18–20, 2001.

Doyle, J. (1998)."Power and contentment," *Politics*, 18(1): 49–56.

Ebbers, G. and McLeay, S. J. (1997). "Accounting and Volksgeist: Territorial claims on accounting regulation," *The Journal of Management and Governance*, 1(1): 67–84.

Eberhartinger, E. (1999). "The impact of tax rules on financial reporting in Germany, France, and the UK," *The International Journal of Accounting*, 34(1): 93–119.

—— (2000). *Ertragssteuerliche Konsequenzen der Internationalisierung der Rechnungslegung* (Vienna: Orac).

——, Gowthorpe, C., and Pilkington, C.(1999). "Accounting regulatory change in Austria: A weakening of tradition." Working paper, presented at 22nd annual EAA congress, 1999.

Egger, A. and Ruppe, H. G. (eds.) (1987). *Reform der Rechnungslegung in Österreich* (Vienna: Orac).

Foucault, M. (1977). *Discipline and punish: The birth of the prison* (Penguin: London).

—— (1988). *Politics, philosophy, culture: Interviews and other writings, 1977–1984* (translated by Sheridan, A. and others; edited with an introduction by Lawrence D. Kritzman; Routledge: New York & London).

Gilfedder, D. and hÓgartaigh, C. Ó. (1998)."The grasshopper and the great cattle: participation and non-participation in the ASB's standard-setting process," *Journal of Management and Governance*, 2: 287–96.

Harding, N. and McKinnon, J. (1997)."User involvement in the standard-setting process: A research note on the congruence of accountant and user perceptions of decision usefulness," *Accounting, Organizations and Society*, 22(1): 55–67.

Hay, C. (1997)."Divided by a common language: Political theory and the concept of power," *Politics*, 17(1): 45–52.

—— (1999)."Still divided by a common language: Discontentment and the semantics of power," *Politics*, 19(1): 47–50.

Janschek, O. (1987). "Bilanzreform in Österreich: Stand der aktuellen Diskussion," in G. Seicht (ed.), *Jahrbuch für Controlling und Rechnungswesen 1987: Bilanzreform, Controlling, Logistik, Arbeitszeitflexibilisierung* (Vienna: Orac).

Karlhofer, F. (1996). "The present and future state of social partnership," in G. Bischof and A. Pelinka (eds.), *Austro-corporatism: Past, Present, Future.* Contemporary Austrian Studies Vol. 4 (New Brunswick, NJ: Transaction Publishers), 119–46.

Lukas, W. and Zetter, R. (eds.) (1997). *Das Rechnungslegungsgesetz: mit den einschlägigen Bestimmungen der Europäischen Union und der Bundesrepublik Deutschland sowie ausführlichen Erläuterungen und Verweisungen,* 2nd ed. (Vienna: Manz).

Lukes, S. (1974). *Power: A radical view* (London & Basingstoke: MacMillan).

MacArthur John, B. (1996)."An investigation into the influence of cultural factors in the international lobbying of the International Accounting Standards Committee: The case of E32," Comparability of financial statements, *The International Journal of Accounting,* 31(2): 213–37.

Mandl, D. (1993). "The new Austrian Financial Reporting Act," *European Accounting Review,* 2: 397–402.

Markovits, A. (1996). "Austrian corportism in comparative perspective," in G. Bischof and A. Pelinka (eds.), *Austro-corporatism: Past, Present, Future.* Contemporary Austrian Studies Vol. 4 (New Brunswick, NJ: Transaction Publishers), 5–20.

McLeay, S., Ordelheide, D., and Young, S. (2000)."Constituent lobbying and its impact on the development of financial reporting regulations: Evidence from Germany," *Accounting, Organisations and Society,* 25: 79–98.

Nowotny, C. (1987)."Die Reform der Rechnungslegung aus der Sicht des Handelsrechts," in A. Egger and H. G. Ruppe (eds.), *Reform der Rechnungslegung in Österreich* (Vienna, Orac), 181–230.

—— and Gruber, E. (1993)."Austria," *European Accounting Review,* special ed. Company law and accounting in nineteenth-century Europe, 292–97.

—— —— (1995)."The history of financial reporting in Austria," in P. Walton (ed.), *European Financial Reporting: A History* (London: Academic Press).

Ordelheide, D. (1999). "Germany" in S. J. McLeay (ed.), *Accounting Regulation in Europe* (Houndmills and London: MacMillan), 99–146.

—— and Pfaff, D. (1994). *European Financial Reporting: Germany* (London: Routledge).

Österreichischer Arbeiterkammertag (1988). Statement concerning the draft of the Austrian Financial Reporting Act. Unpublished.

Platzer, W. (1988). "Der Entwurf zum Rechnungslegungsgesetz 1989: Überblick über die geplanten Änderungen bei Buchführung, Jahresabschluß und Abschlußprüfung," *Steuer- und Wirtschaftskartei,* 22: DK1–16.

Puxty, A. G., Willmott, H. C., Cooper, D. J., and Lowe, T. (1987). "Modes of regulation in advanced capitalism: Locating accountancy in four countries," *Accounting Organizations and Society,* 12(3): 273–91.

"Rechnungslegungsgesetz (1990)". *Österreichisches Recht der Wirtschaft,* (5b): 177–239.

Ryan, C., Dunstan, K., and Stanley, T. (1999)."Constituent participation in the Australian public sector accounting standard-setting process: The case of ED 55," *Financial Accountability & Management,* 15(2): 173–200.

—— —— —— (2000)."Local government accounting standard-setting in Australia: Did constituents participate?" *Financial Accountability & Management,* 16(4): 373–96.

Schaap, A. (2000)."Power and responsibility: Should we spare the king's head?" *Politics,* 20(3): 129–35.

Seicht, G. (1999). "Ziele des Rechnungslegungsgesetzes und die damit angestrebten Verbesserungen der finanziellen Rechenschaftslegung," in R. Bertl and D. Mandl (eds.), *Handbuch zum Rechnungslegungsgesetz: Rechnungslegung, Prüfung und Offenlegung,* 8th ed. (Vienna: Orac).

Seidel, H. (1996). "Social partnership and Austro-Keynesianism," in G. Bischof and A. Pelinka (eds.), *Austro-corporatism: Past, Present, Future.* Contemporary Austrian Studies Vol. 4 (New Brunswick, NJ: Transaction Publishers), 94–118.

Sutton, T. (1984). "Lobbying of accounting standard-setting bodies in the UK and the USA: A Downsian analysis," *Accounting, Organisations and Society*, 9(9): 81–95.

Tálos, E. and Kittel, B. (1996). "Roots of Austro-corporatism: Institutional predonditions and cooperation before and after 1945," in G. Bischof and A. Pelinka (eds.), *Austro-corporatism: Past, Present, Future.* Contemporary Austrian Studies Vol. 4 (New Brunswick, NJ: Transaction Publishers), 21–52.

Tandy, P. R. and Wilburn, N. (1996). "The academic community's participation in standard setting: Submission of comment letters on SFAS Nos. 1–117," *Accounting Horizons*, 10(3): 92–111.

Unger, B. (1999). "Social partnership: Anything left?" in G. Bischof, A. Pelinka, and Karlhofer, F. (eds.), *The Vranitzky Era in Austria.* Contemporary Austrian Studies, 7 (New Brunswick and London: Transaction): 106–35.

Walker, R. and Robinson, P. (1993). "A critical assessment of the literature on political activity and accounting regulation," *Research in Accounting Regulation*, 7: 3–40.

Wallace, R. S. and Gernon, H. (1991). "Frameworks for international comparative financial accounting," *Journal of Accounting Literature*, 10: 209–63.

Walton, P. (1995). "International accounting and history," in P. Walton (ed.), *European Financial Reporting: A History*, (London: Academic Press), 1–10.

Watson, A. (1974). "From legal transplants to legal formants," *The American Journal of Comparative Law*, 43: 469–76.

Watts, R. L. and Zimmerman, J. L. (1978). "Towards a positive theory of the determination of accounting standards," *The Accounting Review*, 53(1): 112–34.

—— —— (1986). *Positive accounting theory* (Prentice-Hall, Englewood Cliffs).

Weetman, P. (2001). "Controlling the standard setting agenda: The role of FRS3," *Accounting, Auditing and Accountability Journal*, 14(1): 85–108.

——, Davie, E. S., and Collins, W. (1996). "Lobbying on accounting issues: Preparer/user imbalance in the case of the Operating and Financial Review," *Accounting, Auditing & Accountability Journal*, 9(1): 59–76.

Standard-Setting Processes and International Accounting Standards

6.1

From Accounting Directives to International Accounting Standards

Karel van Hulle

1. Introduction

The financial reporting scene in the European Union (EU) today appears very different from how it looked before the EU got involved in harmonizing accounting standards in the late 1960s. Although some developments would have taken place anyway, there is no doubt that the EU has been an important driver for change.

At present, a lot of pressure for harmonization comes from capital markets. It is generally recognized that the establishment of an efficient capital market in the EU requires more comparability than currently exists, and that the implementation of the Accounting Directives has not brought about a sufficiently high level of financial reporting by listed companies in the EU. Rather than introduce its own set of high-level accounting standards, the EU decided to "import" International Accounting Standards (IAS). Although this proposal met with considerable support, the final agreement did not come about easily.

The adoption of the Regulation on the application of IAS on June 7, 2002 has not completed the role of the Accounting Directives. Most companies in the EU are unlisted. It may not be necessary to require these companies to apply in their entirety accounting standards that have been conceived to deal with the intricacies of companies that are major players on capital markets. Two important questions arise: What is the interplay between the accounting requirements for listed and unlisted companies, and what is the continued role of the Accounting Directives?

This chapter describes the harmonization process from an EU perspective. It summarizes the historical developments and offers views from the perspective of a person who has been closely associated with the conception, preparation, negotiation, and implementation of this important part of Community legislation. This chapter clearly shows that the regulation of financial reporting is a complex issue and that there is no easy way to bring about accounting harmonization.

2. The Accounting Directives

The EC treaty did not specifically provide for the harmonization of accounting standards. Rather, revising such standards was and is part of company law harmonization. In general, the harmonization of company law should promote freedom of establishment for companies and firms by providing an equivalent level of protection for members (shareholders and employees) and other persons (mainly creditors) in all member states.

The harmonization of accounting standards also serves several specific objectives. It should facilitate trade within the EU as well as cross-border transactions. It should also help to bring about a European capital market.

Harmonization does not necessarily mean uniformity. Initially, only a minimum level of harmonization was deemed necessary. Furthermore, more emphasis was put on equivalence than on comparability. It was believed that the publication of financial statements, which would contain equivalent information combined with specific disclosures in the notes in which different accounting options had been used, was sufficient.

Harmonization takes place through directives. A directive is a legal instrument addressed to the member states that must transpose its provisions into national law within a certain period of time. Although proposals are made by the European Commission, the ultimate decision is taken by the European Parliament and the Council of Ministers.[1] Under the supervision of the European Court of Justice, the Commission must see to it that the directives are implemented in time, and that the implementing legislation is, and remains, in conformity with the directives.

An advantage of this legal instrument is the flexibility it gives to member states in the implementation process. Member states can choose the ways and means to implement the directive (e.g. by combining legislation with accounting standards). Doing so allows them to introduce the

Community rules into their national legal environment in full respect of their national traditions.

A disadvantage of this legal instrument is that timely implementation has been a problem in almost all cases. Further, it is difficult for the Commission to ensure consistent application of the Community rules.

As a result of this process, accounting rules are firmly enshrined in legislation in all EU member states. This fact should not come as a surprise, because this was already the case in most member states before the harmonization process started.

The harmonization process started with the adoption of the Fourth Directive.[2] This Directive applies to some five million limited liability companies. It requires these companies to prepare annual accounts, which must show a true and fair view of the company's assets, liabilities, financial position, and profit or loss. The annual accounts must be accompanied by an annual report. The annual accounts must be audited by a qualified professional and published together with the annual report and an audit report. The Directive also contains a number of exemptions that member states may introduce to favour small- and medium-sized companies.

The Fourth Directive was followed by the Seventh Directive.[3] This Directive introduced a requirement that firms prepare consolidated accounts and a consolidated annual report for those undertakings (parent undertakings) that have the legal power to control another undertaking (subsidiary undertaking). In addition, member states may also require consolidation in firms in which a parent undertaking exercises effective control or where several undertakings are managed on a unified basis (horizontal group). The consolidated accounts must be audited by a qualified professional. They must be published together with a consolidated annual report and an audit report.

Special rules have been developed for banks and insurance companies. The Bank Accounts Directive[4] refers primarily to the Fourth and Seventh Directives. It contains only those rules that were found necessary to take account of the particular characteristics of credit institutions. The Insurance Accounts Directive[5] deals only with the particularities of the insurance industry.

All member states have implemented the Accounting Directives. The difficulties that several member states experienced with the transposition of the Directives into national law gave ample evidence of the importance of this legislation, which clearly goes beyond the pure area of financial reporting. Company law implications (capital maintenance), the relation between accounting and taxation, the accounting treatment of small- and medium-sized enterprises, and the impact of the new accounting requirements on prudential supervision are some of the concerns that were raised in the implementation process.

3. First attempts toward further harmonization

During the negotiations that led to the adoption of the Fourth Directive, several member states raised the question of how they could ensure further progress in harmonization once the Directive had been implemented. It was agreed to set up a Contact Committee under the Directive, which would be composed of representatives of the member states and chaired by a Commission representative.

The functions of this Committee included facilitating the harmonized application of the Directive through regular meetings. These meetings dealt in particular with practical problems arising in connection with its application and advised the Commission, if necessary, on additions or amendments to the Directive. The other Accounting Directives also referred to this Contact Committee.

The Contact Committee met at regular intervals (two or three times a year) and arrived at a number of conclusions concerning the interpretation of provisions in the Accounting Directives, which were included in an Interpretative Communication published by the European Commission.[6] However, it is fair to say that the Committee did not make much progress in further harmonization, particularly because of resistance from two member states.

Germany had experienced serious difficulties in implementing the Accounting Directives, because small- and medium-sized companies opposed the requirement to disclose their financial statements. Germany's official position was that the objectives of the Treaty concerning harmonization of accounting requirements had been fulfilled with the adoption and implementation of the Accounting Directives. There was no further need for harmonization.

The United Kingdom soon discovered that the Accounting Directives were hindering them in developing new accounting standards. The United Kingdom found it difficult to accept that the creative work of the Accounting Standards Board (ASB) could be limited by requirements resulting from the Directives. Therefore, the official line was not to pursue further harmonization through amendments to those Directives. Instead, the United Kingdom sought to keep as much freedom as possible to continue the harmonization process internationally through cooperation with "leading" standard-setters within the so-called Group of 4 (comprising the United Kingdom, Canada, the United States, and Australia/New Zealand), and with organizations such as the International Accounting Standards Committee (IASC).

Because the process was not really moving forward, in January 1990 the European Commission organized a conference in Brussels on the future of the harmonization of accounting standards in the European Community. Experts from the various ministries of the member states, representatives of European organizations of the main users and preparers of accounts, of the accounting profession and academics, and representatives from national accounting standard-setting bodies were invited to express their views on what, if anything, needed to be done at EU level to harmonize accounting standards. On the basis of the discussions at that conference,[7] which was the first one of its kind ever organized in the EU, representatives took a number of important decisions.

3.1. No need to reduce the options in the Accounting Directives

The representatives considered it premature to reduce the options in the Accounting Directives. The options reflected real differences between the member states. Their existence did not prevent comparability.

3.2. The harmonization should be continued

It was agreed that efforts toward further harmonization should continue. Many issues had not been addressed by the Accounting Directives. Thus, there was a serious risk that the harmonization level would diminish if accounting standard-setters adopted new and sometimes divergent accounting standards.

3.3. Creation of an Accounting Advisory Forum

Many of the representatives present at the conference were not directly involved in the work of the EU in the field of accounting. These representatives expressed the wish to be more closely associated with future initiatives to be taken by the Commission. Therefore, in 1990 the Commission decided to set up a new advisory body, the Accounting Advisory Forum. The Forum was chaired by the Commission and comprised twenty-two members. These members represented both the accounting standard-setting bodies of member states and the European organizations for the main users and preparers of accounts (industry, trade unions, banks, insurance companies, stock exchanges, and financial analysts), as well as the accounting profession and academia. It was not easy to limit the membership of the Forum to so few. It was also difficult to identify an accounting standard-setting body for each member state.[8]

The Forum was asked to advise the Commission on technical solutions for problems that had not been dealt with in the Accounting Directives, and to provide guidance on the position to be taken in international accounting harmonization debates. The Forum also provided an arena within which discussions on accounting issues could take place between users and preparers and national standard-setting bodies.[9]

The Forum discussed a number of accounting issues that had been identified as major lacunae in the Fourth Directive: foreign currency translation, government grants, and leasing. The Forum produced a working paper on each of those topics. These papers were published by the Commission. These documents clearly stated that the Forum was not a standard-setting body. Rather, its main function was to advise the Commission on accounting matters and possible ways to facilitate further harmonization. The purpose of the publications was to stimulate discussions among standard-setters, preparers, users, and auditors of accounts in member states.

The last publications of the Forum dealt with Prudence and Matching[10] and with environmental issues in financial reporting. The conclusions of the Forum on the latter topic were included in a Recommendation published by the Commission in 2001.[11]

4. Development of a new accounting strategy

There is no doubt that the quality of the financial information published by limited-liability companies throughout the EU increased considerably with the implementation of the Accounting Directives. However, problems arose at the beginning of the 1990s because of the growing importance of capital markets. Large companies in the EU that were looking for capital on the international capital markets faced the difficulty that international markets did not consider their financial statements, produced on the basis of their national legislation and deriving from the Accounting Directives, as providing the information those markets needed. The markets were asking for more and sometimes different information.

In practice, many global players in Europe were asked to prepare a second set of financial statements in accordance with either U.S. Generally Accepted Accounting Principles (GAAP) or with IAS. This requirement was extremely burdensome and led to confusion about the "correct" numbers. The classic example of this problem was Daimler-Benz, which was the first German company to be listed on the New York Stock Exchange (NYSE). The figures produced on the basis of U.S. GAAP and those that resulted from the application of German GAAP were so different that in the end nobody knew whether the company was making a profit or suffering a loss.

The Commission started consulting with member states and with the business community. Four alternatives were examined:

4.1. Conclusion of a mutual recognition agreement with the United States

The real problem for European global players was access to the U.S. capital market. A solution could consist in obtaining an agreement with the United States on the mutual recognition of financial statements. Attempts made by the Commission very quickly showed that there was little interest in the United States for such an initiative. Financial statements prepared by U.S. companies under U.S. GAAP were in fact already recognized in all member states.

However, this is not the case in the US for financial statements prepared by European companies in accordance with the Accounting Directives. Furthermore, the Directives themselves do not provide a sufficiently comprehensive set of standards to meet US requirements. There are also important differences between member states because of the many options included in the Directives. For the Commission, it quickly became clear that the goal of a mutual recognition agreement with the United States was not a realistic proposition.

4.2. Exclusion of global players from the scope of application of the Accounting Directives

Another solution examined by the Commission was that large listed companies be excluded from the scope of application of the Accounting Directives. These companies would then be free to follow other rules. Although at first this solution appeared attractive, it quickly turned out to be a thorny issue. Such a solution would have implied a quick answer to a number of difficult questions, such as the scope of the exclusion (all listed companies, certain listed companies, companies with important non-EU shareholdings, and so on) and the rules that the excluded companies would then have to apply (IAS and/or U.S. GAAP, other GAAP). Further problems included the need to amend a number of Directives and the inevitable consequence of abandoning the homogeneous approach to financial reporting in the EU.

4.3. An update of the Accounting Directives

One of the problems was that the Accounting Directives were not sufficiently detailed. A solution would have been to amend the Directives to include technical solutions for the various accounting issues that had not yet been dealt with. However, it would have been very difficult to agree on the issues that should have been covered in such a revision. Furthermore, some Member States would certainly have tried to renegotiate those parts of the Directives that they did not like. The preparation and negotiation of such an important revision would have taken a long time, and new issues would probably have arisen by the time the amendments had been fully adopted and implemented in member states.

4.4. Creation of a European Accounting Standards Board

Another option considered by the Commission was the creation of a European Accounting Standards Board. Such a body would have provided the EU with the option of adopting common solutions for the many technical problems that might arise in the accounting field. However, to set up such a body (which would have required legislation) and to develop a comprehensive set of European accounting standards would have taken a great deal of time (and money). In addition, the Commission feared that such a solution would eventually result in the creation of an additional layer between national and international standards.

5. Proposed new accounting strategy

In developing a new accounting strategy, the Commission paid particular attention to respecting the principles of subsidiarity and proportionality set out in the Maastricht Treaty. The Commission wished to avoid as far as possible new legislation, or amendments to existing legislation, at the EU level. The Commission saw no need to develop European standards for the sake of having European standards when other solutions were equally satisfactory.

It was also clear that a more flexible framework was needed, one that could respond rapidly to current and future developments. Unless the framework adopted at the European level could be changed without too many difficulties, there was a risk that the solutions adopted would be set in stone. If these solutions no longer corresponded with today's needs, it would be difficult to justify their existence. Clearly, it was important that the proposed approach provide legal certainty and that it would ensure respect for Community law.

In November 1995, after lengthy discussions with member states and interested parties, the Commission published a Communication[12] in which it proposed a new approach to accounting harmonization. In its Communication the Commission suggested putting its weight behind the international harmonization process, which was already well under way in the International Accounting Standards Council (IASC). Global players in Europe should be allowed to prepare only one set of financial statements, preferably prepared in accordance with IAS and possibly with a distinction between annual and consolidated accounts.

In the Commission's opinion, the production of two sets of financial statements was not only costly, but also confusing. The publication of different figures for different purposes would undermine the investor's confidence in the published financial information. Therefore, it was of the utmost importance that European companies could satisfy differing requirements by producing only one set of financial statements.

The Commission clearly preferred a solution under which large European companies seeking capital on international capital markets could produce their financial statements on the basis of IAS. The preference for IAS was justified by the fact that only the IASC was producing results that had a clear prospect of recognition in the international capital markets within a timescale that corresponded to the urgency of the problem. Through the agreement with the International Organisation of Securities Commissions (IOSCO), there was a real possibility that in a not too distant future the major securities regulators of the world would accept financial statements based on an agreed set of IAS.

At the same time, the preference for IAS meant that the Commission did not advocate the preparation of financial statements by European companies on the basis of U.S. GAAP. American standards had been developed without any European input and were designed to satisfy the needs of the American capital market. These standards are not necessarily suitable in a European context. Furthermore, the application of U.S. GAAP is not independent of the action of the Securities and Exchange Commission (SEC), which supervizes the application of the standards in the United States. However, the Commission was aware of the fact that a growing number of large European companies prepared their financial statements on the basis of U.S. GAAP, particularly those European companies that were listed on the NYSE. To the extent that the financial statements prepared by these companies also conformed with the Accounting Directives, there was, strictly speaking, no problem from a European point of view. Nevertheless, the Commission believed that this could only be a next-best solution, and that preference should be given to a solution that was more international.

The Commission was well aware that, for many companies in Europe, the preparation of financial statements in accordance with IAS would mean that they would have to distinguish between annual accounts and consolidated accounts. This pragmatic solution would indeed be required for those companies based in member states where there was a close linkage between accounting and taxation. In those member states, the annual accounts that companies are required to prepare for approval by the shareholders are attached to the tax return and form the basis for corporate taxation. Thus, any change in the accounting rules was likely to have immediate (mostly negative) consequences on the amount of taxes to be paid.

On the other hand, in most instances, consolidated accounts have the advantage of not being the basis on which the distributable or taxable profit is determined. In those member states that have introduced the option provided for in Article 29(2) of the Seventh Directive, it is already possible for parent companies to adopt different accounting policies in their parent entity and consolidated accounts. The use of these different valuation rules is possible if the rules are in conformity with the Fourth Directive.

6. The proposed new accounting strategy in action

The Council of Ministers endorsed the Commission's proposed new accounting strategy. Two conditions were stated:

1. If the EU was to accept IAS as the preferred set of accounting standards to be applied in consolidated accounts of global players, then the EU must have an increased involvement in the work of the IASC. Therefore, the Commission was granted an observer seat on the Board of the IASC and on the Standards Interpretations Committee (SIC). The Commission was also invited to participate in a number of steering committees.

   In these roles, the Commission representative was assisted by a technical adviser from the private sector. The positions to be taken on particular standards and exposure drafts were discussed prior to the meetings with member states in the context of a new technical subcommittee of the Contact Committee. This technical subcommittee met three or four times a year and prepared a position that the Commission representative could defend to the Board and the SIC. However, it should be pointed out that the Commission representative did not speak on behalf of the EU. The IASC is a private sector organization in which member states are not represented as such. One of the difficulties that the Commission representative experienced was that the representatives of the accounting profession of those member states that were granted a seat on the Board (France, Germany, the Netherlands, the Nordic Federation of Accountants, and the United Kingdom) never voted in the same way. Further, their position often diverged from that which the Commission representative defended on the basis of the discussions held with member states prior to the meeting.

2. The preparation of consolidated financial statements using IAS was only possible to the extent that there were no conflicts between IAS and the Accounting Directives. Therefore, it was important for the Commission to examine with member states to what extent conflicts existed. To do this, a task force was set up, composed of experts from the Commission and member states. The task force concluded that

there were no major conflicts between IAS and the Accounting Directives. As a result, it was possible for a European company to prepare
its consolidated accounts in conformity with IAS without being in
conflict with the Accounting Directives.

To many people this conclusion came as somewhat of a surprise. How
could there be no major conflicts between IAS and the Accounting Directives, when the objectives of IAS and the Accounting Directives were not
the same? That conclusion was possible because the discussion focused
on the consolidated accounts, and because both the Accounting Directives and IAS contained a large number of options. Furthermore, the
conclusion was based on a dynamic interpretation of the Directives. It
was fair to say that a number of accounting issues that had been dealt
with under IAS had not been discussed in detail when the Directives
were elaborated. The relevant IAS could therefore be considered as a
further elaboration of the basic principles contained in the Directives.
Further, these principles were not read from the point of view of any
particular member state, but rather from a European point of view. Since
the Directives were a compromise between different points of view, it was
possible to arrive at a conclusion that was different from that adopted by
any given member state that implemented the Directives.
   The findings of this task force were unanimously endorsed by the
Contact Committee and were published by the Commission.[13] The
examination by the Contact Committee did not contain a value judgment on IAS as such. Rather than examining which set of rules was the
better one, the Contact Committee asked itself to what extent a hypothetical European company that wanted to prepare its financial statements
in accordance with IAS could do so without being in conflict with the
Accounting Directives. There was a presumption that a European company that wanted to apply IAS would be prepared to comply with all the
requirements, even with those which it might consider burdensome. At
the same time, it was clear that companies also had to comply with those
requirements imposed by the Accounting Directives that went beyond
what was required by IAS.
   The fact that there were no major conflicts between IAS and the
Accounting Directives did not mean that there were no conflicts with
national law. The Accounting Directives contained a significant number
of options. It was perfectly possible for member states to have chosen an
option that was not allowed under IAS. In the same way, it was presumed
that in those cases in which the Accounting Directives gave an option to
companies, the latter would apply the option that conformed with IAS.

The absence of major conflicts also resulted from the fact that IAS contained a number of options. Companies could then select those options that conformed with the Accounting Directives.

To provide legal certainty, the Commission published an Interpretative Communication concerning certain provisions in the Accounting Directives. At regular intervals the Commission also published position papers on the conformity between newly adopted IAS and interpretations by the SIC and the Accounting Directives. These position papers were posted on the Commission's website.[14] The last position paper was published in February 2000 and related to the conformity between IAS applicable to accounting periods beginning before July 1, 1999 and the European Accounting Directives.

In its Communication, the Commission announced that it would not hesitate to propose changes in the Accounting Directives, where such changes appeared necessary, particularly when such changes would avoid conflicts with IAS. This was the reason why the Commission proposed an amendment to the Accounting Directives in February 2000. The new amendment allowed for certain financial assets and liabilities to be valued at fair value, in accordance with IAS 39 "Financial instruments: Recognition and measurement." This proposal was adopted by Council and Parliament on September 27, 2001.[15]

Following the Commission's recommendation in the 1995 Communication, seven member states (Austria, Belgium, Finland, France, Germany, Italy, and Luxembourg) adopted legislation or measures that allowed listed companies to depart from the national rules on consolidation and to prepare their consolidated financial statements in accordance with IAS (and U.S. GAAP).[16]

7. Toward a mandatory application of IAS

Because of the growing importance of capital markets for corporate financing in the EU, and to allow EU companies and citizens to benefit fully from the advantages of the introduction of a common currency, in 1999 the Commission presented its Financial Services Action Plan.[17] This Action Plan contained some forty measures, the implementation of which would contribute to the realization of an integrated market for financial services in the EU. At the Lisbon Council in March 2000, the heads of state and governments of member states decided to set 2005 as the deadline for the implementation of this Action Plan.

In the area of financial reporting, the Action Plan proposed that all listed EU companies report under the same accounting framework. Applying a common framework for financial reporting should not only improve the comparability between financial statements of companies operating on the same (European) capital market, it should also allow EU companies to use the same set of financial statements for listing purposes throughout the world. Rather than develop a distinct European accounting framework, it was decided to give a boost to international harmonization by putting the full weight of the EU behind the efforts by the IASC[18] in its drive to develop international accounting standards.

There can be no doubt that the efficiency of capital markets in the EU is seriously hampered by the lack of comparability between financial statements published by listed companies. It is not uncommon for companies listed at the same exchange to apply different accounting standards (national standards of any member state of the European Economic Area (EAA), IAS, or U.S. GAAP). In addition, because of the options in the Directives and the minimum level of harmonization, national standards are still very different. Even where IAS is applied, there are suggestions that, at present, its application is not wholly consistent in practice. The lack of enforcement of the standards applied by companies makes it difficult for investors to rely on the accuracy of the financial information published by companies.

The lack of comparability and the inadequate enforcement are the main reasons why, in a new Communication published in June 2000,[19] the Commission proposed a radical change. The main proposals made in this Communication are summarized as follows:

- All listed EU companies must prepare their consolidated accounts in accordance with IAS
- The requirement to apply IAS would take effect at the latest from 2005 onward
- Member states would be allowed to extend the application of IAS to unlisted companies and to individual accounts
- IAS would be introduced into the legal environment of the EU on the basis of a decision by an endorsement mechanism to be set up at EU level
- A proper enforcement infrastructure must be developed to ensure that accounting standards are applied in the same way in all member states
- The Accounting Directives would be modernized

8. Regulation of the European Parliament and of the Council on the application of IAS

On June 7, 2002, after the European Parliament had approved the text in plenary on March 12, the Council adopted the Commission's proposal for a Regulation on the application of IAS.[20] This is a remarkable achievement. The Commission introduced its proposal in February 2001.[21] Although the negotiation was very complex, the text was adopted in a single reading between Council and Parliament. Such rapid adoption does not happen very often. Why did it happen in this case? No doubt the main reason is that the proposal was supported by all member states as well as by the markets, by the profession, and by users and preparers.[22] It was seen as a milestone in the creation of a single European capital market.

8.1. Legal instrument: A Regulation

The legal instrument chosen by the Commission is quite revolutionary. Rather than proceeding by way of a directive (which is the traditional instrument used for the harmonization of company law, including accounting), the Commission decided to use another legal instrument available under the Treaty of Rome: A regulation. Unlike a directive, which must be transposed into national law before it becomes effective in practice, a regulation is directly applicable in all member states and does not require the intervention of national legislators.

Because the Commission and member states had declared their intention to establish an internal market for financial services by 2005, it was crucial that in the area of financial reporting a common framework would be applicable as of 2005. The only way to achieve this timetable was by adopting a regulation.

A further advantage of this legal instrument is that, in the case of companies that have to comply with IAS, member states would no longer be allowed to impose further financial reporting requirements. In the same way, member states could not restrict in any way the application of IAS by those companies. Therefore, in the case of companies that have to comply with IAS, member states can no longer restrict accounting options available under IAS, nor can they issue new accounting standards.

8.2. Scope of the Regulation

Because the Regulation is primarily a capital-market measure, it applies to all companies governed by the law of a member state whose securities are admitted to trading on a regulated market in the EU. Some 7,000 companies will be directly affected by the Regulation. A far greater number of companies will be indirectly affected because they belong to a group that is now required to apply IAS.

Originally, the Commission wanted to apply the Regulation to all companies that were required to publish a public-offer prospectus, regardless of whether their securities were admitted to trading on a regulated market. This extension of the scope was not accepted. However, in a statement entered into the minutes of the Council, the Commission declared its intention to examine the need for a mandatory application of IAS to all companies that are required to publish a public-offer prospectus. There is certainly no objective reason why investors who have bought the securities issued by such companies should receive less protection.

Foreign companies (and especially U.S. companies) listed within the EU are not required to apply IAS or to reconcile to IAS. Although this might appear strange at first sight, it is in fact part of EU policy aiming at opening up the market in the United States to EU companies that are preparing their financial statements on the basis of IAS. Just as U.S. companies can be listed in the EU without having to apply or to reconcile to IAS, EU companies should be allowed to access the U.S. capital market without having to apply or reconcile to U.S. GAAP.

Member states may permit or require unlisted companies to prepare their financial statements in accordance with IAS. If a member state chooses that option, the regime applicable to the companies concerned is exactly the same as that which applies to listed companies that are required to apply IAS by the regulation. As a result, member states can no longer issue accounting standards for those companies. Their accounting regime is entirely governed by IAS.

Only consolidated accounts must be prepared in accordance with IAS. The annual accounts of listed companies can continue to be governed by national law derived from the Accounting Directives. This situation was unavoidable because of the close link that exists between accounting and taxation in many member states. To the extent that there is such a link, it would be difficult for a company to prepare its annual accounts in accordance with IAS, because doing so would significantly affect the taxation it is required to pay. For the infrequent situations in which a listed company is not a parent of a group and therefore does not prepare consolidated accounts, member states will have to decide whether they want to use the option to extend the scope of the Regulation to the annual accounts prepared by these companies.

It is to be expected that, particularly for regulated industries (banking and insurance), member states will want to subject all similar companies to the same accounting requirements. Accordingly, even unlisted banks and insurance companies may be required to apply IAS. Member states will also come under pressure to decide if they want to keep a homogeneous accounting environment, and if so, whether they want to give up (in part or totally) the link between accounting and taxation.[23] Member states could of course decide to make this change gradually. That is the reason why the Commission has proposed a modernization of the Accounting Directives, which offers an alternative to member states that do not want to move to IAS all at once. They can do so gradually by using the accounting options that will become available as a result of the modernization.

8.3. Which standards must be applied?

In conformity with the 1995 Communication, the Regulation imposes the use of IAS. The Commission was quite clear about this. There should be no choice. All listed companies should be required to apply the same set of accounting standards. Some people advocated a choice between IAS and U.S. GAAP. The existence of a choice was not accepted, for two reasons.

First, U.S. GAAP is the accounting regime of the United States. It does not constitute an international framework because it is too closely linked to the needs of one particular country. Second, offering a choice would be counterproductive. It would not provide the right incentive to move in the direction of international standards.

International Accounting Standards are defined in Article 2 of the Regulation, which refers to the standards and interpretations adopted by the IASB. In the original proposal, the door was also left open for the adoption of "equivalent standards," which were defined as "standards that ensure a high degree of transparency and comparability of financial reporting and are as close as possible to IAS." The Commission deemed this broadening of the definition necessary to allow for the adoption at EU level of accounting solutions for situations not yet covered by an IAS, for instance in the case of the insurance industry. This possibility was not retained in the final version of the Regulation because it was considered that the possibility of issuing accounting rules in those cases was not allowed under the present "*comitology*" regime. This regime is the process by which IAS are "endorsed" and it is discussed further below. If the Commission thinks it necessary for the EU to adopt accounting solutions in areas not covered by IAS, it will be necessary to use the normal procedure provided for in the Treaty, that is a proposal to be adopted by Council and Parliament.

8.4. Endorsement

Although most people agreed that the choice in favor of IAS was right, there was considerable opposition to handing over the accounting standard-setting for listed companies to a private body that was largely self-controlled. Doing so would not conform with the democratic traditions of member states. Laws are made by the Parliament or through delegation by the Parliament. Since such a delegation did not exist, the application of IAS in the EU legal environment could only be possible after a formal endorsement process. To be applied within the EU, IAS must be endorsed.

At the same time, it was unthinkable that an IAS adopted by the IASB would then need to be renegotiated at the EU level. The policy should be that once an IAS had been adopted by the IASB, it should be acceptable to the EU. Therefore, it was extremely important to build into the process a number of guarantees that would contribute to the success of that policy. It should not come as a surprise that a large part of the negotiation surrounding the Regulation was devoted to an agreement on those guarantees.

The first guarantee relates to the position of the EU within the IASC Foundation's structure. It was inconceivable that the EU would not in one way or another be represented within the structure of the IASC Foundation. Such representation has become difficult since the IASC (the organization preceding the IASC Foundation) changed its structure. The new Constitution no longer provides for the possibility of having observers on the standard-setting board. Thus, it was agreed between the Commission and the IASC Foundation that the Commission would have an observer seat on the Standards Advisory Council and on the International Financial Reporting Interpretations Committee. It was also agreed that close contacts would be maintained on a permanent basis between the Commission and the IASB (the accounting standard-setting body of the IASC Foundation). Although the Commission did and does not formally represent the EU in this area, both member states and the Parliament insisted that the Commission should be an active participant on behalf of the EU.

The second guarantee relates to the upstream technical input from interested parties in the EU in the international accounting standard-setting process. In most countries in the EU, it is uncommon for interested parties to intervene in the standard-setting process. In addition, the likelihood of different positions being expressed by member states on any given accounting issue is so obvious that something must be done to ensure that the violins are tuned before the orchestra starts to play. This is the reason why the Commission strongly insisted that the private sector (particularly industry and the accounting profession) should take the initiative to set up a European technical group that would contribute on behalf of the EU to the work of the IASB. The best way to prevent a possible rejection of an IAS by the EU would be to ensure that there had been proper input from the very beginning and that all arguments had been properly discussed.

The private sector reacted favorably to the Commission's suggestion by creating a new body called EFRAG (European Financial Reporting Advisory Group). This body was set up by the main parties interested in financial reporting (industry, accounting profession, standard-setters, stock exchanges, financial analysts).

EFRAG has a Supervisory Board in which the "founding fathers" of the organization are represented. The technical work is done by the Technical Expert Group (TEG), which meets on a monthly basis. To exchange views about the work of the IASB, EFRAG has also taken the initiative to bring together at regular intervals all standard-setting bodies in the EU. The European Commission and CESR (Committee of European Securities Regulators) are represented as observers on the TEG of EFRAG.

The third guarantee is specifically provided for in the Regulation. To make the endorsement procedure viable, it was necessary to put into place a system that would work quickly, but without losing proper consultation and transparency. Proper consultation and transparency were necessary because the standards were adopted by a private organization over which the EU had no direct control. Therefore, it was decided to authorize the European Commission to endorse the standards. Endorsement was to be done on the basis of the so-called "*comitology*" procedure provided for in a Council Decision of June 28, 1999.[24] On the basis of that Decision, it is the Commission that makes the final decision on endorsement. The Commission will be assisted by a Committee called the Accounting Regulatory Committee, in which member states are represented.

During the discussions with the European Parliament, the Commission undertook the obligation to ensure that Parliament would be properly informed about the work of the Accounting Regulatory Committee. A specific *recital* (no. 8) was added to the text that refers to the declaration made by the Commission in the European Parliament on February 5, 2002 concerning the implementation of financial services legislation. This declaration was made on the follow-up of the report presented by Mr. Lamfalussy[25] after the discussions with the European Parliament.

The European Parliament had been worried that it might lose its influence as a result of the increasing complexity of legislation in the financial services area, which was to be carried out through committees rather than through the normal procedure that involves Council and Parliament. A "modus vivendi" was agreed to among the Commission, the Council, and the Parliament, which involves extensive information and reporting to the Parliament. The agreement by the Commission to extend this procedure to the Regulation made it possible to obtain the agreement of the Parliament on the Regulation in one single reading.

The initial proposal from the Commission did not contain any specific conditions that needed to be satisfied before an IAS could be endorsed by the Commission. This situation was changed during the discussions in the Council Working Party. Article 3 of the Regulation now states that an individual IAS can only be adopted if three conditions are satisfied:

1. The standard must not be contrary to the true and fair view principle referred to in the Fourth and Seventh Directives. This assessment ensures that there exists a high degree of conformity with the Accounting Directives. However, rather than requiring strict conformity with each and every provision of the Accounting Directives, the condition is satisfied when the application of the standard under consideration results in the presentation of a true and fair view in the same way as if the Accounting Directives had been applied. The Directives remain applicable to maintain a base level of comparability for all limited liability companies across the EU. This arrangement should help encourage unlisted companies that do not use IAS to move from the minimum requirements of the Accounting Directives to more sophisticated financial reporting such as IAS. The application of IAS can be viewed as a supplementary requirement for listed companies.

In practice, this condition means that a standard will be acceptable if it corresponds to current accounting thinking as laid down
in the Directives. Should a standard go too far beyond such thinking,
endorsement will only be possible if the Commission feels that the
standard introduces a better accounting approach. In that case, the
Commission will propose an amendment to the Accounting Directives to ensure that the Directives reflect that better approach. The
general reference to the true and fair view requirement avoids the
need to look for a detailed conformity assessment for each individual
standard.

2. The standard must also be conducive to the European public good.
   This condition is of a more political nature. The concept extends to
   a consideration of the needs of all parties—the companies, and their
   stakeholders and creditors. Through its adoption of IAS, the EU does
   not want to put its listed companies in a situation in which they will
   not be able to compete on an equal footing for financial resources
   available in either the Community capital markets or the world capital markets. As indicated in the Preamble to the Regulation (*recital
   no. 5*), it is important for the competitiveness of Community capital
   markets to achieve convergence of the standards used in Europe for
   the preparation of financial statements with international accounting
   standards used globally, for cross-border transactions or for listing
   anywhere in the world. This is a strong message to the IASB: convergence, particularly with U.S. GAAP, is needed to ensure that EU
   companies and their competitors in the United States are subject to
   the same rules, and that these rules are equally robust.

Of course, the concept of European public good goes beyond convergence. A standard would not be conducive to the European
public good if it were introducing accounting solutions that, although
technically correct, would raise serious problems. For instance, there
would be problems if the proposed solution did not pass a cost/benefit
analysis or if it were to have negative consequences at a macroeconomic level. There is always the risk that the concept of European
public good might be used as an excuse for not endorsing a standard
that European stakeholders do not want for various reasons. The best
way to ensure that such is not the case is for the IASB to operate in a
transparent way and to listen to the arguments as they are being put
forward. Standard-setting is indeed a political activity. Constituents
must feel that their problems are being taken care of and that the
IASB is acting responsibly by not ignoring the problems, but rather by
trying to address them in an appropriate manner. This process could

well mean that a particular accounting solution needs time before it becomes acceptable.

3. The standard must also meet the criteria of understandability, relevance, reliability, and comparability, which, in accordance with the Conceptual Framework of the IASB, are required of the financial information needed for making economic decisions and assessing the stewardship of management.

8.4.1. Endorsement process

In practice, the endorsement process will start with the Commission formally asking EFRAG for their view on whether an IAS should be endorsed. Once the opinion of EFRAG has been received, the Commission will draft a proposal for adoption of the standard. This proposal will then be discussed by the Accounting Regulatory Committee and voted upon (qualified majority). The Commission will then decide on the basis of the opinion expressed by the ARC.[26]

As there exists no intention to develop euro-IAS, endorsement will always be full endorsement (or no endorsement) of any given standard. To avoid potential difficulties with the endorsement of a standard, the process includes a number of safeguards.

In accordance with Article 7(1) of the Regulation, the Commission must liaise on a regular basis with the ARC on the status of active IASB projects and any related documents issued by the IASB. Liaising ensures that the two governing bodies coordinate positions and facilitate discussions concerning the adoption of standards that might result from these projects and documents. *Recital* no. 15 of the Preamble states that the Commission *must in its deliberations on and in elaborating positions to be taken on documents and papers issued by the IASB in the process of developing international accounting standards take into account the importance of avoiding competitive disadvantages for European companies operating in the global marketplace, and, to the maximum possible extent, the views expressed by the delegations in the ARC.*

In accordance with Article 7(2) of the Regulation, the Commission must report to the ARC in a timely manner if it intends not to propose the adoption of a standard.

As stated in the minutes of the Council, if an IAS that is being considered for adoption is particularly relevant for banks, insurance companies, or securities markets, the Commission will invite to the ARC, as appropriate, a representative of the Banking Advisory Committee, and/or of the Insurance Committee, and/or of the Committee of European Securities Regulators (CESR), as an observer.

Once a standard has been adopted, it will be published in full as a Commission regulation in each of the official languages of the Community, in the Official Journal of the European Communities. The standards will thus become part of Community law, which means that they will also automatically come under the jurisdiction of the European Court of Justice.

To avoid copyright problems, the Commission concluded an agreement with the International Accounting Standards Committee Foundation in which the Foundation waived its rights on the standards as soon as the standard has been published in the Official Journal. Instead, the Foundation ceded its rights to the Community institutions, the member states of the EEA, and third parties for use of the standards within the EEA.

The Regulation took effect on September 14, 2002, that is the third day following its publication in the Official Journal (September 11, 2002). Acting on a request by the Commission, on June 24, 2002 EFRAG advised the Commission to endorse the current standards "en bloc."

In accordance with Article 3(3) of the Regulation, the Commission *must decide at the latest by 31 December 2002 on the applicability within the Community of the international accounting standards in existence upon the entry into force of the Regulation.*

However, the Commission has not yet prepared a proposal to be voted upon by the ARC. The translation of the standards in all official languages proved more time consuming than originally thought. In accordance with the rules of procedure of the ARC, the Commission cannot bring forward a formal proposal unless such translation is available to all members of the ARC before the meeting. Therefore, it is unlikely that a formal endorsement decision about the existing standards will be taken before May 2003, as it is not likely that high-quality translations in all eleven official languages will be available before March or April 2003.

At the first official meeting of the ARC on November 6, 2002, some members argued that they might have difficulties with an endorsement of IAS 39 because that standard did not sufficiently account for the way in which banks in Europe conduct their business. The IASB announced in December 2002 that it will organize several roundtable discussions in March 2003 to discuss problems that have been brought forward by banks and insurance companies concerning both IAS 32 and IAS 39. These roundtable discussions should contribute to making an "en bloc" endorsement decision possible, as suggested by EFRAG.

8.5. First-time application

The requirement that listed companies prepare their consolidated accounts in accordance with IAS will apply for each financial year starting on or after January 1, 2005. To make this possible, the Commission insisted strongly that a suitable procedure should be developed by the IASB for the first-time application by companies of IAS. This topic is now the subject of an Exposure Draft that was issued by the IASB in July 2002. There are two exceptions to the application of IAS in 2005.

The first exception concerns those companies with a secondary listing on a regulated market outside the EU that have been applying another set of internationally accepted standards as the primary basis for their consolidated accounts since a financial year that started prior to the publication of the Regulation in the Official Journal. Member states may allow such companies to continue to apply those standards until the financial year starting on or after January 2007. This exception was primarily requested by German companies listed in the United States. These companies are preparing their consolidated accounts on the basis of U.S. GAAP.

The second exception concerns companies that have only debt securities admitted on a regulated market of any member state. Here again, member states may allow such companies to continue to apply their national standards until 2007.

8.6. Recent developments

Meanwhile the modernisation of the Accounting Directives has been completed by the adoption of Directive 2003/51/EC of the European Parliament and the Council of 18 June 2003 amending Directives 78/660/EEC, 83/349/EEC, 86/635/EEC and 91/674/EEC on the annual and consolidated accounts of certain types of companies, banks and other financial institutions and insurance undertakings (O.J. No. L 178 of 17 July 2003). On 29 September 2003, the Commission adopted its first Regulation (EC/No. 1725/2003) adopting certain international accounting standards in accordance with Regulation (EC) No. 1606/2002 of the European Parliament and the Council (O.J. No. L 261 of 13 October 2003). Attached to this Regulation is the full text of all existing international accounting standards and interpretations with the exception of IAS 32 and 39, which are still under revision by the IASB. In November 2003, the Commission published a document with comments concerning certain Articles of the Regulation (EC) No. 1606/2002 of the European Parliament and the Council of 19 July 2002 on the application of international standards and the Fourth Council Directive 78/660/EEC of 25 July 1978 and the Seventh Council Directive 83/349/EEC of 13 June on accounting. This document can be found on the Commission's website referred to in footnote 14.

9. Concluding observations

The introduction of a requirement that listed EU companies prepare their consolidated accounts in accordance with IAS has started a debate in several member states concerning a possible extension of that requirement to other companies and to annual accounts. An extension of the requirement's scope would mean that member states will no longer be able to impose further standards for those companies, just as they are no longer allowed to impose further standards on listed companies. This restriction might prove difficult in practice, because the transition from the present accounting regime to IAS might be quite a big step.

To allow for a gradual transition to IAS, on May 28, 2002, the Commission introduced a proposal for an amendment of the Accounting Directives. This amendment was aimed at facilitating the transition from national standards to international standards by removing existing conflicts between the Directives and IAS, and by introducing into the Directives accounting options provided for by IAS but not presently available under the Directives. It is expected that many member states will take this route.

There are now further issues that are high on the agenda. These issues include proper enforcement of IAS throughout the EU and the acceptance of IAS financial statements by the United States.

Notes

The views expressed in this contribution are entirely those of the author.

[1] I note that the codecision procedure was introduced after the adoption of the Accounting Directives. No codecision powers existed for the Parliament when these Directives were adopted.

² Fourth Council Directive (78/660/EEC) of July 25, 1978 on the annual accounts of limited liability companies, O. J. No. L 222 of August 14, 1978.

³ Seventh Council Directive (83/349/EEC) of June 13, 1983 on consolidated accounts, O. J. No. L 193 of July 18, 1983.

⁴ Council Directive (86/635/EEC) of December 8, 1986 on the annual accounts and consolidated accounts of banks and other financial institutions, O. J. No. L 372 of December 31, 1986.

⁵ Council Directive (674/91/EEC) of December 19, 1991 on the annual accounts and consolidated accounts of insurance undertakings, O. J. No. L 374 of December 31, 1991.

⁶ Interpretative Communication of the European Commission (98/C16/04) concerning certain articles of the Fourth and Seventh Council Directives on Accounting, O. J. No. C 16 of January 20, 1998.

⁷ See Commission of the European Communities (ed.) 1990. *The future of harmonisation of accounting standards within the European Communities* (Office for Official Publications of the European Community, Luxembourg).

⁸ For instance, when the Forum was set up there was no accounting standard-setting body in Germany or Luxembourg.

⁹ Dieter Ordelheide represented the European Accounting Association in the Forum. He played a prominent role in the discussions at a time when there was little interest in Germany in promoting further harmonization. As the objective of the discussions was not the elaboration of new rules, but a better understanding of each other's positions, the input from a leading academic, such as Dieter Ordelheide, who had a profound knowledge of comparative accounting proved invaluable. As Germany did not have an accounting standard-setting body at that time, it was difficult to find a person in Germany outside the Ministry of Justice who could explain the German position, which was often at odds with that defended by other member states and particularly the United Kingdom.

¹⁰ Commission of the European Communities, Directorate-General XV "Internal Market and Financial Services" (ed.) 1995. *Prudence and Matching. Document of the Accounting Advisory Forum* (XV/7002/95).

¹¹ Commission Recommendation (2001/453/EC) of May 30, 2001 on the recognition, measurement, and disclosure of environmental issues in the annual accounts and annual reports of companies, O. J. No. L 156 of 13 June 2001.

¹² Communication of the European Commission on "Accounting harmonisation: A new strategy vis-à-vis international harmonization," COM 95(508).

¹³ Contact Committee on the Accounting Directives, (1996). *An examination of the conformity between the international accounting standards and the European Accounting Directives* (European Commission, Office for Official Publications of the European Communities, Luxembourg).

¹⁴ http://europa.eu.int/comm/internal_market/en/company/index.htm.

¹⁵ Directive 2001/65/EC of the European Parliament and of the Council of September 27, 2001 amending Directives 78/660/EEC, 83/349/EEC, and 86/635/EEC as regards the valuation rules for the annual and consolidated accounts of certain types of companies as well as of banks and other financial institutions, O. J. No. L 283 of October 27, 2001.

¹⁶ It is interesting to note that no official assessment of the conformity between U.S. GAAP and the Accounting Directives has been carried out.

¹⁷ Communication of the European Commission on "Financial services: Implementing the framework for financial markets. Action plan," COM (1999) 232.

¹⁸ In 2000, an agreement was reached concerning a restructuring of the IASC. The board of the IASC was replaced by a new board (IASB). This new board is now composed almost entirely of full-time members.

19 Communication of the European Commission on "EU financial reporting: The way forward," COM (2000) 359.
20 Regulation (EC) No. 1606/2002 of the European Parliament and of the Council of July 19, 2002 on the application of international accounting standards, O. J. No. L 243, September 9, 2002, p. 1.
21 O. J. No. C 154 E, May 29, 2001, p. 285.
22 See for instance the surveys carried out by PriceWaterhouseCoopers: "International Accounting Standards in Europe—2005 or now?" November 2000 and "2005—Ready or not?" May 2002. www.pwcglobal.com/ias. See also the opinion of the Economic and Social Committee, O. J. No. C 260, September 17, 2001, p. 86.
23 See for instance the White Paper published in Spain by the Ministry of the Economy and the ICAC (Instituto de Contabilidad y Auditoria de Cuentas): Informe sobre la situación actual de la contabilidad en España y líneas básicas para abordar su reforma, Madrid, 2002.
24 Council Decision (1999/468/EC) of June 28, 1999 laying down the procedures for the exercise of implementing powers conferred on the Commission, O. J. No. L 184, July 17, 1999.
25 European Commission, Final Report of the Committee of Wise Men on the Regulation of European Securities Markets, 2001.
26 Article 5 of the Council Decision of June 28, 1999. The Article promulgates the procedures for the exercise of implementing powers conferred to the Commission. It contains a specific procedure for the case in which member states disagree with the Commission or when the European Parliament believes that the Commission has exceeded its powers.

6.2

Academics in the Accounting Policy Process: England and Germany Compared

Michael Power[1]

1. Introduction

It is widely accepted that the accounting rule making process is political. This means that the development of rules is shaped and influenced by many parties with an interest in their economic and other consequences. To study even a small part of this process is a considerable undertaking, involving close attention to the particular rule and to the actions of the actors attempting to shape it. Aside from the tax authorities, investors, regulators, preparers and the general public, accounting academics, as individuals or in groups, may be influential. In this paper I provide a preliminary comparative overview of their role in the accounting policy process in Germany and England.[2]

    This focus is not as marginal to the question of financial accounting rule development as it first appears; the role, or lack of role, of academics, whether temporary or institutionalized, as individuals or as groups, says much about the style of rule making in an accounting jurisdiction and provides a specific standpoint from which broader differences in accounting regulatory systems can be understood. From time to time, representatives of accounting practice demand greater relevance from accounting academics and their research. Although researchers are increasingly responding to these demands (Schipper, 1994), in Anglo-American circles there remains a tendency to talk of a gap between academia and practice. On the one hand it is argued that practical problems exist that demand solutions and there is often criticism of overly theoretical work that can only be read by a small number of colleagues. On the other hand academics often defend the long term percolative influence of their research; they do not operate in a market for 'quick fixes'.

The nature of academia is varied and often contested. For example, against the model of the academic as technical problem solver, it has been suggested that academics, when they support practice, operate largely in a market for excuses (Watts and Zimmerman, 1989) producing research reports which rationalize the practices which, for whatever reason, currently find favour (Stamp, 1985). Academics may also function as critics (some argue that this role is in danger of being lost. See Sikka *et al.*, 1995), as defenders of scientific values and as potential representatives of marginalized groups. Practitioners often do not want challenging and adversarial engagements with academics and proposals that fail to find favour often fall by the wayside as 'too academic'. However, it is always worth recalling Keynes' famous statement that 'practical men, who believe themselves to be quite exempt from any intellectual influences, are usually the slaves of some defunct economist.'

All this means that the relationship between academics and the practices that they study and promulgate is complex and varied; one should be cautious in taking 'gaps' between them at face value (Hopwood, 1988). For example, academics may exercise a long term, if uncertain, influence over practice by training the next generation of accountants. Such a comparative study as this also raises a number of difficult methodological questions. For example, how can the category of 'academic' be defined? In countries such as the Netherlands and Scotland, there is a long tradition of part-time academic appointments. Here academics play a role in the policy process, but it is questionable whether they do this by virtue of being academics. Persons holding academic appointments may play a role in policy processes more by virtue of their social authority than by providing any explicit research input. There is a formal difference between the influence of academics in policy contexts and the influence of their ideas. Roles in the policy process may also vary from explicit formal representation to the provision of supporting research to informal background influence. And formalized roles through representation may not necessarily correspond to the power to determine outcomes.

Another methodological problem is that what counts as research in such contexts can vary greatly, embracing summations of current practice, the development of analytical models, politically driven critique and empirical investigation into the consequences of particular accounting treatments. The financial accounting policy process also has many different stages and components and academics may play different roles in these various stages. For example, arenas for *rule making* may be quite different from fora for *rule interpretation*. Finally, any study such as this is compromised by the fact that policy settings and the roles demanded of academics are constantly changing over time. It is therefore difficult to draw any definitive comparative conclusions. Indeed, cross-border influences provide a constant reminder that accounting jurisdictions are not hermetically sealed off from one another.

These and other issues provide daunting obstacles to meaningful national studies even before any comparative work is undertaken. And yet, even a preliminary study such as this can shed a little light on an aspect of financial accounting rule development, provided that these methodological issues are borne in mind. In this paper, the analysis has a workable, if somewhat artificial, threefold structure which deals with: the broad systemic features of the environment within which accounting academics work; the role of particular groups and networks; the influence of individuals and ideas. Individuals may play specific roles which are only loosely coupled to the systemic links between academics and policy circles. The threefold structure expresses this looseness of fit, as well as admitting a certain 'structuration' in Giddens' sense, between the different levels of influence that academics may have on the accounting policy process.

2. Culture and environment

Specialist academic communities cannot be understood in abstraction from the development of university systems and the teaching of business and accounting within them. Indeed, the distinctive style of accounting academic life depends greatly on its relative proximity to the fields of economics and law and specifically on the development, or lack, of a business economics tradition. In Germany the 'accounting academic' is subsumed within the field of *Betriebswirtschaftslehre* and this has important consequences when making comparisons with England. Part of the reason has to do with the emergence of the two academic fields in each country. In England accounting was much more of a discrete practical, and then academic, specialism than its German counterpart, even when the distinctive 'economic' approach to accounting was developed at the London School of Economics (Napier, 1996). Nevertheless there are also parallels.

Soon after the LSE was founded in 1895, German business schools emerged from varied pressures to create a missing elite in business. A number of schools were created in the late nineteenth and early twentieth centuries (Leipzig, Aachen, Frankfurt, Cologne and Berlin) which were initially independent of universities and state centred traditions of cameralist knowledge (Lindenfeld, 1990; Busse von Colbe, 1996). The Cologne model impressed Ashley, the first professor of Accounting in England at the University of Birmingham (Napier, 1996) and developments in Germany were similar to those in the USA at that time. Military, academic and public service ideals in the universities also provided resistance to these developments; many were against the absorption of 'merely instrumental' ideas into the university curriculum itself. It was not just in Germany that it was doubted whether accounting was really a proper university subject (Lindenfeld, 1990, p. 221). Against the established scholarly institutions of Oxford and Cambridge, part-time evening accounting teaching gradually took hold in England in the 'new' universities, while in Germany independent *Handelshochschule* were established as models of business education.

Despite these similarities the formation of the field of *Betriebswirtschaftslehre*, under the decisive influence of Schmalenbach who placed accounting at the centre of this applied technical subject, provides an important point of contrast. Tensions with other faculties persisted, as no doubt they do today, but the field of business economics has grown as part of the academy in Germany. In England until 1947, teachers of accounting were mainly part-time academic-practitioners and, largely because the accounting professions were already well established, accounting was not integrated, as in Germany, into a broader field of business knowledge. Whereas both accounting and applied microeconomics were related within the field of business economics in Germany, in England economic theory and accounting practice were never close. Economics as a field professionalised around high theory and macroeconomic traditions of analysis (where economic analyses of income were in fact influential on policy). At the LSE in the 1930s, individuals like Edwards developed economic analyses of cost which were critical of existing accounting practice but which found insufficient allies in practice to have an influence at the time (Napier, 1996, p. 466). Although Schmalenbach was also critical of practice, Germany was different because it conquered the problem of the low prestige of applied business education early on, perhaps because of the absence of an Oxbridge model. In contrast, in England a gulf emerged between merely practical bookkeeping and the high economic analysis of income and cost (Napier, 1996). Despite the more recent development of business schools in England a business economics tradition comparable to Germany is yet to emerge to bridge this gap.

Thus, although the teaching of accounting in England, as in Germany, emerged from a series of practical demands, this led to quite different institutionalizations of the academic field. German academics such as Schmalenbach and Bunger could be agents of standardization and the *Handelshochschule* could be instruments of rationalization at the level of technical education (Harston, 1993, p. 154) in a way that their English counterparts could not. The ideas of English economists influenced the development of national income accounting (Napier, 1996, p. 467) but became increasingly remote from the level of enterprise.

These differences between the intellectual fields in which accounting emerged and was taught and researched also have implications for the respective links between academia and the accounting profession in the two countries (Vieten, 1995). There are many factors involved in these differences. One could point to the deeply German conception of economic order as bounded by the state (Lehmbruch, 1992, p. 33) and the fact that regulatory action, as a knowledge-intensive process, still enjoys a high degree of legitimacy in Germany (Dyson, 1992, p. 1) and is characterized by a widespread sense of public obligation. Accounting and audit regulation in Germany was forged in the aftermath of economic collapse, an experience which shaped a sense of collective enterprise. For example, academics were a primary group shaping the 1931 accounting law in Germany (Harston, 1993) and thereby the development of the practical field itself. In contrast, English suspicion of technical expertise, reinforced by the deeply institutionalized links between Oxbridge and the Civil Service, and the validation of theoretical economics, served systemically to marginalize the influence of accounting academics.

Because of these differences accounting professors in Germany could emerge, unlike their English counterparts, as respected representatives of financial accounting *practice* (Busse von Colbe, 1992). For example, Schmalenbach's work typified a natural and original interface between education, research and practice which remains valid today. In short, German accounting academics became more systemically integrated into corporatist regulatory culture than their English counterparts (although here there is probably greater similarity between Scotland and Germany). They have a relatively stronger influence over the professional examination system (Vieten, 1995, p. 500) and German respect for technical elitism supports the role of academics in producing that elite. In England at least, academics and accounting degrees within universities have played a more problematic and ambivalent role in professional examination systems. Indeed, it is significant that proposals in 1996 by the ICAEW to reform the professional education system make no reference to the English and Welsh universities at all.

These broad 'cultural' differences reflect not only a positioning with respect to the field of economics but also that of law. The relatively greater influence of the academic law model in Germany is striking as compared with the UK. If one can accept that law is not merely practice in Germany but a certain model of legitimate conduct and, crucially, normative knowledge production, then it is understandable that the role of many German financial accounting academics will tend to resemble that of their legal colleagues. A great deal of research tends to take the form of a jurisprudential style of commentary and problem solving which explores accounting norms, discusses internal consistency, interprets particular treatments, looks for solutions to new problems within existing legal frameworks and so on. The role of academic work of this nature is to 'stabilise expectations' (Ordelheide, 1996) and the academic is a representative of *Wissenschaft* science in the sense of systematic knowledge. Romantically perhaps, the German academic can be seen more as a guardian of an elaborate and formal accounting system. But one should not also overstate the direct linkages between academic work and practice in Germany. It has been said that this jurisprudential role reaches limits when its logical deductions of accounting practice do not conform to what is generally accepted practice (von Wysocki, 1983, p. 66). However, the point is that German academics tend to operate in the same value system as business itself, and perceive themselves as so doing. This reflects the difference noted above between the embedding of accounting disciplines within *Betriebswirtschaftslehre* and the formative English attachments between accounting and economic *theory*.

A brief glance at journals in the two countries reflect something of these differences. One can distinguish between 'academic' and 'professional' type journals in England. The former reflect the growing influence of Anglo-American traditions of analytical and empirical research which began to dominate the social sciences in the 1960s and which quickly displaced descriptive work. The latter exist to provide commentary and opinion on professional matters. Practitioners rarely contribute to the former although English academics often contribute articles to the latter.

In Germany, this ideal typical distinction is harder to make. Many journals where German accounting academics write fall between these ideal types and there is no specific journal for accounting, no *Zeitschrift für Rechnungswesen*. For example, *Die Betriebswirtschaft* is more 'scholarly' than, say, *Accountancy* but less so than, say, *Accounting and Business Research*. The latter is also good example of a journal which was founded by the ICAEW and which has become more 'academic' over time, a development which has created some tension and has fuelled perceptions of a gap between practice and research.

A full comparative analysis of journals is not possible but these *prima facie* differences reflect the fact that German academics tend to conduct research in the form of normative commentary on accounting matters within the field of *Betriebswirtschaftslehre*. This is slowly changing as individuals open themselves to international influences and conduct empirical and analytical research. In the UK professional academic reputations are not built primarily in this manner, although this was not always so. Professional validation systems for accounting academics depend increasingly on publications in highly rated North American journals. This reflects a relatively greater systemic decoupling between professional commentary and research in the UK as compared with Germany. This is a development which is increasingly the subject of critical commentary by representatives of practice and the North American journal *Accounting Horizons* was established to bridge the so-called gap.

To summarise: despite many similarities, particularly when individuals are considered below, it is possible to point to general systemic or cultural differences between academic accounting in the UK and Germany, differences which bear upon the potential for academics to influence financial accounting rule development. German accounting academics are systemically closer to professional matters both in teaching and knowledge production than the English. They tend to operate in a system of values, reflected in a conception of research as norm interpretation, which is closer to the values of business and the economy than in England. In contrast to the (largely defensive) attempts of English accountants to relocate accounting as a business discipline in recent years, the field of *Betriebswirtschaftlehre* in Germany has always subsumed accounting theory and practice within a broader framework. This provides a case for arguing that the German accounting academic is embedded in a field which is closer in orientation to policy matters, in values and temperament, than the operational environment of his English counterpart.

3. Groups and networks

Notwithstanding general observations about the different culture of academic accounting in Germany and England, it remains to be seen how this culture shapes the *actual* roles played by academics in policy. Zeff (1996) suggests that early attempts to foster accounting research in the UK by the Association of University teachers of Accounting (AUTA) were always resisted by the English Institute. The Accounting Research Association, formed in 1936 at the LSE, was largely ignored. Rather than Baxter's agenda of bringing economic theory to bear on an understanding of accounting, the English profession was, and probably still is, much more interested in the educational dimensions of contact with academics. Zeff (1996) speculates that it was the continuing resistance by the ICAEW to the exposure of students to critical ideas which led to Solomons leaving the UK: 'The long-standing antipathy of some, though not all, of the leading members of the English Institute toward a place in the universities in the education and training of articled clerks. ...' (Zeff, 1996, p. 36) was part of the reason for his departure. It must be said that the position in Scotland was very different and the profession had from the outset close links to universities.

The AUTA was a forerunner of the British Accounting Association (BAA). The BAA has an annual congress but few practitioners attend this event. Nor does this organization lobby systematically to make 'views of professors' known on accounting matters. In this sense, it is an association with no formal input into the policy process. The English and Welsh Institute has a research board and many academics are involved in this, but even sponsored research also has an ambivalent relation to the rule development process. The ICAEW research board is funded largely by an independent trust and not the subscriptions of members. Conferences and workshops take place from time to time and leading academics and technical practitioners meet and discuss controversial financial reporting issues. These events play no formal role but serve to constitute an informal network of opinion and discussion.

On the face of it the BAA corresponds roughly to *Der Verband der Hochschulelehrer für Betriebswirtschaft* (VHBW), the association of German Professors of Business Economics comprising approximately 700 members including Swiss and Austrians. However, in contrast with the BAA, this body consists of full professors only and in the late 1970s created an 'Accounting Commission' (*Die Kommission Rechnungswesen im Verband der Hochschulelehrer für Betriebswirtschaft*—KRVH) to oversee and make recommendations on the implementation of the 4th and 7th Directives within German law. The KRVH in turn created smaller working groups for specific purposes (Chmielewicz, 1988, p. 65).

The creation and functioning of this body, a one-off event in Germany and unusual for its national point of view in a federal system, is nevertheless instructive on the differences between England and Germany. Not only do individual English academics rarely comment on exposure drafts in the market for emerging interpretations but the BAA has not created a sub-body to represent the views of academia as a legitimate player in the system (The UK Conference of Accounting Professors has a policy interest but this is related more to education than to accounting policy itself).

The KRVH emerged from discussion about the role of German academics in society (Ordelheide, 1996). There were concerns about the loss of influence over the development of accounting norms (rather than the market for interpretation) and in the German context the opportunity does not come very often for influencing legislation (Chmielewicz, 1988). The KRVH opted to make particular suggestions rather than drafting laws themselves and to avoid disclosure issues (KRVH, 1979; KRVH, 1980; KRVH, 1983). The German professors sought publicly to play a distinctive role on behalf of science and the economy as a whole in contrast to other lobbyists (KRVH, 1978). However, if the regulation of financial accounting really is political then it cannot be resolved by scientific methods alone (Busse von Colbe, 1992, p. 31). Thus the KRVH debated the need for pragmatism and compromise in its recommendations. Hartl (1986) argues that the KRVH was caught between a pragmatically necessary normative style and a scientific one from which it derived its authority. In the end the former dominated the latter. While KRVH (1978; 1979) make much of the need for objectivity, this demand plays less of a role in later documents (Hartl, 1986, pp. 154–5).

So what of the influence of the KRVH? Causal certainty of influence is impossible to gauge (Chmielewicz, 1988, p. 68; Busse von Colbe, 1992, p. 32) and there were obvious failures in recommendations, such as the (now far-sighted) proposal for a FASB type regulator. There was some success in pressing for a rational reorganization of the law but Ordelheide (1996) shows that, even when professors made recommendations that were apparently uncontested by other groups, they tended to have a lower success rate than other groups when they acted alone. In part the impact of the KRVH was also undermined by a general shift in German politics in 1982 whereby policy issues were increasingly defined in managerial terms.

The success or otherwise of the KRVH matters less than the fact of its existence. The KRVH was recognised as an institutionally legitimate player, the 'other' of sectional industry, in the rule development process and provides an example of the problems that an academic organization faces when directly entering the policy process. German academics also play a role in other networks. For example, the *Schmalenbachgesellschaft-Deutsche Gesellschaft für Betriebswirtschaft* is a private research institute consisting of representatives from the corporate sector and academia (Vieten, 1995, p. 499). The SG/DGBW have a congress each year and the 2000 or so participants are a mixture of academics and businessmen. Again, the contrast with England is striking. The BAA is not like this; there would have to be something like a BAA/ICAEW joint policy research institute. It may be argued that in many ways the technical departments of large accounting firms play the role vacated by English academics in the UK. And yet in the British system of rule development, through the Accounting Standards Board, it is in principle much easier for an English academic to comment on an Exposure Draft than for a German professor to comment on draft law. Very few academics do this, reflecting again the gulf between the values of academia and practice in the UK.

To summarise: if the role of academics is lower key and more individualized (see below) in England as compared with Germany, the greater institutionalization of collective academic voice in Germany does not map directly onto influence. Overall, the German system of rule development through legal process comes in larger chunks than in England and knowledge production is more dispersed (Vieten, 1995, p. 499). This forces the lobbying process to be relatively more institutionalized as compared with the role of inside influence and lobbying clubs, like the Hundred Group of finance directors, in the UK. German academics, through the KRVH and other bodies, play a legitimate and recognized role in this process despite their lack of clear success.

4. Individuals and ideas

In German speaking countries, particularly Austria, there is little doubt that professors enjoy the high social status that accompanies public office. This already gives greater institutional, if unspecific, authority to German professors of accounting as compared with their English counterparts. On the back of this generalized social authority, some German academics reinforce their authority in the accounting field through the production of detailed *Kommentare*. These texts are often economically successful products in their own right and the authors tend to be a mixture of academics, *Wirtschaftsprüfer* and finance directors. As noted above, these commentaries have authority in the system of rule interpretation, although there is also a competitive 'market for interpretations' (Ordelheide and Pfaff, 1994). The *Kommentare* differ on some issues, reflecting in part the allegiances and involvement of different firms. Similar texts in the English context are *UK GAAP* written by the accounting firm Ernst & Young and the annual study of UK financial reporting published by the ICAEW. Although academics edit and contribute to the latter text, it is not in the same style of authoritative interpretation as its German counterpart.

Despite these differences at the level of *Kommentare* in the two countries, certain individuals have acquired status and influence in policy matters in their own right. Here the comparative contrast which holds at the level of culture and of networks is much harder to establish. In Germany Busse von Colbe and Moxter are examples of 'authoritative opinion' in their own right and have no ready equivalents in the UK. Nevertheless individuals like Edey, Carsberg, Macve, Bromwich and others developed formal links with the accounting profession (of which they were members). There is also no clear parallel in Germany with Edward Stamp's critical interventions in the press in the late sixties which led to the formation of the Accounting Standards Committee. For the reasons outlined above, German academics are less likely to be individually critical in this way, at least publicly. An exception is the campaign against banks and supervisory boards conducted by Ekkehard Wenger, Professor of Economics at the University of Würzburg, but generally there is no discernable critical tradition within *Betriebswirtschaftslehre* itself, either in the Stamp mould or in a more radical sense. Indeed, notwithstanding extensive experimentation with alternative social indicators in Germany, this critical tradition has failed to penetrate mainstream accounting. German accounting academics tend to identify more readily with the values and objectives of the economic system and its information requirements. German industry accepts the scientific role of the German academic that is, as a critical but ultimately consensual contributor. The English academic does not function in such a clear system of values. Instead it is the accounting firms which have established themselves as authorities in the market for interpretations, mediating the views of their powerful clients.

One important factor when comparing individuals is their relative allegiance to the fields of economics, law and practice. For example, superficially there are some parallels between Eugene Schmalenbach and Lawrence Dicksee (the first Professor of Accounting at Birmingham in 1902). Both spent a considerable time in practice and were concerned with applied knowledge throughout their lives; both had left school at 17 to work and so on. But Schmalenbach's orientation towards the discipline of economics was a decisive difference; he was an individual whose work was coextensive with the formation of both the scientific and practical fields of *Betriebswirtschaft* and accounting within it (Lindenfeld, 1990, p. 222; Busse von Colbe, 1996, p. 418). Schmalenbach's concept of *Dynamische Bilanz* was essentially a conceptual framework for accounting which placed the income statement at its centre. It established a genre for working in the field.

In England, Dicksee, who 'was rarely seen to consult other men's writings before delivering himself on any subject' (Kitchen and Parker, 1980, p. 53) was succeeded by de Paula, whose manual of auditing was influential, and later by Rowland. These early figures were very much men of the profession and saw themselves in that light; their intellectual allegiance lay, if anywhere, in the direction of company law. These individuals could influence the rule-making process, such as it was, by virtue of inhabiting the same social and intellectual world as the rulemakers. The same could not be said of their successors at LSE, Edwards and later Baxter, whose economic based criticisms of accounting practice and strong advocacy of replacement cost accounting earned them much criticism from the accounting profession. It is probably here that the 'intellectual fault line' unique to the English context is to be found. And yet, the great paradox perhaps, the Accounting Standards Board in the UK was headed by an ex-academic, Sir David Tweedie who was advised by Professor Geoffrey Whittington. There is no German academic, despite all the institutionalized proximity to policy, who has this form of direct influence over accounting rule development, due in large part to the fact that there was, until recently, no German ASB. Yet by comparison with Germany, accounting academics as a body in the UK rarely contribute to the standard setting process (Napier, 1996, p. 472). This emphasises the need to separate analytically the group and individual levels.

Perhaps the real limits to the influence of accounting academics in policy matters is illustrated by the history of inflation accounting. Here, at the heart of thinking about accounting measurement, many accounting academics are both most intellectually at home yet also most remote from the values and norms of practitioners. The experience of hyper-inflation has been a decisive factor in shaping German accounting practice (Busse von Colbe, 1996, p. 417). But it has worked against the institutionalization of price change accounting because this would be to legitimize the instability of the currency value. Thus, although CPP and CCA systems were debated heatedly and advocated by Schmalenbach, Mahlberg and Schmidt (Potthoff and Sieben, 1994, p. 84), these great men found few allies in policy circles: 'Schmidt's work [. . .on CCA. . .] did not influence accounting practice directly during his lifetime. It was later influential in the German IdW pronouncement of 1975 . . .although that was not implemented in practice. More importantly, it seems probable that Schmidt had a significant influence on the thinking of Limberg and the Dutch replacement cost school' (Whittington, 1983, p. 131). Of course, the receptivity of Dutch practice to these ideas is yet another twist in the story of academic influence over practical accounting.

In Germany the existence and advocacy of economic based theory of accounting measurement did not lead to its adoption in practice. This story of failure is similar to that of inflation accounting policy in the UK. One may hypothesize that times of inflation heighten academic influence in policy deliberation where measurement issues are at stake, but this temporary influence does not necessarily lead to lasting change to accounting. It has been suggested that Schmalenbach's concept of dynamic profit failed to be influential in practice because it was out of line with commercial law (Schneider, 1995) even though it was influential on tax law judgements (Busse von Colbe, 1992, p. 34). The lesson is that individuals may have influence by virtue of an unspecific authority but not all of their ideas may have influence. Accounting practice in both Germany and the UK has proven highly insensitive to economics-based arguments for reform.

In summary, the position of individual accounting academics provides a more idiosyncratic picture which upsets some of the neat distinctions between German and English accounting academics developed above. Figure 6.2.1 provides a tentative basis for thinking about the relative locations of different academics, between the three poles of practice, law and economics. The existence of a coherent business economics tradition is represented by an ideal mid-point, here occupied by the figure Schmalenbach. That the English individuals are at the edges of this scheme suggests the absence of a Business Economics tradition (Napier, 1996). While it is dangerous to locate 'most' English and German accounting academics, since these points are shifting, the point is to bring out the contrast between legal and non-legal intellectual centres of gravity. This schema also requires a further fourth dimension in terms of orientation

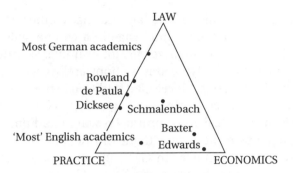

Fig. 6.2.1. Accounting academics and intellectual space.

towards empirical research. For example, it has been said that German academics have been slow to take up empirical research (Busse von Colbe, 1996, p. 420), a fact which has enabled them to function in the market for interpretations. The economics pole in Figure 6.2.1 is really analytical rather than empirical economics and interests in organization theory and practice are not really represented.

Wherever they are on this scheme, academics can be disturbing agents in the accounting policy process if they are schooled in measurement systems which challenge the historic cost convention. But they will only really disturb accounting policy consensus if they have sufficient allies within practice itself, that is they are close to the norms and values of the practitioner corner in Figure 6.2.1 above. In the UK in recent years discounting has begun to play an increasing role in a number of financial accounting areas, marking to market is seriously discussed and comprehensive income is making a comeback in the thinking of the ASB. For all the systemic differences, some English accounting academics as individuals may have more direct influence on policy outcomes than their German counterparts.

5. Conclusions

The very idea of an accounting academic is difficult to hold stable in such a preliminary study as this. Many different models and conceptions exist and even an extensive definition in terms of full time university appointment in a particular field begs many questions. Furthermore, individuals who fall under such a definition do not always behave in accordance with a certain underlying model. One must always allow for the scholarly practitioner, the academic technician and many other idiosyncrasies. Some demands for academics to engage in a certain style of research tend to see the field in 'German' terms, for example, Whittington (1983, p. 145) sees a need for clarifying assumptions and working out a kind of jurisprudence. This is a not a developed tradition in the UK. Equally, elite German professors of accounting are beginning to build reputations in North American analytical and empirical research traditions.

Even when we take these sensitivities to detail into account, there remains a sense of difference. In Germany there seems to be greater *institutionalized* contact between the fields of business, regulation and academia. Academics seem to be valued components of a system even if they are not always influential. In England (one must be careful to make Scotland an exception; it is similar in many respects to the Netherlands as far as this issue is concerned) there is a much looser relationship which often gives rise to tensions. This has to do with broad traditions of academic independence but also with the recent history of the intellectual field of accounting as such. Academic accountants in the UK do not monopolise the production of accounting labour and the market for norm interpretation has been dominated by the firms. These differences also reflect differences in social respect for the views and contributions of academics to policy development.

Are there any normative prescriptions that may be derived from this overview? Perhaps the relative proximity of academics to accounting policy development may indicate a degree of openness of rule development to fundamental issues of measurement and to empirical studies of consequences. However, academics and their ideas will always be compromised in the policy arena where a normative regulatory style is required for clear and legitimate prescriptions, as the KRVH discovered. For this reason, the closer that academics move to the heart of policy making, the more likely it is that they are socialized into the role of regulator, with all that this involves. Another lesson is that, given that financial accounting rules can never be so tightly specified as to remove all discretion, it may be desirable to unburden the rule development process of the ASB and support an explicit market for interpretations around this. The pronouncements of the Urgent Issues Task Force and *UK GAAP* play something of this role. However, English academics with no tradition of engaging in such work increasingly see little to be gained from commentary and the *a priori* deliberations of policy as compared with empirical and analytical work.

In the end, the accounting academic as researcher will always be marginal to the policy process, in the sense of clearly determining outcomes. And yet, what may matter to the financial rule development process is that it is also more than mere politics, a power struggle, and is informed by principles and reasoning. Between the provision of mere legitimating excuses and the direct application of research results, academic input into both rule development and interpretation can support a certain quality of discussion and provide a language and style of deliberation. The role of academics in the financial accounting policy process may be as the defender of a certain normative climate for high quality deliberation.

Notes

1 The author is grateful for the comments and advice of John Flower, Dieter Ordelheide and Theodore Siegel and for the financial support of the Wissenschaftskolleg zu Berlin and of the European Commission.
2 The focus on 'England' rather than Britain is preferred because Scotland and Scottish academics do not fit the general argument developed here. England is intended to refer also to Wales and it has not been overlooked that the ICAEW is the Institute of Chartered Accountants in England *and Wales*. Rather, the terms 'England' and 'English' have been adopted for ease of usage only.

References

Busse von Colbe, W. (1992) 'Relationships between Financial Accounting Research, Standards Setting and Practice in Germany', *European Accounting Review*, Vol. 1, No. 1, pp. 27–38.
—— (1996) 'Accounting and the Business Economics Tradition in Germany', *European Accounting Review*, Vol. 5, No. 3, pp. 413–34.
Chmielewicz, K. (1988) 'Die Kommission Rechnungswesen und das Bilanzrichtlinien-Gesetz', in Domsch, Eisenführ, Ordelheide and Perli (eds.) (1988) *Unternehmenserfolg: Festschrift für Busse von Colbe*. Wiesbaden.
Dyson, K. (1992) 'Theories of Regulation and the Case of Germany: A Model of Regulatory Change' in Dyson, K. (ed.) (1992) *The Politics of German Regulation*. Aldershot: Dartmouth.
Harston, M. E. (1993) 'The German Accounting Profession - 1931 and Before: A Reflection of National Ideologies,' *The Accounting Historians Journal* Vol. 20, No. 2, pp. 139–162.
Hartl, R. (1986) *Die Politikberatung durch die Kommission Rechnungswesen in Verband der Hochschulelehrer für Betriebswirtschaft e.V.* Frankfurt an Main: Verlag Peter Lang.
Hopwood, A. G. (1988) 'Accounting Research and Accounting Practice: The Ambiguous Relationship Between the Two' in Hopwood, A. (ed.) *Accounting from the Outside*. New York: Garland Publishing.

Kitchen, J. and Parker, R. H. (1980) *Accounting Thought and Education: Six English Pioneers.* London: ICAEW.

KRVH (1978) 'Reformvorschläge zur handelsrechtlichen Rechnungslegung', *Die Betriebswirtschaft* Vol. 38, No. 3, pp. 453–55.

—— (1979) 'Reformvorschläge zur handelsrechtlichen Rechnungslegung', *Die Betriebswirtschaft* Vol. 39, No. 1a, pp. 3–41.

—— (1980) 'Stellungnahme zum Vorentwurf eines Bilanzrichtlinie-Gesetzes vom. 5.2.1980', *Die Betriebswirtschaft* Vol. 40, No. 4, pp. 589–597.

—— (1983) 'Stellungnahme zum Regierungsentwurf eines Bilanzrichtlinie-Gesetztes' *Die Betriebswirtschaft* Vol. 43, No. 1, pp. 5–15.

Lindenfeld, D. F. (1990) 'The Professionalization of Applied Economics: German Counterparts to Business Administration', in Cocks, G. and Jarausch, K. H. (eds.) (1990) *German Professions:* 1800–1950. Oxford: Oxford University Press.

Napier, C. (1996), 'Accounting and the Absence of a Business Economics Tradition in the United Kingdom', *European Accounting Review*, Vol. 5, No. 3, pp. 449–481.

Ordelheide, D. (1996) 'Standardisation of Financial Reporting in Germany' European Universities Research Network, Brussels.

—— and Pfaff, D. (1994) *European Financial Reporting: Germany.* London: Routledge/ICAEW.

Potthoff, E. and Sieben, G. (1994) 'Eugen Schmalenbach', in Edwards J. R. (ed.) *Twentieth-Century Accounting Thinkers.* London: Routeledge/ICAEW.

Schneider, D. (1995) 'The history of financial reporting in Germany,' in Walton, P. (ed.) *European Financial Reporting: A History.* London: Academic Press.

Sikka, P., Willmott, H. and Puxty, A. (1995) 'The Mountains are Still There: Accounting Academics and the Bearings of Intellectuals' *Accounting, Auditing and Accountability Journal* Vol. 8, No. 3, pp. 113–140.

Stamp, E. (1985) 'The Politics of Professional Accounting Research: Some Personal Reflection,' *Accounting, Organizations and Society* Vol. 10, No. 1, pp. 111–123.

Vieten, H. (1995) 'Auditing in Britain and Germany Compared: Professions, Knowledge and the State' *European Accounting Review* Vol. 4, No. 3, pp. 485–511.

Von Wysocki, K. (1983) 'Research into the Processes of Accounting Standard Setting in the Federal Republic of Germany' in M. Bromwich and A. G. Hopwood (eds.) *Accounting Standards Setting: An International Perspective.* London: Pitman.

Whittington, G. (1983) 'The Role of Research In Setting Accounting Standards: The Case of Inflation Accounting,' in M. Bromwich and A. G. Hopwood (eds.) *Accounting Standards Setting: An International Perspective.* London: Pitman.

Zeff, S.A. (1996) 'The Early Years of the Association of University Teachers of Accounting: 1947–1959,' Working paper, Houston: Rice University.

Index